PARADIGMS FOR ANTHROPOLOGY

AN ETHNOGRAPHIC READER

Edited by
E. Paul Durrenberger and Suzan Erem

UNIVERSITY PRESS

OXFORD
UNIVERSITY PRESS

Oxford University Press, Inc., publishes works that further
Oxford University's objective of excellence in research, scholarship,
and education.

Oxford New York
Auckland Cape Town Dar es Salaam Hong Kong Karachi
Kuala Lumpur Madrid Melbourne Mexico City Nairobi
New Delhi Shanghai Taipei Toronto

With offices in
Argentina Austria Brazil Chile Czech Republic France Greece
Guatemala Hungary Italy Japan Poland Portugal Singapore
South Korea Switzerland Thailand Turkey Ukraine Vietnam

Copyright © 2010 by Paradigm Publishers

First published by Paradigm Publishers
Published by Oxford University Press,
198 Madison Avenue, New York, New York 10016
http://www.oup.com

Oxford is a registered trademark of Oxford University Press

Library of Congress Cataloging-in-Publication Data available

ISBN 978-0-19-994588-7 hardback
ISBN 978-0-19-994589-4 paperback

CONTENTS

PREFACE FOR INSTRUCTORS

We have collected classic and contemporary examples of anthropology to provide examples of

- What anthropological fieldwork is and where it fits,
- how we can understand different cultures
- and explain their differences;
- the importance of history
- and power;
- relationships of the global and the local
- and where individuals fit.

Some of the selections are classics, but most were written expressly for this collection with students like yours in mind. All the contemporary writers are experienced anthropologists who teach introductory anthropology courses.

We designed the collection so you can use it as

- a series of ethnographic examples if you use no main text;
- a supplement for any of the common introductory textbooks; or
- a complement to our text *Anthropology Unbound: A Field Guide to the 21st Century,* 2nd ed. (Paradigm Publishers, 2010).

All the examples are based on ethnographic fieldwork, and most of them are based on long-term studies in the field.

Each selection can be used to illustrate a variety of different concepts. Eric Wolf's analysis of the rise of Islam, for instance, presents cultural ecology as an approach and provides an example of a revitalization movement; it also discusses the uses of historical materials in anthropology, the importance of understanding historical processes, how states come into being, and the role of religion. Alan Sandstrom's new contribution on Nahua religion likewise explores the role of an established religious tradition, how local religions respond to state religions, cultural ecology, and the importance of long-range local ethnographic understanding and comparative perspectives.

Different instructors may elect to cut different paths through the works we present, but we trust that all the works are sufficiently rich to supplement your own experience and analyses with a broad selection of paradigms for anthropology.

Those who use this volume together with *Anthropology Unbound* will see that some of the selections are the original works we mention in the text. One such example is Malinowski's famous discussion of fieldwork, which many of us had in mind as we found ourselves halfway around the world immersed in unfamiliar languages, smells, foods, and situations and recalled his lines about imagining ourselves suddenly set down surrounded by all our gear. Or as we found ourselves in a hospital, industrial farm, or corporate boardroom imagining that we were beginners with nothing to guide us.

In the first draft of *Anthropology Unbound,* we initially quoted Richardson's appreciation of ethnography in the contemporary world as he assessed it half a century later so frequently that we had to cut most of the quotations we'd selected. Now we have a chance to let students read the original and appreciate his challenge to us all: if we anthropologists don't search for the human secret and tell the human myth, who will, damn it, who will? Richardson lets us all—writers, instructors, and students—know that we are not the only ones who wrestle with demons in the deep of night. Anthropology doesn't get any better than this.

Other landmark articles expose students to original works that we mention in the text (Goodenough, Harris, Rappaport, Wolf, Gunder Frank), and new material provides contemporary examples of concepts we discuss, including the corporate shaping of American culture (Doukas), informal economy (Zlolniski), political ecology (Gezon), and industrial agriculture (Dilly). Josiah Heyman and Howard Campbell's discussion of the U.S.-Mexico border alerts students to the pitfalls of oversimplifying ideas of culture and structure. Several concepts are distributed through the text rather than explicitly discussed in separate sections. This collection includes Kathleen Adams's explicit discussion of agency as well as Bob Marshall's description of the various kinds of cooperatives that are springing up in Japan. Emine Onaran İncirlioğlu illustrates the advantages of long-term ethnographic involvment with an area in her description of changing gender relationships in a Turkish village that has become involved in the global economy in different ways through time. Azizur Molla provides a model for how to transcend the limitations of single locales to study public health issues in a whole country.

Cultural ecology and political ecology call our attention to the evolution of structures. Larry Kuznar's paper helps students understand the role of individuals as well as the importance of complexity. It reassures students that although processes are complex, we can understand them and we have a role in shaping them.

INTRODUCTION
FOR STUDENTS

Thomas Kuhn was a philosopher who was interested in how science progresses. Kuhn's study of the actual history of the sciences persuaded him that progress in any science is more than just adding one fact to a vast collection of other facts until we know all the facts there are to know.

Think about astronomy. In the old days, people thought Earth was at the center of everything. They weren't stupid, either. If you go out and look at the stars and the planets, you will come to the same conclusion. They look like they go around Earth. That's the evidence of our senses.

But modern people don't stare up at the stars that much. From the time we first go to school, we see pictures of planets going around the sun. We make three-dimensional models of the solar system with the sun at the center, and soon that structure seems natural to us. The other planets are a lot like Earth, so our planet isn't unique in this system.

You can't just add facts to the first point of view—that Earth is the center of everything—to get to the second—that our solar system revolves around the sun. That change, Kuhn said, involved a whole change in the way people saw things; it involved seeing different worlds. So the difference between Ptolemy, the guy who put together the Earth-centered idea of the heavens, and Copernicus, the guy who said the sun is at the center, isn't a difference of fact but a difference of how they saw the facts; it's a difference in what they thought or guessed or supposed was the most important way to organize the facts they had.

Kuhn's big finding was that science isn't only about facts; it's also about the assumptions we use to organize and make sense of those facts. So if you want to navigate in a ship, you still use the Ptolemaic system. But if you want to make a calendar so that the days of your calendar more or less match what the seasons are doing, a Copernican system does a better job. And that's exactly what was at stake at the time of Copernicus. His ideas were heretical, but they allowed the church to make a calendar that kept Christmas in the deep of winter and Easter in the spring.

So how do scientists learn these organizing ideas? The usual way is by studying with other people who know what they're doing. That's why you take laboratory courses. People who know about chemistry teach you about it, and you learn from them and from your books. Kuhn figured that what you do in the lab is more important than what you read in books. Doing the experiments in the lab book with the help of your lab instructor teaches you more about chemistry than anything else.

It's through the repetition of those lab experiments that you learn the assumptions of chemistry, those things nobody questions, the basics; anthropologists working in our "laboratory"—the field—call those basics the *cultural code*. If you put together all the practical examples, the unstated assumptions, the things people learn by doing, and the more explicit statements you get in textbooks, you have what Kuhn called a paradigm.

He got the idea from language teaching and learning. When you study a language, you learn examples. For instance, *I go, you go, he/she/it goes*. That example illustrates the difference between when to use *go* and when to use *goes*. That shows you a pattern in a language. Kuhn saw the same process of unconscious learning taking place in science as it does in language, so he borrowed the term *paradigm* to explain it.

If all this is true, how could Copernicus have come up with his new paradigm in the first place? To test any sentence to see if it's grammatical, you can compare it to a paradigm or a part of a paradigm. If you hear someone say, "When Brian and me were outside, we saw a shooting star," you can compare that with the paradigm, and you find that although you would say "Brian saw," you would never say "Me saw." So, you know the proper words must be "When Brian and *I* were outside, we saw a shooting star." But you could understand the incorrect version.

Here is something that doesn't fit the paradigm, but it sounds okay to you. What's wrong with this picture? What's wrong with it is that the way we use the language has changed so that it doesn't fit the paradigm anymore. So we can change the way we use the language, or we can change our paradigm. What are the chances of changing everyone's use of English? Slim to none.

But when that happens in science, when the paradigm doesn't match the observations, people begin to feel uneasy, as you probably did when we gave the example "Brian and me saw" and you thought, "Nothing's wrong with that sentence." When enough people feel uneasy enough, they start to think of other and different organizing ideas. Take this statement: "Obviously, Earth is at the center of the heavens." If we make a calendar based on that assertion, Christmas drifts, just as Jewish and Muslim holidays do today because they're based on the lunar calendar, which is not so tightly keyed to the seasons. Christmas would drift from fall to spring and would never occur at the same time of the seasonal year, and that doesn't make sense. If that's important to you, you figure a different way to make a calendar, and you'll be willing to believe someone who tells you that maybe Earth actually goes around the sun.

Copernicus would never have had a chance to spread his ideas if nobody had cared about the calendar because he had no hard data to support those ideas, just some mystical notion that the sun was the greatest of all things and therefore had to be at the center of everything. Later, some other scientists, like Galileo and Kepler, became worried by things they could see that didn't fit the old paradigm but did fit the new one. But historically, it was the calendar that did the trick.

Then people started to look for different kinds of facts. Ferdinand Magellan said, "The Church says the Earth is flat, but I know that it is round, for I have seen the shadow on the moon, and I have more faith in a shadow than in the Church." The teachings of the astronomers went against the church's doctrine, so these men were considered heretics. Later, many religious people would feel the same way about the teachings of Darwin. Just as Copernicus took Earth out of the center of the heavens, Darwin saw humans as just another kind of animal.

The works of Darwin and Copernicus are examples of what Kuhn called a *scientific revolution*. They were revolutions because they brought about entirely different ways of seeing things, not just minor changes in the old ways of seeing things. Scientific revolutions mean changes in paradigms or the important examples. The lab courses change, the field trips change, and the textbooks change. Sometimes it makes a big difference outside the scientific community. Copernicus's ideas challenged theological thought because he was saying there was no longer an imperfect and changing Earth surrounded by spheres that were more and more pure, where angels and then God were located.

Technically, a *paradigm* is the *cultural code* that makes the example make sense. This book presents a series of examples that we hope will help you formulate the ways of seeing that are important for anthropology. We've brought together a number of examples you can read and think about in the same way as you might so many different lab experiments. Each reading tells you something about the assumptions of the anthropologist who wrote it. Our purpose is to give you some examples that will help you see the organizing ideas that go with the textbook you're using, just as lab manuals go with your other texts. So that's where we got our title, *Paradigms for Anthropology.*

The chapters in this collection go into more detail on some of the things we've discussed in our book *Anthropology Unbound*. We mention Bronislaw Malinowski a couple of times in that book, but here, you can read his own words. In the text, we quote Miles Richardson, but here, you can read the whole article he wrote and see what he said about Malinowski. We discussed examples from the works of Roy Rappaport, Ward Goodenough, Marvin Harris, and many others. Here, you can hear directly from them and from many contemporary anthropologists as well.

Anthropology is anchored in the past but looks to the future. When we understand how social, economic, and political systems work, it's hard to be surprised by current events. When Paul Durrenberger was studying the fishing industry along the northern Gulf Coast of the United States, he wanted to learn about its history. Among the sources he consulted were the records of the Bureau of Freed Men and Abandoned Lands, the U.S. government agency that was set up in the Civil War era to deal with all the issues that arose from having freed slaves and proclaimed as abandoned the lands of those who had fought on the side of the Confederacy. There wasn't a lot about fishing in those records, but there was a report by a general who warned that the occupation army should not put the prewar Southern aristocracy back in power. He developed an analysis of social relations among the aristocrats, ordinary people, and former slaves and suggested that if the previous aristocrats gained power again, they would reinstitute some form of slavery. Subsequent events showed him to be right.

In the first edition of *Anthropology Unbound*, we discussed how finance gains power over substantive capital and how money shamans come to control economic systems. To people who understood those relationships, even people like the millionaire Warren Buffett, the meltdown of the global economy that started in 2008 was no surprise. They could understand what was happening as they read or heard about it in the news.

Anthropology is anchored in the past in two senses. First, we have the advantage of the long time lines that archaeologists develop with their studies of the material evidence of activities that people leave. So we can trace our history back to the very beginnings of our species. We can see how states develop and how the roles of elites, common people, and slaves evolve all over the world, and we can see that the processes are much the same at any time and any place. But anthropology is also anchored in the past because we build on the results of previous ethnographic and archaeological research.

For instance, in the text, we mention Malinowski and his work in the Trobriand Islands. He wasn't the first anthropologist to do fieldwork, but he wrote such a detailed and concise description of what he was about that many who have come after him have benefited from his effort. We start with Malinowski's statement on what fieldwork is about because nobody has done it better. But things change, and Miles Richardson was doing fieldwork in a very different world from Malinowski's. So we include his piece to show the differences.

We're not trying to provide a history of anthropology; rather, we're trying to give you some of the building blocks of the discipline. That's a complex matter. Kuhn pointed out that the development of science is never a neat and straight-line process. Sciences grow in fits and starts.

People think they know what they're doing until they come across something that doesn't fit their expectations, as we discussed in the text. Anthropologists know that expectations are more powerful than realities. That's what culture is all about. And we also know that some people are very committed to their points of view, no matter what. Kuhn said it's the same in science. If you've spent your whole career attempting to prove that Earth is at the center of the cosmos and you know that God made it that way, you really don't want to hear about the sun being at the center of a solar system that is just part of a huge galaxy, or about the shadows of Earth on the moon.

Those concepts don't fit your expectations, and besides, you'd have to admit your life's work is all wrong. If your reputation depends on proving that Earth is at the center, you'll do whatever you must to prove that.

But you won't live forever. And even your former students will die. Then there may be room for new ideas. This is what Kuhn called the process of scientific revolution, in which one set of assumptions, practices, and ideas, or a paradigm, replaces another. Anthropology doesn't even work that smoothly, and we're not going to get into the history of anthropology here. But there are some basic ideas that have proven to be valuable.

One is Malinowski's idea of what fieldwork is all about. Another is the idea advanced by Marvin Harris, Eric Wolf, and Roy Rappaport that we can understand culture in terms of the everyday realities that people have to deal with. Yet another is what Ward Goodenough learned in living on the small Pacific island of Truk—that if we impose our own ideas on things, we can't understand those everyday realities. We don't mean to say these guys invented such ideas. It doesn't work that way. We get ideas from all over the place and use the ones that help us understand things. We're just naming the people whose work we're including here as examples.

We included Miles Richardson's piece for several reasons. First, he admits to being from a religious and working-class background and tells a good story about how anthropology affected him personally. But more than that, he talks about how things in the world of the 1960s and 1970s didn't match up with the ideas in some of the books about the romance of noble primitives living in a world untainted by the ills of civilization. Most of all, Richardson has a view of the magnificence of the task of anthropology, of the very audacity of even trying to really understand the human condition and tell other people about it. He also has the courage to talk about how petty anthropologists can be in dealing with each other—how they fight and squabble about unimportant things to make themselves feel important and how they ignore important things because they're afraid. Just as Kuhn said.

In *Anthropology Unbound*, we offered our take on the knowledge anthropologists have accumulated for some two hundred years about who we are and how we came to be the way we are as a species. One of Paul's graduate school friends was fond of saying that the invention of the printing press made class meetings and lectures obsolete. Whatever someone could tell you in a lecture, you could read in a book. A lot of the things that colleges and universities do are based on obsolete models. Another graduate student friend of Paul's said that universities were invented by the best minds of the twelfth century and had not been updated since. In those pre-printing-press days, people would walk across Europe or China just to read a book. The lecture system was invented as a kind of copying machine for books. A person would stand at a lectern and read from a book, and students would write out their own copies of the book.

We've come a long way since then with copy machines, computer scanners, and the Internet. Now you can access online a lot of the articles we discussed at the American Anthropological Association's Anthrosource, an online database of all anthropological journals that fall within the purview of the association and its member organizations. All members of the association have access to it, and many college and university libraries subscribe to it. If your library does subscribe, you have a lot of the history of American anthropology at your fingertips. The Web site not only has articles from the *American Anthropologist,* considered the main journal in our field, but also material from the newsletters and journals of the association's more than thirty-five component sections covering various topical and geographic interests.

Almost every anthropologist has done some kind of fieldwork, whether in *archaeology* or *sociocultural anthropology.* She could have excavated Maya, Aztec, Egyptian, or other sites of ancient civilizations. He might have lived with peasants in Latin America, Europe, Africa, or Asia. She might have worked in a factory or hospital in China, Turkey, or the United States or in a fish-processing plant in Iceland or Canada.

Your instructor will tell you about his or her own work because only that firsthand experience can communicate the excitement of anthropology. The textbook can provide information about some of the places your instructor hasn't been. And this reader can give you some of the details we haven't been able to go into in the text itself. One of the great advantages of being human is that we can use language to learn from the experience of others. And one of the advantages of writing is that we can read what the people who came before us thought or what people in distant places think. So this reader can save you the trouble of finding the old journals and looking up the articles we think are important. We've also put less emphasis on the ones you can access on the Web.

We've collected some work of current anthropologists as well. We asked them to write short articles especially for this collection. This material is just as important as the old stuff because it gives you an idea of what people are doing in anthropology today and because it will help you develop the kind of understanding that makes events of the future unsurprising.

These particular folks are still alive. They grew up in an age of globalization and technology, unlike Goodenough and Malinowski, and are facing the challenges of doing local ethnography in a rapidly shrinking, ever-industrializing world. If you find yourself totally engrossed in one of their stories, maybe it's time you consider becoming an anthropologist, if you haven't already. Anthropology gives you a way of seeing the world that you can apply to anything that comes at you in life. We hope we and our colleagues here will help expand that view for you a bit, no matter where you end up.

The subtitle of *Anthropology Unbound* is *A Field Guide to the 21st Century,* and that's what the new contributions round out. They take us right into the middle of the chaos of the global system that swirls around us all to explain new things like industrial swine production in the American Midwest, how corporations shape the cultural code of the United States, what computer simulations can teach us, how people in Bangladesh get water and the difference it makes in their health, how Turkish villagers as well as people on the southern U.S. border and Mexican immigrants in California are dealing with globalization, how people in Mexico make use of their ancient beliefs to guide them through uncertain times, and how international agencies make a difference in what is and isn't a drug in Madagascar. These contributions illustrate the breadth and reach of anthropology and the way it can help us to understand what is going on right now on our planet. Together, they provide a field guide to the twenty-first century and models for how to do anthropology. We hope that you enjoy them and, more, that they help you understand your world. Along with the older works, they provide paradigms for anthropology.

I

Fieldwork

1

THE EARLY PARADIGM
ON A PACIFIC ISLAND
EXCERPT FROM *ARGONAUTS*
OF THE WESTERN PACIFIC

Bronislaw Malinowski

I

Further East, on the South coast, there lives the industrious, seafaring population of the Mailu, who link the East End of New Guinea with the central coast tribes by means of annual trading expeditions.[1] Finally, the natives of the islands and archipelagoes, scattered around the East End, are in constant trading relations with one another. We possess in Professor Seligman's book an excellent description of the subject, especially of the nearer trade routes between the various islands inhabited by the Southern Massim.[2] There exists, however, another, a very extensive and highly complex trading system, embracing with its ramifications, not only the islands near the East End, but also the Louisiades, Woodlark Island, the Trobriand Archipelago, and the d'Entrecasteaux group; it penetrates into the mainland of New Guinea, and exerts an indirect influence over several outlying districts, such as Rossel Island, and some parts of the Northern and Southern coast of New Guinea. This trading system, the Kula, is the subject I am setting out to describe in this volume, and it will be seen that it is an economic phenomenon of considerable theoretical importance. It looms paramount in the tribal life of those natives who live within its circuit, and its importance is fully realised by the tribesmen themselves, whose ideas, ambitions, desires and vanities are very much bound up with the Kula.

II

Before proceeding to the account of the Kula, it will be well to give a description of the methods used in the collecting of the ethnographic material. The results of scientific research in any branch of learning ought to be presented in a manner absolutely candid and above board. No one would dream of making an experimental contribution to physical or chemical science, without giving a detailed account of all the arrangements of the experiments; an exact description of the apparatus used; of the manner in which the observations were conducted; of their number; of the length of time devoted to them; and of the degree of approximation with which each measurement was made. In less exact sciences, as in biology or geology, this cannot be done as rigorously, but every student will do his best to bring home to the reader all the conditions in which the experiment or the observations were made. In Ethnography, where a candid account of such data is perhaps even more necessary, it has unfortunately in the past not always been supplied with sufficient generosity, and many writers do not ply the full searchlight of methodic sincerity, as they move among their facts but produce them before us out of complete obscurity.

It would be easy to quote works of high repute, and with a scientific hallmark on them, in which wholesale generalisations are laid down before us, and we are not informed at all by what actual experiences the writers have reached their conclusion. No special chapter or paragraph is devoted to describing to us the conditions under which observations were made and information collected. I consider that only such ethnographic sources are of unquestionable scientific value, in which we can dearly draw the line between, on the one hand, the results of direct observation and of native statements and interpretations, and on the other, the inferences of the author, based on his common sense and psychological insight.[3] Indeed, some such survey, as that contained in the table, given below (Div. VI of this chapter) ought to be forthcoming, so that at a glance the reader could estimate with precision the degree of the writer's personal acquaintance with the facts which he describes, and form an idea under what conditions information had been obtained from the natives.

Again, in historical science, no one could expect to be seriously treated if he made any mystery of his sources and spoke of the past as if he knew it by divination. In Ethnography, the writer is his own chronicler and the historian at the same time, while his sources are no doubt easily accessible, but also supremely elusive and complex; they are not embodied in fixed, material documents, but in the behaviour and in the memory of living men. In Ethnography, the distance is often enormous between the brute material of information—as it is presented to the student in his own observations, in native statement, in the kaleidoscope of tribal life—and the final authoritative presentation of the results. The Ethnographer has to traverse this distance in the laborious years between the moment when he sets foot upon a native beach, and makes his first attempts to get into touch with the natives, and the time when he writes down the final version of his results. A brief outline of an Ethnographer's tribulations, as lived through by myself, may throw more light on the question, than any long abstract discussion could do.

III

Imagine yourself suddenly set down surrounded by all your gear, alone on a tropical beach close to a native village, while the launch or dinghy which has brought you sails away out of sight. Since you take up your abode in the compound of some neighbouring white man, trader or missionary, you have nothing to do, but to start at once on your ethnographic work. Imagine further that you are a beginner, without previous experience, with nothing to guide you and no one to help you. For the white man is temporarily absent, or else unable or unwilling to waste any of his time on you. This exactly describes my first initiation into field work on the south coast of New Guinea. I well remember the long visits I paid to the villages during the first weeks; the feeling of hopelessness and despair after many obstinate but futile attempts had entirely failed to bring me into real touch with the natives, or supply me with any material. I had periods of despondency, when I buried myself in the reading of novels, as a man might take to drink in a fit of tropical depression and boredom.

Imagine yourself then, making your first entry into the village, alone or in company with your white cicerone. Some natives flock round you, especially if they smell tobacco. Others, the more dignified and elderly, remain seated where they are. Your white companion has his routine way of treating the natives, and he neither understands, nor is very much concerned with the manner in which you, as an ethnographer, will have to approach them. The first visit leaves you with a hopeful feeling that when you return alone, things will be easier. Such was my hope at least.

I came back duly, and soon gathered an audience around me. A few compliments in pidgin English on both sides, some tobacco changing hands, induced an atmosphere of mutual amiability. I tried then to proceed to business. First, to begin with subjects which might arouse no suspicion, I started to "do" technology. A few natives were engaged in manufacturing some object or other. It was easy to look at it and obtain the names of the tools, and even some technical expressions about the proceedings, but there the matter ended. It must be borne in mind that pidgin English is a very imperfect instrument for expressing one's ideas, and that before one gets a good training in framing questions and understanding answers one has the uncomfortable feeling that free communication in it with the natives will never be attained; and I was quite unable to enter into any more detailed or explicit conversation with them at first. I knew well that the best remedy for this was to collect concrete data, and accordingly I took a village census, wrote down genealogies, drew up plans and collected the terms of kinship. But all this remained dead material, which led no further into the understanding of real native mentality or behaviour, since I could neither procure a good native interpretation of any of these items, nor get what could be called the hang of tribal life. As to obtaining their ideas about religion, and magic, their beliefs in sorcery and spirits, nothing was forthcoming except a few superficial items of folklore, mangled by being forced into pidgin English.

Information which I received from some white residents in the district, valuable as it was in itself, was more discouraging than anything else with regard to my own work. Here were men who had lived for years in the place with constant opportunities of observing the natives and communicating with them, and who yet hardly knew one thing about them really well. How could I therefore in a few months or a year, hope to overtake and go beyond them? Moreover, the manner in which my white informants spoke about the natives and put their views was, naturally, that of untrained minds, unaccustomed to formulate their thoughts with any degree of consistency and precision. And they were for the most part, naturally enough, full of the biased and prejudged opinions inevitable in the average practical man, whether administrator, missionary, or trader, yet so strongly repulsive to a mind striving after the objective, scientific view of things. The habit of treating with a self-satisfied frivolity what is really serious to the ethnographer; the cheap rating of what to him is a scientific treasure, that is to say, the native's cultural and mental peculiarities and independence—these features, so well known in the inferior amateur's writing, I found in the tone of the majority of white residents.[4]

Indeed, in my first piece of Ethnographic research on the South coast, it was not until I was alone in the district that I began to make some headway; and, at any rate, I found out where lay the secret of effective field work. What is then this ethnographer's magic, by which he is able to evoke the real spirit of the natives, the true picture of tribal life? As usual, success can only be obtained by a patient and systematic application of a number of rules of common sense and well-known scientific principles, and not by the discovery of any marvelous shortcut leading to the desired results without effort or trouble. The principles of method can be grouped under three main headings; first of all, naturally, the student must possess real scientific aims, and know the values and criteria of modern ethnography. Secondly, he ought to put himself in good conditions of work, that is, in the main, to live without other white men, right among the natives. Finally, he has to apply a number of special methods of collecting, manipulating and fixing his evidence. A few words must be said about these three foundation stones of field work, beginning with the second as the most elementary.

IV

Proper conditions for ethnographic work. These, as said, consist mainly in cutting oneself off from the company of other white men, and remaining in as close contact with the natives as possible, which really can only be achieved by camping right in their villages.... It is very nice to have a base in a white man's compound for the stores, and to know there is a refuge there in times of sickness and surfeit of native. But it must be far enough away not to become a permanent milieu in which you live and from which you emerge at fixed hours only to "do the village." It should not even be near enough to fly to at any moment for recreation. For the native is not the natural companion for a white man, and after you have been working with him for several hours, seeing how he does his gardens, or letting him tell you items of folklore, or discussing his customs, you will naturally hanker after the company of your own kind. But if you are alone in a village beyond reach of this, you go for a solitary walk for an hour or so, return again and then quite naturally seek out the natives' society, this time as a relief from loneliness, just as you would any other companionship. And by means of this natural intercourse, you learn to know him, and you become familiar with his customs and beliefs far better than when he is a paid, and often bored, informant.

There is all the difference between a sporadic plunging into the company of natives, and being really in contact with them. What does this latter mean? On the Ethnographer's side, it means that his life in the village, which at first is a strange, sometimes unpleasant, sometimes intensely interesting adventure, soon adopts quite a natural course very much in harmony with his surroundings.

Soon after I had established myself in Omarakana (Trobriand Islands), I began to take part, in a way, in the village life, to look forward to the important or festive events, to take personal interest in the gossip and the developments of the small village occurrences; to wake up every morning to a day, presenting itself to me more or less as it does to the native. I would get out from under my mosquito net, to find around me the village life beginning to stir, or the people well advanced in their working day according to the hour and also to the season, for they get up and begin their labours early or late, as work presses. As I went on my morning walk through the village, I could see intimate details of family life, of toilet, cooking, taking of meals; I could see the arrangements for the day's work, people starting on their errands, or groups of men and women busy at some manufacturing tasks.... Quarrels, jokes, family scenes, events usually trivial, sometimes dramatic but always significant, formed the atmosphere of my daily life, as well as of theirs. It must be remembered that as the natives saw me constantly every day, they ceased to be interested or alarmed, or made self-conscious by my presence, and I ceased to be a disturbing element in the tribal life which I was to study, altering it by my very approach, as always happens with a newcomer to every savage community. In fact, as they knew that I would thrust my nose into everything, even where a well-mannered native would not dream of intruding, they finished by regarding me as part and parcel of their life, a necessary evil or nuisance, mitigated by donations of tobacco.

Later on in the day, whatever happened was within easy reach, and there was no possibility of its escaping my notice. Alarms about the sorcerer's approach in the evening, one or two big, really important quarrels and rifts within the community, cases of illness, attempted cures and deaths, magical rites which had to be performed, all these I had not to pursue, fearful of missing them, but they took place under my very eyes, at my own doorstep, so to speak.... And it must be emphasised whenever anything dramatic or important occurs it is essential to investigate it at the very moment of happening, because the natives cannot but talk about it, are too excited to be reticent, and too interested to be mentally lazy in supplying details. Also, over and over again, I committed breaches of etiquette, which the natives, familiar enough with me, were not slow in pointing out. I had to learn how to behave, and to a certain extent, I acquired "the feeling" for native good and bad manners. With this, and with the capacity of enjoying their company and sharing some of their games and amusements, I began to feel that I was indeed in touch with the natives, and this is certainly the preliminary condition of being able to carry on successful field work.

V

But the Ethnographer has not only to spread his nets in the right place, and wait for what will fall into them. He must be an active huntsman, and drive his quarry into them and follow it up to its most inaccessible lairs. And that leads us to the more active methods of pursuing ethnographic evidence. It has been mentioned at the end of Division III that the Ethnographer has to be inspired by the knowledge of the most modern results of scientific study, by its principles and aims. I shall not enlarge upon this subject, except by way of one remark, to avoid the possibility of misunderstanding. Good training in theory, and acquaintance with its latest results, is not identical with being burdened with "preconceived ideas." If a man sets out on an expedition, determined to prove certain hypotheses, if he is incapable of changing his views constantly and casting them off ungrudgingly under the pressure of evidence, needless to say his work will be worthless. But the more problems he brings with him into the field, the more he is in the habit of moulding his theories according to facts, and of seeing facts in their bearing upon theory, the better he is equipped for the work. Preconceived ideas are pernicious in any scientific work, but foreshadowed problems are the main endowment of a scientific thinker, and these problems are first revealed to the observer by his theoretical studies.

In Ethnology the early efforts of Bastian, Tylor, Morgan, the German Völkerpsychologen have remoulded the older crude information of travellers, missionaries, etc., and have shown us the importance of applying deeper conceptions and discarding crude and misleading ones.[5]

The concept of animism superseded that of "fetishism" or "devil worship," both meaningless terms. The understanding of the classificatory systems of relationship paved the way for the brilliant, modern researches on native sociology in the field work of the Cambridge school. The psychological analysis of the German thinkers has brought forth an abundant crop of most valuable information in the results obtained by the recent German expeditions to Africa, South America and the Pacific, while the theoretical works of Frazer, Durkheim and others have already, and will no doubt still for a long time inspire field workers and lead them to new results. The field worker relies entirely upon inspiration from theory. Of course he may be also a theoretical thinker and worker, and there he can draw on himself for stimulus. But the two functions are separate, and in actual research they have to be separated both in time and conditions of work.

As always happens when scientific interest turns towards and begins to labour on a field so far only prospected by the curiosity of amateurs, Ethnology has introduced law and order into what seemed chaotic and freakish. It has transformed for us the sensational, wild and unaccountable world of "savages" into a number of well ordered communities, governed by law, behaving and thinking according to consistent principles. The word "savage," whatever association it might have had originally, connotes ideas of boundless liberty, of irregularity, of something extremely and extraordinarily quaint. In popular thinking, we imagine that the natives live on the bosom of Nature, more or less as they can and like, the prey of irregular, phantasmagoric beliefs and apprehensions. Modern science, on the contrary, shows that their social institutions have a very definite organisation, that they are governed by authority, law, and order in their public and personal relations, while the latter are, besides, under the control of extremely complex ties of kinship and clanship. Indeed, we see them entangled in a mesh of duties, functions, and privileges, which correspond to an elaborate tribal, communal, and kinship organisation. Their beliefs and practices do not by any means lack consistency of a certain type, and their knowledge of the outer world is sufficient to guide them in many of their strenuous enterprises and activities. Their artistic productions again lack neither meaning nor beauty.

It is a very far cry from the famous answer given long ago by a representative authority who, asked, what are the manners and customs of the natives, answered, "Customs none, manners beastly," to the position of the modern Ethnographer! This latter, with his tables of kinship terms, genealogies, maps, plans and diagrams, proves the existence of an extensive and big organisation, shows the constitution of the tribe, of the clan, of the family; and he gives us a picture of the natives subjected to a strict code of behaviour and good manners, to which in comparison the life at the Court of Versailles or Escurial was tree and easy.[6]

Thus the first and basic ideal of ethnographic field work is to give a clear and firm outline of the social constitution, and disentangle the laws and regularities of all cultural phenomena from the irrelevances. The firm skeleton of the tribal life has to be first ascertained. This ideal imposes in the first place the fundamental obligation of giving a complete survey of the phenomena, and not of picking out the sensational, the singular, still less the funny and quaint. The time when we could tolerate accounts presenting us the native as a distorted, childish caricature of a human being is gone. This picture is false, and like many other falsehoods, it has been killed by Science. The field Ethnographer has seriously and soberly to cover the full extent of the phenomena in each aspect of tribal culture studied, making no difference between what is commonplace, or drab, or ordinary, and what strikes him as astonishing and out of the way. At the same time, the whole area of tribal culture *in all its aspects* has to be gone over in research. The consistency, the law and order which obtain within each aspect make also for joining them into one coherent whole.

An Ethnographer who sets out to study only religion, or only technology, or only social organisation cuts out an artificial field for inquiry, and he will be seriously handicapped in his work.

VI

Having settled this very general rule, let us descend to more detailed consideration of method. The Ethnographer has in the field, according to what has just been said, the duty before him of drawing up all the rules and regularities of tribal life; all that is permanent and fixed; of giving an anatomy of their culture, of depicting the constitution of their society. But these things, though crystallised and set, are nowhere *formulated*. There is no written or explicitly expressed code of laws, and their whole tribal tradition, the whole structure of their society, are embodied in the most elusive of all materials; the human being. But not even in human mind or memory are these laws to be found definitely formulated. The natives obey the forces and commands of the tribal code, but they do not comprehend them; exactly as they obey their instincts and their impulses, but could not lay down a single law of psychology. The regularities in native institutions are an automatic result of the interaction of the mental forces of tradition, and of the material conditions of environment. Exactly as a humble member of any modern institution, whether it be the state, or the church, or the army, is *of* it and *in* it, but has no vision of the resulting integral action of the whole, still less could furnish any account of its organisation, so it would be futile to attempt questioning a native in abstract, sociological terms. The difference is that, in our society, every institution has its intelligent members, its historians, and its archives and documents, whereas in a native society there are none of these. After this is realised an expedient has to be found to overcome this difficulty. This expedient for an Ethnographer consists in collecting concrete data of evidence and drawing the general inferences for himself. This seems obvious on the face of it, but was not found out or at least practised in Ethnography till field work was taken up by men of science. Moreover, in giving it practical effect, it is neither easy to devise the concrete applications of this method, nor to carry them out systematically and consistently.

Though we cannot ask a native about abstract, general rules, we can always enquire how a given case would be treated. Thus for instance, in asking how they would treat crime, or punish it, it would be vain to put to a native a sweeping question such as, "How do you treat and punish a criminal?" for even words could not be found to express it in native, or in pidgin. But an imaginary case, or still better, a real occurrence, will stimulate a native to express his opinion and to supply plentiful information. A real case indeed will start the natives on a wave of discussion, evoke expressions of indignation, show them taking sides—all of which talk will probably contain a wealth of definite views, of moral censures, as well as reveal the social mechanism set in motion by the crime committed. From there, it will be easy to lead them on to speak of other similar cases, to remember other actual occurrences or to discuss them in all their implications and aspects. From this material, which ought to cover the widest possible range of facts, the inference is obtained by simple induction. The *scientific* treatment differs from that of good common sense, first in that a student will extend the completeness and minuteness of survey much further and in a pedantically systematic and methodical manner; and secondly, in that the scientifically trained mind will push the inquiry along really relevant lines, and towards aims possessing real importance. Indeed, the object of scientific training is to provide the empirical investigator with a *mental chart*, in accordance with which he can take his bearings and lay his course.

To return to our example, a number of definite cases discussed will reveal to the Ethnographer the social machinery for punishment. This is one part, one aspect of tribal authority. Imagine further that by a similar method of inference from definite data, he arrives at understanding leadership in war, in economic enterprise, in tribal festivities—there he has at once all the data necessary to answer the questions about tribal government and social authority. In actual field work, the comparison of such data, the attempt to piece them together, will often reveal rifts and gaps in the information which lead on to further investigations.

From my own experience, I can say that, very often, a problem seemed settled, everything fixed and clear, till I began to write down a short preliminary sketch of my results. And only then, did I see the enormous deficiencies, which would show me where lay new problems, and lead me on to new work. In fact, I spent a few months between my first and second expeditions, and over a year between that and the subsequent one, in going over all my material, and making parts of it almost ready for publication each time, though each time I knew I would have to rewrite it. Such cross-fertilisation of constructive work and observation, I found most valuable, and I do not think I could have made real headway without it. I give this bit of my own history merely to show that what has been said so far is not only an empty programme, but the result of personal experience. In this volume, the description is given of a big institution connected with ever so many associated activities, and presenting many aspects. To anyone who reflects on the subject, it will be clear that the information about a phenomenon of such high complexity and of so many ramifications, could not be obtained with any degree of exactitude and completeness, without a constant interplay of constructive attempts and empirical checking. In fact, I have written up an outline of the Kula institution at least half a dozen times while in the field and in the intervals between my expeditions. Each time, new problems and difficulties presented themselves.

The collecting of concrete data over a wide range of facts is thus one of the main points of field method. The obligation is not to enumerate a few examples only, but to exhaust as far as possible all the cases within reach; and, on this search for cases, the investigator will score most whose mental chart is clearest. But, whenever the material of the search allows it, this mental chart ought to be transformed into a real one; it ought to materialise into a diagram, a plan, an exhaustive, synoptic table of cases. Long since, in all tolerably good modern books on natives, we expect to find a full list or table of kinship terms, which includes all the data relative to it, and does not just pick out a few strange and anomalous relationships or expressions. In the investigation of kinship, the following up of one relation after another in concrete cases leads naturally to the construction of genealogical tables. Practised already by the best early writers, such as Munzinger, and, if I remember rightly, Kubary, this method has been developed to its fullest extent in the works of Dr. Rivers. Again, studying the concrete data of economic transactions, in order to trace the history of a valuable object, and to gauge the nature of its circulation, the principle of completeness and thoroughness would lead to construct tables of transactions, such as we find in the work of Professor Seligman.[7] It is in following Professor Seligman's example in this matter that I was able to settle certain of the more difficult and detailed rules of the Kula. The method of reducing information, if possible, into charts or synoptic tables ought to be extended to the study of practically all aspects of native life. All types of economic transactions may be studied by following up connected, actual cases, and putting them into a synoptic chart; again, a table ought to be drawn up of all the gifts and presents customary in a given society, a table including the sociological, ceremonial, and economic definition of every item. Also, systems of magic, connected series of ceremonies, types of legal acts, all could be charted, allowing each entry to be synoptically defined under a number of headings. Besides this, of course, the genealogical census of every community, studied more in detail, extensive maps, plans and diagrams, illustrating ownership in garden land, hunting and fishing privileges, etc., serve as the more fundamental documents of ethnographic research.

A genealogy is nothing else but a synoptic chart of a number of connected relations of kinship. Its value as an instrument of research consists in that it allows the investigator to put questions which he formulates to himself *in abstracto,* but can put concretely to the native informant. As a document, its value consists in that it gives a number of authenticated data, presented in their natural grouping. A synoptic chart of magic fulfils the same function. As an instrument of research, I have used it in order to ascertain, for instance, the ideas about the nature of magical power. With a chart before me, I could easily and conveniently go over one item after the other, and note down the relevant practices and beliefs contained in each of them. The answer to my abstract problem could then be obtained by drawing a general inference from all the cases.[8] ... I cannot enter further into the discussion of this question, which would need further distinctions, such as between a chart of concrete, actual data, such as is a genealogy, and a chart summarising the outlines of a custom or belief, as a chart of a magical system would be.

Returning once more to the question of methodological candour, discussed previously in Division II, I wish to point out here, that the procedure of concrete and tabularised presentation of data ought to be applied first to the Ethnographer's own credentials. That is, an Ethnographer, who wishes to be trusted, must show clearly and concisely, in a tabularised form, which are his own direct observations, and which the indirect information that forms the bases of his account.... With the help of ... the many references scattered throughout the text, as to how, under what circumstances, and with what degree of accuracy I arrived at a given item of knowledge, there will, I hope remain no obscurity whatever as to the sources of the book.

Chronological List of Kula Events Witnessed by the Writer

First Expedition, August 1914–March 1915.
March 1915. In the village of Dikoyas (Woodlark Island) a few ceremonial offerings seen. Preliminary information obtained.
Second Expedition, May 1915–May, 1916.
June 1915. A Kabigidoya visit arrives from Vakuta to Kiriwina. Its anchoring at Kavataria witnessed and the men seen at Omarakana, where information collected.
July 1915. Several parties from Kitava land on the beach of Kaulukuba. The men examined in Omarakana. Much information collected in that period.
September 1915. Unsuccessful attempt to sail to Kitava with To'uluwa, the chief of Omarakana.
October–November 1915. Departure noticed of three expeditions from Kiriwina to Kitava. Each time To'uluwa brings home a haul of *mwali* (armshells).
November 1915–March 1916. Preparations for a big overseas expedition from Kiriwina to the Marshall Bennett Islands. Construction of a canoe; renovating of another; sail making in Omarakana; launching; *tasasoria*

on the beach of Kaulukuba. At the same time, information is being obtained about these and the associated subjects. Some magical texts of canoe building and Kula magic obtained.

Third Expedition, October 1917-October 1918.

November 1917–December 1917. Inland Kula; some data obtained in Tukwaukwa.

December 1917–February 1918. Parties from Kitava arrive in Wawela. Collection of information about the *yoyova.* Magic and spells of Kaygau obtained.

March 1918. Preparations in Sanaroa; preparations in the Amphletts; the Dobuan fleet arrives in the Amphletts. The *uvalaku* expedition from Dobu followed to Boyowa.

April 1918. Their arrival; their reception in Sinaketa; the Kula transactions; the big intertribal gathering. Some magical formulae obtained.

May 1918. Party from Kitava seen in Vakuta.

June–July 1918. Information about Kula magic and customs checked and amplified in Omarakana, especially with regard to its Eastern branches.

August–September 1918. Magical texts obtained in Sinaketa.

October 1918. Information obtained from a number of natives in Dobu and Southern Massim district (examined in Samarai).

To summarise the first, cardinal point of method, I may say each phenomenon ought to be studied through the broadest range possible of its concrete manifestations; each studied by an exhaustive survey of detailed examples. If possible, the results ought to be tabulated into some sort of synoptic chart both to be used as an instrument of study, and to be presented as an ethnological document. With the help of such documents and such study of actualities, the clear outline of the framework of the natives' culture in the widest sense of the word and the constitution of their society can be presented. This method could be called *the method of statistic documentation by concrete evidence.*

VII

Needless to add, in this respect, the scientific field work is far above even the best amateur productions. There is, however, one point in which the latter often excel. This is in the presentation of intimate touches of native life, in bringing home to us these aspects of it with which one is made familiar only through being in close contact with the natives, one way or the other, for a long period of time. In certain results of scientific work—especially that which has been called "survey work"—we are given an excellent skeleton, so to speak, of the tribal constitution, but it lacks flesh and blood. We learn much about the framework of their society, but within it, we cannot perceive or imagine the realities of human life, the even flow of everyday events, the occasional ripples of excitement over a feast, or ceremony, or some singular occurrence. In working out the rules and regularities of native custom, and in obtaining a precise formula for them from the collection of data and native statements, we find that this very precision is foreign to real life, which never adheres rigidly to any rules. It must be supplemented by the observation of the manner in which a given custom is carried out, of the behaviour of the natives in obeying the rules so exactly formulated by the ethnographer, of the very exceptions which in sociological phenomena almost always occur.

If all the conclusions are solely based on the statements of informants, or deduced from objective documents, it is of course impossible to supplement them in actually observed data of real behaviour. And that is the reason why certain works of amateur residents of long standing, such as educated traders and planters, medical men and officials, and last, but not least, the few intelligent and unbiased missionaries to whom Ethnography owes so much, surpass in plasticity and in vividness most of the purely scientific accounts. But if the specialised field worker can adopt the conditions of living described above, he is in a far better position to be really in touch with the natives than any other white resident. For none of them lives right in a native village, except for very short periods, and everyone has his own business, which takes up a considerable part of his time. Moreover, if, like a trader or a missionary or an official he enters into active relations with the native, if he has to transform or influence or make use of him, this makes a real, unbiased, impartial observation impossible, and precludes all-round sincerity, at least in the case of the missionaries and officials.

Living in the village with no other business but to follow native life, one sees the customs, ceremonies and transactions over and over again, one has examples of their beliefs as they are actually lived through, and the full body and blood of actual native life fills out soon the skeleton of abstract constructions. That is the reason why, working under such conditions as previously described, the Ethnographer is enabled to add something essential to the bare outline of tribal constitution, and to supplement it by all the details of behaviour, setting and small incident. He is able in each case to state whether an act is public or private; how a public assembly behaves, and what it looks like; he can judge whether an event is ordinary or an exciting and singular one; whether natives bring to it a great deal of sincere and earnest spirit, or perform it in fun; whether they do it in a perfunctory manner, or with zeal and deliberation.

In other words, there is a series of phenomena of great importance which cannot possibly be recorded by questioning or computing documents, but have to be observed in their full actuality. Let us call them *the imponderabilia of actual life*. Here belong such things as the routine of a man's working day, the details of his care of the body, of the manner of taking food and preparing it; the tone of conversational and social life around the village fires, the existence of strong friendships or hostilities, and of passing sympathies and dislikes between people; the subtle yet unmistakable manner in which personal vanities and ambitions are reflected in the behaviour of the individual and in the emotional reactions of those who surround him. All these facts can and ought to be scientifically formulated and recorded, but it is necessary that this be done, not by a superficial registration of details, as is usually done by untrained observers, but with an effort at penetrating the mental attitude expressed in them. And that is the reason why the work of scientifically trained observers, once seriously applied to the study of this aspect, will, I believe, yield results of surpassing value. So far, it has been done only by amateurs, and therefore done, on the whole, indifferently.

Indeed, if we remember that these imponderable yet all important facts of actual life are part of the real substance of the social fabric, that in them are spun the innumerable threads which keep together the family, the clan, the village community, the tribe—their significance becomes clear. The more crystallised bonds of social grouping, such as the definite ritual, the economic and legal duties, the obligations, the ceremonial gifts and formal marks of regard, though equally important for the student, are certainly felt less strongly by the individual who has to fulfill them. Applying this to ourselves, we all know that "family life" means for us, first and foremost, the atmosphere of home, all the innumerable small acts and attentions in which are expressed the affection, the mutual interest, the little preferences, and the little antipathies which constitute intimacy. That we may inherit from this person, that we shall have to walk after the hearse of the other, though sociologically these facts belong to the definition of "family" and "family life," in personal perspective of what family truly is to us, they normally stand very much in the background.

Exactly the same applies to a native community, and if the Ethnographer wants to bring their real life home to his readers, he must on no account neglect this. Neither aspect, the intimate, as little as the legal, ought to be glossed over. Yet as a rule in ethnographic accounts we have not both but either the one or the other—and, so far, the intimate one has hardly ever been properly treated. In all social relations besides the family ties, even those between mere tribesmen and, beyond that, between hostile or friendly members of different tribes, meeting on any sort of social business, there is this intimate side, expressed by the typical details of intercourse, the tone of their behaviour in the presence of one another. This side is different from the definite, crystalised legal frame of the relationship, and it has to be studied and stated in its own right.

In the same way, in studying the conspicuous acts of tribal life, such as ceremonies, rites, festivities, etc., the details and tone of behaviour ought to be given, besides the bare outline of events. The importance of this may be exemplified by one instance. Much has been said and written about survival. Yet the survival character of an act is expressed in nothing so well as in the concomitant behaviour, in the way in which it is carried out. Take any example from our own culture, whether it be the pomp and pageantry of a state ceremony, or a picturesque custom kept up by street urchins, its "outline" will not tell you whether the rite flourishes still with full vigour in the hearts of those who perform it or assist at the performance or whether they regard it as almost a dead thing, kept alive for tradition's sake. But observe and fix the data of their behaviour, and at once the degree of vitality of the act will become clear. There is no doubt, from all points of sociological, or psychological, analysis, and in any question of theory, the manner and type of behaviour observed in the performance of an act are of the highest importance. Indeed behaviour is a fact, a relevant fact, and one that can be recorded. And foolish indeed and shortsighted would be the man of science who would pass by a whole class of phenomena, ready to be garnered, and leave them to waste, even though he did not see at the moment to what theoretical use they might be put!

As to the actual method of observing and recording in field work these *imponderabilia of actual life and of typical behaviour,* there is no doubt that the personal equation of the observer comes in here more prominently, than, in the collection of crystalised, ethnographic data. But here also the main endeavour must be to let facts speak for themselves. If in making a daily round of the village, certain small incidents, characteristic forms of taking food, of conversing, of doing work ... are found occurring over and over again, they should be noted down at once. It is also important that this work of collecting and fixing impressions should begin early in the course of working out a district. Because certain subtle peculiarities, which make an impression as long as they are novel, cease to be noticed as soon as they become familiar. Others again can only be perceived with a better knowledge of the local conditions. An ethnographic diary, carried on systematically throughout the course of one's work in a district would be the ideal instrument for this sort of study. And if, side by side with the normal and typical, the ethnographer carefully notes the slight, or the more pronounced deviations from it, he will be able to indicate the two extremes within which the normal moves.

In observing ceremonies or other tribal events, ... it is necessary, not only to note down those occurrences and details which are prescribed by tradition and custom to be the essential course of the act, but also the Ethnographer ought to record carefully and precisely, one after the other, the actions of the actors and of the spectators. Forgetting for a moment that he knows and understands the structure of this ceremony, the main dogmatic ideas underlying it, he might try to find himself only in the midst of an assembly of human beings, who behave seriously or jocularly, with earnest concentration or with bored frivolity, who are either in the same mood as he finds them every day, or else are screwed up to a high pitch of excitement, and so on and so on. With his attention constantly directed to this aspect of tribal life, with the constant endeavour to fix it, to express it in terms of actual fact, a good deal of reliable and expressive material finds its way into his notes. He will be able to "set" the act into its proper place in tribal life, that is to show whether it is exceptional or commonplace, one in which the natives behave ordinarily, or one in which their whole behaviour is transformed. And he will also be able to bring all this home to his readers in a clear, convincing manner.

Again, in this type of work, it is good for the Ethnographer sometimes to put aside camera, note book and pencil, and to join in himself in what is going on. He can take part in the natives' games, he can follow them on their visits and walks, sit down and listen and share in their conversations. I am not certain if this is equally easy for everyone—perhaps the Slavonic nature is more plastic and more naturally savage than that of Western Europeans—but though the degree of success varies, the attempt is possible for everyone. Out of such plunges into the life of the natives—and I made them frequently not only for study's sake but because everyone needs human company—I have carried away a distinct feeling that their behaviour, their manner of being, in all sorts of tribal transactions, became more transparent and easily understandable than it had been before. All these methodological remarks, the reader will find again illustrated in the following chapters.

VIII

Finally, let us pass to the third and last aim of scientific field work, to the last type of phenomenon which ought to be recorded in order to give a full and adequate picture of native culture. Besides the firm outline of tribal constitution and crystallised cultural items which form the skeleton, besides the data of daily life and ordinary behaviour, which are, so to speak, its flesh and blood, there is still to be recorded the spirit—the natives' views and opinions and utterances. For, in every act of tribal life, there is, first, the routine prescribed by custom and tradition, then there is the manner in which it is carried out, and lastly there is the commentary to it, contained in the natives' mind. A man who submits to various customary obligations, who follows a traditional course of action, does it impelled by certain motives, to the accompaniment of certain feelings, guided by certain ideas. These ideas, feelings, and impulses are moulded and conditioned by the culture in which we find them, and are therefore an ethnic peculiarity of the given society. An attempt must be made therefore, to study and record them.

But is this possible? Are these subjective states not too elusive and shapeless? And, even granted that people usually do feel or think or experience certain psychological states in association with the performance of customary acts, the majority of them surely are not able to formulate these states, to put them into words. This latter point must certainly be granted, and it is perhaps the real Gordian knot in the study of the facts of social psychology. Without trying to cut or untie this knot, that is to solve the problem theoretically, or to enter further into the field of general methodology, I shall make directly for the question of practical means to overcome some of the difficulties involved.

First of all, it has to be laid down that we have to study here stereotyped manners of thinking and feeling. As sociologists, we are not interested in what A or B may feel *qua* individuals, in the accidental course of their own personal experiences—we are interested only in what they feel and think *qua* members of a given community. Now in this capacity, their mental states receive a certain stamp, become stereotyped by the institutions in which they live, by the influence of tradition and folklore, by the very vehicle of thought, that is by language. The social and cultural environment in which they move forces them to think and feel in a definite manner. Thus, a man who lives in a polyandrous community cannot experience the same feelings of jealousy, as a strict monogynist, though he might have the elements of them. A man who lives within the sphere of the Kula cannot become permanently and sentimentally attached to certain of his possessions, in spite of the fact that he values them most of all. These examples are crude, but better ones will be found in the text of this book.

So, the third commandment of field work runs: Find out the typical ways of thinking and feeling, corresponding to the institutions and culture of a given community, and formulate the results in the most convincing manner. What will be the method of procedure? The best ethnographical writers—here again the Cambridge school with Haddon, Rivers, and Seligman ranks first among English Ethnographers—have always tried to quote *verbatim* statements of crucial importance. They also adduce terms of native classification; sociological, psychological and industrial *termini technici,* and have rendered the verbal contour of native thought as precisely as possible. One step further in this line can be made by the Ethnographer, who acquires a knowledge of the native language and can use it as an instrument of inquiry. In working in the Kiriwinian language, I found still some difficulty in writing down the statement directly in translation which at first I used to do in the act of taking notes. The translation often robbed the text of all its significant characteristics—rubbed off all its points—so that gradually I was led to note down certain important phrases just as they were spoken, in the native tongue. As my knowledge of the language progressed, I put down more and more in Kiriwinian, till at last I found myself writing exclusively in that language, rapidly taking notes, word for word, of each statement. No sooner had I arrived at this point, than I recognised that I was thus acquiring at the same time an abundant linguistic material, and a series of ethnographic documents which ought to be reproduced as I had fixed them, besides being utilised in the writing up of my account.[9] This *corpus inscriptionum Kiriwiniensium* can be utilised, not only by myself, but by all those who, through their better penetration and ability of interpreting them, may find points which escape my attention, very much as the other *corpora* form the basis for the various interpretations of ancient and prehistoric cultures; only, these ethnographic inscriptions are all decipherable and clear, have been almost all translated fully and unambiguously, and have been provided with native cross-commentaries or *scholia* obtained from living sources....

IX

Our considerations thus indicate that the goal of ethnographic field work must be approached through three avenues:

1. *The organisation of the tribe, and the anatomy of its culture* must be recorded in firm, clear outline. The method of *concrete, statistical documentation* is the means through which such an outline has to be given.
2. Within this frame, the *imponderabilia of actual life*, and the *type of behaviour* have to be filled in. They have to be collected through minute, detailed observations, in the form of some sort of ethnographic diary, made possible by close contact with native life.
3. A collection of ethnographic statements, characteristic narratives, typical utterances, items of folklore and magical formula has to be given as a *corpus inscriptionum*, as documents of native mentality.

These three lines of approach lead to the final goal, of which an Ethnographer should never lose sight. This goal is, briefly, to grasp the native's point of view, his relation to life, to realise *his* vision of *his* world. We have to study man, and we must study what concerns him most intimately, that is, the hold which life has on him. In each culture, the values are slightly different; people aspire after different aims, follow different impulses, yearn after a different form of happiness. In each culture, we find different institutions in which man pursues his life-interest, different customs by which he satisfies his aspirations, different codes of law and morality which reward his virtues or punish his defections. To study the institutions, customs, and codes or to study the behaviour and mentality without the subjective desire of feeling by what these people live, of realising the substance of their happiness—is, in my opinion, to miss the greatest reward which we can hope to obtain from the study of man.

These generalities the reader will find illustrated in the following chapters. We shall see there the savage striving to satisfy certain aspirations, to attain his type of value, to follow his line of social ambition. We shall see him led on to perilous and difficult enterprises by a tradition of magical and heroical exploits, shall see him following the lure of his own romance. Perhaps as we read the account of these remote customs there may emerge a feeling of solidarity with the endeavours and ambitions of these natives. Perhaps man's mentality will be revealed to us, and brought near, along some lines which we never have followed before. Perhaps through realising human nature in a shape very distant and foreign to us, we shall have some light shed on our own. In this, and in this case only, we shall be justified in feeling that it has been worth our while to understand these natives, their institutions and customs, and that we have gathered some profit from the Kula.

Notes

1. Cf. "The Mailu," by B. Malinowski, in Transactions of the R. Society of S. Australia, 1915; Chapter iv. 4, pp. 612 to 629.
2. Op. cit. Chapter xl.

3. On this point of method again, we are indebted to the Cambridge School of Anthropology for having introduced the really scientific way of dealing with the question. More especially in the writings of Haddon, Rivers and Seligman, the distinction between inference and observation is always clearly drawn, and we can visualise with perfect precision the conditions under which the work was done.

4. I may note at once that there were a few delightful exceptions to that, to mention only my friends Billy Hancock in the Trobriands; M. Raffael Brudo, another pearl trader; and the missionary, Mr. M. K. Gilmour.

5. According to a useful habit of the terminology of science, I use the word Ethnography for the empirical and descriptive results of the science of Man, and the word Ethnology for speculative and comparative theories.

6. The legendary "early authority" who found the natives only beastly and without customs is left behind by a modern writer, who, speaking about the Southern Massim with whom he lived and worked "in close contact" for many years, says: "We teach lawless men to become obedient, inhuman men to love, and savage men to change." And again: "Guided in his conduct by nothing but his instincts and propensities, and governed by his unchecked passions. . . ." "Lawless, inhuman and savage!" A grosser misstatement of the real state of things could not be invented by anyone wishing to parody the Missionary point of view. Quoted from the Rev. C. W. Abel, of the London Missionary Society, "Savage Life in New Guinea," no date.

7. For instance, the tables of circulation of the valuable axe blades, op. cit., pp. 531, 532.

8. In this book, . . . the reader will find only a few samples of synoptic tables. . . . Here, I have not wanted to overload the account with charts, etc., preferring to reserve them till the full publication of my material.

9. It was soon after I had adopted this course that I received a letter from Dr. A. H. Gardiner, the well-known Egyptologist, urging me to do this very thing. From his point of view as archaeologist, he naturally saw the enormous possibilities for an Ethnographer of obtaining a similar body of written sources as have been preserved to us from ancient cultures, plus the possibility of illuminating them by personal knowledge of the full life of that culture.

2

HOW IT WORKS IN THE GLOBAL WORLD
ANTHROPOLOGIST—THE MYTH TELLER

Miles Richardson

I was lying in the sack, staring at the walls, trying to fight the boredom of my last year in the United States Air Force.[1] It's a hard job, fighting boredom, especially the military kind. I had tried just about everything: the bars, the hobby shop, the NCO club, the base library, even the TV in the dayroom. And the job got harder as the time for my discharge became shorter. So I was there, waiting, with a mind as empty as I could get it. Then it was there. Fresh. Immediate. Complete. It was almost frightening, almost unbelievable, but it became bigger, more exhilarating, more definite. Then it was me, and I decided. I was going to be an anthropologist.

My decision to be an anthropologist continues to amaze me. Even now, twenty years later, I'm still not sure where that idea came from. Certainly my background was not an intellectual one. My father had found his fourth grade education sufficient to move him from a tenant farm to the railroad shops. He read the newspaper and the Bible, and that's all. And I had his scorn for intellectual things. I did read a lot, more than my friends, and the closest I came to an academic award was being second to the top most user of the library at David Crockett High School in Palestine, Texas. Of course, I wasn't reading Shakespeare. I liked historical and frontier novels, but my favorites were westerns—ones by Max Brand, Peter Field, Luke Short, Zane Grey, and especially Will James. Among my classes in school, I liked vocational agriculture. I sent off for extension pamphlets and taught myself how to recognize crazy chick disease and to grow lespedeza. Otherwise I was content to copy term papers, make up book reports, and pester my English teacher, a sweet lady who talked about *Gone With The Wind* with tears in her eyes. So perhaps it is not surprising that in my senior year, having finished my football eligibility and with nothing else to live for, I quit high school and joined the Air Force.

Yet I know that in this background were the reasons why I became an anthropologist. The principal reason was that I was raised as a Southern Baptist. You would think that a person with an intense religious upbringing would become someone compatible with that background, like a school teacher maybe, or a minister, or best of all, a football player. And people often do. One of my brothers was a preacher, and my sister married one. But it didn't work out that way with me. Actually, that's not too uncommon either. I suspect that for every minister the Southern Baptists have produced, they have turned out five atheists. Pound for pound, the Baptists have probably put more souls in hell than has any other religion. And I'm one of them.

It was in my early adolescence that I discovered I was evil. Because I was evil, I was going to die. Those people who had placed their trust in their personal Savior, those who believed in him and were saved, would live forever. Not me; I was going to die. I tried hard not to be evil. I did not swear, I did not smoke, and certainly I did not drink. I didn't play dominoes nor go to the movies on Sunday. I went to church twice on Sunday plus attending the morning Sunday School and the evening Training Union. I tried to think pure thoughts, and that's what really counted: what you were inside. In the Baptist doctrine good works don't save you; it is your inner surrender to Jesus, placing yourself totally in his hands, that brings you peace and everlasting life. No matter how often you go to church, how frequently you pray, or how much money you put in the collection plate, you are not saved until you turn yourself over to Jesus. The only way you know you are saved is that you know. But how could I be sure of such a thing? Surely a saved person always thought clean thoughts, and here I was, looking at girls with lust on my mind and even stealing glances at the big-bosomed preacher's wife. How could I be saved? What could I do to escape death?

"Look to Jesus," the preacher said. But Jesus was a Lévi Strauss paradox. Jesus-Christ-God was perfect femininity. He was kind, sweet, and full of love. Safe on his gentle breast I would lie. He so loved me that he bled and died on Calvary's tree; he was the gentle Savior who would hear my humble cry. Jesus-Christ-God was perfect masculinity. He was Father, King, Lord, and Master. He was Victor over death and his blood was full of power. He taught gentleness and peace; he sent people to burn forever in hell. How could I touch such a figure? How could I get him to respond? I tried. I searched for a way that I could feel this God and know that I was not abandoned, and alone, and apart, and dead. I have never tried anything harder nor wanted anything more. But I did not succeed, and then I knew I hated God.

My discovery was my salvation. Moved by the bright joy of perfect hate, I put aside Will James and began to read to find out why people were what they were (and why I was what I was). I read erratically, bits and pieces of this and that, stumbling, giving up, and then going in different directions, burning with conflicting emotions, and most of all, alone. Early in my search, I read Thomas Paine's *Age of Reason,* and his challenge to established religion thrilled me. Somewhere along the line I tried E. B. Tylor's *Primitive Culture,* but its nineteenth century sentence structure was too much. Later I found a list of definitions that I had carefully taken from it: "Animism: the belief in spirits; Fetishism: the worship of stone and objects." Just before I decided to become an anthropologist, I was reading travel adventure books by Dana and Ginger Lamb, husband and wife, who struggled through deserts, bandits, and inhospitable jungles to find lost cities in Latin America. The picture of myself paddling up a tropical river with some pretty blonde thing on the bow of my dugout was irresistible.

If my idea of anthropology was limited to flashes of myself in romantic situations, my feelings about it and what I wanted from it were full and strong. I wanted freedom. To me, anthropology was liberation. It was going to free me from the view of man groveling before a God that, on the one hand was sweetly sissy and on the other remotely brutal, from a religion that makes the gentle touching between a man and a woman evil, and from a culture that wants to destroy all who read and question. It was going to free me from the memory of seeing families scratching out a living on a half acre of scrub cotton and of hearing my father say to a neighbor, "You know Will, the principal over at Swanson's Springs? He's one of them. He comes to the front door. He doesn't go around to the back, like a good nigger."

Although anthropology was my way out, my freedom would come not from forgetting these things, nor would it come from being a part of movements to change them. I would never be a joiner. After the First Baptist Church, I had had it with formal organizations. Later, in graduate school, when my best friend asked if I would join CORE and the sit-ins that were beginning in New Orleans in the early 1960s, I told him no, that I was going to finish my dissertation. My freedom from the things that nearly destroyed me (and that continue to haunt me) would come from studying them, from wrestling with them in order to expose their secret. At that point, just short of stomping on them and destroying them, for some reason my private battle stops. Today, I have no love for the Southern Baptists, but I can almost say "Billy Graham" without sneering.

After having decided to be an anthropologist and after being discharged, I took my Korean GI Bill and started to get an education. I knew Harvard didn't want no high school dropout from Palestine, Texas, so I enrolled in a local junior college. I worked my way up from there, through undergraduate college and into graduate school. I went into the field, not with a blonde thing, but with a beautiful, brown-haired wife from England, and together we made it through. I struggled with a dissertation, and there I was, some ten years after it had happened, an anthropologist.

Now that I was one, now that I am one, what is it, being an anthropologist?

Being an anthropologist is to be critical, critical of one's self, of one's profession, and of one's society. Critical and suspicious, almost paranoiac. The anthropologist is an academician. He is nearly always located in a university, and the nature of university life, isolated to a degree from the rest of society but dependent in large measure for its existence on that society, each year coming to grips with a new set of students, naive and sophisticated, demanding and apathetic, produces an individual drawn tight with contradictions: a person who arrogantly attacks ignorance but wistfully pleads with the state legislature or the board of trustees, who teaches the love of learning but jealously erects walls between academic departments, and who believes that the search of knowledge is an end in itself but worries at night that his colleagues are advancing faster, gaining more prestige, and earning more money than he. But the critical sensitivity of the anthropologist seems to go beyond that of the academician. You have only to attend the annual meetings of the American Anthropological Association to realize that in the anthropologist you have more than just your ordinary, run-of-the-classroom professor.[2]

Each year, at the time of Thanksgiving, anthropologists in the United States gather together in order to reexamine their collective soul. In search of expiation, individuals stand before their colleagues and accuse each other of exploiting the people whom they study for their own selfish advancement, of being unwitting tools of neocolonial powers, and worse, of being committed countersubversives employed by the CIA or the Defense Department to study ways in which the United States can continue to maintain control over its client countries. Strong stuff for a boy from east Texas. To be sure, such self-vilification is not restricted to anthropologists; other professional societies also annually lay out their reason for being and pick it apart, looking for defects. And there are anthropologists, perhaps the confident minority, who feel no need for self-analysis and attend the meetings in order to exchange ideas with their friends. Yet the accusations that anthropologists hurl at each other contrast so sharply with the image of the anthropologist as a sympathetic spokesman for the small, the weak, and the forgotten that I have to try to explain it.

That's a big order. Such an explanation would have to examine the makeup of academia and of American society. Like everyone else, anthropologists are part and parcel of the society in which they move about (Wolf 1969). No more than their informants can anthropologists escape the biases of their home culture. Also anthropologists vary; so their discontent varies. Do the physical anthropologist (the solid scientist), the archeologist (the dirt scientist), and the linguist (the elegant scientist) share the same discontent of the ethnologist (the uncertain scientist)? Perhaps in a way they do; they are all concerned about the future of anthropology. Yet probably because I am one, I can't escape the feeling that the ethnologist is at least more vocal about what worries him. Indeed, the ethnologist occupies a key position in the science. Because he considerably outnumbers anthropologists in the other specialities and because he has the general knowledge necessary to teach the introductory course, the ethnologist is frequently the person through whom the student meets anthropology. The student may specialize in one of the other fields, but he will enter that field with an ethnological notion of what anthropology is about. So although my partial explanation of anthropological self-criticism will limit itself to the ethnologist, it should be applicable to a degree to the rest of anthropology.

The distinguishing feature of ethnological research is ethnographic field-work. In the field the relationship most critical to the ethnographer, the one that actually changes him from tourist to ethnographer, is the relationship with his informant. Whenever you think of the ethnologist in the field, you think of him as an ethnographer talking long hours with his informant. The ethnographer does many other things. He collects figures about rainfall, crop yield, population density, migration, educational levels, and per capita income; he scans newspaper articles about local issues, important persons, and recent events; and he reads historical accounts about past patterns of kinship, religious life, social stratification, and livelihoods. He watches to see how busy the market is, how friends behave, what happens at the soccer match, if men drink on Sunday, and whether the devout are always women. But sooner or later the ethnographer feels that he must spend more time with his informant, for the informant has the type of knowledge that the ethnographer must have in order to understand this community.

Who is this person who defines, even creates, the ethnographer?[3] First, he is an informant, not an informer. An informer squeals to the cops. He passes on information about the activities of criminals to the police, and then the police arrest the criminals. An informant may pass on information about illegal activity to the ethnographer, but the ethnographer never arrests anyone. The informant is not an informer partly because the ethnographer is not a cop. This means that the ethnographer defines the informant. How can that be? If the informant defines the ethnographer, and the ethnographer the informant, how do they ever find each other? Sometimes they don't. Only after considerable trial and error does the ethnographer-informant relationship emerge.

The informant is not a subject. A subject is a person, or an animal, perhaps even a plant, that the experimenter takes out of its natural surroundings and puts into a laboratory so that the experimenter is better able to control the variables that may influence the subject's responses. In order to avoid subject bias, the experimenter sometimes tells the subject—when it is a person— that the experimenter is testing one response when in reality he is testing another. An informant is always a person, never an animal, who cannot ex- ist apart from his natural surroundings. The ethnographer may deceive the informant, but he does so at his peril, for the informant is free to reciprocate and deceive the ethnographer.

The informant is not an interviewee. An interviewee answers questions, frequently highly structured, that an investigator asks, or frequently reads, from a form. This exchange, the interview, may last for as long as two or three hours, but often it is shorter, and when it is finished so is the tie between the interviewee and the investigator. Only the single strand of the interview connects them, but several strands tie the ethnographer and the informant together. An informant talks with the ethnographer about a wide range of topics, wandering here, backtracking there. The ethnographer listens more than he talks. When the conversation gradually ends, the ethnographer may ask the informant who in the local community is a good doctor, what is the best day to go to the market, and could he keep an eye on the ethnographer's house while the ethnographer goes to the capital for the next two days. The informant may ask does the United States still have the death penalty, why are so many black people poor in America, and could the ethnographer give him a ride to the city.

The informant is not necessarily a friend. The ties that bind the ethnographer and the informant may create a friendship, and it is difficult to see how an ethnographer or an informant could work with someone they hate. Yet the relationship in itself is not one of friendship. The ethnographer must ask probing questions; he cannot, as one does with friends, accept the informant as the person he is, but the ethnographer must find out, he has to find out, why the informant believes what he does. He goes to the informant seeking knowledge, and the informant becomes his instructor.

The informant is the teacher of the ethnographer. His job is to teach this stranger all that he knows. He explains the strategy of building a house, the characteristics of an extended family, and the meaning of the festival of the dead; he details how he makes pottery, how he reckons kin, and how he confronts sorrow; and he ponders with the ethnographer why cattle are sacred, why brothers are loyal, and why flowers are evil. For his job as teacher, the informant may be paid, not only in favors but also in cash. But he is not an employee; the ethnographer cannot fire him. With the informant as his teacher, the ethnographer struggles to comprehend the details and the meanings of a culture in which he is a student. In the concrete facts of this particular culture, in the knowledge of this particular informant, there is somewhere, if only the ethnographer were wise enough to see it, a key to the whole human story (Geertz 1965).

Without the informant, the ethnographer cannot carry out his task. The ethnographer can go only so far with figures, newspapers, and histories, and even with observations. To complete his work, he has to turn to the informant; without the informant, he cannot be an ethnographer. Because the informant is so central to the ethnographer's reason for being, any change in the informant or in his relationship to the ethnographer, and any change in his society's relationship to the ethnographer's, will create anxiety in the ethnographer, and through him stress in ethnology, and ultimately conflict in anthropology. This is what has happened, and this is why anthropology's self-criticism is at its present strident pitch.

The traditional pattern of relationships between the informant and the ethnographer, like so many of our activities, grew out of the nineteenth century. This was a vigorous period of development for Western civilization. Externally, it was characterized by renewed expansion, by a rejuvenated colonialism; internally it was marked by the development of academic disciplines, one of which was anthropology. As anthropology developed into a science, it became more and more conscious of the need to collect hard data against which it could check its various theories about the biological and cultural development of men. Because Western civilization was only one array of data among many, only one culture in a world of cultures, anthropologists needed data outside of Western civilization. Earlier, they had relied on the accounts of travelers and missionaries; now they began to collect the data themselves. Because of the state of the world (the ordered relationships among societies, the facilities that the growing number of anthropologists had access to, and the development of transportation) the ethnographers were now able to go to other societies and to study their ways of life. Many of these societies were subordinate to one or another of those that comprised Western civilization, and so at its very beginnings ethnography was the study of subjected people controlled by the ethnographer's society. It was in this environment that the pattern of ethnographic fieldwork developed.

The setting in which the ethnographer and the informant came together was polarized by power and cultural differences. The two societies, the ethnographer's and the informant's, were asymmetrically paired: the ethnographer's was powerful, the informant's weak. The two cultures were likewise different: the ethnographer's literate, massive, and complex; the informant's often preliterate, delicate, and direct. The two individuals were equally dissimilar: the ethnographer was white, spoke an Indo-European language, and was highly educated; the informant was black, red, or yellow, spoke Ibo, Sioux, or Yapese, and was illiterate. However, the ethnographer-informant relationship was structured opposite to the thrust of their setting. The informant occupied the higher, dominant position and the ethnographer the lower, subordinate one. As a member of a distinct, exotic culture, the informant was a man of wisdom, schooled in the traditions of his people. The ethnographer was a trained student; his education had keyed him to discover, to find out, to learn the things that the informant knew (Mead 1972).

The ethnographer was in the field to gather data in order to test out different theories about the biological and cultural development of men. Although these theories were most fully expressed in Western civilization, the theories—evolutionary, diffusionist, historical—were not models for Western neocolonialism. On the contrary. Seen in the context of their times, the earlier theorists were caught up in the effort to document the march of mankind, and with their theories they did battle against religious dogmatism, degeneration, and racism. Who can match their record? You have only to read the last sentence of Tylor's *Primitive Culture* to learn that anthropology is a "reformer's science," that the study of culture is a way to combat absolutism and is a path to freedom. The ideology in late nineteenth- and early twentieth-century anthropology was not the ideology of colonial oppression, but of scientific humanism (Stocking 1963, 1966).

As a result of the interplay between the ethnographer, as a scientific humanist, and the informant, as a man of wisdom, striving to communicate across the structural gap that separated their societies, the pattern of fieldwork developed. As time moved, as the early years of the twentieth century came and went, as the colonial powers fought each other for dominance over the informants' societies, the ethnographer tried to find a niche for himself. Guided internally by the need for scientific objectivity, he self-consciously defined himself as different from other whites—from the trader, the missionary, the bureaucrat—and as a person dedicated not to exploiting, not to converting, not to administering, but to understanding the informant's culture. Although in some cases heavily modified by the impact of Western civilization, the informant's culture was still complete, still with its own tools, houses, kinsmen, and religious festivals. The great myths that glorified the history of his people were still fresh on his tongue; the deeds of the great heroes, men and women who fought for their culture, still sparkled in his eyes. The ethnographer took on the task of studying this culture, of describing it in all of its richness before it began to crumble and die. This task led the ethnographer into the interior of the culture, and he began to see it as an elegant balance of technology, kinship, and religion, as a work of art whose beauty lay in the way in which the parts were counterbalanced and interrelated. Yet, the ethnographer's own society, powerful, aggressive, commercial (but also humane), was ripping apart this centuries old portrait of harmony. Caught between his humanistic appreciation of the informant's culture and his membership in a society destroying that culture, between life and death, the ethnographer searched for understanding, and perhaps forgiveness.

The ethnographer sought understanding in the theories of cultural holism and in the methodology of cultural relativism. The holistic theories viewed particular cultures as forming patterns or configurations in which cultural traits were interrelated in either a value-thematic sense or in a functional-causal one. These theories emerged as a reaction against the "shreds and patches" view of culture in which cultural traits, such as the tipi, the travois, the circular shield, were independent units that diffused across the landscape (and sometimes across oceans). Ethnologists of the earlier schools had been using cultural traits to reconstruct the history of cultures. With the exception of the Olympian figure of Kroeber, ethnologists of the holistic school had little interest in the native past and were downright hostile to the idea of cultural evolution. They also seemed uninterested in the ways in which the informant's culture responded to its position at the bottom of the asymmetrical power structure. When they did write about change, it was into the specific past of particular cultures that they looked, as in the case of Africanisms; or it was how individuals in the subordinate society were becoming members of the superordinate society, as in the case of acculturation. This was true of the value-thematic-configurationist school in the United States; the British functionalist approach had even less use for history. "Pseudohistory" was what Radcliffe-Brown called the efforts of the cultural historians (1952: 3). Working at a time when their own society was everywhere penetrating into the societies of their informants, the holistic ethnologists paradoxically adopted a timeless view of culture. A particular culture was a beautiful monad, a configuration of balanced interrelationships, vibrant, delicate, but contained.

Given such a view of culture, the methodological premise of cultural relativism was a logical development. As a tool for research, cultural relativism said that in order to understand any one particular aspect of a culture, you had to see how it was related to the other aspects. In order to understand the Plains Indians' response to death, the gashing of heads and legs, the cutting off of fingers, the destruction of the dead person's lodge, the reluctance of the widow to leave the grave, you had to see how these traits were related to the overall pattern of Dionysian individualism in Plains Indian culture. And in order to understand the Pueblo Indians' reaction to death, the somber funeral feast, the ceremonial closing of the lodge door prohibiting the dead from reentering his home, the firm speech of the chief telling the bereaved that the dead is gone and "They shall not remember any more," you have to view these traits against the Apollonian harmony of Pueblo culture (Benedict 1934: 110–112).

As a tool for research, cultural relativism was a significant advance in ethnography. And it remains so today. It belongs to that set of ethnographic core values that says to take cultures as they come, don't prejudge them, don't impose your own ethnocentric categories upon them. In order to comprehend any item of a people's culture, you have to view that item in its sociocultural context. Cultural relativism is as much a part of the ethnographer's tool kit as are field notes, tape recorders, and cameras.

But cultural relativism was more than a methodological tool for research; it was a moral justification for being an anthropologist. Caught in the interplay between scientific humanism, the drive for human freedom, and the encounter with a living, exotic culture threatened by the same civilization that produced the drive, the ethnographer found a sense of mission in cultural relativism. His mission was to preach the doctrine of cultural differences, to lecture to his own society that there is no one path to the solution of human problems. He spoke clearly, "Here is a way of life that through the centuries has found some of the secrets of human existence. The way of our society is not the only way. Look upon this culture and be humble." This was the ethnographer's reason for being: a sort of cultural interpreter who sought to bring the intricate beauty of a fully integrated culture to the notice of his people, so that they would be less arrogant and would administer their power with more sympathy.

The cultural relativists did not study how the power of their society structured the cultures of their informants; rather, they attacked the problem of power obliquely. Horrified by the ethnocentrism of their own colonialist society, the cultural relativists protested that all cultures express equally valid solutions to the human problem and that people (and especially ethnographers) cannot be God and decide which culture is the best. Since the cultures that they studied were still whole, distinct cultures (or could be so reconstructed from the accounts of older informants), they felt strong in their arguments. Perhaps they were naive. But they were the first people in history to immerse themselves systematically, consciously, into a totally foreign culture for the explicit purpose of understanding that culture on its own terms, without any official purpose other than being an ethnographer, without any cultural hull they could hide in when the going got rough—naked, exposed, raw. Reborn by the field experience they returned from that experience as a new breed of humans. Their hope, their mission, lay in convincing other people of the validity of that experience.

So were the ethnographers before World War II and before the Nazis. Out of the spread of Western neocolonialism and from the development of anthropology as a discipline, they evolved a new method of learning: fieldwork. Fieldwork began as a means of gathering data in order to prove or disprove theories of biological and cultural evolution. In time it developed into a fixed pattern with a theory of cultures, with a methodological tool, and with a moral justification. Practiced most brilliantly by Margaret Mead, it was described most romantically by Bronislaw Malinowski:

> Soon after I had established myself in Omarakana (Trobriand Islands), I began to take part, in a way, in the village life, to look forward to the important or festive events, to take personal interest in the gossip and the developments of the small village occurrences; to wake up every morning to a day, presenting itself to me more or less as it does to the native. I would get out from under my mosquito net, to find around me the village life beginning to stir, or the people well advanced in their working day according to the hour and also to the season, for they get up and begin their labours early or late, as work presses. As I went on my morning walk through the village, I could see intimate details of family life, of toilet, cooking, taking of meals; I could see the arrangements for the day's work, people starting on their errands, or groups of men and women busy at some manufacturing tasks. Quarrels, jokes, family scenes, events usually trivial, sometimes dramatic but always significant, formed the atmosphere of my daily life, as well as of theirs. It must be remembered that as the natives saw me constantly every day, they ceased to be interested or alarmed, or made self-conscious by my presence, and I ceased to be a disturbing element in the tribal life which I was to study, altering it by my very approach, as always happens with a newcomer to every savage community. In fact, as they knew that I would thrust my nose into everything, even where a well-mannered native would not dream of intruding, they finished by regarding me as part and parcel of their life, a necessary evil or nuisance, mitigated by donations of tobacco. (1961: 7–8)

The traditional pattern of fieldwork, the asymmetrical pairing of the two societies, the great differences between the two cultures, the informant as a man of wisdom and the ethnographer as his student, and the moral justification for being an anthropologist became a part of the subculture of ethnography and of anthropology. This became the image of the ethnographer in the field and the model he used to guide his activities. This was the notion that I carried into the field, and like many of my contemporaries, I found it archaic.

I was just beginning to wake up when a great voice boomed into the patio and blasted me into my mosquito net. "People of San Pedro. Arise! Men to the fields. Children to school. And come to mass Sunday. If you don't, you will turn into Communists or Protestants." A nice guy in other ways, the new priest enjoyed hearing his voice amplified to godlike proportions by the loud speaker located on top of the church steeple, a block from my house. I fought my way through the mosquito net and got my feet on the floor. I leaned down and pulled my machete out from under the mattress. I looked at it a minute, vaguely wondering what I would do if some of the thieves that supposedly lived in San Pedro ever decided to rob me. Doña Leonor had warned me about them, "Listen *míster,* you've got to be more careful. Yesterday I passed by your house and saw that your window was open. The thieves will look in and see all your things, and at night they will climb over the patio wall and cut your throat." I hung the machete up and let my dog out into the back yard. He was a big, black, but very friendly Labrador that in a period of homesickness, I had named "Tex." He had a loud, deep bark that Doña Leonor approved of. I belched up last night's *aguardiente* and almost threw up as the sweet, sticky taste of white rum spread into my mouth. I turned on my water faucet and looked with dismay at the brown sludge that came out of it. With my teeth still furry, I went down the street to buy the morning bread. "The bread hasn't come yet, *míster"* snapped the store lady. She turned to another customer, "Look at this, would you." She spread the newspaper out before his disbelieving eyes. "Colombia! What a rotten country!" she exclaimed. I peeked over their shoulders at the front page photograph of a naked body with its head by its feet. The caption explained that a bandit group, led by *capitán Tarzán,* had murdered peasants in a mountain village and had mutilated the bodies. The store lady went on several minutes about how the rich were hiring the bandits to drive peasants away from their land, so that the rich could buy the property at a bargain price.

Later that morning, I thought I would be like Malinowski and walk through the village, etc., so I got Tex and went out. The men had left for their work, the women were cleaning house behind closed doors and windows, and the kids were in school. But at least Tex enjoyed it. Being a Labrador, he couldn't resist jumping into a large spring boxed in with concrete. As I called him out, a man walking by muttered, *"Gringos!* Washing their dogs in water that people bath in." Back at my house, I was writing field notes, when Seneca came. "I can't go with you today to visit the tobacco factory. I've got to go to Tuluá and get some medicine for my mother. We're out of money. Look, *doctor,* could you loan me two hundred pesos. Thanks. Look, *doctor,* could you speak to your *jefe,* to the chief of your organization, about me. I know that if you will do that, he'll hire me. You'll do that, will you? That's all it will take. Just a word on your part. You are out of cigarettes? Here, I've got one." Seneca left. For a minute I stood at the doorway and looked at the deserted plaza and across the plaza to the valley and then at the Andes mountains, rising up to meet the clouds. I shut the door, picked up my guitar, and thought about Hank Williams and Palestine, Texas.

The traditional model of fieldwork, up in the clouds of Malinowskian romanticism, did not signify when applied to the reality of the world emerging in the 1950s and the 1960s. The traditional pattern grew out of the neocolonialism of the late nineteenth century; the new pattern of fieldwork struggles to take form in the revolutionary turbulence of the second half of the twentieth century.

The setting in which the ethnographer and the informant work today is still polarized by cultural and power differences. However, these differences are far less sharp than before. The two societies remain asymmetrically paired, but the informant's society has gained considerable power while the ethnographer's society has lost some. The society of the informant is now at least nominally free of the ethnographer's, and, in some cases, it may exercise considerable independence for varying lengths of time. The Arab oil embargo of 1973-1974 is one example. How much real power and true freedom the developing societies have is difficult to assess. Yet in comparison with their status in the traditional pattern of fieldwork, the societies of the informants have gained power.

Moreover, the ethnographer of today comes from a background considerably different from that traditionally associated with anthropology in the United States. At least according to anthropological folklore, ethnographers of the older tradition were largely from the upper classes. Their families were families of solid substance, or they were connected to ones that were. Several had wealthy patrons. The environment in which they grew up was an intellectual one; their relatives were people who valued learning. Nearly all were born in the great cities of the northeast, and ethnically they often were Jewish, German, or Old American. Frequently, they were close, personal friends or close, personal enemies. Beginning after World War II and especially since the Korean War, changes in American society, the rising standard of living, more governmental support for education, and increased urbanization have widened the recruiting base for anthropology (Nash and Wintrob 1972). No doubt many continue to come from the upper classes, but also many emerge from the lower levels. They come from backgrounds that ordinarily do not supply academicians. While probably few are ex–Southern Baptists, many are children of parents who earned modest incomes and who placed little faith in education. A substantial number were born in smaller cities and towns in different parts of the country, and while still predominantly white, they are more ethnically diverse than were previous anthropologists. Compelled by the contradictory forces within them, they break the ties with their background and look for a style of life to replace the one of their rough and ready fathers. They adopt the academic style, but it wears unevenly. They overcompensate here, undercompensate there. They are what they scorn in others; they are status-aspiring; they are Archie Bunkers with PhDs. When they go into the field, they carry these scars with them. Insecure in themselves, perhaps they find insecure people to study.

The same changes that have broadened the recruiting base for anthropologists have also popularized anthropology. Earlier, general knowledge about anthropology was restricted to a few who believed that anthropology was to the social sciences what physics was to the natural sciences: intellectual, competent, cool. Currently, while still retaining some of its elitist charm and derring-do, anthropology, like the submarine sandwich, is becoming massified. It seems to be on its way to becoming just another social studies requirement that freshmen have to take, with the anthropologist just another vague, gray figure, barely perceptible against the backdrop of blackboard and chalk dust.

Similarly, the informant—the embodiment of a culture that through the centuries has worked out its deep, smooth solutions to the problems of human existence—is now a tarnished figure barely visible against the backdrop of television, rock music, Charlton Heston, and beer bottles. Even though his race is often different, culturally the informant and his society resemble more and more the ethnographer and his society. While in *recent* times, the ethnographer's society may have secured special forms of music, new types of literature, and new clothing styles from the informant's society, these are small in comparison to the current massive export of cultural items, from computers to Bat Man, from the ethnographer's society to the informant's (Camacho 1972). The ethnographer is finding that the informant's culture contains the very attributes that he tried to avoid by leaving his own small town: getting ahead even if it means walking on people; forgetting kinship ties with the poor and maximizing those with the rich; ranking men on how well they can fight and fuck, and ranking women on how empty-headed they can pretend to be; and damning all who study and question.

Either because of the wholesale incorporation of cultural traits or because of the more subtle but effective process of modernization, the informant's culture becomes an impoverished version of the ethnographer's (Richardson 1967). The sphere of the informant's knowledge is less and less distinctive and more and more restricted. It becomes more difficult for the pair to perform the roles of the man of wisdom instructing his most talented student. Occasionally the structure collapses, and the pair find themselves playing out the farce of the ethnographer as patron and the informant as the unfortunate, who begs favors. The proud primitive now whines; the sensitive student now commands. The massification of the ethnographer. The proletarianization of the informant. Disillusion. Bitterness.

The collapse of the traditional pattern of fieldwork against the reality of the contemporary field experience is a major cause of the feeling of disaster and guilt that permeates ethnology, and through ethnology, American anthropology. The traditional pattern justified the ethnographer's being an ethnographer through the message of cultural relativism which rested on the theory of cultures, of shining monads, intricate, complete, dazzlingly crystal against the black sky of nature. Once these monads began to merge into a uniform, brown sameness, how could the doctrine of cultural differences have any appeal? Once the informant was a man who fought with Geronimo. Now he is a Saturday drunk in the white man's jail. How can the ethnographer profess that every culture has equally valid solutions to the human problem? How can the ethnographer find a special niche for himself in the informant's society? He bumps into others seeking the same niche, sociologists, political scientists, and local ethnographers (the last, exasperated by the constant demands of foreign social scientists, wish that they all would take their problems and go elsewhere). How can the ethnographer be reborn by immersing himself in a truly different culture, when nearly all cultures are becoming the same and the informant looks more and more like the people from across the tracks? How can he handle the guilt generated by seeing how his society exploits the informant's society, when there is no flash of exotic culture to lure his attention away from shacks built from cardboard and lives built from braggadocio and abnegation?

He can't. The collapse of the traditional model of fieldwork, with its moral justification grounded on the theory and experience of cultural differences, against the uncompromising reality of the contemporary structure has left the ethnographer, ethnology, and to a degree, anthropology without a sense of mission. Without an implicit, shared sense of doing what is right, anthropology in the United States has become unhooked from itself. Different anthropologists race each other in their willingness to accept the most devastating criticism. Some happily agree with the sociologists that we should stop trying to be novelists and become scientists (people who wear white smocks and hire interviewers). Others are painfully delighted with the assertion from minority groups that only a Black can understand the soul of the Black (a statement tediously similar to that of the white supremacists who say that only the Southerner can understand the South). Still others suicidally rejoice when one of their fellow anthropologists proclaims that the end of anthropology is at hand.

Currently, anthropologists are at each other's throats with three competing justifications for being an anthropologist: (1) Anthropology is a science and needs no other justification. It seeks to broaden and deepen human knowledge about humans through a search for general principles that are applicable to the study of any particular sociocultural system. Anthropologists as anthropologists should stay clear of political matters, such as passing resolutions about racial injustice or genocide. This is the traditional justification, and today's critics swarm around it like oilmen around sheiks. It is toy-playing in the ivory tower, or worse, its neutral stance is a front for the establishment. (2) Anthropology should be an applied science. While there is nothing wrong with studying baboons, Folsom points, Adena pottery, and cross-cousin marriage, the basic purpose of anthropology is the application of its knowledge to easing the pain of transition from the primitive peasant condition to the complex modern one. At one time the applied approach was the radical one. Indeed, if another bit of anthropological folklore is accurate, the Society for Applied Anthropology was formed in protest to the failure of the American Anthropological Association to take the applied field seriously. Today, however, the daring young men of yesterday are the gray beards of the establishment. The best that an applied anthropologist can hope for from his critics is to be called a liberal lackey—a person whose heart bleeds for the underdog but whose pocketbook is filled with establishment paychecks. (3) Anthropology should be in the service of the revolution. This recent justification (which like relevance and streaking is already at the what-else-is-new level) argues that not only did anthropology grow out of colonialism, but that it is also colonialistic. To regain its soul, anthropology must place itself at the service of the society it studies. It should be prepared to fight for the informant and his society—even if the informant doesn't feel like fighting. Critics quickly point to the arrogance of the revolutionary anthropologist—a person who *knows* what *his* people need. Labels like bourgeois adventurer and radical chic fly around his head and bug him constantly.

Where do we go from here? As an ethnologist, I'm not sure. Maybe that is the best way to be. I like what Dell Hymes says,

> I would hope to see the consensual ethos of anthropology move from a liberal humanism, defending the powerless, to a socialist humanism, confronting the powerful and seeking to transform the structure of power. Yet one can have no illusion of unanimity on all issues. In World War I, as Norman Thomas once put it, socialists were killing each other as cheerfully as Christians.... In a given country three conscientious anthropologists might choose three different loyalties—one to a government, one to a group seeking to overthrow it or to secede from its control, and one to a village that wished to be left alone by both.... Nor can we ignore obligations to our families, which we might put ahead of all others. (Hymes 1972: 52-53)

We can begin by saying goodbye to Malinowskian primitive anthropology. Once we have purged ourselves of the traditional model, we are ready to accept the contemporary world on its own terms—a basic anthropological notion. When we do this, something magical happens. The real world shifts a bit, and there he is—the informant—the man of wisdom, clear and distinct, ready, if we will but listen, to instruct us once again in the old, old lesson of being human. Maybe he can't tell us everything there is to know about his culture, but he can tell us something of the mystery of the human enterprise. He is no subject or interviewee, but a person—man or woman—who knows that this is the way life is. All we need to do is to listen.

But how to listen, that's the question. As a scientist, as an applied anthropologist, as a revolutionary? What stance should the ethnographer take, not only as an ethnographer listening to his informant, but also as an anthropologist with a mission? That is a decision that each anthropologist must make for himself. But we must expect tension among ourselves, between us and American society, and even between us and our informants and their societies—particularly their elites. As long as ethnographers continue to occupy the precarious junction between superordinate and subordinate societies, we are going to have the stomachaches of contradictions and ambiguities. These contradictions and ambiguities will make us dissatisfied, and restless, and critical, so that being an anthropologist is like being the marshal of Dodge City back in the rough days of radio drama: "It's a chancy job. It makes a man watchful—and a little lonely."

There is another stance that the anthropologist might take. It is older, much older than being a pure scientist, applied scientist, or revolutionary. That is the stance of the myth teller. The myth teller, the epic poet, stood on the fringes of his society and told of the great struggles between gods and humans, how they fought and how they loved. The poet knew these experiences; he felt their heat and pull, but something within him drove him to the margins of society where he could see all that was happening. There he recorded in his head what took place. What he saw moved him. Before him stood the great hero. Two-thirds god, the hero wanted to do everything, learn everything, and understand everything. Because of the god part that was in him, he could not accept death and strove to conquer it; but because of the human part, he failed. He was the tragic hero, magnificent in strength, splendid in appearance, courageous in heart, but with one fatal flaw: he was one-third man. The myth teller saw in the struggles of the hero the lot of man. Man's lot is that he question; but it is equally his lot that he receive no answer (Richardson 1972).

Being human is being heroic. Back at the time when ice chilled the air and when great mammals trembled the earth with their tread, the human epic began. Out of the turbulence of the Pleistocene we arose. Firm of foot, skillful of hand, quick of thought, and with images dazzling in our eyes, we moved out of Africa and out of the Pleistocene, until now we have explored the earth, walked on the moon, and touched Jupiter, and beyond. We are a biological success. We have made our mark for all to see. Who can challenge what we have done?

The reason for our success is our ability to symbolize experience, to dream of what might be and then to act as if the dreams were real (White 1949; Burke 1966; and Duncan 1968). In us all the flow, and crash, and thunder of the primate experience has become externalized and objectified (Hallowell 1968; Holloway 1969; and Richardson 1974). We have taken the private learning, the inward emotions, the life experience of the individual primate and through the magic of symbols have externalized it onto our behavior, our sounds, and our tools. What once was mating is now marriage, what once were calls are now words, and what once were termite sticks are now atomic bombs.

The ability to symbolize, to have culture, has made us what we are. We know the world because of culture; because of culture we also know fear. The fear that we humans know is not solely the fear of imminent danger: it is the fear of being evil, of being dead, of being alone. While culture allows us to talk to each other, it also prohibits us from being with one another. We can no longer reach out and touch our other selves; we can only encounter what we imagine others to be. We can't approach our other selves directly, but only as we symbolize the others to be: man, woman, black, white, friend, enemy. No matter how hard we try we cannot escape labeling and being labeled. Labeling is as much a part of us as shells are a part of turtles. Shells allow turtles to exploit a niche in the environment; culture allows us to do the same. No more than the turtle can take off his shell can humans stop symbolizing. Only when the turtle becomes extinct and we blow ourselves up will we both be free of shells and culture. Culture is our blessing; it is also our curse, our fatal flaw.

Like the hero seeking after eternal life, we seek to escape loneliness. Walled in by our prison of culture, we can't reach others. We try, we struggle, we stick out our hands, but find nothing. But we try again, and again find nothing. What made us human, the power to envision a better world, won't let us rest. We push ourselves to the limit of our individual cells and try once more, but again there is nothing. What made us human, the ability to label and to act on those labels, guarantees that we fail.

Reality eludes us since we left the warm comfort of the primate troop. As we struggle to cope with the problem of being human, as we try to adapt to the human condition, we evolve cultural patterns that go in contradictory directions. *We are cruel.* We wage war on our own kind, shooting other people with arrows, cutting their bodies with obsidian swords, blasting them apart with land mines. We starve members of our own societies, building economic systems that produce fat billionaires and thin babies, crying in the night. We grind psyches in the grist mill of religion, tearing apart souls for the Glory of God, in the Highest. *We are magnificent.* With a digging stick and a pebble tool we beat the African savanna at its own game. With torch and red ochre we drew on the cave walls of Europe delicate pictures of wild beasts. With shining metal and finely tuned instruments we went to the moon. Before our story ends, perhaps we will feel Mars beneath us and even walk under the light of a new star. *We are love.* We are brothers; we are sisters. Listen to those of us who speak for all: "As a man I work for the party; as a poet I work for man," Cesar Vallejo, Peruvian Marxist. "From where the sun now stands I will fight no more forever," Chief Joseph, American Indian. "Free at last! Free at last! Thank God Almighty, I'm free at last!" Martin Luther King, Jr., Southern Black. We are these things and more. How can a single species do and be so many contradictory things? The ability to symbolize makes us what we are. It accounts for our successes; it is the reason for our failures. Being a human is an impossible task, but it is our task.

The anthropologist's job is to tell of that task, to glorify man by composing and reciting with skill and passion the human myth. Like the poet recording the exploits of the epic hero, the anthropologist mythicizes the human record. He takes the discrete bits of human data, the pelvic girdle, Acheulean handaxes, Eskimo kinship, and phonemic contrasts, and narrates the human story, how we came to be, how we fought in the past, how we live today. As teller of the human story, the anthropologist cannot falsify what we are. He seeks to find the full range of human variation, the cruelty, the magnificence, the love that is in us all and in all of our cultures. But the anthropologist is not a passive recorder of human data; he searches for the human secret.

As myth teller, the anthropologist feels the heat and pull of human effort. As an ethnographer, he stands between the juncture of superordinate and subordinate societies, and he experiences the contradictory stresses of that position. He must not isolate himself from those stresses by putting on a white smock and directing interviewers from the sterile atmosphere of an air-conditioned office. If children consider him just another village idiot, if adults laugh at his childlike mistakes, if he is a consistent victim of Montezuma's Revenge (or the Old World variant, the Pharaoh's Curse), at least he lives in the world of people. Nor can the ethnographer be principally occupied with directing cultural traffic from the superordinate to the subordinate society. Neither can he forget in his anxiety to speak for the poor that the rich also fall within the range of human variation. To recite the human epic, the anthropologist needs the passion of the radical, the practicality of the liberal, and the detachment of the scientist. But in the end, he must remain a teller, perhaps a revolutionary teller, but a poet and not a change agent.

In telling the human myth, of how men wrestle with the problem of being human, of how people envision a society of love but live in a society of hate, of how they conceive of a collective soul but live in individual cells, the anthropologist may find his own salvation. In writing of the struggles of others, he may find ways to cope with his own demons that torture him at night. In reciting the heroism of humans, he may learn to live heroically, to know that Gods live forever, but humans die bravely.

If the anthropologist does not tell the human myth, then who will?

> Who will see human gentleness in a Ramapithecus jaw?
> Who will look with wonder at the Sorcerer of Les Trois Frères?
> Who will hunt meat with the Siriono and weep when a Sánchez dies?
> Who will see a verb in a pebble tool, or fight for Papiamentu, or learn the lesson of he be gone?
> Who will watch the ghosts dance?
> Who will defend the Neanderthal?
> Who will argue about the pre-Columbian chicken, or pre-Clovis man, or maize in Africa?
> Who will believe in the bifid penis?
> Who will watch the birds glide over the New Guinea highlands? Who will feast with the Yanomamö or go north with Nanook? Who will journey with Don Juan?
> Who will record these things and more?
> Who will search for the human secret? Who will tell the human myth?
> Who will, damn it, who will?

Notes

1. I completed the first draft of this article while on sabbatical leave, fall semester, 1973, and I thank Dr. Irwin A. Berg, Dean of the College of Arts and Sciences, and the administration of Louisiana State University for granting the sabbatical. Sam Hilliard, Joyce Rockwood Hudson, Valerie Richardson, and Donald Vermeer made helpful comments. I particularly thank Ward Goodenough and Charles Hudson for

their encouragement and Charles for his sharp editorial eye. Illusions do not elude him. Of course, I am solely responsible for this attempt to write about anthropology. Because being an anthropologist is an intense thing, I have tried to write intensely, and, I hope, skillfully. Maybe I'm a frustrated novelist, but I can't help but feel (along with Langness 1973) that there is a place in professional journals for articles that make the reader grunt and say goddamn. If I were still a Southern Baptist, I would say that I was writing an inspirational piece, somewhere between Billy Graham's "The Hour of Decision" and Martin Luther King's "I Have a Dream."

2. My notion of the tone of anthropology in the United States comes from attending the meetings of the American Anthropological Association and from reading the letters to the editor in the *Newsletter* and the debates that go on in *Current Anthropology*. My characterization of the background of both earlier and contemporary anthropologists draws heavily on anthropological folklore, and as folklore has purposes other than truth telling, the characterizations are no doubt inaccurate in detail. Anthropologists have published little on their social background and their place in American society. However, a growing literature exists on ethnographers in the field. When reading these accounts, one occasionally thinks of the reports in *True Magazine*, like "My Years Among the Man Eating Amazons of Brazil." But this literature is a far cry from, and a vast improvement over, the time not long ago when there were only Malinowski's account and the chapter on interview techniques and field relationships by Paul in *Anthropology Today* (1953). As background material for this article, I have sampled this literature: Berreman (1962), Casagrande (1960), Freilich (1970), Jarvie (1969), Kimball and Watson (1972), King (1965), Kloos (1969), Nash (1963), Powdermaker (1966), and Spindler (1970).

3. The description of the informant and of the ethnographer-informant relationship draws on the literature cited in note 2 and on my fieldwork, a year and a half in Colombia (1962–1963) and three summers in Costa Rica (1967, 1972, 1973).

References

Aceves, Joseph B. 1974. *Identity, Survival, and Change: Exploring Social/Culture Anthropology.* Morristown, NJ: General Learning Press.

Benedict, Ruth. 1934. *Patterns of Culture.* Boston: Houghton Mifflin.

Berreman, Gerald. 1962. *Behind Many Masks.* Society for Applied Anthropology, Monograph No. 4.

Burke, Kenneth. 1966. *Language as Symbolic Action.* Berkeley: University of California Press.

Camacho, Daniel. 1972. *La Dominación Cultural en el Subdesarrollo.* San José, Costa Rica: Editorial Costa Rica.

Casagrande, Joseph B., ed. 1960. *In the Company of Man: Twenty Portraits of Anthropological Informants.* New York: Harper Torchbooks.

Duncan, Hugh D. 1968. *Symbols in Society.* New York: Oxford University Press.

Freilich, Morris, ed. 1970. *Marginal Natives: Anthropologists at Work.* New York: Harper and Row.

Geertz, Clifford. 1965. "The Impact of the Concept of Culture on the Concept of Man." In *New Views of Man,* John R. Platt, ed. Chicago: University of Chicago Press.

Hallowell, A. Irving. 1968. "Self, Society, and Culture in Phylogenetic Perspective." In *Culture: Man's Adaptive Dimension,* M. F. Ashley Montagu, ed. New York: Oxford University Press. (First published 1960.)

Holloway, R. L., Jr. 1969. "Culture: A *Human* Domain." *Current Anthropology* 10: 395-412.

Hymes, Dell, ed. 1972. *Reinventing Anthropology.* New York: Random House.

Jarvie, I. C. 1969. "Problems of Ethical Integrity in Participant Observations." *Current Anthropology* 10: 505-508.

Kimball, Solon T., and James B. Watson, eds. 1972. *Crossing Cultural Boundaries: The Anthropological Experience.* New York: Chandler.

King, Arden. 1965. "The Anthropologist as Man: The Ultimate Paradox." Paper presented at the Sixty-Fourth Annual Meeting, American Anthropological Association, Denver, Colorado.

Kloos, Peter. 1969. "Role Conflicts in Social Fieldwork." *Current Anthropology* 10: 509-512.

Langness, L. L. 1973. "Fact, Fiction, Style, and Purpose: Some Comments on Anthropology and Literature." Paper presented at the Seventy-Second Annual Meeting, American Anthropological Association, New Orleans, Louisiana.

Malinowski, Bronislaw. 1961. *Argonauts of the Western Pacific.* New York: E. P. Dutton. (First published 1922.)

Mead, Margaret. 1972. "Fieldwork in High Cultures." In *Crossing Cultural Boundaries: The Anthropological Experience,* Solon T. Kimball and James B. Watson, eds. New York: Chandler.

Nash, Dennison. 1963. "The Ethnologist as Stranger: An Essay in the Sociology of Knowledge." *Southwestern Journal of Anthropology* 19: 149-167.

Nash, Dennison, and Ronald Wintrob. 1972. "The Emergence of Self-Consciousness in Ethnography." *Current Anthropology* 13: 527-542.

Paul, Benjamin. 1953. "Interview Techniques and Field Relationships." In *Anthropology Today,* A. L. Kroeber, ed. Chicago: University of Chicago Press.

Powdermaker, Hortense. 1966. *Stranger and Friend: The Way of an Anthropologist.* New York: W. W. Norton.

Radcliffe-Brown, A. R. 1952. *Structure and Function in Primitive Society.* London: Cohen and West.

Richardson, Miles. 1967. "The Significance of the 'Hole' Community in Anthropological Studies." *American Anthropologist* 69: 41-54.

———. 1972. "Gilgamesh and Christ: Two Contradictory Models of Man in Search of a Better World." In *Aspects of Cultural Change,* Joseph B. Aceves, ed. Southern Anthropological Society Proceedings No. 6. Athens: University of Georgia Press. (Reprinted in Aceves 1974.)

———. 1974. "Images, Objects, and the Human Story." In *The Human Mirror: Material and Spatial Images of Man,* Miles Richardson, ed. Baton Rouge: Louisiana State University Press.

Spindler, George, ed. 1970. *Being an Anthropologist: Fieldwork in Eleven Cultures.* New York: Holt, Rinehart, and Winston.

Stocking, George W., Jr. 1963. "Matthew Arnold, E. B. Tylor and Uses of Invention." *American Anthropologist* 65: 783-799.

———. 1966. "Franz Boas and the Culture Concept in Historical Perspective." *American Anthropologist* 68: 867-882.

White, Leslie. 1949. *The Science of Culture.* New York: Farrar, Straus, and Cudahy.

Wolf, Eric. 1969. "American Anthropologists and American Society." In *Concepts and Assumptions in Contemporary Anthropology,* Stephen Tyler, ed. Southern Anthropological Society Proceedings No. 3. Athens: University of Georgia Press.

II

Cultural Codes

3

WHERE PACIFIC
ISLANDERS LIVE
RESIDENCE RULES

Ward H. Goodenough

Determining a community's rule or rules of residence in marriage has long been established as a basic requirement for any satisfactory descriptive account of its social system.[1] That residence practices are important determinants of the various forms of family and kinship organization has long been postulated by ethnologists and recently been given impressive statistical documentation by Murdock.[2]

Needless to say, studies such as his are dependent upon the reliability with which ethnographic facts are reported and interpreted. Ethnologists now take it for granted that a reliable report of residence customs is based on a house by house census of the community studied. When we read that such a census reveals a given ratio of residence types, I think most of us feel secure in what we regard as reliable information.

It was quite a shock, therefore, when I recently found myself differing considerably with John Fischer about the incidence of residence forms in a community on Truk (Romonum Island) where we both collected data within the space of three years. Our respective tabulations appear on the following page.[3]

On the basis of my figures we would not hesitate to classify Trukese society as essentially matrilocal, since nearly three-quarters of the married couples are apparently living in matrilocal residence. On the basis of Fischer's figures, with little more than half the married couples in matrilocal residence and almost a third living patrilocally, I would myself be inclined to classify Trukese society as bilocal. In short, two censuses of the same community within three years result in differences of a magnitude sufficient to suggest a different classification of its residence customs. Fischer's and my conclusions were both based on accepted census procedure. Either there were radical changes in residence practice and physical shifts of household accordingly in three years' time or we were honestly interpreting similar census data in very different ways.

Table 3.1

| | Goodenough | | Fischer | |
Type of Residence	Cases	Percent	Cases	Percent
Matrilocal	46	71	36	58
Patrilocal	1	1.5	20	32
Avunculocal	10	15	0	—
Neolocal	4	6	6	10
Other arrangement	3	5	0	—
Ambiguous	1	1.5	0	—
Total	65	100	62	100

As to the first alternative, Fischer's census reveals a move by an entire extended family group from one location to another (a practice for which there is ample past precedent), a shift in residence of several people as a result of the consolidation of two related lineages (a move that was already planned when I was on Romonum), and the residential separation of a segment of Romonum's largest lineage from its parent body, together with segments of two other lineage groups. Whether these three segments form one extended family is not clear from Fischer's census. His notes also reveal seven marriage dissolutions, three by death and four by divorce, and six new marriages. In order to ascertain whether the difference in our figures was a result of these changes or due to differences of interpretation, I have classified the residences in Fischer's census in accordance with the same principles which I used with my own data. The results for a total of sixty married couples are as follows:[4] 40 cases (67 percent) in matrilocal residence, 9 cases (15 percent) in avunculocal, 4 cases (7 percent) ambiguously in matrilocal or avunculocal, 1 case (1 percent) in patrilocal, 3 cases (5 percent) in neolocal, and 3 cases (5 percent) in some other arrangement. With due allowance for the ambiguous seven percent, the results are virtually identical with those based on my data of three years earlier. Considering the numerous shifts which had taken place, involving sixteen couples in addition to those whose marital status changed as already noted, the consistency of the percentages obtained for the two censuses is remarkable.

Only one interpretation is possible. The differences in Fischer's and my results cannot be attributed to differences in the raw census data. They arise from an honest difference in how to interpret the data.

The most obvious point at which we might differ in our respective interpretations would appear to be on the distinction between patrilocal and

avunculocal residence. Indeed, in my own published report on Trukese social organization, I used the term patrilocal where I might better have used
avunculocal.[5] But Fischer reports avunculocal residence for another island
in the Truk area, and, in any case, confusion of avunculocal with patrilocal
residence could not account for the significant difference between his and my
reported incidence of matrilocal residence. Here, indeed, is a serious matter.
Two trained anthropologists seem unable to agree as to what is and what is
not a case of matrilocal residence. Yet few ethnological concepts have been
more precisely defined than those pertaining to residence. How, then, is it
possible for us to disagree?

One possibility is that we used different kinds of additional information
about Trukese society as a basis for interpreting the census data. If this is
true, it means that residence forms cannot be reliably determined from the
usual type of census information collected by ethnographers. A second possibility is that the established definitions of residence forms are so phrased
as to make unclear how they should be applied to the enumeration of individual residences. Thus, without being aware of it, we might actually be
using different concepts of residence at the applied level though starting in
the abstract with similar ones.

We shall see that both of these factors have been at work. Fischer and I
have been using different kinds of additional data to interpret the census
material and we have also been working in practice with somewhat different
concepts of residence.

Few concepts in ethnology are more clear-cut and seemingly straightforward than are those pertaining to residence. Moreover, we have yet to develop
methods which rival in sophistication those already established for empiri-
cally determining patterns of family and kin organization. If these concepts
and methods are still wanting, we are confronted with a serious challenge.
Their reconsideration would appear to be in order.

First, there is the question of the adequacy of census data alone as a basis
for determining a society's residence rules. In considering it, I would like
to turn from Truk for a moment and use the Nakanai people of New Britain
Island in Melanesia for illustrative purposes.[6]

Nakanai communities are made up of several hamlets, which are clustered
closely together. Each hamlet's site is said to be the property of the matrilineal
descendants of its founder or cofounders, but a census showed no consistent
pattern of residence with respect to hamlet. Each hamlet had a group of relatives as its nucleus, but the genealogical relationships between them were
of every conceivable kind. Now it ultimately turned out that there is indeed
a pattern, that a man regularly brings his wife to live in the hamlet where
his father is residing. He and his wife remain there until his father dies. If
his father moves elsewhere, they move with him. When the father dies, the
couple may continue to reside as before, particularly if the father was without
sister's sons or if the husband has no matrilineal association with any hamlet
in his father's village. More often, however, the couple removes to the hamlet

in which the husband's immediate matrilineage has hereditary land rights, or to one where there is a concentration of his male sibmates.

Several things obscure this pattern. Since many people die before their children marry, a man is likely to start residing with a father substitute, who may be his father's brother, mother's brother, older brother or parallel cousin on either side, cross-cousin, stepfather, or older sister's husband, whoever among them took charge of feeding him as a child and/or negotiating his marriage. The number of cases in which a man and his wife are actually residing in the hamlet of the groom's father or maternal uncle is relatively few. All of the older men and many of the younger have no living fathers or uncles. One man, for example, has taken his two wives to live where no other man of his sib is represented and where his father never resided at any time. His own brother is residing elsewhere, in the hamlet with which their father was associated. The man in question resided there formerly and moved to the present hamlet after a quarrel. On the face of it, his is a case of neolocal residence. But from the genealogies we learn that his mother's brother and mother's mother's brother were associated with this hamlet, though they had died long before he moved there. Thus his apparent neolocal residence actually conforms to the pattern of a move from patrilocal to avunculocal residence, for he is now living where his mother's brothers would be, if he had any.

Furthermore, no amount of census data would reveal that residences with parallel cousins and brothers-in-law were residences with father substitutes and hence in conformity with patrilocal principles. So frequently is the pattern obscured by the death of close relatives that our census data from Nakanai with its record of sib membership and living close kinsmen proved useless by itself for analyzing residence. The pattern began to emerge only after analysis of the genealogical data, where the dead had equal weight with the living and where questions about where a man lived elicited a list of two or more hamlets rather than just one. When I then redrafted my genealogical charts by hamlet rather than by sib, the essentially patri-avunculocal character of residence in Nakanai became finally apparent. With only census data to work with, the Nakanai must have remained one of those so-called loosely structured societies so frequently reported for Melanesia. We are confronted with the unavoidable conclusion, then, that careful census data, though indispensable to ethnographic insight, are not in themselves clear evidence of a society's residence rules, and that reports of residence based directly on such evidence alone are scientifically unreliable.

It is clear, then, that more than census data may be needed for even the semblance of pattern in residence to emerge. It is also clear that after a pattern does emerge, interpretation of particular residences with respect to that pattern requires additional sociological and cultural information. With the Nakanai, for example, it is important to know whether the husband's father is living or dead. If he is dead, did he die before or after the husband got married? If he died before, who acted as father substitute for the husband? Is the father substitute living or dead? Are the husband's uncles living or dead? Where do or did they reside? Where does the husband's lineage have land? These are the sociological facts which we must know. Behind them are the cultural facts from which we learn their relevance: the nature of the father-son relationship in Nakanai, the father's responsibility for his son's passage into marriage, which requires paying a bride price. As long as the father lives he assumes at least nominal responsibility for these things, however much of the burden is, in fact, carried by other kinsmen. When the father dies, these responsibilities are formally assumed by someone else. Just who else depends on a great many considerations which we need not go into here. Whoever that person is, however, he is likely to become a father substitute as far as future residence decisions are concerned. Residence with him is, therefore, an expression of the patrilocal principle regardless of what the actual genealogical tie with him may be, or kinship term used for him. Once we understand this, we discover that most Nakanai men who live to marry spend some time in what I regard as patrilocal residence, many ultimately going on to what I regard as avunculocal residence in the hamlets associated with their respective matrilineal lineages.[6a]

It should by now be clear that the determination of residence rules poses two different problems. The first problem has to do with recognizing the pattern of residence in a society. We have seen that census data alone may not be sufficient for this. The second problem has to do with classifying the residence of individual couples. We have here seen how essential are sociological and cultural data apart from census and genealogical materials in order to know whether individual cases do or do not conform to the pattern discerned. Such information, moreover, may serve to show how cases which appear to conform to one pattern really conform to another. This brings us back to the problem as it appeared in Truk where Fischer and I, both aware of the presence of patrilocal and matrilocal forms, cannot agree on which is which in specific cases. Even where we agree as to what the patterns are, we cannot agree as to what cases conform to them. In this instance, the same sociological and cultural data were available to both of us. Where we differed was in regard to what aspects of it we considered relevant for classifying a couple's residence. This difference, I believe, may have stemmed in part from a different resolution of ambiguities which arise when we try to apply our residence concepts. Let me illustrate the problem with an example from Truk.

At the time of my census, I encountered a household in which there resided an elderly man with his second wife, and his three sons by his first marriage. The eldest son was married, and his wife resided there too. The composition of this household was typical of that of a patrilocal extended family. The natural thing to do, therefore, would be to count the two married couples as two cases of patrilocal residence. In doing this, we are taking as our criterion for classification the type of extended family which the household presents as indicated by the relationships between its members. In this instance, both couples are residing in outward conformity with the pattern of a patrilocal extended family and are each, therefore, presumably in patrilocal residence.

Here, of course, we have operationally defined residence forms in terms of conformity with household patterns as defined by genealogical connections between the household members. But if we take as our criterion of patrilocal residence the fact that the bride has removed on marriage "to or near the parental home of the groom," to quote Murdock's definition,[7] then the pattern of household composition is no longer a reliable basis for classifying individual residence. We must know who moved where at the time of marriage. When we ask about this in relation to the above Trukese household, we learn that both present wives moved into the house from elsewhere, their husbands already residing there, and the patrilocal picture is reinforced. On the basis of this definition of patrilocal residence there is no apparent need to seek further information. Certainly the son's case is clear. He lived here with his parents and when he married he brought his wife to his parents' home.

But let us now look at some additional facts. The father's first wife belonged to a matrilineal lineage which owns the house and land in which this extended family lives. Nearby is another house in which lives a lineage sister of the dead first wife with her husband and children. We discover that the women of this lineage have lived here together with their husbands in a hamlet cluster and that the father moved here in matrilocal residence with his first wife. His sons belong to the owning lineage. When his first wife died, this lineage allowed him to continue to be with his children. When his son married, he brought his wife not to his father's house but to his own matrilineal lineage's place of localization. The house in which his father was residing was available to him because he had no sisters living there. Had he had sisters there, he would have had to build a separate house, for adult brothers and sisters may not sleep under the same roof. Now, if all the men in a matrilineal lineage brought their wives to live on their lineage land, the result would be an avunculocal extended family. Our seemingly perfect example of a patrilocal extended family turns out to be the result of an initial matrilocal residence by the father (subsequently filiolocal) and an avunculocal residence by the son.[8] But the son's residence is recognizable as avunculocal only when we see what would be the alignments which would result if everyone were residing in the same relationship to their matrilineal kin groups as he.

This example shows that we have a genuine problem when we try to apply our residence concepts to classifying individual marriages for purposes of statistical analysis. Our concepts, which in the abstract appear so precise, become very slippery when we try to use them in this way. If we stop to take into account the context in which these concepts were developed, I think both the reason for the problem and its solution become clear.

Our concepts have been designed for the purpose of classifying prevailing or ideal usages in different societies as a means of grouping these societies for comparative purposes. To do this it is necessary for the usages in question to have been adequately described beforehand. The concepts belong to the same order of abstraction as do such linguistic rubrics as "agglutinating" or "inflecting," which cannot be applied intelligently until the grammatical processes have first been analyzed in other terms. Concepts used for comparative purposes, moreover, must be based on criteria which are independent of any particular culture. That is why we define types of residence in terms of physical alignments of persons differentiated by genealogical (biological) considerations. The criteria are of necessity extracultural.

It is, therefore, a procedural fallacy to use these concepts as a basis for classifying the residence choices of individual members of a society. They do not choose on the basis of criteria which are outside their culture, which exist only in the heads of anthropologists. They choose on the basis of the criteria which are provided by their particular culture and which may be quite different—indeed probably are—from those used by the anthropologist in classifying their culture. This means that if I wish to apply the label "patrilocal" to one of the real choices within a culture, I must recognize that it means something different from patrilocal residence in the context of ethnological comparison. I must explain what I mean by the term in the context of individual choice. But I must do more than this.

Whatever may be the purposes of an ethnographer in describing a culture, he has the duty of describing it in terms which fit the phenomena. If he is going to describe residence, for example, he cannot work with an *a priori* set of residence alternatives, albeit he has defined them with the utmost care. He has to find out what are the actual residence choices which the members of the society studied can make within their particular sociocultural setting. The only way he can do this is to construct a theory of their residence behavior in accordance with the scientific canons of theory construction. This means that he must try to conceive categories of residence and criteria of choice which give the simplest and most accurate account of their behavior. He must try to validate them by using them to predict the future residence choices of betrothed persons, or by predicting where pairs of persons would live if they were married to each other and seeing whether his predictions agree with those which members of the society would also make for such hypothetical marriages. Once he has isolated what are the several residence choices provided by the culture, he is in a position to ascertain their order of precedence and conditions under which the order of precedence changes. Anything less than this cannot claim to be an adequate description of a society's residence rules. Once such a description has been made, one can put whatever labels one wishes on the categories isolated, just as in linguistics once a phoneme has been isolated and described the assignment of an alphabetical symbol to it is a matter of convenience. Working with such descriptions, moreover, the comparativist can see clearly what he is doing when he classifies cultures in accordance with the concepts appropriate to his enquiry.

Let us consider, then, what are the categories of residence choice as I understand them to exist in Truk. Let us see what lies behind the labels which I used without explanation in the tabulations at the beginning of this paper.

Let us dispense with the labels entirely for the time being and thus avoid any possibility of further nominalistic confusion.

In my published report on Truk,[9] I indicated that the cornerstone of its social structure is the property-owning corporation, which, because it perpetuates its membership by a principle of matrilineal descent and is a segment of the community rather than being widely extended across community lines, I chose to call a lineage. No individual can exist independent of some lineage affiliation. If he goes to another community he must either affiliate with one of its lineages or remain outside the community pale without food, shelter, or protection. If it has enough adult members and access to a suitable site, a lineage has its own dwelling house (or cluster of houses) which is regarded as the place where it is physically located. A large lineage may contain two or even three separately localized sublineages. Lineages may move from one site to another as they gain right of access to different plots of land; house sites are not regarded as permanent. There are several ways in which a lineage may have right of access. It may itself own the ground under full or provisional title;[10] one of its members may hold personal title to the ground; or a sublineage may be the owner. A lineage may also be localized on land which belongs to a man who has married into it. When this happens, the understanding is invariably that the man's children, who are members of the lineage, have received the land in gift from their father, so that in localizing here the lineage has moved, in effect, to land belonging to one of its members. With the tendency nowadays for the lineage to be localized in a cluster of smaller houses instead of a single large one as in former times, the site may consist of several adjacent plots under separate ownership; but each case will conform to the pattern above—three adjacent plots, for example, being held by the lineage, one of its members, and one of its husbands respectively. The need for juggling of this kind has also been increased on Romonum Island with the movement of all house sites to the beach, during the decade before World War II. The point of importance to note, however, is that a man who is living on land which he got from his father is in all probability not living in the extended family associated with his father's lineage, but in that associated with his or his wife's. Let us now see what are the possible choices of residence open to a married couple within this setting.

The first thing to note is that the choice is always between extended family households. Couples do not go off and set up in isolation by themselves. The only exceptions to this are native pastors and catechists whose residence is determined by their occupation. (They find it necessary, however, to try to make some arrangements for domestic cooperation with a neighboring household.) The important question for a married couple, then, is: to what extended families does it have access? It has access by right to the extended family associated with the lineage of either the bride or the groom. A member of a lineage which is not localized becomes a dependent of his or her father's lineage for purposes of shelter. The extended families associated with the wife's father's lineage and husband's father's lineage form, therefore, a pair of secondary possibilities for choice of residence. At any one time, however, a couple has but two alternatives: on the one hand the wife's lineage or, if it is not localized, then her father's lineage, and on the other hand the husband's lineage or, if it is not localized, then his father's. Other things being equal, as long as one party to the marriage belongs to a lineage which is localized, this lineage will be chosen before joining the other's father's lineage. Resort to a father's lineage of either spouse is, therefore, a fairly rare occurrence. Other things being equal, moreover, a couple will regularly choose to live with the extended family associated with the wife's lineage rather than that associated with the husband's. It is regarded as proper for one's children to grow up in the bosom of their own lineage in close association with their lineage "brothers" and "sisters," with whom they are expected to maintain absolute solidarity, no matter what the circumstances, for the rest of their lives. Given matrilineal descent as the principle of lineage membership, regular residence with the extended family associated with the husband's lineage would keep lineage brothers separated from one another until adulthood and lineage sisters would not normally live and work together either as children or adults. Choosing to reside with the wife's localized lineage, therefore, is consistent with the high value placed on lineage solidarity.

But what are the considerations which make other things unequal? Under what circumstances do people regularly choose in favor of the husband's localized lineage even though the wife's lineage is localized? And under what circumstances do couples prefer to reside with a wife's father's lineage household rather than the household associated directly with the husband's lineage? What are the factors, in short, which favor a husband instead of his wife and a secondary instead of a primary affiliation?

Most instances of residence with the husband's lineage household occur in cases where the wife's lineage is not localized because it does not have enough adult women to run a separate household or lacks access to suitable land. But there are other circumstances favoring such residence. Ultimate responsibility and authority in a lineage are vested in its adult men. If residence with the wife's kin would take the husband too far away from where his own lineage house is located, it may appear advisable for him to bring his wife to live at the latter place. As the physical distance between the husband's and wife's lineage households increases and as the importance of the husband in his lineage affairs increases, the greater the likelihood that residence will be with the husband's kin. Where the husband or his lineage is in a position to provide the children with far more land than the wife's lineage, and at the same time the husband and wife come from communities too widely separated to make it possible to reside in one and maintain the land in the other, residence will be with the husband's kin. If the husband's lineage will soon die out, so that his children will take over its lands, these children may organize as a new lineage temporarily operating jointly with the survivors of their father's lineage. Such of these children as are women may bring their husbands into what may be regarded either as the wife's or wife's father's localized lineage (the former as one looks to the future, the latter as one looks to the past).

Finally, it may happen that a young couple may be requested to reside with elder relatives in a household in which they do not have any *right* to live. In Fischer's census, for example, I note the case of an elderly man residing with his wife's localized kin group. He and his wife have no children. Nor are there junior kin in his wife's lineage who do not have greater responsibilities to others in the household (judging from my genealogical data). Living with them are this old man's sister's daughter and her newly acquired husband. As head of her lineage, the old man has obviously pulled her into this household with the consent of his wife and her kin (who are thus relieved of undue responsibility). She has no other reason for being there, and the arrangement will terminate when either the old man or his wife dies. Temporary arrangements like this one, made for mutual convenience and with the consent of those concerned, may be on the increase today. I suspect, however, that one hundred years ago they would also have accounted for the residence of up to five percent of the married couples.

The foregoing, then, are the considerations which I believe the Trukese have in mind when they decide where they are going to live. By postulating them, I am able to give a straightforward accounting of Trukese residence behavior as I experienced it. I find, moreover, that they make the results of the many residential and marital changes revealed in Fischer's census thoroughly intelligible, a fact not without significance for the validity of this view of Trukese residence behavior.

If we accept as valid the formulation of their residence principles presented here, then it is clear that in making their residence decisions the Trukese do not choose between living with the parents of the husband or the parents of the wife. With what parents, if any, a couple resides is a fortuitous by-product of a choice made with other considerations in mind. While there may be specific inquiries for which we might find it desirable to ascertain the frequency with which different parent-child residential alignments occur in Truk, such alignments have nothing directly to do with Trukese residence rules nor are they descriptive of them.[11] Truk is, therefore, in obvious contrast with Nakanai, where couples choose to live in the hamlet where the husband's father resides, regardless of the latter's reason for being there.

It should also be clear that while land ownership in Truk is a factor which limits the number of sites where a lineage can be localized as an extended family, individual couples are concerned with what extended family they will join, not with whose land they will live on (except in the case of intercommunity or interisland marriages as already noted). To use land ownership as a basis for differentiating types of residence choice, therefore, seems to me to be artificial.[12] Undoubtedly there are societies, however, where land plays a more direct role in the residence choices of individual couples.

Since it is extended families between which the Trukese choose, we may list the types of residence which are descriptive of the possibilities inherent in their social structure as follows:

1. Residence with the extended family associated with the wife's lineage.
2. Residence with the extended family associated with the husband's lineage.
3. Residence with the extended family associated with the wife's father's lineage.
4. Residence with the extended family associated with the husband's father's lineage.
5. Residence by arrangement with a specific kinsman in an extended family in which one is otherwise without residential right.
6. Residence independent of any extended family—only a hypothetical possibility until recent times, now involving church officials and a few persons seeking to break with traditional ways.

In discussing residence rules in my earlier report on Trukese social structure,[13] I lumped types one and three above under the heading "matrilocal" and referred to types two and four together as "patrilocal," using these terms in a sense equivalent to that for which Adam has coined the expressions "uxorilocal" and "virilocal."[14]

This brings us to the problem facing the comparativist. Granting that these are the types of residence inherent in Trukese social structure, by what means are we to equate them with the very different possibilities inherent in Nakanai social structure or that of any other society?

To solve this problem we must have a system of residence classification into which the types belonging to any and every particular culture can be readily fitted. The typology already established, taking as its criteria the several possible alignments of primary and secondary relatives in spatial proximity, is in every respect ideally suited for this purpose. The only thing that has been wrong with it has been the improper use made of it in ethnographic description. But this does not answer the question of how we are in practice to go about fitting the types we get for a specific culture into these types we use for comparative purposes.

Since the comparative system is based on alignments of primary and secondary kin, we must examine each cultural type that emerges in ethnographic description to see what alignments it would logically produce under the ideal conditions in which all couples choose it and everyone has a full complement of living kinsmen. Let us apply this procedure to the first four types we have established for Truk and see what happens.

Type 1. If everyone lived with the extended family associated with the wife's matrilineage, the result would be an alignment of matrilineally related women with their husbands; the mother-daughter link would stand out.

Type 2. If everyone lived with the extended family associated with the husband's matrilineage, the result would be an alignment of matrilineally related men with their wives; the link would be between mother's brother and sister's son.

Type 3. If everyone lived with the extended family associated with the wife's father's lineage, the result would be an alignment of women whose fathers belonged to the same matrilineage. Strange as this grouping may appear, the Trukese have standard expressions for this kind of relationship; the women would all be *pwiipwi winisam*, "siblings through fathers," or *jëfëkyren eew cëk sööpw*, "heirs (as distinct from members) of the same lineage."

Type 4. If everyone lived with the extended family associated with the husband's father's lineage, the result would now be a similar alignment of men who were *pwiipwi winisam*, whose fathers belonged to the same matrilineage. The link would be through father's brother, father's mother's brother, father's mother's mother's brother, etc.

Notably absent from the alignments of kin possible are groupings of patrilineally related men with their wives and of patrilineally related women with their husbands. Such alignments could result only by having everyone in Truk resort to residence type 5, living by special arrangement in an extended family in which they were without residential rights, and doing so in relation to the same set of relatives. It appears, therefore, that as long as extended families based on matrilineal lineages remain the object of residential choice in Truk, no matter what changes occur in the preference given to affiliation through the husband or wife, there cannot develop extended families containing systematic alignments of patrilineally related men or women. Such can only arise through a cultural change of a more profound nature: a change in the object of choice itself, so that, for example, couples no longer see the choice as one between localized lineages but as one between the husband's and wife's parents (wherever they may be residing).

Trukese residence types 1 and 2 are clearly best regarded as equivalent to the matrilocal and avunculocal types of comparative ethnology. By analogy it is possible to regard types 3 and 4 as the logical counterparts of amitalocal and patrilocal residence in a society where localized matrilineal kin groups are the objects of residential choice. The comparable analogues of matrilocal and avunculocal residence will be equally peculiar in a society where the objects of choice are localized patrilineal groups.

These considerations led me to list the incidence of type 4 under the patrilocal heading in the tables at the beginning of this paper. In view of the general association of patrilocal residence with the systematic alignment of patrilineally related men, such practice may lead only to further confusion and for this reason be unwise. The point remains, however, that patrilocal residence in this more usual sense can occur in Truk only following upon a fundamental change in its cultural principles governing the object of residential choice. After such change, Truk would necessarily be a different society for purposes of comparative study, whose residence principles would have to be worked out anew within the framework of its now different social system. The residence types that would fit that system would resemble those which fit its present one no more closely than do those of any other society. While we may balk at calling residence type 4 patrilocal because of the groove in which our thinking about residence has long slid, there is no logical reason for not doing so. Within the framework of Trukese culture as it is presently organized, type 4 is the structural analogue of what in other social systems we would not hesitate to call patrilocal residence.

It has been my immediate purpose in this paper to examine the problem of reliability in ethnographic reporting as it relates to customs of residence in marriage. In doing so, I have necessarily touched on matters which have significance for the study of culture generally. In concluding this discussion, therefore, it may be well to say something directly about them.

We noted first that census data of the usual kind are not sufficient for a reliable formulation of residence customs. We needed additional information. The additional information needed was different for the two societies examined. What was relevant in one was irrelevant in the other. We saw, moreover, that there is no *a priori* way of deciding what of all the possible kinds of information will be relevant; this is a matter to be determined in the light of all the other things an ethnographer is learning about the society he is studying. Every ethnographer knows that as he keeps learning and trying to find order in what he learns, he eventually arrives at a way of viewing his material such that a coherent structure emerges. This is just another way of saying that cultural description is the formulation of theory of a complex sort by which we seek to account for what we observe and what our informants tell us. It is this fact, so much a part of our everyday professional experience, whose significance for ethnographic method I think we have tended to overlook—an oversight which seems to be responsible for many discrepancies in ethnographic reporting of the sort illustrated here. I think we have tended to regard theory as beginning at the comparative or cross-cultural level and to see the methodology of ethnographic description as largely a matter of accurate recording and truthful reporting. I trust that Fischer's and my experience is sufficient to show that being a careful and honest reporter is only the beginning. One must be a theoretician as well.

But here again our disciplinary bias has done us a disservice. Since we have tended to regard theory as belonging to the domain of comparative study and have looked on ethnography as the means by which we obtain data to support or refute the kinds of propositions which have preoccupied the various schools of comparativists, we have consequently been inclined to try to order our data within the conceptual framework of comparative study. Thus we are inclined to feel that we have made a descriptive ethnographic statement when we say that residence in a society is prevailingly patrilocal, when what we are really saying, of course, is that the society has residence customs of a nature undisclosed but such that we feel they ought to be classified as patrilocal for comparative purposes. Thus we confuse the role of the ethnographer with that of the ethnologist. In view of the problem discussed here, it appears that this can be our undoing.

For this reason I have tried to show that what we do as ethnographers is, and must be kept, independent of what we do as comparative ethnologists. An ethnographer is constructing a theory that will make intelligible what goes on in a particular social universe. A comparativist is trying to find principles common to many different universes. His data are not the direct observations of an ethnographer, but the laws governing the particular universe as the ethnographer formulates them. It is by noting how these laws vary from one universe to another and under what conditions, that the comparativist arrives at a statement of laws governing the separate sets of laws which in turn govern the events in their respective social universes. Although they operate at different levels of abstraction, both ethnographer and comparativist are engaged in theory construction. Each must, therefore, develop concepts appropriate to his own level of abstraction, and in the case of the ethnographer to his particular universe. When we move from one level to the other we must shift our conceptual frameworks in accordance with systematic transformation procedures. Shortcutting in this has, I think, been another major reason for imprecision in our researches.

Despite such imprecisions, comparative study has managed to go forward to a remarkable degree. It is precisely because of the advances there made that we are now having to take serious stock in such matters as ethnographic reliability. I think, in this regard, that we are reaching a point comparable to that reached by linguists a short generation ago. Linguistics, with its already monumental achievements in comparative philology, took a great step forward as a science because linguists recognized that every language presents a new structure unlike any other, and that only by developing rigorous methods for arriving at precise theoretical statements of these structures would it be possible significantly to advance farther the study of language in general. I think we may be coming to a point where substantial progress in cultural anthropology will likewise require concentrating on descriptive ethnography as a legitimate scientific end in itself.

Notes

1. This is a considerably revised version of a paper originally presented at the annual business meeting of the American Ethnological Society in New York City, January 11, 1955. The author is indebted to Dr J. L. Fischer for making available his census material from Romonum Island on Truk and for explaining at considerable length in personal correspondence the procedures he followed in interpreting his

material. Dr G. P. Murdock and Dr D. M. Schneider both offered constructive criticism of the original version of this paper.

2. G. P. Murdock, *Social Structure* (New York, 1949).

3. J. L. Fischer, *Native Land Tenure in the Truk District* (Mimeographed, Civil Administration, Truk), p. 23. My own figures, hitherto unpublished, are taken from field notes collected in 1947 by Dr G. P. Murdock and myself as members of the research team from Yale University in the Coordinated Investigation of Micronesian Anthropology sponsored by the Office of Naval Research and the Pacific Science Board of the National Research Council. Additional financial aid was furnished by Yale University and the Wenner-Gren Foundation for Anthropological Research.

4. My total of sixty as against Fischer's sixty-two apparently results from the fact that he included some widowed persons in his count. The three men widowed since the time of my census were all still residing as they had been, in each case matrilocally. I am able to use his census material because of the information in my own notes about all of the individuals concerned.

5. W. H. Goodenough, *Property, Kin and Community on Truk* (Yale University Publications in Anthropology, no. 46, 1951), pp. 127-128.

6. The material on the Nakanai is from field notes collected during the spring and summer of 1954 under the joint auspices of the University Museum and Department of Anthropology of the University of Pennsylvania, the American Philosophical Society, and the Tri-Institutional Pacific Program.

6a. This picture of Nakanai residence is based on preliminary analysis of the field data. Further analysis, now in progress, indicates that it will require refinement, without, however, affecting the point illustrated here.

7. Op. cit., p. 16.

8. Fischer's census shows that the father has since moved into matrilocal residence in his present marriage.

9. Op. cit.; see especially pp. 66-80 for a fuller exposition of the material briefly summarized here.

10. See my discussion of Trukese property, op. cit., especially pp. 33-47.

11. Their irrelevance for understanding residence possibilities among the Lapps, also, has recently been pointed out by Robert N. Pehrson, "Bilateral Kin Grouping as a Structural Type," *Journal of East Asiatic Studies* 3 (1954), pp. 199-202. He also has difficulty applying the concepts of patrilocality, matrilocality, etc. to the principles governing residence decisions among the Lapps.

12. Fischer, recognizing that additional sociological information was needed to interpret the residence picture, decided to use information about who now held the land and from whom they had gotten it, collecting this information when he made his census. This *a priori* decision on his part is one of the differences between us in interpreting the residence situation.

13. Op. cit., pp. 127-128.

14. Leonard Adam, "Virilocal and Uxorilocal," *American Anthropologist* 49 (1947), p. 678.

4

ANTHROPOLOGY
GETS RELIGION
CULTURAL ECOLOGY, PANTHEISM,
AND PAPER DOLLS AMONG
THE NAHUA PEOPLE OF MEXICO

Alan R. Sandstrom

Religion is one of those aspects of human life that is difficult to study and make sense of. For many people with deep religious convictions, the problem hardly exists. Some feel confident that they already know the truth and are following the only correct path. For anthropologists and outsiders, however, the task of examining religious belief and ritual practice in cultures other than their own poses special difficulties. Colorful religious rituals are often the most creative expressions in people's daily lives of their most deeply held cultural values and worldview. Such rituals call out for attention and explanation. And yet the beliefs underlying these often spectacular dramas seem to defy common sense. Otherwise reasonable people suddenly appear to be exotic or even irrational when their justifications for religion are examined closely.

This seeming barrier to cross-cultural understanding is a problem that has confronted anthropology since its very beginning as a scientific discipline. Of the various solutions that have been proposed, none to date has proven fully satisfactory. My own experiences among the Nahua people of Mexico are typical of a profound problem faced by anthropologists: How do we describe and explain cultural phenomena in value-free terms and yet make sense of beliefs that appear on the surface to be nonsensical? One solution I have proposed to the dual problem of describing and explaining Nahua religion comes from the most unlikely of places, namely, the Himalayas of northern India. As I discuss in the following pages, it was a tortuous route leading to an insight about Nahua religion that began in the tropical forests of Mesoamerica and led to the mountain valleys of the Roof of the World.

The Nahua Indians living in Mexico and Central America are generally viewed as hardworking, pragmatic people. As I illustrate, their rituals are spectacular events, aesthetically pleasing and filled with majesty, but they also contain puzzling episodes that people explain through arresting myths and oral narratives (Sandstrom 1991). For example, Nahua shamans, or as I prefer to call them, "ritual specialists," cut enormous numbers of anthropomorphic figures from sheets of paper. They count them out carefully and lay them on beautifully decorated altars. Then, reminiscent of their pre-Hispanic forebears, they sprinkle them with animal blood (Sandstrom and Sandstrom 1986). Why would people dedicate blood offerings to paper dolls? It was a mystery I set out to solve.

Another example illustrates how straightforward explanations provided by people can be puzzling. Although the Nahua are expert farmers, Nahua understandings of crop fertility are elaborate and seem strange to us. Their myths tell of the *pilhuehuentsitsi* (little ancient ones), twelve tiny old men wearing garments with rubber sleeves who march across the sky carrying walking sticks. They haul water from the Gulf of Mexico on their backs, and as they pass overhead, they create thunder and lightning by striking their sticks. They deliver the water to a cave at the top of the sacred mountain Postectli, where a female water spirit named Apanchanej (water dweller), who has a fishtail instead of legs, delivers it to the cornfields in the form of precious rain. Apanchanej is a manifestation of Tonantsij (our sacred mother), an earth spirit who gave birth to the seeds that produce the life-sustaining crops people plant in their fields. Yet when she gave birth to corn in the form of a beautiful blond-haired boy named Chicome Xochitl (Seven Flower), Tonantsij's mother became insanely jealous and tried to kill him. Seven Flower's grandmother (a kind of sorceress) threw him in the water, ground him on a stone metate, and tried to roast him alive in the sweat bath. Each time, the boy came back to life. In the end, he tricked his murderous grandmother into entering the overheated sweat bath, where she burned to death. A toad threw her ashes into the Gulf of Mexico, whereupon they turned into a huge lizard. It is on her back—the rough surface of the earth—where we human beings live out our lives. A water spirit becomes the earth mother, and a homicidal grandmother who tries to destroy the life-giving corn is transformed into the earth. What can it all mean?

It is hard to avoid treating members of another culture in a condescending way when they reveal what beliefs they hold about the spirit realm, fate, misfortune, or the causes of human disease. Other people's myths and religious stories always seem bizarre and almost childlike to outsiders. They are the features of a foreign culture most likely to offend and even threaten people who do not share them. Examples surely include religious food taboos, genital mutilation as a religious rite, human sacrifice among the ancient Aztecs, jihad and purdah in Islam, and (closer to home) the snake-handling cultists who speak in tongues, polygyny in Mormonism, and the cults surrounding figures such as Jim Jones or David Koresh and the Branch Davidians. How are we to understand these unusual, even upsetting, religious beliefs and practices without falling into a facile and self-affirming ethnocentrism? Can it be that everyone in the world is insane except us?

The Problem of Nahua Religion

None of these questions is easy to answer, but I have found that ethnographic work among the Nahua has helped clarify issues and provided a way to think about the problematic aspects of religion in different cultures. The Nahua speak the Nahuatl language, and many of them are contemporary descendants of the great Aztec civilization that ruled over the largest empire in the New World before the arrival of the Europeans in Mesoamerica in the early sixteenth century. Nahuatl is related to Ute, Paiute, Comanche, Shoshone, and other languages spoken in the American Southwest. There are today more than 1.5 million speakers of the language. Many Nahua live in small, rural communities and make their living through farming and temporary wage labor on ranches and neighboring towns and cities.

As a graduate student, I was very excited to have the opportunity to conduct ethnographic field research in a Gulf Coast Nahua community in northern Veracruz, Mexico. My plan was to study the slash-and-burn system of horticulture and attempt to relate it to Nahua religion and worldview. The Nahua call their religion *tlaneltokili* in Nahuatl, meaning "belief, devotion, or worship"; when speaking Spanish, they call it simply *costumbres,* or "customs." I came to learn that the Nahua system of beliefs and ritual practice is firmly rooted in the pre-Hispanic period and that many of their deities, myths, and sacred offerings are virtually identical to those reported by sixteenth-century chroniclers. Of course, after nearly five hundred years of history, the contemporary religion had undergone significant changes. Yet the continuities were striking.

The aim of my research was to investigate a contemporary Native American religion, but I also hoped to help solve some of the problems that have plagued scholars studying the belief systems of the great pre-Hispanic civilizations of Mesoamerica. Researchers had struggled to comprehend Aztec religion even though a rich historical record survives describing Aztec culture. Spanish friars and their trained Nahua assistants left voluminous detailed documents, but because the Spanish clergy were missionaries, they were particularly interested in better understanding the Aztec religious system so as to replace it with their form of medieval Catholicism. The Native American religion proved challenging to characterize and even more difficult to wipe out. The pantheon of deities was unstable, and key figures often appeared in multiple, contradictory, and incommensurate guises that seemed to shade into one another. Versions of even central myths were inconsistent, beliefs appeared disorganized, and rituals seemed utterly incoherent. In short, the historical accounts reflect the difficulty of outsiders trying to understand other people's religion. It was my aim as a graduate student to study living descendants of the Aztecs and gain insights that would help straighten it all out.

An Anthropologist Enters the Field

It was the summer of 1970 when I arrived at a remote Nahua village of six hundred people that I call Amatlán. For my initial two field trips I was alone, but during all subsequent visits I was accompanied by my wife, Pamela, and later our son Michael. After facing a difficult adjustment to life in a foreign culture one hundred miles from the nearest paved road, where few spoke Spanish, much less English, and where there was no electricity, running water, bathrooms, or even outhouses, I set about my work. Not surprisingly, I found that much of Nahua life was very agreeable and seemed reasonable given the level of technology and limited resources that people had at their disposal. Their houses were made of poles lashed on a frame with steeply pitched, thatched roofs. The dwellings were quite comfortable for the climate, efficiently constructed using available materials and technology, and they lasted many years before having to be replaced. The same held for food production. The Nahua and other Native Americans in the region practice slash-and-burn horticulture, a type of gardening that is combined with gathering, fishing, and hunting. The men cut the forest with a steel machete, dry the trees and brush, burn them, and plant corn, beans, squash, and other crops in the ashes with a digging stick. The women help in the harvest when the crop is ready. There are two growing seasons each year. This was certainly not the way crops are grown in Iowa, but again reasonable given the constraints faced by individual farmers.

I soon learned that the staple in the Nahua diet is corn. Corn is also at the center of their religious conceptions, as we see shortly. Corn means sustenance to them, and the grain is evidence of a cosmos that provides the means for life and happiness. Things were going well, and I was gathering lots of information on Nahua technology, but I could not help but notice that there was no religious activity. I would occasionally hear lilting guitar and violin music coming from far off in the dense tropical forest that could have had some religious association, but I was unable to confirm my suspicions. People knew I was interested in witnessing a ritual, but nobody was saying anything. I had now been resident for nearly six months and had begun to despair. I thought I had discovered the first culture in the world with no religion at all. So much for my carefully worked-out plan.

As an anthropology graduate student, I knew that there are about six thousand cultures in the world today and that every one of them in the ethnographic record has some kind of religious system. Countless numbers of cultural traditions existed in prehistory—a time that spans more than 99 percent of the human past—and we can safely assume that each of these cultures also had religion. Although individuals may or may not be religious, cultures always are. It follows that religion must contribute something very important to our survival as a species. If there were groups without religion, they are no longer with us. What was the problem with these Nahua? The question was killing me.

Then I got a break. A friend informed me that the community was going to hold a four-day celebration for Tonantsij, called in Spanish La Virgen de Guadalupe (the Virgin of Guadalupe), in a small thatch-roofed shrine that I had not yet come upon. Needless to say, I was intrigued by the prospect. It was getting toward the end of December at this point, and so the celebration looked like it might be related to the Christian celebration of Christmas. I knew the Nahua had been missionized actively for centuries, and so it stood to reason that they were simply rural Christians. Of course, this discovery would have been fatal to my overall research project. La Virgen is a manifestation of Mary, and so her identity fit well with the Christmas theory. However, I knew that Tonantsij is a pre-Hispanic earth deity, and this fact would point to an indigenous origin. The winter solstice falls in midwinter, which is why Christmas is observed at that time, but it might be the reason for an ancient ritual as well. Only by witnessing the event could I determine its nature and reduce the ambiguity.

The day arrived and I went to the shrine. Soon the people formed a procession that included a guitarist and violinist playing those same lilting melodies I had heard before. There was an old lady holding a smoking copal incense brazier, a girl carrying a box containing a plaster statue of the Virgin of Guadalupe, two other girls carrying a pair of statues depicting Mary and Joseph, and about another dozen young girls with lighted beeswax candles. Over four days, the procession visited each house in the village to bring the blessing of Tonantsij and thus fertility to that family. Male dancers with elaborate folded-paper and mirror headdresses, each holding a rattle and flower ornament carved from wood, performed through the night until dawn, at which time the procession resumed making its way house to house. On the final day, the people returned to the shrine. Inside the rustic building along one wall was a large altar made of two handmade tables. Above the altar was a long arch covered with greenery and pinwheels made of palm and marigold flowers. On the altar table and beneath it were dozens of burning beeswax candles that cast a yellow light. A tall wooden cross placed between the altar tables reached from the floor to the roof of the shrine. I knew that traditional Mexican celebrations of Christmas involved *posadas* (literally, inns), whereby processions of people go house to house to commemorate the biblical story of Joseph and Mary in search of lodging on the eve of Jesus' birth. The Nahua celebration seemed reminiscent of that custom.

The affair was my first Nahua ritual, and this observance at least appeared to be a mixture of Spanish Catholicism and Native American elements. But the evening was not over yet. Dozens of people gathered in the shrine, each bowing respectfully before the altar and placing a lighted beeswax candle on it. The musicians played while the dancers performed, and the lone old woman swayed before the altar censing everyone with the aromatic copal smoke. There was an air of anticipation as the tall figure of Reveriano entered the shrine. He was dressed in traditional white shirt and pants and carried a woven sisal bag over his shoulder. I later learned that he was the most power-ful and respected ritual specialist in Amatlán. He squatted down before the altar, took out a sheaf of colored papers, and with a pair of scissors proceeded to cut several dozen elaborate paper images. The images were humanlike, with many complex patterns cut into each figure that seemed diagnostic of their identity or purpose. They represented a variety of specific wind spirits, which, I later found out, were the angry and dangerous souls of villagers who had died violent or premature deaths. He carefully laid them out, sprinkled or daubed them with a series of offerings while chanting the whole time, and then suddenly ripped them into tiny bits. After dancing wildly all around the shrine, Reveriano gave instructions to the others to set out on the altar an elaborate feast of the best food and drink.

This was my initial encounter with the paper dolls, and although I did not know any of the details of the ritual, I realized that I had witnessed something extraordinary. What better and more dramatic way to come to the realization that the Nahua worldview was something radically different, not merely a reflection of my own. Paper was nearly a sacred substance in most pre-Hispanic Mesoamerican societies. Each temple employed paper cutters, and paper was one of the most important items of tribute that flowed from the provinces into the imperial capitals. The paper was made into garments for priests, banners and flags, clothing for statues, and books containing sacred knowledge. Paper was so linked to the Native American religion that the Spaniards outlawed its manufacture and use by Indians on pain of their being brought before the Inquisition. Within a few years, paper was nowhere to be found. And yet here in Amatlán, in a remote corner of the state of Veracruz, paper remained the central focus of religious rituals. I later found paper being used in the same way by neighboring Otomí, Tepe-hua, Huastec, and Totonac peoples. Reveriano was dedicating offerings to dangerous wind spirits, thought by the Nahua to cause disease and death, in order to keep them away from the main offering dedicated to Tonantsij. By deflecting these entities, he protected the villagers and ensured that the offerings were properly received by the earth mother.

This sequence of events did not look like any Christmas that I had ever seen, either in the United States or in Mexico. With further research, I learned that the altar is a model of the Nahua cosmos. The arch is *ilhuicactli,* the sky realm, and the marigold pinwheels represent the stars. The altar tabletop represents *tlalticpac,* the earth's surface, or, as the myths describe it, the back of the earth monster. Finally, the sacred space beneath the altar represents the earth itself. The tall cross placed between the altar tables is the *axis mundi,* a kind of cosmic center pole that connects the sky, earth, and underworld realms. I also learned of the close connection between the Virgin of Guadalupe and the pre-Hispanic deity Tonantsij. The statues of Joseph and Mary were reinterpreted by the Nahua as the lord and lady of work. With years of additional ethnographic investigation, I have come to realize that Nahua rituals in the region are largely Native American in meaning and function, with a small admixture of Spanish Catholicism. But like everything else connected with religion in the New World, there is an ambiguity built into the system. The result is decidedly not Christian, despite the best efforts of the missionaries for a half millennium. Nevertheless, the Nahua and other groups in the region have enthusiastically incorporated some Christian elements into their beliefs, spirit pantheons, and ritual practices.

Contemporary Nahua religion, as it turns out, is complex; it involves a whole range of ritual occasions, including pilgrimages to sacred mountains, dedication of offerings in caves and at the summits of mountains, divination, sorcery and countersorcery practices, disease prevention and curing, crop fertility rituals, calendrical rituals, rites of reversal and rites of passage, and many additional observances. It also includes a complex system of myths that help explain the rituals. In this chapter, I focus on the paper images that are at the heart of so many Nahua ritual events in order to show how they help bridge the gulf between spirit and human domains.

From the outset of our research, Pamela and I endeavored to make systematic collections of the paper images with the goal of determining the extent of the pantheon and perhaps clarifying what seemed especially murky areas of Nahua belief. We became regulars at village ritual observances. The people had become experts at hiding their rituals from outsiders to protect against interference from missionaries or traveling priests. There had even been periods of time in the recent past when civil authorities attempted to prosecute followers of the traditional religion. These facts help explain why I had such a hard time getting invited to my first ritual. However, we soon joined the circuit and before long had witnessed dozens of ritual events. We got to know the major ritual specialists and enlisted their aid in adding to our growing collection of paper images. We eventually learned how to make the flower and palm adornments that are so important for the proper Nahua offering, and so we soon were in demand whenever an event was planned.

As the years went by, we made the acquaintance of many ritual specialists and our collection of paper images grew into the thousands. There seemed no end to them. One powerful ritual specialist and a particularly talented paper cutter is Encarnación Téllez Hernández. His cuttings are true works of art as well as being effective expressions of the abstract ideas and meanings that lie behind Nahua religion. We became close friends, and he did his best to inform us about the more esoteric aspects of his belief system. He wanted us to take the paper dolls back home with us so that we could tell Americans about his religion, which he told us in heartfelt terms was "a very beautiful thing."

After witnessing countless rituals during many separate field stays spanning nearly four decades, and despite the best efforts of the Nahua themselves to help us, we were still not able to develop a fully coherent picture of this religious system. We might have concluded that the pantheon is unstable, that deities have multiple contradictory and incommensurate guises and seem to shade into one another, and that the myths are inconsistent, beliefs appear disorganized, and rituals seem incoherent. We found ourselves in the identical situation faced by scholars working on the Aztec religion of the sixteenth century. The religion and its philosophical principles seemed intractable despite our best effort and years of trying to understand it. Examination of the paper figures did not seem to help. We had collected images representing corn, beans, the earth, the sun, the moon, water, sacred hills and caves, dew, hail, rain, clouds, wrath, envy, dead souls, wind spirits, houses, woodpiles, musical instruments, and blood-sucking transforming sorcerers. The list apparently had no end. Then one day when Encarnación was cutting us yet another neat stack of paper dolls to take back to the United States, I exclaimed with exasperation in my voice, "How many of these are there?" He stopped his work, and with a quizzical look on his face, he replied, "They are all the same." Then he used the Spanish word *señal* to describe them, meaning "sign" or "mark." So the paper dolls were all the same, and they were signs or marks. What could it all mean?

The very possibility of meaningful cross-cultural communication seemed to be at stake. We had been working in Amatlán for fifteen years at the time Encarnación made this remark. It is worth mentioning at this point that ethnography is a two-way process. The Nahua asked us nearly as many questions about our own society as we asked about theirs. One memorable encounter occurred when Pamela told a group of women about the popularity of Tupperware parties. She explained that a woman would invite her friends and relatives over and serve food, expect her guests to look over the offerings, and pay money to take some home. The women sat and stared, listening politely during Pamela's explanation. After thanking her for telling them about this custom, they left with stricken looks on their faces. No decent person would invite kinswomen to a party to sell them plastic containers. On another occasion I was speaking to a group of men at Encarnación's house. They wanted to know what religion was like in North America, particularly Protestantism. I recounted what I knew and mentioned that some Protestants believe the Bible to be true in every detail, even miracles. They were familiar with many Christian personages, such as Jesus and Mary, whom they have reinterpreted and equate respectively with the sun, Tonatij, and Tonantsij, the earth mother. They wanted to know about the miracles that people believed in. I mentioned the opening of the sea and the drowning of the Pharaoh's army, Jesus walking on water, the multiplication of loaves and fishes, and people being raised from the dead. There was a slight pause of disbelief, but nobody even commented on what I said, and they went right on to other more plausible topics of conversation. As an anthropologist, I certainly know how our own cherished beliefs can sound foolish to people from other cultures. But I had never had the fact so clearly illustrated to me as that evening in Amatlán. It is a truism in anthropology that the best way to learn about your own culture is to immerse yourself in another one.

Anthropology and Cultural Ecology

In my view, the purpose of the anthropological study of culture is to document the thoughts and behaviors of human groups and develop explanations for similarities and differences among them. For example, why are Anglo North American and Eskimo kinship systems identical? These are two vastly different societies. Why do Iroquois people trace descent through the female line? Anthropologists are interested in how and why cultures evolve, that is, transform from one system to another. There are many scientific problems to identify if our goal is understanding causation in human social life. I should mention that not everyone agrees with this goal. Anthropology was hit in the mid-1980s by a virulent postmodern attack that rejected science—particularly social science—and all generalized knowledge as examples of Euro-American colonial imposition on the world's peoples. People in any society tend to think that things just happen, that their society and religion are universal, correct, and eternal, but in my view, and from the stance of scientific anthropology, social and cultural phenomena are caused, not random. There are reasons that things are the way they are, but the members of a culture are rarely aware of them. Anglos and Eskimos have the same system of kinship partly because it adapts them to highly mobile lifestyles. The Iroquois matrilineal kinship system may be caused by males being absent for long periods of time during the year.

The question for us to pose, then, is, *What causes religions to be the way they are?* Or to put the matter more precisely, *What factors have caused Nahua religion to exist in its present form, and how is it different today compared with five hundred years ago?* I think the approach that holds the greatest promise in identifying the causes of religious belief and practice is the research strategy called "cultural ecology." This approach has been around since the nineteenth century, and it is based on a materialist perspective that makes it analogous to field biology studies for studying human population adaptations. The idea is that culture can be understood as a strategy for survival. Culture adapts individuals in societies to given requirements for making a living in a given environment with a given level of technology. People's needs for food, water, shelter, and the imperative to raise children must be met first if a group is to survive. The material conditions of life lead people to develop social and cultural institutions and traditions such as kinship and religious systems that are consonant with the pragmatic requirements of their lives.

The inspiration for this theoretical perspective is Karl Marx, but chapter-and-verse Marxists would reject cultural ecology as "mechanical" (or worse, "vulgar") materialism because it denies the dialectical nature of human social dynamics. Despite these criticisms, I think cultural ecology is the correct approach to understand the similarities and differences among the world's inventory of cultures. There is great cultural variability, but the variation is not infinite. Historically unrelated groups with similar modes of production have statistically predictable similarities in their social organizations or ideological systems. For example, there is variation in the ideological systems of hunting and gathering peoples, but there are remarkable commonalities among them as well; one such characteristic is the marked egalitarianism among the world's hunter-gatherer bands. Cultural ecologists would like to know how these similarities come about.

In my view, the biggest scientific problem in the social sciences today is understanding the connection between material conditions of life and the socially shared beliefs, worldview, religious symbols, value and meaning systems, aesthetic standards, and all of the ideological phenomena that are part of every culture in the world. Using standard cultural-ecological terminology we can ask, *What is the relationship between a culture's infrastructure and superstructure?* The "infrastructure" is that part of culture that acts as the interface between human beings and nature, including technology, work patterns, environmental factors, modes of production, and modes of reproduction. The "superstructure" is composed of myths, symbols, philosophy, music, art, ideology, and religion. Some scholars add a third, intermediate level that falls between the infrastructure and superstructure, and they call it "structure." The structure of a culture is the social system that includes divisions of labor, political organization, kinship systems, political economy, educational systems, and social classes. All cultures can be understood in terms of their infrastructure, structure, and superstructure. Anthropologists call this analytical division the "universal pattern." The question boils down to, *How does the infrastructure cause the superstructure?* Another way to phrase the problem is that because individuals are capable of an infinite number of ideas, *Why do some ideas become social?* We think that ideas are socially shared only if they are compatible with the infrastructure.

Cultural-ecological theory asserts that religious traditions must make sense in the context of people's lives, a context that is conditioned by the way they make a living. Understanding how this works is a long-term problem in the social sciences that, if solved, promises to bring a new understanding of our own society as well as all others. As our work progressed, we were dismayed to learn how much solid ethnographic information was lacking on the contemporary Nahua. Other researchers had previously published reports on more acculturated groups, but even this information was scattered and incomplete. We lacked basic information on the kinship system. Very little useful material had been published on the relations of the Nahua with other indigenous groups or Hispanic elites that held the monopoly on social, political, and economic power in the region. The Nahua religion practiced in the rural outback was essentially unknown to scholars. To move forward with the larger project, we would have to rework completely some generally held understandings (and misunderstandings) of the Native American religious systems in Mesoamerica.

Our level of frustration grew, and for a few years we gave up entirely on the project. We took advantage of an opportunity to open a new research front among the Tibetans in exile in the Himachal Pradesh region of northwestern India. Our fieldwork in the foothills of the Himalayas lasted for eight months. Like many visitors to Asia, we became enthralled with the colorful kaleidoscope of landscapes, peoples, and religions of the region. We conducted ethnographic research on Tibetan Buddhism, interviewed monks and high reincarnate lamas, attended rituals, and read extensively. It was totally fascinating, but all the while the Nahua puzzles continued to haunt us. In the end, the seemingly irrational move to a new field area provided a key experience that helped to clarify Nahua religion.

I will not be able to describe in this brief chapter the complexities of analysis that would solve the problem of infrastructural causation. Much work remains to be done. But I can tell you something of what we have learned about Nahua religion and how it places the Nahua in relation to what in our own society we call the "forces of nature" and in relation to the Nahua means of horticultural production First, I examine how myths help the Nahua to understand and record conceptions of natural processes. Second, I focus on the critical importance of geographical features of the landscape in the Nahua religion and worldview. Third, I show how our discoveries about religion in India helped to clarify the idea of pantheism and the fundamental mystery of the paper dolls and the sophistication of Nahua religion.

The Nahua View of Natural Processes

How do the Nahua interpret and talk about natural processes? It is important to understand that most peoples of the world have not experienced a scientific revolution such as the one that transformed modern society, first in Europe and later in the United States and elsewhere. People in all cultures have detailed empirical knowledge about natural phenomena, and they have complex technology based on that knowledge. Due to historical circumstances, people in the West, and increasingly in other parts of the world, talk about the phenomena of nature using the vocabulary of science. We speak to each other about meteorology, solar energy, photosynthesis, molecular biology, and genes. The Nahua talk about the same processes and phenomena but without using the terms and concepts deriving from a scientific worldview. The detailed knowledge they have about the world is encoded in their myths and rituals. For example, the Nahua say the sun provides the energy that animates the world. This energy is observable in the form of heat that showers down upon the earth's surface. When a seed is planted in the ground and provided with water, the sun will bring the plant to life with its heat. Corn, the staple crop, absorbs the solar heat, and when people eat the corn in the form of tortillas or tamales, this energy is transferred through the bloodstream into the tissues to produce body heat. In the Nahua conception, human beings have multiple souls; one of these is the *tonali,* which means "heat soul." When a person dies, he or she loses the life-giving connection to the sun and turns cold. The Nahua have a saying that encapsulates this process, *sintli ne toeso,* which means "corn is our blood." It is easy to see that the Nahua view of the conversion of solar energy into consumable plant life and its relation to human nutrition and survival is closely analogous to the Euro-American scientific view.

According to the Nahua, disease is caused in most cases by invisible wind spirits that invade the body. The Nahua have developed a two-pronged strategy for treating illness. The first is through skilled use of the many medicinal herbs that grow wild or that the Nahua cultivate in their gardens. The second is through symbolic means. Ritual specialists devote a majority of their professional practice to diagnosing and curing patients of disease or preventing illness by symbolically drawing wind spirits away from people. They portray these entities through the medium of cut paper so that people can have a better conception of what ails them. The winds are associated with filth and pollution or elements of disorder and disruption of the normal working of the natural and social worlds. At the most elevated level, the Nahua link disease with the disruption of social and natural processes. Symbolic curing takes place in the context of the extended family and is designed to eliminate disharmony and return the patient to health. Most Europeans and North Americans attribute disease to invisible entities that are associated with pollution and invisible to the naked eye. By both incorporating medicinal plants and rallying the family in the curing effort, the Nahua have anticipated the so-called new medicine, which attempts to treat patients as both biological and social beings. The Nahua view does not substitute for Western biomedicine, but it parallels and reinforces it in many ways.

The Nahua experience of the world is expressed through religious and mythic symbols. The twelve little men in rubber-sleeved clothing who carry water from the Gulf of Mexico to the sacred water mountain are clearly metaphors for clouds that bring the rain. In fact, water vapor from the Gulf is lofted upward by the Sierra Madre Oriental mountain range to the west of Veracruz state, and this phenomenon accounts for the exceptionally heavy rainfall in the region. The rain appears to come from the mountains, and this observation has been incorporated into the myth system. The earth, in conjunction with sun and rain, does literally give birth to the corn, and the processes of germination and growth have been incorporated in the personage of Tonantsij. Corn is thrown in water, buried in the earth, ground on a stone metate, and heated over the fire, and yet it returns every year to support the people. Thus, the adventures of Seven Flower with his vicious grandmother simply reflect the persistence of corn in the face of abuse by the humans who depend on it. In case anyone forgets that Seven Flower is the corn plant, in a society where virtually everyone has black hair, his hair is blond, like corn silk.

The Sacred Landscape

The Nahua have thoroughly incorporated the landscape into their religious system. To some extent, every group brings aspects of the landscape into their beliefs and myths. Anthropologists call such systems of sacred geography the "cognized environment." Hunting and gathering peoples often have particularly elaborate cognized environments. The Nahua represent an extreme in this regard. Every hill, plain, spring, stream, boulder, or other geographical feature is named by them and plays a role in their myths and rituals. When walking along, people comment on each feature they pass and point out the spots that figure in their mythic stories. They often name their homesteads by some nearby geographical feature (for example, *atlalco,* meaning "muddy place"), and it is common for people to take such names as their own (e.g., Juan Atlalco). This toponymic or place-name system illustrates the close association the Nahua have with their local environment and reveals the important role that the landscape plays in their consciousness, identity, and daily life.

For the Nahua, the place of the landscape in their religious conceptions is illustrated by their ideas about water mountains, such as Postectli in northern Veracruz. They say that mountains are the sources of all that is good and positive in the world. Mountains have caves near their summits that are literally filled with life-giving water. These caves are particularly sacred and are believed to be the source not only of rain, seeds, and fertility, as we have see, but also of treasure and other valued items. The Nahua say that the earth is a living body whose soil is its flesh; water, its blood; and stones, its bones. The mountains are its head; the earth, its body; and the underworld, its feet. Nahua farmers dedicate constant offerings to the earth to make amends for burning it and poking it with digging sticks to plant corn. A funeral ritual is basically a plea to the earth to forgive the deceased for offenses to the earth during his or her life. As we have already seen, the Nahua view the earth's surface as the back of a living crocodilelike monster surrounded by water.

Although I would not make the case that the Nahua understanding of the earth and landscape is identical to our own, many scientists are now saying that we should view the earth as a living entity. Green movement supporters argue that complex geological and ecological systems are at least analogous to living creatures. The Gaia movement directly makes the case that the earth is alive, and this movement could turn into a religion in the future. The North American Earth Day observance began in 1970 and is already taking on religious overtones. "What Would Jesus Do?" is an initiative that links mainstream religion with the ecology movement. And even the Southern Baptist Convention, once staunchly opposed to the idea of global warming, acknowledged in 2008 that climate change is a reality that must be addressed. By incorporating the landscape into their deepest religious convictions and by viewing the earth as a living entity, the Nahua recognize that all living systems, including human beings, are related to each other and to the natural processes of the planet. Suddenly, their religion begins to make more sense.

But the question remains: Why do the Nahua use such seemingly bizarre metaphors to convey empirical observations of the earth and its living creatures? It is important to remember that this group has no writing system to preserve knowledge. The Nahua have incorporated their wisdom into the most powerful ideological system at their disposal: religion. Insights about the workings of the universe are stored in the form of striking narrations that are easy to remember and thus to recount to one another and to the next generation.

Pantheism in Nahua Religion

Nahua religion is fundamentally pantheistic in character. It was in India that we first saw pantheism in action. Tibetan Buddhism and Hinduism are pantheistic religions, and our exposure to practitioners of those religions proved to be a key breakthrough in our research among the Nahua. We later found out that this solution to the problem of defining religion in Mesoamerica was hinted at in an obscure article published in 1910 by a German researcher named Hermann Beyer. The idea was later rediscovered and elaborated by anthropologist Eva Hunt (1977) in her insightful book *The Transformation of the Hummingbird*. Scholars studying Mesoamerican religions have had difficulty understanding the concept of deity because of the seemingly contradictory nature of the historical record and the various labels that they use to categorize religions. Some call them "animistic" (the belief that everything has a soul) or "animatistic" (the belief in *mana* or an impersonal force). Most often, they are characterized as "polytheistic" (the belief in a pantheon of discrete deities usually arranged in a hierarchy). The fact is that none of these formulations fit the data very well, and attempts by scholars to apply these labels to the pre-Hispanic civilizations have led to much of the confusion over the nature of the Mesoamerican cases. A major difficulty with our project was that we also did not know how to characterize Nahua religion. It was among the Tibetans living in exile in India that we learned of another way to interpret the Mesoamerican data.

So what is pantheism? It is a profound philosophical and religious system that differs radically from theistic or deity-centered religions such as Christianity, with its doctrine of a supreme transcendent god. In pantheism, the cosmos itself is the deity; the creator and the creation are one in the same. In Christianity, the creator and creation are separate, and many Christian theologians consider pantheism to be a heresy. The cosmos in pantheism is a seamless, indivisible totality, and everybody and everything partakes of deity. All diversity is an illusion, a product of our sense organs and the way our brains work. Thus, there is no distinction between animate and inanimate; everything is suffused with deity, even objects. Pantheism helps explain the sacred landscape for the Nahua. For them, it is literally alive—part of a living universe—and everything is permeated with the sacred principle.

The name for this sacred principle in Nahuatl is Totiotsij, "our sacred deity," a word based on the root *teotl,* translated by sixteenth-century Spaniards as "God." But the friars were unaware that it was a radically different concept of the deity from their own. For the Nahua, the great animator of the universe, the entity that breathes life into the cosmos, is the sun. The people believe that the sun (Tonatij in Nahuatl) provides a divine heat and the power of life to every object and entity. Not surprisingly, the Nahua have incorporated many elements of Spanish Catholicism into their religion. Their name for the sun when asked in Spanish is Jesús (or Jesus Christ). But the sun to them is simply the largest and most spectacular aspect or manifestation of the great unity that incorporates and defines everything in existence. At a profound level, people, animals, objects, and forces are identical and incapable of being separated. The Nahua concept of water in its multiple states provides an excellent example of pantheistic thinking. Natural phenomena such as dew, hail, clouds, fog, thunder, and lightning are all understood as aspects of the single substance of water, and they are each visualized in a distinctive way in the medium of cut paper. Apparent diversity masks the underlying unity.

One problem with pantheistic systems is that they tend to be very abstract and far removed from daily life. People are more generally concerned with problems such as illness, human and crop fertility, and avoidance of danger. To connect the abstract with the pragmatic, people in pantheistic religions often create portrayals of relevant aspects of the world that have a direct bearing on one's life. In Hinduism, there are literally millions of portrayals of various deities in statues and paintings. Hindu temples are filled with these objects, and yet they all represent aspects or temporary manifestations of the great indivisible whole. Tibetan Buddhists also produce scroll-like thanka paintings and sacred statues to represent aspects of the Buddha, but these are all ephemeral or transitory appearances derived from the single great unity that lies at the heart of existence. Theistic religions (such as monotheistic Christianity) also produce sacred art and portray significant figures, but these are meant to represent real people and personages such as saints. In pantheism, everything in the universe partakes of the great divine totality. For Hindus it is Brahma, for Buddhists it is Buddha, and for the Nahua this sacred principle is Totiotsij. This imperative to visualize abstract aspects of the pantheistic cosmos helps to explain the Nahua paper doll complex.

Just like their Hindu and Tibetan Buddhist counterparts, Nahua ritual specialists portray spirits relevant to a particular ritual to make the religious system seem less remote and more immediate for participants. When curing a patient, ritual specialists cut out paper images of disease-causing wind spirits to symbolize the danger posed by these pathogens. When dedicating an offering to ensure fertility of the fields, they create images in paper of the earth, the seed, and the water spirits. The variations on the design of paper images are limited only by the imagination of the ritual paper cutter. Ritual specialists create hundreds or even thousands for a single ritual offering and usually destroy the paper figures after they have served their purpose, symbolizing in a direct way the return to the unity from which the figure represented was temporarily extracted. The only exception to this practice, attesting to the ephemeral nature of reality, is the wooden box filled with paper images of the seed spirits (each dressed in tiny cloth outfits) that each ritual specialist keeps permanently on his or her home altar. These paper images serve as a constant reminder of the beneficent nature of the cosmos that provides what human beings need to survive. The point they underscore is that there is only one sacred entity; everything else is derivative. The ritual specialist Encarnación meant it when he said that "the paper figures are all the same," but it took us years to learn how to listen to him.

At the core of Nahua rituals is the *tlamanilistli*, a word that means simply "offering." So it appears that rituals are a kind of social exchange with spirit entities in the Nahua view. Rituals overseen by a Nahua specialist trained in the esoteric aspects of curing and crop increase vary in complexity depending on what the people are seeking. The rituals are essentially offerings dedicated to the spirit representatives of the processes of nature in order to obligate them so that they will continue to provide abundant harvests, rain, sun, health, children, and prosperity. Human beings and spirits are caught up in an elaborate and delicate cycle of exchanges.

Conclusion

So what can we say about the religion of the Nahua? Their religion clearly addresses daily pragmatic concerns of the Nahua horticultural way of life, such as crop fertility, human health, and balance with the forces of nature. The religion practiced by the Nahua situates people in their natural and social environment, explains natural occurrences, and allows people to participate in complex processes of the world while not strictly controlling them. It helps people grasp plant reproduction or human disease, for example, and represent such phenomena in symbolic terms. It permits people to participate in and enter into reverential exchange with forces of a world created and conditioned by the way they make their living.

Nahua religion gives expression to the important conception that people are part of the natural order, incorporated into a complex system of exchange with natural forces. In pantheism, human beings are identical to nature; they do not stand apart. Nahua religious ideas show how everything is interrelated. The Nahua say that people are corn. In chanting and poetry, they call people *tlalchamantli*, which means "earthly sprout." Human beings are corn in a different form, a transformation of the corn plant. Our bodies are modeled on corn. The tassel is our head, the stalk is our body, and the roots are our feet.

The Nahua conceive of the ripe corn ready for harvest as *ilamatl,* a sacred old lady who holds in her arms a precious baby swaddled in leaves. For the Nahua, the sun lives in us as our heat soul. Our blood is like the water that surrounds us, and our flesh is like the earth that sustains us. As human beings we are intimately linked to the local landscape. In us are the forces of the cosmos making everything alive. All of these ideas and many more are encoded in Nahua religion.

People's religious ideas are not random, nor can they be reduced to historical accident. In the end, the problem of connecting infrastructure with superstructure must be approached by ethnological comparison of cross-cultural cases. We must compare historically unrelated horticultural societies to test theories about ritual symbols, the sacred landscape, and pantheism. For us, the work has just begun on this project because it has taken us so long to come to a fuller understanding of the Nahua system. However, comparisons are useless unless they are based on high-quality, detailed ethnographic data on groups such as the Nahua. Individual studies such as ours are critical to the endeavor.

We have conclusive evidence that infrastructural changes cause superstructural adjustments. Our own technological and demographic infrastructure has been undergoing radical change over the past century, and thus we should expect the religious superstructure to respond. Our productive system is transforming from a manufacturing into a service and information economy. The globalization of economic and political processes is accelerating alarmingly. If cultural-ecological theory is correct, we should look for new religions to emerge and for established ones to reflect these profound transformations. The rise of millennial cults, nativistic movements, religious revivalism, and crises in doctrinal identity may be signs of things to come. The Nahua, too, are swept up in these global changes, and, not surprisingly, new religious forms are emerging in Mexico, too. A few years ago in a neighboring village, a young Nahua woman, Amalia Bautista, was the focus of a revitalization movement that declared her the living manifestation of the corn sprit Seven Flower. She has been silenced by the Catholic Church and quietly sequestered in a convent. Popular movements like this are difficult to control, and they can threaten entrenched powers.

A striking feature of pantheistic systems is that adherents do not recognize a clear distinction between good and evil. For pantheists, forces of nature— like all human beings—are a mixture of positive and negative qualities. Deity permeates everything, and therefore evil contains good, and anything good must also have an evil aspect. Even Tonantsij may kill a person who fails to enter into ritual exchange with her. Miquilistli, the Nahua spirit of death, has significant power that can be used to cure desperately ill people. For Buddhists and Hindus, sin is said to be caused by ignorance, not evil. This feature of pantheism does not mean that people are incapable of telling right from wrong, but rather that they are sensitive to how complex such a judgment is. Likewise, cultural relativism in anthropology does not mean that one cannot make moral judgments about the practices of other cultures. Cultural relativism is a scientific stance and does not imply moral relativism. But cultural relativism adds a level of complexity to judgments about good and evil and cautions against the common but mistaken assumption that one's own culture is the sole measure of truth.

The title of this chapter, "Anthropology Gets Religion," has a double meaning. One meaning is that anthropologists will get what religion is all about through painstaking cross-cultural studies in which we extract ourselves from our own largely unconscious cultural systems. The second meaning is that anthropology is getting religion by returning to its roots as an empirical scientific field. The discipline is once again moving ahead with significant studies that address serious scientific problems. We are finding our way back to our original calling.

References

Hunt, Eva. 1977. *The Transformation of the Hummingbird: Cultural Roots of a Zinacanteco Mythical Poem*. Ithaca, NY: Cornell University Press. This is a classic book on Mesoamerican religious symbolism with a pioneering discussion of pantheism.

Sandstrom, Alan R. 1991. *Corn Is Our Blood: Culture and Ethnic Identity in a Contemporary Aztec Indian Village*. Norman: University of Oklahoma Press. This work is an ethnography of a Nahua community where the traditional religion is an important part of daily life.

Sandstrom, Alan R., and Pamela Effrein Sandstrom. 1986. *Traditional Papermaking and Paper Cult Figures of Mexico*. Norman: University of Oklahoma Press. This book tells the history of Mexican paper and how it is used in religious rituals among contemporary indigenous peoples. It contains an early sample of some of the paper images that we have collected over the years.

III

Explaining Cultures

5

SACRED COWS IN INDIA
THE MYTH OF THE SACRED COW

Marvin Harris

NEW DELHI, Dec. 1—Prime Minister Indira Gandhi appealed today to India's holy men to stop fasting and agitating against cow slaughter.

In an effort to halt the spreading wave of fasts by the saffron-clad Hindu Sadhus, Mrs. Gandhi wrote directly to Muni Shushil Kumar, president of the All-Party Cow Protection Campaign Committee.

The Muni has announced his intention of starting a fast tomorrow to demand a nationwide ban on the slaughter of cows, which are revered by Hindus as symbols of abundance but whose meat is often eaten by India's Moslem minority.

On Nov. 7 thousands of demonstrators, led by a group of holy men smeared with white ash and draped with garlands of marigolds, rioted in front of Parliament. Eight persons were killed and 47 injured.

The New York Times
December 2, 1966

Among the popular myths of cultural anarchy, none is more widely accepted than that of the Indian sacred cow. Protected by Hindu taboo from being slaughtered and eaten, these supposedly useless animals wander about at will, impeding traffic and, it is reported, damaging crops. Indeed, in some parts of India, aged cattle are even housed in *gosadans*—bovine old-age homes.

But the myth of the sacred cow is part of a widespread overemphasis on the mismanagement of food production by primitive and peasant peoples. One often hears, especially in these times of vast aid programs for the underdeveloped countries of the world, that irrational ideologies and customs prevent the effective use of available food resources.

In the case of the sacred cow, it must be admitted that the Indian dairy industry is among the least efficient in the world. In India, the average annual yield of whole milk per cow has been reported at 413 pounds, as compared with an average of over 5,000 pounds in Europe and the United States. Furthermore, of the 79.4 million cows maintained in 1961, only 20.1 million were milk producers. Among the 47.2 million cows over three years old, 27.2 million were dry and/or not calved. If we go on to accept the proposition that India can make no profit from the negligible slaughter of its enormous cattle supply, we have completed the case for the great cattle bungle. Hence the conclusion of a 1959 Ford Foundation report on India's food problem:

"There is widespread recognition, not only among animal husbandry officials, but among citizens generally, that India's cattle population is far in excess of the available supplies of fodder and feed.... At least one third, and possibly as many as one half, of the Indian cattle population may be regarded as surplus in relation to feed supply."

This view is endorsed by government agronomists, and the Indian Ministry of Information insists that "the large animal population is more a liability than an asset in view of our limited land resource." Because of the perpetual food shortage for humans in India, refusal to slaughter cattle seems to prove that the mysterious has triumphed over the practical. Some would even have us believe that in order to preserve his cow the individual farmer is prepared to sacrifice his own life. Such is the myth of the sacred cow.

A better understanding of the cow complex in India involves the answers to the following two questions: (1) Is it true that the rate of reproduction and survival of the Indian population is lowered as a result of the competition between man and cattle for scarce resources? (2) Would the removal of the Hindu taboo on slaughter substantially modify the ecology of Indian food production?

The answer to the first question is that the relation between man and cattle—both cows and bullocks—is not competitive, but symbiotic. The most obvious part of this symbiosis is the role played by male cattle in cultivation. Indian farming is based on plow agriculture, to which cattle contribute up to 46 per cent of the labor cost, exclusive of transport and other activities. Obviously, tractors are not a realistic alternative.

Despite the existence of 96.3 million bullocks, of which 68.6 million are working animals, India suffers from a shortage of such animals. It is generally agreed that a pair of bullocks is the minimum unit for cultivation. But a conservatively estimated 60 million rural households dispose of only 80 million working cattle and buffaloes. This would mean that as many as two-thirds of India's farmers may be short of the technical minimum. Moreover, under existing property relations the bullocks cannot be shared among several households without further lowering the productivity of marginal farms. M. B. Desai, an Indian economist, explains why: "Over vast areas, sowing and harvesting operations, by the very nature of things, begin simultaneously with the outbreak of the first showers and the maturing of crops respectively and especially the former has got to be put through quickly during the first phase of the monsoon. Under these circumstances, reliance by a farmer on another for bullocks is highly risky and he has got, therefore, to maintain his own pair."

We see, then, that the draft animals, which appear to be superfluous from the point of view of what would be needed in a perfectly engineered society, turn out to be considerably less than sufficient in the actual context of Indian agriculture.

But what of the cows? The first thing to note is again obvious. No cows, no bullocks. Of course, the issue is not so easily settled. Although the need for bullocks establishes the need for cows, it does not establish the need for 80 million of them. We are, however, coming closer to the answer, because we now know that to the value of the milk and milk products produced by the cows, we must add the value of the 69 million male traction animals also produced.

Among the other immediate and important contributions of the cow is the dung. In addition to the relatively minor value of dung as plaster in house construction, this material is India's main cooking fuel. India's grain crops cannot be metabolized by human beings without cooking. Coal and oil are, of course, prohibitively expensive for the peasant family. Thus, dung alone provides the needed energy, and cattle provide the dung on a lavish scale. Of the 800 million tons annually bequeathed the Indian countryside, 300 million are consumed in cookery. This amount is the Btu equivalent of 35 million tons of coal or 68 million tons of wood, an impressive amount of Btu's to be plugged into an energy system.

Of the remaining 500 million tons of dung, the largest part is used for manuring. It has been claimed that 160 million tons of this manure is "wasted on hillsides and roads," but it must be noted that some of this probably reenters the ecological system, since, as we shall see in a moment, the cattle depend upon hillsides and roads for much of their sustenance. (Needless to say, the intensive rainfall agriculture characteristic of large parts of the subcontinent is dependent upon manuring. So vital is this contribution that one scholar argues that substitutes for the manure consumed as fuel "must be supplied, and lavishly, even at a financial loss to government.")

In the present context, the most important point to note about the fuel and manure functions of India's cattle is that old, dry, barren animals do not cease to provide dung. On this score alone, one might expect more caution before the conclusion is reached that the sacred cow is a useless luxury.

Two additional contributions by cattle, including cows, remain to be mentioned. In 1962 India produced 16 million cattle hides. Much of this output is consumed in the manufacture of leather products vital to the traditional farming technology. In addition, despite the Hindu proscription, a considerable amount of beef *is* eaten. Those who stress the quaintness of the beef-eating taboo fail to give proper emphasis to the millions of people in India who have no caste to lose. Not only are there some 55 million members of exterior or untouchable groups, many of whom will consume beef if given the opportunity, but there are also several millions more who are pagan, Christian, or Moslem. It seems likely that a high proportion of the 20 million bovines that die each year get eaten. Moreover, it is quite clear that not all these cattle die a natural death. On the contrary, the very extent of the agitation for antislaughter bills reveals how widespread the slaughter actually is.

We see that to the contribution of the cow as a producer of milk, we must add the production of meat, bullocks, manure, fuel, and hides. The extent of the symbiosis between man and cow, however, is not thereby demonstrated. There still remains the possibility that all these needs could be met at a lower energy or monetary cost per peasant household by reducing the number of aged cows that the peasant tolerates in his ménage. To prove that the ecosystem under discussion is essentially adaptive for human life it must be shown that resources consumed by the cows, old and young, do not, from the point of view of the peasant's balance sheet, outweigh the enumerated contributions. This proof is fairly easy to establish.

Note, first of all, that one of the most persistent professional complaints against the sacred cow is that the beasts wander all over the place, cluttering up the markets, railroad stations, and roadsides. Many authorities seem not to inquire why all this wandering takes place from the point of view of the cow, since presumably she has remained uninformed of her sacred privileges. The cow is wandering about because she is hungry and is looking for food—in the ditches, around the base of telegraph poles, between the railroad ties, along the hillsides, in every nook and cranny where something edible has reared its head. The sacred cow is an exploited scavenger, a mere walking skeleton for most of the year, precisely because her ecological niche is removed from that of human food crops.

An ecological explanation of why so many cows are kept is now possible: Each farmer needs his own pair of bullocks. Lacking cash, he cannot afford to buy these animals. Rather than risk going into debt at usurious rates, he prefers to try to breed bulls (which he will exchange later for bullocks). Since all the available land is given over to human food crops, the breeding cows must scavenge for their food. Being undernourished, they breed, irregularly. The farmer refrains from culling uncalved animals since they convert grain by-products and scrub vegetation into useful dung. Meanwhile, there is always a chance that the cow will eventually conceive. If a female calf is born, the scrub and chaff are converted into milk, while the calf is gradually starved to death. In the long run, the more cows an individual farmer owns, the greater the likelihood that he can replace his bullocks without going into debt.

This explanation does not involve references to ahimsa, the Hindu doctrine of the sanctity of life. Instead, the large number of cows and bullocks is seen as the result of ecological pressures generated by the human population's struggle to maintain itself. Ahimsa may thus be regarded as an ideological expression of these pressures; in other words, ahimsa itself derives power and sustenance from the material rewards it confers upon both men and animals.

In answer to the second question under consideration, it would thus seem that the basic ecology of Indian cattle production is not a mere reflex of the Hindu taboo on slaughter. Removing that taboo might temporarily alter the ecosystem. In the long run, however, the rate at which cattle are presently slaughtered in India is governed by the ability of the peasantry to slaughter them without impairing the production of traction animals, fuel, fertilizer, and milk. It is a well-known fact that the least efficient way to convert solar energy into comestibles is to impose an animal converter between plant and man. Hence, it is wrong to suppose that India could, without major techno-environmental innovations, support any large number of animals whose principal function was to supply animal protein. It has already been shown that the supply of beef is now one of the functions of the cattle complex, but this must necessarily remain a marginal or tertiary attribute of the ecosystem. As a matter of fact, it is obvious that any large-scale drift toward animal slaughter before the traction, fuel, and manure needs of the productive cycle were met would immediately jeopardize the lives of tens of millions of Indians.

6

RITUAL REGULATION OF ENVIRONMENTAL RELATIONS AMONG A NEW GUINEA PEOPLE

Roy A. Rappaport

Most functional studies of religious behavior in anthropology have as an analytic goal the elucidation of events, processes, or relationships occurring within a social unit of some sort.[1] The social unit is not always well defined, but in some cases it appears to be a church, that is, a group of people who entertain similar beliefs about the universe, or a congregation, a group of people who participate together in the performance of religious rituals. There have been exceptions. Thus Vayda, Leeds, and Smith (1961) and O. K. Moore (1957) have clearly perceived that the functions of religious ritual are not necessarily confined within the boundaries of a congregation or even a church. By and large, however, I believe that the following statement by Homans (1941: 172) represents fairly the dominant line of anthropological thought concerning the functions of religious ritual:

> Ritual actions do not produce a practical result on the external world—that
> is one of the reasons why we call them ritual. But to make this statement is
> not to say that ritual has no function. Its function is not related to the world
> external to the society but to the internal constitution of the society. It gives
> the members of the society confidence, it dispels their anxieties, it disciplines
> their social organization.

No argument will be raised here against the sociological and psychological functions imputed by Homans, and many others before him, to ritual. They seem to me to be plausible. Nevertheless, in some cases at least, ritual does produce, in Homans' terms, "a practical result on the world" external not only to the social unit composed of those who participate together in ritual performances but also to the larger unit composed of those who entertain similar beliefs concerning the universe. The material presented here will show that the ritual cycles of the Tsembaga, and of other local territorial groups of Maring speakers living in the New Guinea interior, play an important part in regulating the relationships of these groups with both the nonhuman components of their immediate environments and the human components of their less immediate environments, that is, with other similar territorial groups. To be more specific, this regulation helps to maintain the biotic communities existing within their territories, redistributes land among people and people over land, and limits the frequency of fighting. In the absence of authoritative political statuses or offices, the ritual cycle likewise provides a means for mobilizing allies when warfare may be undertaken. It also provides a mechanism for redistributing local pig surpluses in the form of pork throughout a large regional population while helping to assure the local population of a supply of pork when its members are most in need of high quality protein.

Religious ritual may be defined, for the purposes of this paper, as the prescribed performance of conventionalized acts manifestly directed toward the involvement of nonempirical or supernatural agencies in the affairs of the actors. While this definition relies upon the formal characteristics of the performances and upon the motives for undertaking them, attention will be focused upon the empirical effects of ritual performances and sequences of ritual performances. The religious rituals to be discussed are regarded as neither more nor less than part of the behavioral repertoire employed by an aggregate of organisms in adjusting to its environment.

The data upon which this paper is based were collected during fourteen months of field work among the Tsembaga, one of about twenty local groups of Maring speakers living in the Simbai and Jimi Valleys of the Bismarck Range in the Territory of New Guinea. The size of Maring local groups varies from a little over 100 to 900. The Tsembaga, who in 1963 numbered 204 persons, are located on the south wall of the Simbai Valley. The country in which they live differs from the true highlands in being lower, generally more rugged, and more heavily forested. Tsembaga territory rises, within a total surface area of 3.2 square miles, from an elevation of 2,200 feet at the Simbai river to 7,200 feet at the ridge crest. Gardens are cut in the secondary forests up to between 5,000 and 5,400 feet, above which the area remains in primary forest. Rainfall reaches 150 inches per year.

The Tsembaga have come into contact with the outside world only recently; the first government patrol to penetrate their territory arrived in 1954. They were considered uncontrolled by the Australian government until 1962, and they remain unmissionized to this day.

The 204 Tsembaga are distributed among five putatively patrilineal clans, which are, in turn, organized into more inclusive groupings on two hierarchical levels below that of the total local group.[2] Internal political structure is highly egalitarian. There are no hereditary or elected chiefs, nor are there even "big men" who can regularly coerce or command the support of their clansmen or co-residents in economic or forceful enterprises.

It is convenient to regard the Tsembaga as a population in the ecological sense, that is, as one of the components of a system of trophic exchanges taking place within a bounded area. Tsembaga territory and the biotic community existing upon it may be conveniently viewed as an ecosystem. While it would he permissible arbitrarily to designate the Tsembaga as a population and their territory with its biota as an ecosystem, there are also nonarbitrary reasons for doing so. An ecosystem is a system of material exchanges, and the Tsembaga maintain against other human groups exclusive access to the resources within their territorial borders. Conversely, it is from this territory alone that the Tsembaga ordinarily derive all of their foodstuffs and most of the other materials they require for survival. Less anthropocentrically, it may be justified to regard Tsembaga territory with its biota as an ecosystem in view of the rather localized nature of cyclical material exchanges in tropical rainforests.

As they are involved with the nonhuman biotic community within their territory in a set of trophic exchanges, so do they participate in other material relationships with other human groups external to their territory. Genetic materials are exchanged with other groups, and certain crucial items, such as stone axes, were in past obtained from the outside. Furthermore, in the area occupied by the Maring speakers, more than one local group is usually involved in any process, either peaceful or warlike, through which people are redistributed over land and land redistributed among people.

The concept of the ecosystem, though it provides a convenient frame for the analysis of intraspecific trophic exchanges taking place within limited geographical areas, does not comfortably accommodate intraspecific exchanges taking place over wider geographic areas. Some sort of geographic population model would be more useful for the analysis of the relationship of the local ecological population to the larger regional population of which it is a part, but we lack even a set of appropriate terms for such a model. Suffice it here to note that the relations of the Tsembaga to the total of other local human populations in their vicinity are similar to the relations of local aggregates of other animals to the totality of their species occupying broader and more or less continuous regions. This larger, more inclusive aggregate may resemble what geneticists mean by the term population, that is, an aggregate of interbreeding organisms persisting through an indefinite number of generations and either living or capable of living in isolation from similar aggregates of the same species. This is the unit which survives through long periods of time while its local ecological *(sensu stricto)* subunits, the units more or less independently involved in intraspecific trophic exchanges such as the Tsembaga, are ephemeral.

Since it has been asserted that the ritual cycles of the Tsembaga regulate relationships within what may be regarded as a complex system, it is necessary, before proceeding to the ritual cycle itself, to describe briefly, and where possible in quantitative terms, some aspects of the place of the Tsembaga in this system.

The Tsembaga are bush-fallowing horticulturalists. Staples include a range of root crops, taro *(Colocasia)* and sweet potatoes being most important, yams and manioc less so. In addition, a great variety of greens are raised, some of which are rich in protein. Sugar cane and some tree crops, particularly *Pandanus conoideus,* are also important.

All gardens are mixed, many of them containing all of the major root crops and many greens. Two named garden types are, however, distinguished by the crops which predominate in them. "Taro-yam gardens" were found to produce, on the basis of daily harvest records kept on entire gardens for close to one year, about 5,300,000 calories[3] per acre during their harvesting lives of 8 to 24 months; 85 per cent of their yield is harvested between 24 and 76 weeks after planting. "Sugar-sweet potato gardens" produce about 4,600,000 calories per acre during their harvesting lives, 91 per cent being taken between 24 and 76 weeks after planting. I estimated that approximately 310,000 calories per acre is expended on cutting, fencing, planting, maintaining, harvesting, and walking to and from taro-yam gardens. Sugar-sweet potato gardens required an expenditure of approximately 290,000 calories per acre.[4] These energy ratios, approximately 17:1 on taro-yam gardens and 16:1 on sugar-sweet potato gardens, compare favorably with figures reported for swidden cultivation in other regions.[5]

Intake is high in comparison with the reported dietaries of other New Guinea populations. On the basis of daily consumption records kept for ten months on four households numbering in total sixteen persons, I estimated the average daily intake of adult males to be approximately 2,600 calories, and that of adult females to be around 2,200 calories. It may be mentioned here that the Tsembaga are small and short statured. Adult males average 101 pounds in weight and approximately 58.5 inches in height; the corresponding averages for adult females are 85 pounds and 54.5 inches.[6]

Although 99 per cent by weight of the food consumed is vegetable, the protein intake is high by New Guinea standards. The daily protein consumption of adult males from vegetable sources was estimated to be between 43 and 55 grams, of adult females 36 to 48 grams. Even with an adjustment for vegetable sources, these values are slightly in excess of the recently published WHO/FAO daily requirements (Food and Agriculture Organization of the United Nations 1964). The same is true of the younger age categories, although soft and discolored hair, a symptom of protein deficiency, was noted in a few children. The WHO/FAO protein requirements do not include a large "margin for safety" or allowance for stress; and, although no clinical assessments were undertaken, it may be suggested that the Tsembaga achieve nitrogen balance at a low level. In other words, their protein intake is probably marginal.

Measurements of all gardens made during 1962 and of some gardens made during 1963 indicate that, to support the human population, between .15 and .19 acres are put into cultivation per capita per year. Fallows range from 8 to 45 years. The area in secondary forest comprises approximately 1,000 acres, only 30 to 50 of which are in cultivation at any time. Assuming calories to be the limiting factor, and assuming an unchanging population structure, the territory could support—with no reduction in lengths of fallow and without cutting into the virgin forest from which the Tsembaga extract many important items—between 290 and 397 people if the pig population remained minimal. The size of the pig herd, however, fluctuates widely. Taking Maring pig husbandry procedures into consideration, I have estimated the human carrying capacity of the Tsembaga territory at between 270 and 320 people.

Because the timing of the ritual cycle is bound up with the demography of the pig herd, the place of the pig in Tsembaga adaptation must be examined.

First, being omnivorous, pigs keep residential areas free of garbage and human feces. Second, limited numbers of pigs rooting in secondary growth may help to hasten the development of that growth. The Tsembaga usually permit pigs to enter their gardens one and a half ʳo two years after planting, by which time second-growth trees are well established there. The Tsembaga practice selective weeding; from the time the garden is planted, herbaceous species are removed, but tree species are allowed to remain. By the time cropping is discontinued and the pigs are let in, some of the trees in the garden are already ten to fifteen feet tall. These well-established trees are relatively impervious to damage by the pigs, which, in rooting for seeds and remaining tubers, eliminate many seeds and seedlings that, if allowed to develop, would provide some competition for the established trees. Moreover, in some Maring-speaking areas swiddens are planted twice, although this is not the case with the Tsembaga. After the first crop is almost exhausted, pigs are penned in the garden, where their rooting eliminates weeds and softens the ground, making the task of planting for a second time easier. The pigs, in other words, are used as cultivating machines.

Small numbers of pigs are easy to keep. They run free during the day and return home at night to receive their ration of garbage and substandard tubers, particularly sweet potatoes. Supplying the latter requires little extra work, for the substandard tubers are taken from the ground in the course of harvesting the daily ration for humans. Daily consumption records kept over a period of some months show that the ration of tubers received by the pigs approximates in weight that consumed by adult humans, i.e., a little less than three pounds per day per pig.

If the pig herd grows large, however, the substandard tubers incidentally obtained in the course of harvesting for human needs become insufficient, and it becomes necessary to harvest especially for pigs. In other words, people must work for the pigs and perhaps even supply them with food fit for human consumption. Thus, as Vayda, Leeds, and Smith (1961: 71) have pointed out, there can be too many pigs for a given community.

This also holds true of the sanitary and cultivating services rendered by pigs. A small number of pigs is sufficient to keep residential areas clean, to suppress superfluous seedlings in abandoned gardens, and to soften the soil in gardens scheduled for second plantings. A larger herd, on the other hand, may be troublesome; the larger the number of pigs, the greater the possibility of their invasion of producing gardens, with concomitant damage not only to crops and young secondary growth but also to the relations between the pig owners and garden owners.

All male pigs are castrated at approximately three months of age, for boars, people say, are dangerous and do not grow as large as barrows. Pregnancies, therefore, are always the result of unions of domestic sows with feral males. Fecundity is thus only a fraction of its potential. During one twelve-month period only fourteen litters resulted out of a potential 99 or more pregnancies. Farrowing generally takes place in the forest, and mortality of the young is high. Only 32 of the offspring of the above-mentioned fourteen pregnancies were alive six months after birth. This number is barely sufficient to replace the number of adult animals which would have died or been killed during most years without pig festivals.

The Tsembaga almost never kill domestic pigs outside of ritual contexts. In ordinary times, when there is no pig festival in progress, these rituals are almost always associated with misfortunes or emergencies, notably warfare, illness, injury, or death. Rules state not only the contexts in which pigs are to be ritually slaughtered, but also who may partake of the flesh of the sacrificial animals. During warfare it is only the men participating in the fighting who eat the pork. In cases of illness or injury, it is only the victim and certain near relatives, particularly his co-resident agnates and spouses, who do so.

It is reasonable to assume that misfortune and emergency are likely to induce in the organisms experiencing them a complex of physiological changes known collectively as "stress." Physiological stress reactions occur not only in organisms which are infected with disease or traumatized, but also in those experiencing rage or fear (Houssay et al. 1955: 1096), or even prolonged anxiety (National Research Council 1963: 53). One important aspect of stress is the increased catabolization of protein (Houssay et al. 1955: 451; National Research Council 1963: 49), with a net loss of nitrogen from the tissues (Houssay et al. 1955: 450). This is a serious matter for organisms with a marginal protein intake. Antibody production is low (Berg 1948: 311), healing is slow (Large and Johnston 1948: 352), and a variety of symptoms of a serious nature are likely to develop (Lund and Levenson 1948: 349; Zintel 1964: 1043). The status of a protein-depleted animal, however, may be significantly improved in a relatively short period of time by the intake of high quality protein, and high protein diets are therefore routinely prescribed for surgical patients and those suffering from infectious diseases (Burton 1959: 231; Lund and Levenson 1948: 350; Elman 1951: 85ff; Zintel 1064: 1043ff).

It is precisely when they are undergoing physiological stress that the Tsembaga kill and consume their pigs, and it should be noted that they limit the consumption to those likely to be experiencing stress most profoundly. The Tsembaga, of course, know nothing of physiological stress. Native theories of the etiology and treatment of disease and injury implicate various categories of spirits to whom sacrifices must be made. Nevertheless, the behavior which is appropriate in terms of native understandings is also appropriate to the actual situation confronting the actors.

We may now outline in the barest of terms the Tsembaga ritual cycle. Space does not permit a description of its ideological correlates. It must suffice to note that Tsembaga do not necessarily perceive all of the empirical effects which the anthropologist sees to flow from their ritual behavior. Such empirical consequences as they may perceive, moreover, are not central to their rationalizations of the performances. The Tsembaga say that they perform the rituals in order to rearrange their relationships with the supernatural world. We may only reiterate here that behavior undertaken in reference to their "cognized environment"—an environment which includes as very important elements the spirits of ancestors—seems appropriate in their "operational environment," the material environment specified by the anthropologist through operations of observation, including measurement.

Since the rituals are arranged in a cycle, description may commence at any point. The operation of the cycle becomes clearest if we begin with the rituals performed during warfare. Opponents in all cases occupy adjacent territories, in almost all cases on the same valley wall. After hostilities have broken out, each side performs certain rituals which place the opposing side in the formal category of "enemy." A number of taboos prevail while hostilities continue. These include prohibitions on sexual intercourse and on the ingestion of certain things—food prepared by women, food grown on the lower portion of the territory, marsupials, eels, and, while actually on the fighting ground, any liquid whatsoever.

One ritual practice associated with fighting which may have some physiological consequences deserves mention. Immediately before proceeding to the fighting ground, the warriors eat heavily salted pig fat. The ingestion of salt, coupled with the taboo on drinking, has the effect of shortening the fighting day, particularly since the Maring prefer to fight only on bright sunny days. When everyone gets unbearably thirsty, according to informants, fighting is broken off.

There may formerly have been other effects if the native salt contained sodium (the production of salt was discontinued some years previous to the field work, and no samples were obtained). The Maring diet seems to be deficient in sodium. The ingestion of large amounts of sodium just prior to fighting would have permitted the warriors to sweat normally without a lowering of blood volume and consequent weakness during the course of the fighting. The pork belly ingested with the salt would have provided them with a new burst of energy two hours or so after the commencement of the engagement. After fighting was finished for the day, lean pork was consumed, offsetting, at least to some extent, the nitrogen loss associated with the stressful fighting (personal communications from F. Dunn, W. MacFarlane, and J. Sabine, 1965).

Fighting could continue sporadically for weeks. Occasionally it terminated in the rout of one of the antagonistic groups, whose survivors would take refuge with kinsmen elsewhere. In such instances, the victors would lay waste their opponents' groves and gardens, slaughter their pigs, and burn their houses. They would not, however, immediately annex the territory of the vanquished. The Maring say that they never take over the territory of an enemy for, even if it has been abandoned, the spirits of their ancestors remain to guard it against interlopers. Most fights, however, terminated in truces between the antagonists.

With the termination of hostilities a group which has not been driven off its territory performs a ritual called "planting the *rumbim.*" Every man puts his hand on the ritual plant, *rumbim (Cordyline fruticosa* [L.], A. Chev; *C. terminalis,* Kunth), as it is planted in the ground. The ancestors are addressed, in effect, as follows:

> We thank you for helping us in the fight and permitting us to remain on our territory. We place our souls in this *rumbim* as we plant it on our ground. We ask you to care for this *rumbim.* We will kill pigs for you now, but they are few. In the future, when we have many pigs, we shall again give you pork and uproot the *rumbim* and stage a *kaiko* (pig festival). But until there are sufficient pigs to repay you the *rumbim* will remain in the ground.

This ritual is accompanied by the wholesale slaughter of pigs. Only juveniles remain alive. All adult and adolescent animals are killed, cooked, and dedicated to the ancestors. Some are consumed by the local group, but most are distributed to allies who assisted in the fight.

Some of the taboos which the group suffered during the time of fighting are abrogated by this ritual. Sexual intercourse is now permitted, liquids may be taken at any time, and food from any part of the territory may be eaten. But the group is still in debt to its allies and ancestors. People say it is still the time of the *bamp ku,* or "fighting stones," which are actual objects used in the rituals associated with warfare. Although the fighting ceases when *rumbim* is planted, the concomitant obligations, debts to allies and ancestors, remain outstanding; and the fighting stones may not be put away until these obligations are fulfilled. The time of the fighting stones is a time of debt and danger which lasts until the *rumbim* is uprooted and a pig festival *(kaiko)* is staged.

Certain taboos persist during the time of the fighting stones. Marsupials, regarded as the pigs of the ancestors of the high ground, may not be trapped until the debt to their masters has been repaid. Eels, the "pigs of the ancestors of the low ground," may neither be caught nor consumed. Prohibitions on all intercourse with the enemy come into force. One may not touch, talk to, or even look at a member of the enemy group, nor set foot on enemy ground. Even more important, a group may not attack another group while its ritual plant remains in the ground, for it has not yet fully rewarded its ancestors and allies for their assistance in the last fight. Until the debts to them have been paid, further assistance from them will not be forthcoming. A kind of "truce of god" thus prevails until the *rumbim* is uprooted and a *kaiko* completed.

To uproot the *rumbim* requires sufficient pigs. How many pigs are sufficient, and how long does it take to acquire them? The Tsembaga say that, if a place is "good," this can take as little as five years; but if a place is "bad," it may require ten years or longer. A bad place is one in which misfortunes are frequent and where, therefore, ritual demands for the killing of pigs arise frequently. A good place is one where such demands are infrequent. In a good place, the increase of the pig herd exceeds the ongoing ritual demands, and the herd grows rapidly. Sooner or later the substandard tubers incidentally obtained while harvesting become insufficient to feed the herd, and additional acreage must be put into production specifically for the pigs.

The work involved in caring for a large pig herd can be extremely burdensome. The Tsembaga herd just prior to the pig festival of 1962–63, when it numbered 169 animals, was receiving 54 per cent of all of the sweet potatoes and 82 per cent of all of the manioc harvested. These comprised 35.9 per cent by weight of all root crops harvested. This figure is consistent with the difference between the amount of land under cultivation just previous to the pig festival, when the herd was at maximum size, and that immediately afterwards, when the pig herd was at minimum size. The former was 36.1 per cent in excess of the latter.

I have estimated, on the basis of acreage yield and energy expenditure figures, that about 45,000 calories per year are expended in caring for one pig 120–150 pounds in size. It is upon women that most of the burden of pig keeping falls. If, from a woman's daily intake of about 2,200 calories, 950 calories are allowed for basal metabolism, a woman has only 1,250 calories a day available for all her activities, which include gardening for her family, child care, and cooking, as well as tending pigs. It is clear that no woman can feed many pigs; only a few had as many as four in their care at the commencement of the festival; and it is not surprising that agitation to uproot the *rumbim* and stage the *kaiko* starts with the wives of the owners of large numbers of pigs.

A large herd is not only burdensome as far as energy expenditure is concerned; it becomes increasingly a nuisance as it expands. The more numerous pigs become, the more frequently are gardens invaded by them. Such events result in serious disturbances of local tranquility. The garden owner often shoots, or attempts to shoot, the offending pig; and the pig owner commonly retorts by shooting, or attempting to shoot, either the garden owner, his wife, or one of his pigs. As more and more such events occur, the settlement, nucleated when the herd was small, disperses as people try to put as much distance as possible between their pigs and other people's gardens and between their gardens and other people's pigs. Occasionally this reaches its logical conclusion, and people begin to leave the territory, taking up residence with kinsmen in other local populations.

The number of pigs sufficient to become intolerable to the Tsembaga was below the capacity of the territory to carry pigs. I have estimated that, if the size and structure of the human population remained constant at the 1962–1963 level, a pig population of 140 to 240 animals averaging 100 to 150 pounds in size could be maintained perpetually by the Tsembaga without necessarily inducing environmental degradation. Since the size of the herd fluctuates, even higher cyclical maxima could be achieved. The level of toleration, however, is likely always to be below the carrying capacity, since the destructive capacity of the pigs is dependent upon the population density of both people and pigs, rather than upon population size. The denser the human population, the fewer pigs will be required to disrupt social life. If the carrying capacity is exceeded, it is likely to be exceeded by people and not by pigs.

The *kaiko* or pig festival, which commences with the planting of stakes at the boundary and the uprooting of the *rumbim*, is thus triggered by either the additional work attendant upon feeding pigs or the destructive capacity of the pigs themselves. It may be said, then, that there are sufficient pigs to stage the *kaiko* when the relationship of pigs to people changes from one of mutualism to one of parasitism or competition.

A short time prior to the uprooting of the *rumbim*, stakes are planted at the boundary. If the enemy has continued to occupy its territory, the stakes are planted at the boundary which existed before the fight. If, on the other hand, the enemy has abandoned its territory, the victors may plant their stakes at a new boundary which encompasses areas previously occupied by the enemy. The Maring say, to be sure, that they never take land belonging to an enemy, but this land is regarded as vacant, since no *rumbim* was planted on it after the last fight. We may state here a rule of land redistribution in terms of the ritual cycle: *If one of a pair of antagonistic groups is able to uproot its rumbim before its opponents can plant their rumbim, it may occupy the latter's territory.*

Not only have the vanquished abandoned their territory; it is assumed that it has also been abandoned by their ancestors as well. The surviving members of the erstwhile enemy group have by this time resided with other groups for a number of years, and most if not all of them have already had occasion to sacrifice pigs to their ancestors at their new residences. In so doing they have invited these spirits to settle at the new locations of the living, where they will in the future receive sacrifices. Ancestors of vanquished groups thus relinquish their guardianship over the territory, making it available to victorious groups. Meanwhile, the *de facto* membership of the living in the groups with which they have taken refuge is converted eventually into *de jure* membership. Sooner or later the groups with which they have taken up residence will have occasion to plant *rumbim*, and the refugees, as co-residents, will participate, thus ritually validating their connection to the new territory and the new group. A rule of population redistribution may thus be stated in terms of ritual cycles: *A man becomes a member of a territorial group by participating with it in the planting of rumbim.*

The uprooting of the *rumbim* follows shortly after the planting of stakes at the boundary. On this particular occasion the Tsembaga killed 32 pigs out of their herd of 169. Much of the pork was distributed to allies and affines outside of the local group.

The taboo on trapping marsupials was also terminated at this time. Information is lacking concerning the population dynamics of the local marsupials, but it may well be that the taboo which had prevailed since the last fight—that against taking them in traps—had conserved a fauna which might otherwise have become extinct.

The *kaiko* continues for about a year, during which period friendly groups are entertained from time to time. The guests receive presents of vegetable foods, and the hosts and male guests dance together throughout the night.

These events may be regarded as analogous to aspects of the social behavior of many nonhuman animals. First of all, they include massed epigamic, or courtship, displays (Wynne-Edwards 1962: 17). Young women are presented with samples of the eligible males of local groups with which they may not otherwise have had the opportunity to become familiar. The context, moreover, permits the young women to discriminate amongst this sample in terms of both endurance (signaled by how vigorously and how long a man dances) and wealth (signaled by the richness of a man's shell and feather finery).

More importantly, the massed dancing at these events may be regarded as epideictic display, communicating to the participants information concerning the size or density of the group (Wynne-Edwards 1962: 16). In many species such displays take place as a prelude to actions which adjust group size or density, and such is the case among the Maring. The massed dancing of the visitors at a *kaiko* entertainment communicates to the hosts, while the *rumbim* truce is still in force, information concerning the amount of support they may expect from the visitors in the bellicose enterprises that they are likely to embark upon soon after the termination of the pig festival.

Among the Maring there are no chiefs or other political authorities capable of commanding the support of a body of followers, and the decision to assist another group in warfare rests with each individual male. Allies are not recruited by appealing for help to other local groups as such. Rather, each member of the groups primarily involved in the hostilities appeals to his cognatic and affinal kinsmen in other local groups. These men, in turn, urge other of their co-residents and kinsmen to "help them fight." The channels through which invitations to dance are extended are precisely those through which appeals for military support are issued. The invitations go not from group to group, but from kinsman to kinsman, the recipients of invitations urging their co-residents to "help them dance."

Invitations to dance do more than exercise the channels through which allies are recruited; they provide a means for judging their effectiveness. Dancing and fighting are regarded as in some sense equivalent. This equivalence is expressed in the similarity of some pre-fight and pre-dance rituals, and the Maring say that those who come to dance come to fight. The size of a visiting dancing contingent is consequently taken as a measure of the size of the contingent of warriors whose assistance may be expected in the next round of warfare.

In the morning the dancing ground turns into a trading ground. The items most frequently exchanged include axes, bird plumes, shell ornaments, an occasional baby pig, and, in former times, native salt. The *kaiko* thus facilitates trade by providing a market-like setting in which large numbers of traders can assemble. It likewise facilitates the movement of two critical items, salt and axes, by creating a demand for the bird plumes which may be exchanged for them.

The *kaiko* concludes with major pig sacrifices. On this particular occasion the Tsembaga butchered 105 adult and adolescent pigs, leaving only 60 juveniles and neonates alive. The survival of an additional fifteen adolescents and adults was only temporary, for they were scheduled as imminent victims. The pork yielded by the Tsembaga slaughter was estimated to weigh between 7,000 and 8,500 pounds, of which between 4,500 and 6,000 pounds were distributed to members of other local groups in 163 separate presentations. An estimated 2,000 to 3,000 people in seventeen local groups were the beneficiaries of the redistribution. The presentations, it should be mentioned, were not confined to pork. Sixteen Tsembaga men presented bridewealth or child-wealth, consisting largely of axes and shells, to their affines at this time.

The *kaiko* terminates on the day of the pig slaughter with the public presentation of salted pig belly to allies of the last fight. Presentations are made through the window in a high ceremonial fence built specially for the occasion at one end of the dance ground. The name of each honored man is announced to the assembled multitude as he charges to the window to receive his hero's portion. The fence is then ritually torn down, and the fighting stones are put away. The pig festival and the ritual cycle have been completed, demonstrating, it may be suggested, the ecological and economic competence of the local population. The local population would now be free, if it were not for the presence of the government, to attack its enemy again, secure in the knowledge that the assistance of allies and ancestors would be forthcoming because they have received pork and the obligations to them have been fulfilled.

Usually fighting did break out again very soon after the completion of the ritual cycle. If peace still prevailed when the ceremonial fence had rotted completely—a process said to take about three years, a little longer than the length of time required to raise a pig to maximum size—*rumbim* was planted as if there had been a fight, and all adult and adolescent pigs were killed. When the pig herd was large enough so that the *rumbim* could be uprooted, peace could be made with former enemies if they were also able to dig out their *rumbim*. To put this in formal terms: *If a pair of antagonistic groups proceeds through two ritual cycles without resumption of hostilities their enmity may be terminated.*

The relations of the Tsembaga with their environment have been analyzed as a complex system composed of two subsystems. What may be called the "local subsystem" has been derived from the relations of the Tsembaga with the nonhuman components of their immediate or territorial environment. It corresponds to the ecosystem in which the Tsembaga participate. A second subsystem, one which corresponds to the larger regional population of which the Tsembaga are one of the constituent units and which may be designated as the "regional subsystem," has been derived from the relations of the Tsembaga with neighboring local populations similar to themselves.

It has been argued that rituals, arranged in repetitive sequences, regulate relations both within each of the subsystems and within the larger complex system as a whole. The timing of the ritual cycle is largely dependent upon changes in the states of the components of the local subsystem. But the *kaiko*, which is the culmination of the ritual cycle, does more than reverse changes which have taken place within the local subsystem. Its occurrence also affects relations among the components of the regional subsystem. During its performance, obligations to other local populations are fulfilled, support for future military enterprises is rallied, and land from which enemies have earlier been driven is occupied. Its completion, furthermore, permits the local population to initiate warfare again. Conversely, warfare is terminated by rituals which preclude the reinitiation of warfare until the state of the local subsystem is again such that a *kaiko* may be staged and completed. Ritual among the Tsembaga and other Maring, in short, operates as both transducer, "translating" changes in the state of one subsystem into information which can effect changes in a second subsystem, and homeostat, maintaining a number of variables which in sum comprise the total system within ranges of viability. To repeat an earlier assertion, the operation of ritual among the Tsembaga and other Maring helps to maintain an undegraded environment, limits fighting to frequencies which do not endanger the existence of the regional population, adjusts man-land ratios, facilitates trade, distributes local surpluses of pig throughout the regional population in the form of pork, and assures people of high quality protein when they are most in need of it.

Religious rituals and the supernatural orders toward which they are directed cannot be assumed *a priori* to be mere epiphenomena. Ritual may, and doubtless frequently does, do nothing more than validate and intensify the relationships which integrate the social unit, or symbolize the relationships which bind the social unit to its environment. But the interpretation of such presumably *sapiens*-specific phenomena as religious ritual within a framework which will also accommodate the behavior of other species shows, I think, that religious ritual may do much more than symbolize, validate, and intensify relationships. Indeed, it would not be improper to refer to the Tsembaga and the other entities with which they share their territory as a "ritually regulated ecosystem," and to the Tsembaga and their human neighbors as a "ritually regulated population."

Notes

1. The field work upon which this paper is based was supported by a grant from the National Science Foundation, under which Professor A. P. Vayda was principal investigator. Personal support was received by the author from the National Institutes of Health. Earlier versions of this paper were presented at the 1964 annual meeting of the American Anthropological Association in Detroit, and before a Columbia University seminar on Ecological Systems and Cultural Evolution. I have received valuable suggestions from Alexander Alland, Jacques Barran, William Clarke, Paul Collins, C. Glen King, Marvin Harris, Margaret Mead, M. J. Meggitt, Ann Rappaport, John Street, Marjorie Whiting, Cherry Vayda, A. P. Vayda and many others, but I take full responsibility for the analysis presented herewith.

2. The social organization of the Tsembaga will be described in detail elsewhere.

3. Because the length of time in the field precluded the possibility of maintaining harvest records on single gardens from planting through abandonment, figures were based, in the case of both "taro-yam" and "sugar-sweet potato" gardens, on three separate gardens planted in successive years. Conversions from the gross weight to the caloric value of yields were made by reference to the literature. The sources used are listed in Rappaport (1966: Appendix VIII)

4. Rough time and motion studies of each of the tasks involved in making, maintaining, harvesting, and walking to and from gardens were undertaken. Conversion to energy expenditure values was accomplished by reference to energy expenditure tables prepared by Hipsley and Kirk (1965: 43) on the basis of gas exchange measurements made during the performance of garden tasks by the Chimbu people of the New Guinea highlands.

5. Marvin Harris, in an unpublished paper, estimates the ratio of energy return to energy input ratio on Dyak (Borneo) rice swiddens at 10:1. His estimates of energy ratios on Tepotzlan (Meso-America) swiddens range from 13:1 on poor land to 29:1 on the best land.

6. Heights may be inaccurate. Many men wear their hair in large coiffures hardened with pandanus grease, and it was necessary in some instances to estimate the location of the top of the skull.

References

Berg, C. 1948. "Protein Deficiency and Its Relation to Nutritional Anemia, Hypoproteinemia, Nutritional Edema, and Resistance to Infection." In *Protein and Amino Acids in Nutrition,* ed. M. Sahyun, 290–317. New York.

Burton, B. T., ed. 1959. *The Heinz Handbook of Nutrition.* New York.

Elman, R. 1951. *Surgical Care.* New York.

Food and Agriculture Organization of the United Nations. 1964. "Protein: At the Heart of the World Food Problem." *World Food Problems* 5. Rome.

Hipsley, E., and N. Kirk. 1965. "Studies of the Dietary Intake and Energy Expenditure of New Guineans." South Pacific Commission, Technical Paper 147. Noumea.

Homans, G. C. 1941. "Anxiety and Ritual: The Theories of Malinowski and Radcliffe-Brown." *American Anthropologist* 43: 164–172.

Houssay, B. A., et al. 1955. *Human Physiology.* 2nd ed. New York.

Large, A., and C. G. Johnston. 1948. "Proteins as Related to Burns." In *Proteins and Amino Acids in Nutrition,* ed. M. Sahyun, 386-396. New York.

Lund, C. G., and S. M. Levenson. 1948. "Protein Nutrition in Surgical Patients." In *Proteins and Amino Acids in Nutrition,* ed. M. Sahyun, 349-363. New York.

Moore, O. K. 1957. "Divination—A New Perspective." *American Anthropologist* 59: 69-74.

National Research Council. 1963. *Evaluation of Protein Quality.* National Academy of Sciences—National Research Council Publication 1100. Washington.

Rappaport, R. A. 1966. "Ritual in the Ecology of a New Guinea People." Unpublished diss., Columbia University.

Vayda, A. P., A. Leeds, and D. B. Smith. 1961. "The Place of Pigs in Melanesian Subsistence." In *Proceedings of the 1961 Annual Spring Meeting of the American Ethnological Society,* ed. V. E. Garfield, 69-77. Seattle.

Wayne-Edwards, V. C. 1962. *Animal Dispersion in Relation to Social Behaviour.* Edinburgh and London.

Zintel, Harold A. 1964. "Nutrition in the Care of the Surgical Patient." In *Modern Nutrition in Health and Disease,* 3rd ed., ed. M. G. Wohl and R. S. Goodhart, 1043-1064. Philadelphia.

IV

The Importance of History

7

THE ORIGIN OF ISLAM
THE SOCIAL ORGANIZATION OF MECCA
AND THE ORIGINS OF ISLAM

Eric R. Wolf

The present paper attempts to analyze some aspects of the early development of Islam in terms of certain anthropological concepts. It would like to take issue with the popular view best expressed in the words of Harrison[1] that "Mohammedanism is little more than the Bedouin mind projected into the realm of religion." It is concerned primarily with the change from a type of society organized on the basis of kin relationships to a type of society possessed of an organized, if rudimentary, state. It will attempt to show that this change took place in an urban environment and was causally connected with the spread of trade. No cross-cultural comparisons will be attempted, though it is hoped that the material presented may have applicability elsewhere, especially in the study of areas in which settled populations and pastoral peoples interact.

Many writers have dealt with the rise of Islam primarily in terms of diffusion. Thus Torrey analyzed "the Jewish foundations of Islam."[2] Bell dealt with "the origin of Islam in its Christian environment."[3] Hirschberg discussed Jewish and Christian teaching in pre-Islamic Arabia and early Islamic times.[4] Grimme, Nielsen, and Philby have traced Islamic elements to southern Arabia as the principal source of diffusion.[5] Kroeber has included Islam in the "exclusive-monotheistic pattern" which is said to characterize Judaism, Christianity, and Mohammedanism and serves as an instance of his concept of "systemic patterns" of diffusion.[6] The work of these writers is aimed at an understanding of the derivation of some of the culture elements utilized by Islam, or has pointed to the existence of elements analogous to Islam in other religious traditions developed within the same general area.

Our present emphasis is somewhat different. We are interested primarily in the way in which people relate themselves to each other in terms of the material culturally available to them, and how such systems of relationship change due to the impact of internal and external factors. The present approach is thus functional and historical. It is also evolutionary. The writer is interested in one case history, to show up certain changes in social organization which appear to occur at the threshold of transition from one level of organization to another.

The presentation does not aspire in any way to completeness. It must needs disregard large areas of culture which are peripheral to the present problem. Thus, for example, the change in the position of women from pre-Islamic times to the period of Islam has been disregarded here. Certain areas of culture are isolated for observation, so that hypotheses on the character of systemic change may be derived.

The Economic Basis of Meccan Society

During the first century AD, the discovery of the regular change of the monsoon made possible the rise of regular coastwise trade around the Arabian peninsula. This lowered freight rates sufficiently to cause the main overland route from Yemen to Syria to lose much of its importance. While most of the coastwise trade passed into non-Arab hands, the Arab inhabitants of the Hejaz seized what was left of the carrying trade along the main caravan route. This marginal economic development led to the establishment of a permanent settlement in the valley of Mecca, around the year 400 AD.[7]

This permanent settlement was founded by members of the tribe of Koreish, an impoverished subdivision of the larger pastoral tribe Kinana. Before settling at Mecca, the Koreish lived as pastoral nomads in scattered migratory kin groups which added to their livelihood by selling protection to passing caravans.[8] The social organization of these groups appears to have followed the general pattern of such organization among the Bedouins of the pre-Islamic period. They were "local groups habitually moving together,"[9] composed of a chief and his family, free families, protected strangers who were not blood relatives, and slaves.[10] The chief, usually the oldest or most respected male of the group, was responsible for the care of poor, widows, and orphans, for hospitality to strangers, for payments of blood money,[11] and for the maintenance of order within the group.[12] Yet, then as now, "it is only in war, or on the march, which is conducted with all the precautions of war, that the sheikh of a tribe exercises an active authority."[13] Chief and free families were linked together by bonds of kinship. Those individuals who travelled with the group but were not blood relatives of the rest were tied to them by a number of ritual kin relationships which we shall have occasion to discuss more fully at a later point. These relationships enabled the component elements of the group to "combine on the model or principle of an association of kindred,"[14] and made it possible for outsiders to "feign themselves to be descended from the same stock as the people on whom they were engrafted."[15]

The name of Koreish has received two interpretations, both of sociological rather than etymological interest. One interpretation traces the name back to a word meaning "to collect together." The Koreish are said to carry this name, either because their ancestor "collected together" all migratory kinship units around an already existing religious sanctuary at Mecca[16] or because they "collected together commodities from all sides for sale."[17] Another interpretation derives the name from a word meaning "to trade and make profit."[18] The two interpretations adequately characterize the Koreish as a tribe of traders, living in a permanent settlement.

The settled character of their life set them off from the pastoral nomads of the desert, those who "stayed on the heights of the Hedjaz."[19] "They have lived in towns, when only the heads of the Benu Amr lived in them, and others still led an unsettled existence. They have built many habitations in them, and dug wells," sang one pre-Islamic poet.[20] Another said that if he had chosen to stay with the Koreish, he would not have had to wander about the desert in search of pasture, spending the night at "brackish water . . . in an evil lodging."[21] The Koreish themselves set up "a set of arbitrary regulations of the following kind; they declared themselves exempt from the obligation which required that they make sour milk, turn milk into butter, and live in tents made of camel hair, thus renouncing all the customs of the Bedouin desert nomads, from whom they wanted to distinguish themselves completely."[22]

The permanent settlement at Mecca existed solely for the purposes of commerce. A pre-Islamic poet testified to this: "If Mecca had any attractions to offer, Himyarite princes at the head of their armies would long since have hurried there. There winter and summer are equally desolate. No bird flies over Mecca, no grass grows. There are no wild beasts to be hunted. Only the most miserable of all occupations flourishes there, trade."[23] When Mohammed attempted to ruin Mecca by destroying its Syrian trade, after his flight from Mecca to Medina, a merchant of the Koreish clan of Umaiya said:

> Mohammed has stopped up our trade, his men do not leave the coast clear, and the inhabitants have a pact with them and are largely in understanding with them, so we don't know where to go; but if we remain at home, we shall eat up our capital and cannot maintain ourselves in Mecca over a long period of time, because it is only a settlement for the purpose of carrying on trade, with Syria in the summer time and with Abyssinia in winter.[24]

Without trade, the Meccans would have perished in their "unfruitful valley."[25]

The Koreish appear to have become the dominant traders in western Arabia by stages. First, they sold protection to caravans. Then they began to offer wares "for sale along the overland routes leading through their territory."[26] Finally, they entered the large markets located outside their area, coming into direct trade contacts with Syria and Abyssinia,[27] and with Persia.[28] The Koreish

> skimmed the fat off the fairs of the neighboring places. Mina, Maganna, Dhul Magaz and not least Ukaz were like outposts of Meccan trade. In all these places we find the Koreish; they concentrated business in their hands. The esteem in which they were held can be seen from the fact that the weapons which had to be surrendered for the duration of the markets and the pilgrimage were deposited with a Koreish.[29]

The Koreish thus played an important part in centralizing the economy of the peninsula. Their trading ventures turned Mecca into "a city, secure and at ease, to which supplies come from every side";[30] into a "place of crowding";[31] filled with "their movements, their comings and goings";[32] into "the mother city."[33]

The main article of trade carried north from Mecca was leather, especially tanned camel, cattle, and gazelle hides,[34] products of numerous tanneries located in the towns between Taif and Aden. Other export items were precious metals, dry raisins, and incense.[35] Items of trade carried to Mecca were cereals, oil, wine, mule skins, silk, and luxury goods.[36]

Large amounts of capital were invested in this trade. Caravans comprised up to 2,500 camels[37] and were valued up to 50,000 mithkal, or the equivalent of 2,250 kg of gold.[38] Sprenger has attempted to calculate the annual volume of trade flowing in and out of Mecca:

> We must assume that the Meccans sent annually more than 1,200,000 kg of goods to Syria, and imported as much from there. But we set the value at only 10 mithkal per 100 kg, because they also traded in cereals. Export and import in this direction amounted to roughly a quarter of a million mithkal [or the equivalent of 11,250 kg of gold]. If trade with the south was of equal importance, then they had an annual turnover of half a million. The profits were seldom less than 50 percent, and thus they earned a pure increment of at least 250,000 mithkal.[39]

The sums of needed capital for these operations were brought together through the "development of credit institutions [by means of which] the most humble sums could be turned into capital down to the participation of a dinar or a piece of gold, or even . . . half a ducat of gold."[40] "Few caravans set forth in which the whole population, men and women, had not a financial interest. On their return, every one received a part of the profits proportionate to his stake and the number of shares subscribed."[41] Thus, for example, a caravan in the year 624 AD

> numbered 1,000 camels, almost every man of Koreish had participated in it, even if only with small stakes. 50,000 dinars are said to have been invested in it; most of it belonging to the family of Sa'id b. al Oc Abu Uxaixa, either his own or borrowed in return for a share of half the profit. The Banu Makzum are

said to have had 200 camels and 4000 to 5000 mithkal of gold invested in it, al Xarith b. Amir b. Naufal and Umayya b. Xalaf each 1000 mithkal. A number of caravans, belonging to individual Meccan families, were united in this one caravan; the market destination was Gaza.[42]

This "union of the Koreish, their union in equipping caravans winter and summer"[43] centralized trading operations in the hands of the few best equipped to carry on such large-scale ventures.

Money in this society had not yet reached the stage of the universal commodity. Yet precious metals served as a means by which the value of other commodities could be measured. Byzantine and Persian coins were in use,[44] and gold was mined in the Hejaz.[45] As yet, however, "it was not customary to buy and sell with them [coins] except by considering the coins as bullion,"[46] i.e., by weighing rather than by counting them. This may perhaps be attributed to the lack of a central political power whose imprint might have served to standardize the value of the different coins in circulation. At any rate, commodities like food, milk, and wine were sold.[47] Bad harvests around Mecca are said to have caused the prices of bread to rise.[48] Clothing was sold.[49] Abū Sufyān is said to have sold a house for 400 dinars, with 100 dinars for down payment, and the rest payable in installments.[50] Slaves were sold in what was Arabia's largest slave market.[51] Camels obtained in raids were sold in the open market in Mecca,[52] and the price of horses is said to have been determined by market conditions.[53] Camels were hired out for caravan duty.[54] Ransom was calculated in money terms on certain occasions.[55] Certain occupations, such as sheepherding, guiding caravans, wall building, leeching, etc., were paid in wages.[56] While wages in Medina were usually paid in kind, in Mecca they were usually paid in money.[57]

Credit, pricing, and wages set up relationships between individuals and groups of individuals which were not comprised within the preceding system of kin relationships. Under the impact of commercial development, Meccan society changed from a social order determined primarily by kinship and characterized by considerable homogeneity of ethnic origin into a social order in which the fiction of kinship served to mask a developing division of society into classes, possessed of considerable ethnic diversity.

Accumulation of wealth and power in some clans of the Koreish tribe divided the Koreish into rich and poor. To some extent, this was mirrored in the pattern of settlement.[58] The two dominant Koreish clans, Makhzum and Umaiya, occupied the "inner city" around the central sanctuary of the Ka'ba, and were called "Koreish of the center." The other eight and poorer Koreish clans occupied the "outer city" and were called "Koreish of the outskirts." The real functional units of Meccan society, however, were no longer clans as such, nor localized groups of kin, but clusters of rich merchants, their families and their dependents. The dependent population was made up of several groups. Differentiation of status, minor among the pastoral nomads, assumed major importance in Mecca. First, there were the slaves. Secondly, there existed a group of mercenaries, many of whom were of slave origin.[59] Thirdly, merchants maintained the necessary personnel for their caravans. Fourthly, there were middlemen, like the future Caliph Omar. Fifthly, there were people who had come under the domination of the wealthy through debts, like the dependents of al-'Abbās who had brought them under his sway through usury.[60] Sixthly, there existed a group of people who worked for wages. Finally, there were the clients or protected persons, called *mawālī* (sing. *mawlā*).

This group of clients deserves special consideration. A client stood in a relation of dependency, called *jiwār*, to a patron or protector. The word for client is derived from a root signifying "closeness." Two kinds of closeness were distinguished. A pre-Islamic poet speaks of "cousins of our cousins, of the same stock by birth, and a cousin knit to us by an oath."[61] Clients, called cousins by oath, are contrasted with cousins by birth.[62] The client-patron relationship in its pure form involved a tie of ritual kinship, sealed by commingling of blood and by an oath sworn at the central religious sanctuary, the Ka'ba.[63]

Within Mecca, there were thirteen major groups of clients, each affiliated to a patron family or patron clan.[64] The clients were of diverse origins. Some were freed slaves.[65] Others were outlaws from tribal groups who sought refuge. Some were individuals who had moved into the protection of the group through matrilocal marriage. Some were adopted persons.[66]

Just as settlement in Mecca was nominally organized on a genealogical basis, with two clans at the center and eight clans at the outskirts, so the functioning social groups within Meccan society tended to be formally organized on the principle of the fiction of kinship by blood. This fiction was the only means by which, apart from slavery, individuals could be related to each other. Within the social clusters, the clients represented a group not linked by birth but through ritual kin arrangements.

Due to the commercial orientation of Meccan society, this patron-client tie, formally based on a fictional relation of kin, actually took on more and more the guise of an exploitative relation between members of different class groups. This relationship was reinforced by the prevalence of wage payment and by the institution of debt slavery.[67] It has been pointed out repeatedly that the bulk of Mohammed's first converts came from this group of clients and from the slaves of the city.[68] Caetani has even argued that Mohammed himself was a client of the Koreish, rather than a blood relative,[69] and in this he is supported by a curious remark by Mohammed: "And they say, 'Had but this Koran been sent down to some great one of the two cities ...!',"[70] as well as by other evidence.[71] When Mohammed first embarked on his career, the excitement among the slaves of Mecca was so intense that a leading slave owner who had one hundred slaves removed them from the city because he feared that they might become converts.[72] When Mohammed besieged Taif, he called on the slaves of the town to desert to his camp where they would receive their freedom.[73]

The mechanism of kinship between patron and client provided backing for the individual who was poor or powerless. It put the weight of a powerful group of ritual kin behind him. The isolated individual without such backing was exposed to attack or to unobstructed killing in a blood feud.[74] Yet the same mechanism was also potentially disruptive of social stability. If a client was attacked, the protecting group had to make a show of force. This demonstration of force, in turn, involved the protecting group in ever-widening circles of conflict. For example, during an encounter between Mohammed and the Koreish, the client of a leading Koreish merchant was killed by the Muslims. His brother demanded that the dead man's patron exercise the duty of blood revenge. The merchant tried to avoid this duty, fully cognizant of the fact that its exercise would only involve Mecca more deeply in war with the Muslims, but was forced to give in.[75] Like the relationship between sworn allies *(ḥilf)* which involved mutual aid between two equal parties and which we shall touch on more fully later, the relations between patron and client acted as a double-edged sword. The extension of kinship bonds to the individual merely increased the possibility of conflict between groups organized on the kinship model.

As Mecca came to be characterized by growing heterogeneity of status, its population also became more heterogeneous ethnically. Mention is made of Syrian caravan leaders; of travelling monks and curers; of Syrian merchants; foreign smiths and healers; Copt carpenters; Negro idol sculptors; Christian doctors, surgeons, dentists and scribes; Christian women married into a Koreish clan; Abyssinian sailors and mercenaries.[76] Abyssinian, Mesopotamian, Egyptian, Syrian, and Byzantine slaves were sold in the market place.[77] The market center of Mecca exercised an attraction on groups and individuals beyond the Arabian periphery, as well as within the confines of the peninsula itself.

Religious Development in Meccan Society

Economic development set off related tendencies in the field of religion. Gibb has spoken of "the abandonment of local shrines and the growing practice of pilgrimage to central shrines venerated by groups of tribes (of which the Ka'ba in Mecca was one of the most important)."[78]

The leading Koreish held the ranking positions in the Meccan religious hierarchy as well as the dominant positions in the economic system. The Umaiya clan, especially, appears to have owed its predominance, at least in part, to its possession of special religious prerogatives in the past. One pre-Islamic poet swears "by the holy month of the sons of Umaiya" and another is quoted as saying that the Banu Umaiya in Koreish were like the [priestly] family of the Banu Khafajah in the tribe of 'Uqail.[79] At any rate, the strongly monopolistic character of this Koreish religious oligarchy is evident in their attempt to pass their religious offices down to their first born in the direct line of descent.[80] The major offices, that of the priesthood, the presidency of the council house, and the offices concerned with the distribution of food and water to the pilgrims, were apparently developed by the Koreish themselves, and were preempted by them. Three minor offices which seem to have been traditional in the worship of the Ka'ba[81] were held by three minor tribal groups. The religious society of the *Hums,* again headed by the Koreish, further served to reinforce their dominance in the religious sphere.[82]

Like other Arabian sanctuaries, the Ka'ba was surrounded by a sacred area, called the *ḥarām.* Within this precinct no blood could be shed. As the economic importance of Mecca grew, the Koreish self-consciously sought to extend the sacred precinct as a means for increasing the stability of social relations in their trading territory. They sought to "put their warehouses, their strong boxes, at greater distance from their turbulent neighbors."[83] The story of Amr b. Luhaiy illustrates the secular interest involved in this effort. It shows that the Meccan traders ringed the Ka'ba with the idols of other tribal groups, in order to increase the importance of the sanctuary and to attract more visitors to the growing city.[84]

The extension of the concept of an inviolable zone in which blood feuds were outlawed, and new fights could not develop, appears to have resulted from the development of trade and to have fostered a further development of it. Wellhausen writes:

> Within the tumultuous confusion which fills the desert, the festivities at the beginning of each season represent the only enjoyable periods of rest. A peace of God at this time interrupts the continuous feuds for a fair period of time. The most diverse tribes which otherwise did not trust each other at all, make common pilgrimage to the same holy places without fear, through the land of friend and foe. Trade raises its head, and general and lively exchange results.... The exchange of commodities is followed by an exchange of ideas. A community of ideological interest develops that comprises all of Arabia.[85]

The Koreish developed a special pact with other tribal groups to guarantee the inviolability of pilgrims on their journeys to the religious center.[86] Their attempts to maintain peace earned them the scorn of the more warlike desert tribes. "No one has yet lived through a terror [raid] by them," said a Hudail poet.[87] "They are people who do not know how to fight," said a Jew of Medina.[88] "Your courage fails you in battle," sneered another poet, "at best, you are [only] good at figuring in the ranks of the processions!"[89]

In stressing the Ka'ba as the center of their power, the Koreish broke with the traditional notion of a territory belonging to a certain kin group, and representing its inviolable property.

> Under holy protection, there had here developed a general security under law, unheard of in Arabia where law does not otherwise extend beyond the tribe and this limit can only be extended through clientage. No stranger stood here in need of a pass, none needed the protection of a native patron, ... everyone

was secure in this free state of God, and if he was subjected to injustice and force, he always found someone who backed him up.[90]

The Koreish thus laid the basis for a transition from a concept of territoriality circumscribed by kin relations to a concept of territoriality in which considerations of kinship do not play a prominent part. Caetani states that they "admitted that if Arabs not of their own kin were born in the precinct of the Ka'ba or in its vicinity, they had the same rights as the Koreish, in order to validate the idea that settlement near the Ka'ba gave them precedence over all other Arabs."[91]

Parallel to the abandonment of local shrines and growing centralization of worship, there occurred an increasing tendency to stress one deity above others. There existed religious symbols denoting the different social units of the older kinship society. Thus, each Koreish clan appears to have had its special clan symbol,[92] and each Meccan household had its household god.[93] The extension of kinship ties into ritual kin ties of clientage had led to a special predominance of "the conception of god and worshipper as patron and client."[94] But as the new and non-kin-based relations began to emerge in increased strength, the importance of one god, Allah, grew concomitantly. Allah was preeminently the guardian of social relations which extended beyond the scope of kinship. In terms of the pre-Islamic formulae, he is "the guardian of faith and the avenger of treason," the god in whose name people are supposed to "fulfill their contracts, honor their relatives by oath, and feed their guest."[95]

> Allah is the Zeus Xenios, the protector of *gar* and *daif,* of client and guest. Within the lineage and to a lesser degree within the tribe, *rahim,* the piety of family relationship, the holiness of the blood, exercises protection. But when rights and duties exist which go beyond the lineage, then Allah is the one who imposes them and guarantees them. He is the protector of *giwar* [the patron-client relationship] by which the natural circle of the community is widened and supplemented in a fashion which benefits above all the client and the guest.[96]

We have seen that the economic centralization of western Arabia through trade was accompanied by a related tendency in the centralization of religious worship. Here we venture the hypothesis that the emergence of social classes out of the network of a society based primarily on actual or fictive ties of kinship was accompanied, in the sphere of religion, by an increased emphasis on the deity associated with non-kin relationship.

The Organization of Power in Meccan Society

The way in which power is organized in a given society must be considered both in terms of internal, or endogenous, and in terms of external or exogenous factors.[97]

In terms of internal development, the lines of political power in Mecca tended to coincide with the lines of economic power. In theory, power in Mecca was located in a town council, made up of adult males. In actuality, however, the council was dominated by the same wealthy merchants who ruled over the clusters of kin and dependents, and who held the main religious offices. They decided general policy and made alliances. They represented the "union of the Koreish" and their representatives made formal trade agreements with the Abyssinian and the Persian courts.[98] They permitted foreigners to address the town council on specific matters; and received the taxes which all foreigners who were not kin or ritual kin had to pay if they wanted to trade in the area.

Despite its oligarchic character, the council had no direct legislative power and lacked a central executive organ. In a society which was rapidly moving away from primary reliance on kinship ties, its power was still largely kin-based. It lay in the council's ability to break a recalcitrant by refusing to grant him protection. The mechanism for enforcing such decisions was the blood feud, and law was maintained only by the unwillingness of potential culprits to risk the dangers of an encounter with the powerful "Koreish of the center." The limitations of this negative power as a means of effective social control are shown clearly in the story of the supposed boycott against Mohammed at the end of his Meccan period. Whether apocryphal or not,[99] the story demonstrates that "the ideological movement created by the prophet tore apart the ancient Arab order which was based on kinship. Most members of the boycotted lineage did not believe in Mohammed ... and on the other hand, some of Mohammed's most fervent adherents like Abu Bekr and Umar were left untouched by this rule of conduct, since they did not belong to his lineage."[100]

Just as the blood feud as a means of social control in a class-divided society could not govern internal friction, so kin-based mechanisms used to ensure security against the outside world failed of their purpose. We have already seen that the patron-client relation, extending protection to individuals or groups, at the same time extended the possibility of intertribal conflict. The same may be said of the so-called *ḥilf* relationship. The *ḥilf* generally designates a relation of cooperation between roughly equal partners, in contrast to the patron-client relation which involves a stronger and a weaker party.[101] Such a pact of cooperation could be entered into temporarily for a specific purpose like joint action in war or for the purpose of protecting a caravan. Or it could develop into a permanent tie between tribes and tribal groups.[102] The tie was sanctified by a ceremony in which both parties mixed their blood,[103] and might be surrounded by a mythology of common descent.[104] Wellhausen has spoken of the Arab genealogy as a statistical device,[105] and both he and Caetani[106] have stressed the fictional character of descent in Arabia in general. The Koreish maintained such pacts, for example, with many members of the tribe Sulaim who possessed mineral resources and commanded the road from Medina as well as access to Nejd and the Persian

Gulf;[107] with individual Syrian merchants;[108] with a Bedouin marauder like al-Barrad; and others.

While these kin-based mechanisms permitted the formation of more extensive social bonds, they were also charged with potential for further friction. Fights between far-off desert tribes, involving partners to a pact with the Koreish, involved the Koreish against their better interests. When a chain of petty insults started a war between the tribes Kinana and Hawazin, the Koreish had to enter the fight on the side of their Kinana relatives. When their sworn ally al-Barrad plundered the caravan of the king of Hira, they were drawn into the quarrel on his side. Thus the system of ritual kin on which the Koreish relied for increased security at the same time counteracted their interest in peaceful relations of trade.

Lammens has discussed the reaction against direct blood revenge and the growing preference for settlement of blood feuds through arbitration and payment of blood money which came to the fore in pre-Islamic Arabia.[109] It is possible that this reaction was related to a growing realization that the prevailing kinship mechanisms proved disruptive of the peace they were supposed to maintain. It may also have been conditioned by the growing utility and ubiquity of money, by means of which blood claims could be reduced more easily to a common denominator.

An element in the social organization of Mecca which was not disguised as a kinship unit was the military force at the disposal of the Koreish, the so-called Ahabis. This group of soldiers may have consisted either of splinter elements drawn from different tribal groups; or they may have been Abyssinian mercenaries, if one may put credence in Lammens' interpretation of the textual material.[110] They may have resembled the "men of different Arab elements which followed the kings ... a type of Praetorian guard" characteristic of the Himyarite kingdom of Kinda and the Persian satellite kingdom of Hira.[111] Their main function was to provide protection for caravans[112] and to assist the Koreish in warfare. The cadre for these troops was drawn from the Kinana, genealogical relatives of the Koreish. While these military guards were thus nontribal in character, and were organized on the basis of a non-kin principle, they were integrated into the social structure by subordinating them to the command of tribesmen related by kinship to the Meccan oligarchy.

If interaction with the tribal groups near Mecca could be phrased in terms of ritual kin relations, interaction with societies beyond the Arabian periphery meant contact with developed state organizations. These were, first, the satellite states of the greater powers, like the Himyarite Kinda, the Persian Hira, and the Byzantine Ghassan; secondly, the great powers themselves: Byzantium and Persia in the north and first Himyar and later Abyssinia in the south. Hira and Ghassan were outposts which kept the pastoral nomads in check. Built up by nomads themselves, they were used "as barriers against their brothers who pushed after them."[113] They also set the "terms of trade" against the pastoral nomads in the exchange of products between desert and agricultural area. The cultivated zone furnishes the nomads with cereals and handicraft products, permitting them free access to pasture, meadowland and watering places after harvest. The nomads in turn supply the settled area with livestock and livestock products. When the nomads are strong, they rig the terms of exchange against the settlers, by adding tribute in kind to their other demands. Sometimes they may be compensated by outright payment by a larger power. When the settled area is strongly organized politically, it can exploit the need of the nomads for pasture to exact tribute from them in turn.[114] Thus the kings of Hira received leather, truffles, and horses from the nomads,[115] in exchange for pasturing rights in Iraq. Ghassan and Hira even fought each other over the right to exact tribute from a certain area.[116]

These satellites had certain characteristics in common. They maintained armed "Praetorian guards" consisting of detribalized elements[117] and a system of taxation.[118] Their very existence constituted a dilemma for the larger dominant power. If they grew too strong politically, they had to be incorporated into the domain of the dominant power.[119] When they were incorporated, the lack of an independent buffer was immediately felt in new exactions and incursions on the part of the nomads.

The state of Kinda demands some special consideration. It represents the first attempt of which we know to set up a more encompassing social structure in central Arabia, with a center of gravity in the Nejd, around the end of the 5th century AD. The first Kinda prince apparently owed his dominance over the tribal groups included in the Kinda coalition to the desire of the kingdom of Himyar in south Arabia to erect a buffer against Persia.[120] As soon as the coalition was organized, it began to raid Byzantine and Persian territory.[121] "It is evident that not only all Nejd but also great parts of al-Higaz, al-Bahrain, and al-Yamama were subject to al-Harit's [Kindite] sceptre,"[122] and the Kinana, mother tribe of the Koreish, the Asad and the Kais-'Ailan of the Hejaz are mentioned as part of the federation.[123] The Kinda state maintained a "Praetorian guard" similar to that of the Hira and Ghassan, and tax collectors.[124] It broke up as quickly as it had developed, apparently due to an inability to collect the requisite taxes from its component nomadic groups.[125]

The position of Mecca in relation to these organized areas is of considerable importance. Lattimore has pointed out, in connection with another area of interaction between nomads and settled populations, that the probability for independent sociopolitical development increases beyond a certain distance from the dominant center.[126] In this connection, it is significant that Meccan power rose after the Kindite power disintegrated, and that it was able to maintain its independence from Abyssinia, Byzantium, and Persia. Ghassanid expansion reached as far south as al-Ela, Khaibar and Hajel,[127] but never reached Mecca. At least one attempt was made to include Mecca in the Byzantine zone, but it failed. 'Uthmān Ibn Huwairith attempted to seize leadership in Mecca by threatening it with Byzantine reprisals against its Syrian trade. The attempt was foiled, permitting the Umaiya clan to rise to unchallenged domination in the city.[128] The Abyssinian attempt to attack the Persians from the south[129] was similarly doomed to failure. The legend of the Battle of the

Elephants in which God is said to have saved the Ka'ba from destruction by the Abyssinians appears to reflect the fact that the Abyssinians had reached the outer limits of their ability to expand. With leather as its principal export to the north, and with cereals as its principal import, Mecca participated in the general exchange between pastoral and settled area. Its relative distance from the center, and its ability to capitalize on a peripheral trade route permitted the independent growth of state organization in this zone.

The Emergence of the Islamic State

The religious revolution associated with the name of Mohammed made possible the transition from Meccan society as we have described it to a society possessed of the elements which permit state organization. The success of Mohammed's prophetic mission permitted these elements to crystallize out of the preceding social network in which kin relationships had become increasingly fictional and disruptive.

The emergence of Islam completed the centralization of worship by making Mecca the sole religious center. It completed the trend towards worship of the deity governing non-kin relations by making this deity the supreme and only god, "the personification of state supremacy."[130] In Islam—"voluntary surrender" or "self-surrender" to a supreme deity[131]—all men were to be clients of God, the only patron. "And warn those who dread being gathered to their Lord, that patron or intercessor they shall have none but Him," says the Koran.[132] "God is the patron of believers."[133]

"There are no genealogies in Islam," states a traditional saying.[134] The very act of adherence to Islam implied an individual decision into which considerations of kin did not enter. The story of the boycott of the Prophet's lineage shows how completely the principles of kin relationships failed to cope with the new force. "Truly, the most worthy of honor in the sight of God is he who fears him most,"[135] not the individual whose lineage is the most famous or the most powerful. When Mohammed entered Mecca, he declared: "God has put an end to the pride in noble ancestry, you are all descended from Adam and Adam from dust, the noblest among you is the man who is most pious."[136] Adherence to Islam was not a matter of kin relationships: "Mohammed is not the father of any man among you, but he is the Apostle of God."[137] Islam set kinsman against kinsman. "The swords of the sons of his father were drawn against him," mourns a song about the battle of Badr, "oh God! Love among relatives was deeply injured there!"[138] A son turned Muslim could approve the death of his father who had fought with the Koreish against the new faith.[139]

As Islam built on ties other than those of kinship, it had to put a limit on the disruptive exercise of power and protection implicit in the blood feud. On the occasion of his entrance into Mecca, Mohammed "declared all demands for interest payments, for blood revenge or blood money stemming from pagan times as null and void."[140] The same demand was expressed in a letter to the people of Najran: "There are no interest payments and no demands for blood revenge from pagan times."[141] God permits a relaxation of the *lex talionis*.[142]

> A believer killeth not a believer but by mischance: and whoso killeth a believer by mischance shall be bound to free a believer from slavery; and the blood money shall be paid to the family of the slain, unless they convert it into alms. But if the slain believer be of a hostile people, then let him confer freedom on a slave who is a believer; and if he be of a people between whom and your-selves there is an alliance, then let the blood money be paid to his family, and let him set free a slave who is a believer: and let him who hath not the means, fast two consecutive months. This is the penance enjoined by God; and God is Knowing, Wise![143]

The passage cited shows that the incipient Islamic state did not suppress the *talio* as such. It even left the settlement of such disputes to the families concerned. It did, however, insist that the manner in which they were settled conformed to the "penance enjoined by God," and attempted to convert the demand for blood into a demand for wergild. In pre-Islamic times, the duty of carrying on the blood feud passed from father to son in direct inheritance.[144] Islam demanded early and peaceful settlement. The moratorium on blood feud was so much part of the new creed that certain tribes postponed their affiliation with Mohammed, until they had settled all questions of blood revenge.[145]

Another set of kinlike relations superseded by Islam were the relations involving past allies. There was to be "no *ḥilf* in Islam."[146]

The social relations within Arab tribal life represented by the *taḥalluf (ḥilf)* "were of necessity as undesirable to representatives of Mohammed's ideas as the particularism of the tribes. For they furthered feuding between the tribes and were to be overcome in Islam by the brotherhood of all who professed Islam."[147]

The core of the new society was the militant brotherhood of Muhaǰǰirīn and Ansār. The Muhaǰǰirīn were the Muslims who fled with Mohammed from Mecca to Medina. The Ansār were their Medinese hosts. Armed, and without ties of kin to bind them, they resembled the "Praetorian guard" of the kings of Hira and Kinda. They were the storm troops of Islam. A Hudail poet compared them to his own tribes. The Hudail were called "a luxurious people of [many] subdivisions." The Muslims were "a multitude drawn to-gether from many sources of [warriors] clad in iron."[148] They rent the ties of kinship which had bound them in the past. The Ansār were commanded to inform on those "who have been forbidden secret talk, and return to what they have been forbidden, and talk privately together with wickedness, and hate and disobedience towards the Apostle."[149] "The foundations of society, faithful cooperation of kin, were so undermined that they were not safe from espionage on the part of their closest relatives."[150] Disaffected individuals were threatened with use of force.[151]

It is interesting to note how, initially, attempts were made to invent a new functional kind of kinship for this group. Mohammed ordered "that those who migrated with him and the believers in Medina should regard themselves as brethren and therefore able to inherit from one another, while all the bonds of relationship between the Muhadjurun and their relatives left in Mecca were to be regarded as broken."[152]

The Koran states: "Verily, they who have believed and fled their homes and spent their substance for the cause of God, and they who have taken in the prophet and been helpful to him, shall be near of kin the one to the other."[153] They were to form a special aristocracy: "They who have believed, and fled their homes, and striven with their substance and with their persons on the path of God, shall be of highest grade with God."[154]

The new society which arose in Medina and was given organized form by means of a town charter promulgated by Mohammed,[155] was called *umma*, i.e., community. The community included not only Muslims, but non-Muslims as well. The *umma* comprised the whole territory of Medina, embracing all who lived within it.[156] These were all included in the incipient Islamic state, "one community over against mankind." The core of the new community were the Muslims, "a unit with its own laws within the whole society, destined of necessity to disrupt the ties of the whole."[157]

The elements of state power developed gradually. In his deportment as a prophet, Mohammed followed pre-Islamic precedents.

> The mantic knowledge [of the pagan seer, called *kahin*] is based on ecstatic inspiration.... They are interrogated in all important tribal and state occasions ... in private the *kahins* especially act as judges.... They interpret dreams, find lost camels, establish adulteries, clear up other crimes.... The prophet Mohammed disclaimed being a *kahin*. But ... his earliest appearance as a prophet reminds us strongly of the manner of the soothsayer. He was an ecstatic and had "true dreams" like them.... Even the forms which he was still using for administering justice and settling disputes in Medina during the early years of his stay there correspond in their main features to those of the pagan *kahin* and *hakam*.[158]

Mohammed himself acted as judge in a few known cases only.[159] Yet his very word, said to be the word of God, acted as law in the new state. During his lifetime, the prophet himself was the final judicial authority. He deposed lineage chiefs and replaced them with his own candidates.[160] He appointed officials, in the majority of cases apparently on a temporary basis.[161] The incipient state did not take on itself direct governing power over groups which became affiliated with it. Usually, its "emissaries exercised a sort of supervision and collected taxes."[162] In many cases, local authorities continued, themselves becoming officials of the new state.[163] In one case, a Christian chief became collector of the Islamic tax from his own people.[164]

The subordination of the right of the blood feud to the power of the state brings out more clearly the character of the new organization. The blood feud implied exercise of power based on kinship. The consequence of its exercise was warfare between kin groups. With the limitation of the blood feud under Islam "there was accomplished a separation of war and blood revenge which had been impossible in such clarity before. The notion of blood revenge is still applied to war. The faithful are each other's avengers of blood on the war path of God, but tribal law and family sentiment are wholly ignored."[165]

The family remained the executor of the civil feud, but the use of force in the form of war became an attribute of the state. Due to the limited development of the judicial power in the new state, writers have often misunderstood the meaning of warfare in Islam. 'Abdurraziq has criticized traditional views of *jihād* (the holy war) as a war of conversion by fire and sword, as follows: "All evidence shows that the purpose of the holy war was not to be religious propaganda and to bring the people to believe in Allah and his prophet alone. The holy war is carried on only for the purpose of affirming the authority of the state and of enlarging the kingdom.[166] ... A government must base itself on its armed force and ability to exercise power."[167]

The new state was capable not only of the essential show of force, but also possessed of effective taxing power. One fifth of all booty was assigned to the Prophet as "the part of God." Among pre-Islamic Bedouins, one fourth or one fifth of all booty[168] was assigned to the chief "as a kind of state treasure which was of course in the hands of physical individuals due to the lack of judicial persons."[169] The chief was supposed to use this wealth to settle blood feuds, grant hospitality, feed guests and the poor, and care for widows and orphans.[170] The prophet's "fifth" represents the transfer of this mechanism from the level of the kin group to the level of the state. In pre-Islamic times, areas of pasture located in the sacred precincts around sanctuaries could be used as common pastures not monopolized by any one tribe.[171] In Islam, the sacred precincts and the pastures located in them became state property, with "Allah the legal successor of the pagan deity,"[172] where tax camels and other livestock could be kept.[173]

Muslims had to pay a so-called poor tax or alms tax (*zakāt*), as one of their five essential religious duties. It soon became a graduated income tax.[174] Payment or nonpayment of this tax quickly became the chief test of adherence to Islam. When Mohammed died, many affiliated tribal groups broke away from the new state, maintaining their newly acquired religious faith, but refusing to pay taxes. Mohammed, during his lifetime, had already castigated "the Arabs of the desert ... who reckon what they expend in the cause of God as tribute, and wait for some change of fortune to befall you."[175] The leaders of the revolts against the state proclaimed their missions "like Mohammed in the name of Allah and not in the name of some pagan deity.... They wanted to carry on divine worship, but not to pay taxes."[176] The new officials "caused anger among the populace, especially in their capacity as tax collectors."[177] Among the Tamim, "after the death of Mohammed the question was whether the tax camels which had been brought together were to be handed over at the proper station or not; this was the criterion of faith in Islam or of defection."[178] When the Muslims won, the camels were handed over.[179]

The use of the poor tax to finance the newly established state structure implies the transference of a mechanism which had previously functioned on the lineage level to the level of the state. The tribal chief or head of the subtribe was responsible for the care and feeding of the poor. The necessary sums were obtained from a portion of the booty allocated to him for such purposes. He was also responsible for hospitality to strangers. Under Islam, care for the poor as well as the responsibility for entertaining strangers was shifted to the level of the state.

The use of taxation for this purpose led to an argument among scholars as to whether Mohammed could be called a socialist.[180] It must be pointed out that Mohammed did not touch the basic dynamic of the society which had produced him. To followers who feared that combining the religious pilgrimage with irreligious trade might be a sacrilege, he is supposed to have said: "There are no sins for you during the festivals of pilgrimage."[181] Mohammed, Abu Bekr, and Omar all owed their personal wealth to trade. Torrey has pointed to the abundance of "commercial-theological" terms in the Koran.[182] Mohammed and his adherents continued to trade while in exile in Medina, an often overlooked fact.[183] Continued trade, as well as the plundering of Meccan caravans, fortified the position of the faithful in Medina, where wide-travelled merchants were used as well as valued spies and informers on other areas.[184] Mohammed, did, however, transfer to the state the responsibility for the care of the poor whose status had become increasingly exploitative under the guise of traditional kin relationships. We have seen above that he declared all interest payments stemming from pagan times to be null and void. Usury was made illegal: "God hath allowed selling, but forbidden usury."[185] Both acts seem to have been aimed at undercutting the Koreish power and raising resistance against it. Poor Muhajjirīn were also granted a special part of the spoils,[186] and poor Muslims were assigned land.[187]

Non-Muslims paid a special tax, but were integrated into the new state without forced conversion. Where they resisted the encroachment of the new state by force, they were indeed subjected to serious economic disabilities, as, for example, were the Jews of Khaibar.[188] But the popular notion that the beginnings of Islam were marked by wholesale conversions, achieved by force, is wholly unwarranted. The Koran says: "Dispute not, unless in kindly sort, with the people of the Book; save with such of them as have wrongfully dealt with you,"[189] and "let there be no compulsion in religion."[190] If these non-Muslims paid taxes, as did the Christians of Aila, the Jews of Adruh, Garba, and Makna, and the Jewish and Christian communities of southern Arabia, their security was guaranteed. They became "people [living] under contractually guaranteed protection."[191] Such relationships had previously been phrased in terms of kin or ritual kin relationships between patrons and clients, as in the case of the protective relation in existence between the Jewish communities of Medina and Khaibar and their Bedouin patrons.[192] Under Islam, this type of relation was transferred to the level of the state.

Conversion to Islam was in fact not primarily a religious demand, but a political one. During the initial Medinese period

> Mohammed does not call on the tribes to convert themselves to Islam.... He concludes with them pacts of protection and mutual aid in aggression, in which he guarantees his clients security of person and property and promises them the protection of God and his messenger. In exchange, they assume the duty of putting themselves at the disposal of the prophet when he calls on them to fight. Excepted are wars in the cause of religion![193]

Only after the unsuccessful siege of Medina by the Koreish did Mohammed begin to demand that affiliated tribes take on Islam "as a sign of political affiliation."[194] Conversion "only served as a manifestation of political affiliation with Mohammed and remained therefore limited to the circles which sought this affiliation. The remainder paid the *gizja* [the special tax paid by non-Muslims]. Mohammed was more interested in the tax which these tribes brought in than in their belief."[195]

Mohammed was statesman enough to grant the status of Muhajjirīn to the Aslam, a tribe which owned pasture grounds on the road from Medina to Mecca and without whose cooperation the war against the Koreish could not have been carried on,[196] and to permit the inhabitants of Taif to include the sacred precinct around their pagan sanctuary into the sacred precinct of Mecca, thus getting the same prerogatives as the inhabitants of Mecca.[197] Within the various tribal groups and settlements which joined Mohammed, only certain minorities accepted Islam as a religious faith. These were usually groups attempting to improve their status within their own societies.[198] Mohammed had already begun in Mecca to "introduce himself to individuals [among the Bedouins] of whom he knew that they were held in great esteem and to lecture them about his vision of God's guidance and mercy."[199] The use of the state treasury to win over such interested nomad leaders is implied in the Koran: "But alms are to be given only to the poor and needy, and to those who collect them, and to those whose hearts are won for Islam, and for ransoms, and for debtors, and for the cause of God, and the wayfarer."[200] The inclusion of petty chiefs in participation in booty served to attract "ambitious sheiks who were then interested in spreading Islam among the members of their tribe. These in turn sought their allies among the Muslims, in order to maintain themselves against the ruling families with their help."[201] Their titles to properties and perquisites acquired through their affiliation with Islam depended on the continued existence of the Islamic state, and were strengthened by the progress of Islam. When the death of Mohammed threatened the young state with disintegration, these minorities acted to keep the tribal groups within the new structure. Victory was based on the ability of the Muslims to keep the adherence of "the loyal minorities among the Bedouin tribes, with whom they were superior to the majorities, because these never allied themselves, nor closed their ranks with determination.... There were also Bedouins who, together with the Muslims, carried on successful operations against dissenters within their own tribe."[202]

The alliance with Bedouin tribes, finally, enabled the young state to challenge the dominant powers along the Arab periphery. This task would have been impossible without the active cooperation of tribes in Syria[203] and tribes ranging along the Persian frontier.[204]

The center of the Islamic state, however, remained in the settled communities, where it had originated. It might be said that the state was "oasis bound." Marçais has noted that "if the Muslim army contingents ... comprised a nomad majority, the cadres were recruited among the settled people of the Hejaz, Medinese agriculturists, town merchants of Mecca and Taif."[205] Von Grunebaum states:

> Islam, from its very outset unfolding in an urban milieu, favored city development. The legislation of the Koran envisages city life. The nomad is viewed with distrust.... Only in a city, that is, a settlement harboring a central mosque, jami', fit for the Friday service and a market (and preferably a public bath) can all the requirements of the faith be properly fulfilled. Migration into town, hijra, is recommended and almost equalized in merit to that more famous migration, again called hijra, of the Prophet from Mecca to Medina. To forsake town for country is severely condemned.[206]

Conclusion

Our brief historical survey has shown that the tendencies which Mohammed brought to fruition were reaching their peak of development in pre-Islamic times. Commercial development in urban settlements had caused the emergence of class groupings from the preceding network of kin relations. Centralization of worship and the emergence of a deity specifically linked with the regulation of non-kin relations as the chief deity went hand in hand with the centralization of trade and the disintegration of the kinship structure. Yet in the political sphere, the use of kinship mechanisms in situations which increasingly exposed their nonfunctional character in the new setting led to disruption and conflict, rather than to further organization and consolidation.

The religious revolution associated with the name of Mohammed permitted the establishment of an incipient state structure. It replaced allegiance to the kinship unit with allegiance to a state structure, an allegiance phrased in religious terms. It limited the disruptive exercise of the kin-based mechanism of the blood feud. It put an end to the extension of ritual kin ties to serve as links between tribes. It based itself instead on the armed force of the faithful as the core of a social order which included both believers and unbelievers. It evolved a rudimentary judicial authority, patterned after the role of the pre-Islamic soothsayer, but possessed of new significance. The limitation of the blood feud permitted war to emerge as a special prerogative of the state power. The state taxed both Muslims and non-Muslims, in ways patterned after pre-Islamic models, but to new ends. Finally, it located the center of the state in urban settlements, surrounding the town with a set of religious symbols that served functionally to increase its prestige and role.

The revolution accomplished, power quickly passed out of the hands of the armed brotherhood of the faithful into the hands of the Koreish who had fought against them. It may be said that Mohammed accomplished for the Meccan traders that which they could not accomplish themselves: the organization of state power.

Notes

1. Harrison, 1924, p. 42.
2. Torrey, 1933.
3. Bell, 1926.
4. Hirschberg, 1939.
5. Grimme, 1892; Nielsen, 1927; Philby, 1947.
6. Kroeber, 1948, p. 314.
7. Lammens, 1926, p. 13.
8. Lammens, 1928, p. 239.
9. Smith, 1903, p. 43.
10. Levy, 1933, vol. 1, p. 278.
11. Procksch, 1899, pp. 7–9.
12. Ashkenazi, 1946–49, p. 665.
13. Smith, 1903, p. 68.
14. Maine, 1888, p. 127.
15. Idem, p. 126.
16. Wüstenfeld, 1864, p. 28.
17. Idem, p. 25.
18. Ibn Hishām, 1864, vol. 1, p. 46.
19. Ibn Hishām, 1864, p. 85.
20. Ibid.
21. Mufaḍḍalīyāt, 1918, p. 254.
22. Caetani, 1905, p. 148.
23. Essad Bey, 1936, p. 44.
24. Wāḳidī, 1882, p. 100.
25. Koran 14, 40; p. 229.
26. Wüstenfeld, 1864, p. 35.
27. Ibid.
28. Idem, p. 38.
29. Wellhausen, 1884–99, vol. 3, p. 88.
30. Koran 16, 113; p. 208.
31. Idem, 3, 90; p. 395.
32. Idem, 3, 196; p. 405.
33. Idem, 42, 5; p. 271.
34. Sprenger, 1869, vol. 3, p. 94.

35. Lammens, 1928, pp. 22-23; Sprenger, 1869, p. 95.
36. Lammens, 1928, pp. 22-23; Sprenger, 1869, p. 95.
37. Wāḵidī, 1882, p. 34.
38. Idem, p. 39.
39. Sprenger, 1869, p. 96.
40. Lammens, 1924, p. 233.
41. Lammens, 1926, p. 16.
42. Wāḵidī, 1882, p. 39.
43. Koran 61, 1; p. 36.
44. Balādhurī, 1916-24, p. 233.
45. Buhl, 1930, p. 51.
46. Balādhurī, 1916-24.
47. Ibn Hishām, 1864, vol. 2, pp. 3, 7; Mufaḍḍalīyāt, 1918, p. 34.
48. Wüstenfeld, 1864, p. 36.
49. Ibn Hishām, 1864, p. 9.
50. Wāḵidī, 1882, p. 340.
51. Lammens, 1928, p. 12.
52. Ibn Hishām, 1864, pp. 21-22.
53. Mufaḍḍalīyāt, 1918, p. 308.
54. Idem, p. 318.
55. Wāḵidī, 1882, p. 76.
56. Bukhārī, 1903-14, vol. 2, pp. 62-64; Sprenger, 1869, vol. 1, p. 275.
57. Sprenger, 1869, vol. 3, p. 141.
58. Wüstenfeld, 1864, pp. 58-75, passim.
59. Lammens, 1928, p. 244.
60. Buhl, 1930, p. 109.
61. Mufaḍḍalīyāt, 1918, p. 34.
62. Goldziher, 1889, vol. 1, p. 105.
63. Smith, 1903, pp. 50-51.
64. Wüstenfeld, 1864, pp. 59-75, passim.
65. Smith, 1903, p. 51.
66. Idem, pp. 49-52, passim.
67. Lammens, 1924, pp. 236-237.
68. Caetani, 1905, p. 240; Procksch, 1899, pp. 81-82.
69. Caetani, 1905, pp. 68-69.
70. Koran, 43, 30; p. 136.
71. Caetani, 1905, pp. 233-234, note 1 to p. 225.
72. Sprenger, 1851, p. 159.
73. *Encyclopedia of Islam*, vol. 1, p. 80.
74. Buhl, 1930, pp. 36.37.
75. Procksch, 1899, p. 38.
76. Lammens, 1928, pp. 12-32, passim.
77. Idem, pp. 18-19.
78. Gibb, 1948, p. 113.
79. Mufaḍḍalīyāt, 1918, pp. 125-126.
80. Wüstenfeld, 1864, p. 34.
81. Caetani, 1905, p. 105; Wellhausen, 1884-99, vol. 3, p. 77.
82. Caetani, 1905, p. 148.
83. Lammens, 1928, p. 239.

84. Ibn Hishām, 1864, vol. 1, p. 39.
85. Wellhausen, 1884-99, vol. 3, p. 183.
86. Caetani, 1905, p. 165.
87. Hell, 1933, p. 10.
88. Ibn Hishām, 1864, vol. 2, p. 2.
89. Lammens, 1928, p. 145.
90. Wellhausen, 1884-99, vol. 3, p. 88.
91. Caetani, 1905, p. 148.
92. Lammens, 1928, p. 145.
93. Wākidī, 1882, p. 370.
94. Smith, 1927, p. 79.
95. Wellhausen, 1884-99, vol. 3, p. 191.
96. Wellhausen, 1884-99, vol. 3, p. 190.
97. Wittfogel, 1932, pp. 542-551.
98. Wüstenfeld, 1864, pp. 35, 38.
99. Caetani, 1905, pp. 290-291; Buhl, 1930, p. 175.
100. Buhl, 1930, p. 176.
101. Pedersen, 1914, p. 29; Bräunlich, 1934, p. 191.
102. Bräunlich, 1934, p. 194.
103. Pedersen, 1914, p. 21; Smith, 1903, pp. 60-61.
104. Nallino, 1941, pp. 77-78.
105. Wellhausen, 1884-99, vol. 4, p. 27.
106. Caetani, 1905, p. 59.
107. *Encyclopedia of Islam,* vol. 4, p. 518.
108. Lammens, 1914, p. 79.
109. Lammens, 1928, p. 232.
110. Lammens, 1928, pp. 244-283, passim.
111. Rothstein, 1899, pp. 136-137.
112. Lammens, 1928, p. 283.
113. Rothstein, 1899, p. 130.
114. Dussaud, 1907, pp. 3-4.
115. Fraenkel, 1886, p. 178.
116. Rothstein, 1899, pp. 130-131.
117. Idem, pp. 136-137.
118. Ibid.
119. Idem, pp. 117-120; Nöldeke, 1887, p. 31.
120. Olinder, 1927, pp. 37-40.
121. Idem, p. 57.
122. Idem, p. 75.
123. Idem, p. 74.
124. Idem, p. 81.
125. Idem, pp. 77-78.
126. Lattimore, 1940, pp. 238-240.
127. Musil, 1926, p. 259.
128. Sprenger, 1869, vol. 1, p. 91.
129. Tabarī, 1879, pp. 204-205.
130. Wellhausen, 1927, p. 8.
131. Smith, 1927, p. 80; Lyall, 1903, p. 784.
132. Koran 6, 51; p. 321.

133. Idem, 2, 258; p. 367.
134. Levy, 1933, vol. 2, p. 79.
135. Koran 49, 13; p. 470.
136. Wākidī, 1882, p. 338.
137. Koran 33, 40; p. 438.
138. Ibn Hishām, 1864, vol. 1, p. 390.
139. Idem, p. 340.
140. Wākidī, 1882, p. 338.
141. Sperber, 1916, p. 91.
142. Koran 2, 173-174; p. 356.
143. Koran, 4, 94; p. 421.
144. Lammens, 1928, p. 202.
145. Idem, p. 197.
146. *Encyclopedia of Islam,* vol. 2, p. 308.
147. Goldziher, 1889, p. 69.
148. Hell, 1933, p. 6.
149. Koran 58, 9; p. 451.
150. Sprenger, 1869, vol. 3, p. 27.
151. Ibn Hishām, 1864, vol. 1, pp. 266-267.
152. *Encyclopedia of Islam,* vol. 3, p. 508.
153. Koran 8, 73; p. 381.
154. Koran 9, 20; p. 472.
155. Wellhausen, 1884-99, vol. 4, pp. 68-73.
156. Idem, p. 74.
157. Buhl, 1930, p. 210.
158. *Encyclopedia of Islam,* vol. 2, pp. 625-626.
159. Caetani, 1905, pp. 645-646.
160. Margoliouth, 1905, p. 216.
161. 'Abdurraziq, 1934, p. 168.
162. Wellhausen, 1884-99, vol. 3, p. 29.
163. Wellhausen, idem, p. 30.
164. Ḥusain, 1938, pp. 126-127.
165. Procksch, 1899, p. 66.
166. 'Abdurraziq, 1934, p. 175.
167. Idem, p. 176.
168. Mufaḍḍalīyāt, 1918, p. 237.
169. Procksch, 1899, p. 9.
170. Idem, pp. 7, 59.60.
171. Wellhausen, 1884-99, vol. 3, p. 104.
172. Idem, p. 104.
173. Kremer, 1875-77, vol. 1, p. 57.
174. Idem, pp. 51-52.
175. Koran 9, 99; p. 481.
176. Wellhausen, 1884-99, vol. 6, p. 7.
177. Idem, p. 31.
178. Idem, p. 13.
179. Idem, p. 15.
180. Grimme, 1892; Snouck Hurgronje, 1894, pp. 48-70, 149-178.
181. Bukhārī, 1903-14, p. 20.

182. Torrey, 1892.
183. Lammens, 1924, pp. 257–260.
184. Ibid.
185. Koran 2, 276; p. 369.
186. Koran 59, 8; p. 432.
187. Bālādhurī 1916.24, vol. 1, p. 37.
188. Ibn Hishām, 1864, vol. 2, p. 170ff.
189. Koran 29, 45; p. 265.
190. Koran, 2, 257; p. 367.
191. Buhl, 1930, p. 346.
192. Lammens, 1928, pp. 70–71, 79.
193. Sperber, 1916, p. 4.
194. Idem, p. 5.
195. Ibid.
196. Idem, pp. 18–19.
197. Idem, p. 72.
198. Idem, pp. 33–79, passim.
199. Ibn Hishām, 1864, vol. 1, p. 211.
200. Koran 9, 60; p. 477.
201. Sperber, 1916, p. 74.
202. Wellhausen, 1884–99, vol. 6, p. 11.
203. Kremer, 1875–77, pp. 85–96.
204. Musil, 1927, pp. 284–285, 292.
205. Marçais, 1928, p. 88.
206. Von Grunebaum, 1946, pp. 173–174.

References

'Abdurraziq, 'Ali. 1934. "L'Islam et les bases du pouvoir." *Révue des Études Islamiques* 8, pp. 163–222.

Ashkenazi, Touvia. 1946–49. "La tribu arabe: ses éléments." *Anthropos* 41–44, pp. 657–672.

Bālādhurī, Ahmad Ibn Yaḥya Ibn Jābir al- [d. 892]. 1916–24. *The Origins of the Islamic State*, translated and annotated by Hitti and Murgotten, Studies in History, Economics, and Public Law, Faculty of Political Science, Columbia University, vol. 68; 2 vols. New York: Longmans Green.

Bell, Richard. 1926. *The Origin of Islam in Its Christian Environment*. London: Macmillan.

Bräunlich, Erich. 1934. "Beiträge zur Gesellschaftsordnung der arabischen Beduinenstämme." *Islamica* 6, pp. 68–111, 182–229.

Buhl, Frants. 1930. *Des Leben Muhammeds*. Leipzig: Quelle and Meyer.

Bukhārī, Muhammad Ibn Ismāil al- [810–870]. 1903–14. *Les traditions islamique*, translated and annotated by Houdas and Marçais, Publications de l'École des Langues Orientales Vivantes, 4th series; 4 vols. Paris: Imprimerie Nationale.

Caetani, Leone. 1905. *Annali dell' Islam*, vol. 1. Milan: Hoepli.

Dussaud, Rene. 1907. *Les arabes en Syrie avant l'Islam*. Paris: Leroux.

Encyclopedia of Islam. 1913–34. 4 vols. Leiden: Brill.

Essad Bey. 1936. *Mohammed*. New York: Longmans Green.

Fraenkel, Siegmund. 1886. *Die aramäischen Fremdwörter im Arabischen*. Leiden: Brill.

Gibb, H. A. R. 1948. "The Structure of Religious Thought in Islam, Part II: Muhammad and the Quran." *The Muslim World* 38, pp. 113-123.

Goldziher, Ignaz. 1889. *Muhammedanische Studien*. 2 vols. Halle a. S.: Niemeyer.

Grimme, Hubert. 1892. "Mohammed: das Leben." *Darstellungen aus dem Gebiete der Nichtchristlichen Religionsgeschichte*, vol. 7. Munster i. W.: Aschendorffsche Buchhandlung.

Harrison, Paul W. 1924. *The Arabs at Home*. New York: Crowell.

Hell, Joseph. 1933. *Neue Hudailiten-Diwane*. 2 vols. Leipzig: Harrassowitz.

Hirschberg, J. W. 1939. "Jüdische und Christliche Lehren im vorund frühislamischen Arabien." *Polska Akademia Umiejetności, Prace Komisiji Orientalistycznej* 32.

Ḥusain, S. M. 1938. "Early Arabic Odes." *University of Dacca Bulletin* 19.

Ibn Hishām, 'Abd al-Malik [d. 834]. 1864. *Das Leben Mohammeds nach Mohammed Ibn Ishak*, translated by Weil. 2 vols. Stuttgart: Metzler.

Koran. 1937. London: Everyman's Library.

Kremer, Alfred, Freiherr Von. 1875-77. *Culturgeschichte des Orients unter den Chalifen*. 2 vols. Vienna: Braümuller.

Kroeber, Alfred. 1948. *Anthropology*. New York: Harcourt Brace.

Lammens, Henri. 1914. *Le berceau de l'Islam: l'Arabie occidentale à la veille de l'hégire*, vol. 1. Rome: Scripta Pontificii Instituti Biblici.

——. 1924. "La Mecque à la veille de l'hégire." *Mélanges de l'Université Saint Joseph* 9, fasc. 3.

——. 1926. *Islam: Beliefs and Institutions*. New York: Dutton.

——. 1928. *Les chrétiens à la Mecque à la veille de l'hégire: l'Arabie occidentale avant l'hégire*. Beyrouth: Imprimerie Catholique.

Lattimore, Owen. 1940. *Inner Asian Frontiers of China*. New York: American Geographical Society.

Levy, R. 1933. *An Introduction to the Sociology of Islam*. 2 vols. London: Williams and Norgate.

Lyall, Sir Charles J. 1903. "The Words 'Hanif' and 'Muslim.'" *Journal of the Royal Asiatic Society*, pp. 771-784.

Maine, Henry Sumner. 1888. *Ancient Law*. New York: Henry Holt.

Marçais, W. 1928. "L'islamisme et la vie urbaine." *Communication, Comptes Rendus, Académie des Inscriptions et Belles-lettres*, pp. 86-100.

Margoliouth, D. S. 1905. *Mohammed and the Rise of Islam*. New York: Putnam.

Mufaḍḍalīyāt. 1918. *An Anthology of Ancient Arabian Odes, compiled by al-Mufaḍḍal Ibn Muhammad:* Vol. 2, *Translation and Notes*, translated and annotated by Lyall. Oxford: Clarendon Press.

Musil, Alois. 1926. "The Northern Hejaz: A Topographical Itinerary." *American Geographical Society Oriental Explorations and Studies* 1.

——. 1927. "The Middle Euphrates: A Topographical Itinerary." *American Geographical Society Oriental Explorations and Studies* 3.

Nallino, Carlo Alfonso. 1941. *Raccolta di Scritti Editi e Inediti*, Vol. 3: *Storia dell' Arabia Preislamica e Storia e Instituzioni Musulmane*. Rome: Publicazioni dell' Instituto per l'Oriente.

Nielsen, Ditlef, ed. 1927. *Handbuch der altarabischen Altertumskunde*. Copenhagen: Nyt Nordisk Forlag.

Nöldeke, Theodor. 1887. "Die Ghassanischen Fürsten aus dem Hause Gafna." *Abhandlungen, Kaiserliche Preussische Akademie der Wissenschaft zu Berlin, Phil. u. Hist. Klasse* 2.

Olinder, Gunnar. 1927. "The Kings of Kinda of the Family of Akil al-Murār." *Lunds Universitets Årsskrift, Ny Fôljd, Fôrsta Avdelningen* 23, no. 6.

Pedersen, Johs. 1914. "Der Eid bei den Semiten." *Studien zur Geschichte und Kultur des islamischen Orients* 3.

Philby, H. St. J. B. 1947. *The Background of Islam.* Alexandria: Whitehead Morris.

Procksch, Otto. 1899. "Über die Blutrache bei den vorislamischen Arabern und Mohammeds Stellung zu ihr." *Leipziger Studien aus dem Gebiete der Geschichte,* vol. 5, part 4. Leipzig: Teubner.

Rothstein, Gustav. 1899. *Die Dynastie der Lahmiden in al-Hira.* Berlin: Reuther und Reichard.

Smith, William Robertson. 1903. *Kinship and Marriage in Early Arabia.* London: Black.

———. 1927. *Lectures on the Religion of the Semites.* New York: Macmillan.

Snouck Hurgronje, C. 1894. "Mohammed était-il socialiste?" *Rêvue de l'Histoire des Religions* 30, pp. 48–70, 149–178.

Sperber, Jakob. 1916. *Die Schreiben Mohammeds an die Stämme Arabiens.* Berlin: Reichsdruckerei.

Sprenger, Aloys. 1851. *The Life of Mohammed.* Allahabad: Presbyterian Mission Press.

———. 1869. *Das Leben und die Lehre des Mohammed.* 3 vols. Berlin: Nicolai.

Tabarī, Muḥammad Ibn Jarīr al- [839–923]. 1879. *Geschichte der Perser und Araber zur Zeit der Sasaniden,* translated and annotated by Nöldeke. Leiden: Brill.

Torrey, Charles C. 1892. *The Commercial-Theological Terms in the Koran.* Leiden: Brill.

———. 1933. *The Jewish Foundations of Islam.* New York: Jewish Institute of Religion Press.

Von Grunebaum, Gustave E. 1946. *Medieval Islam.* Chicago: University of Chicago Press.

Wākidī, Muḥammad Ibn 'Umar al- [752–829]. 1882. *Muhammed in Medina,* translated and abbreviated by Wellhausen. Berlin: Reimer.

Wellhausen, Julius. 1884–99. *Skizzen und Vorarbeiten.* 6 vols. Berlin: Reimer.

———. 1927. *The Arab Kingdom and Its Fall.* Calcutta: University of Calcutta.

Wittfogel, Karl August. 1932. "Die Entstehung des Staates nach Marx und Engels." In *Festschrift für Carl Grünberg,* pp. 538–551. Leipzig: Hirschfield.

Wüstenfeld, Ferdinand. 1864. *Geschichte der Stadt Mekka nach den arabischen Chroniken,* vol. 4. Leipzig: Brockhaus.

8

COMMUNITY IN MEXICO AND INDONESIA

CLOSED CORPORATE PEASANT COMMUNITIES IN MESOAMERICA AND CENTRAL JAVA

Eric R. Wolf

One of the salient aims of modern anthropology conceived as a science, is to define recurrent sequences of cause and effect, that is, to formulate cultural laws.[1] This paper is concerned with recurrent features in the social, economic, and religious organization of peasant groups in two world areas, widely separated by past history and geographical space: Mesoamerica[2] and Central Java.[3] These have been selected for comparison, because I have some measure of acquaintance with Mesoamerica through field work, and a measure of familiarity with the literature dealing with the two areas.

The cultural configuration which I wish to discuss concerns the organization of peasant groups into closed, corporate communities. By peasant I mean an agricultural producer in effective control of land who carries on agriculture as a means of livelihood, not as a business for profit.[4] In Mesoamerica, as in Central Java, we find such agricultural producers organized into communities with similar characteristics. They are similar in that they maintain a body of rights to possessions, such as land. They are similar because both put pressures on members to redistribute surpluses at their command, preferably in the operation of a religious system, and induce them to content themselves with the rewards of "shared poverty." They are similar in that they strive to prevent outsiders from becoming members of the community, and in placing limits on the ability of members to communicate with the larger society. That is to say, in both areas they are corporate organizations, maintaining a perpetuity of rights and membership; and they are closed corporations, because they limit these privileges to insiders, and discourage close participation of members in the social relations of the larger society.

Outright communal tenure was once general in both areas. In Java, such tenure still survived in a third of all communities in 1927, while land in more than a sixth of all communities was still redistributed annually. Such land consisted of the community's most valuable land, the irrigated rice fields.[5] Yet even where communal tenure has lapsed, jurisdiction over land by the community remains important. Communities may deny or confirm the rights of heirs who have left the village to inherit village lands;[6] they may take back and issue land to someone else if a member leaves the community;[7] or they may take back land issued if a member commits a crime.[8] Aliens may settle in such a community as sharecroppers, but may not inherit or buy the land they work.[9] Community members have priority in the purchase of village lands.[10] And members do not have the right to pledge their land as security.[11]

Estimates concerning the survival of land-holding communities in Meso-america tend to vary greatly. McBride estimated that in Mexico, in 1854, there were some 5,000 "agrarian corporations" in possession of 11.6 million hectares, but that in 1923 land-holding communities survived only in "certain out-of-the-way parts of the country."[12] Tannenbaum, in turn, calculated that in 1910 about 16 percent of all Mexican villages and 51 percent of the rural Mexican population lived in "free villages," that is, villages not included in some large estate.[13] This computation has been criticized by Simpson who follows Luis Cabrera in holding that "by the end of the Díaz regime [in 1910] ... 90 per cent of the villages and towns on the central plateau had no communal lands of any kind."[14] A recent estimate holds that in 1910 41 percent of land-holding communities still maintained communal tenure, though on an illegal basis.[15] Today, there is a general tendency to maintain communal tenure on hillsides and forests, but to grant private ownership over valley bottoms and garden plots.[16] Even in such cases, however, communities can and do prohibit the sale of land to outsiders and limit the right of members to pledge land as a security on loans.[17] In contrast to Central Java, periodic reallotment of land to community members seems to be rather rare in Mesoamerica.[18]

Peasant communities in both areas show strong tendencies to restrict membership in the community to people born and raised within the boundaries of the community. The community is territorial, not kinship-based.[19] Rules of community endogamy further limit the immigration of new personnel. These rules are characteristic of Mesoamerica; they occur only occasionally in Central Java.[20]

Membership in the community is also demonstrated by participation in religious rituals maintained by the community. In Java, each community is charged with the maintenance of proper relations with its spirits and ancestors. The rituals which serve this function cannot be carried on by the individual.[21] Each year the land is ritually purified (*slametan bresih desa*), the community spirit is feasted (*sedekah bum*), and offerings are made to the souls of the dead (*njadran*).[22] The religious official—in the past usually the chief, but nowadays more often the land supervisor and diviner of the community[23]—is looked upon as "a personification of the spiritual relation of the people to their land."[24] In Mesoamerica, there is no evidence of ancestor worship or propitiation as such.[25] Yet each community tends to support the cult of one or more saints. The functions associated with these cults are delegated to members of the community. A man gains social prestige by occupying a series of religious offices charged with these functions; these tend to be ranked in a prescribed ladder of achievement. Often, they carry with them a decisive voice in the political and social affairs of the community.[26] Apparently only members of the community are normally admitted to such religio-political participation.

In both areas, the community motivates its members to expend surpluses in the operation of a prestige economy. The prestige economy operates largely in support of the communal religious cult, and allied religious activities. In Central Java, where cattle are symbolic of land-ownership,[27] wealth is expended conspicuously in cattle sacrifices, as well as in a large number of ritual feasts (*slametans*) offered by private individuals to ward off evil or difficulties, to celebrate special events in the life cycle, to mark holidays, and to emphasize stages in the production of rice.[28] Similarly, pilgrimages to Mecca earn prestige at the cost of large stores of surplus wealth. In 1927, the cost of such a pilgrimage was estimated at 1,000 florin. In that year, 60,000 Indonesians made the voyage, spending 60 million florin in the process, "an enormous sum for so poor a country."[29] In Mesoamerica, adult members of the community generally undertake to finance part of the cult of one or more saints, when they assume religious office. Expenditures may prove economically ruinous, though they earn great social prestige for the spender.[30]

In both areas, we not only encounter a marked tendency to exclude the outsider as a person, but also to limit the flow of outside goods and ideas into the community. This tendency is often ascribed to "inherent peasant conservatism" or to adherence to "static needs," but may actually represent the complex interplay of many factors. Villagers are poor, and unable to buy many new goods. The goods purchased must be functional within peasant life. Peasant needs in both areas are met by marketing systems which serve only the peasantry, and which are organizationally and culturally distinct from other marketing systems within the larger societies to which they belong. Such markets also have similar characteristics. They tend to offer a very high percentage of objects manufactured by peasant labor within the peasant household. They show a high proportion of dealings between primary producers and ultimate consumers. They are characterized by small purchases due to the limited amount of consumer purchasing power. In both areas, moreover, we find regular market days in regional sequence which make for a wide exchange of an assortment of local products, probably much larger than any storekeeper could hope to keep in his store.[31] Such markets can only admit goods which are congruous with these characteristics. The goods sold must be cheap, easily transportable, adaptable to the limited capital of the seller. Only goods such as these will reach the peasant household.

In both areas, moreover, peasant communities maintain strong attitudes against accumulated wealth. In Mesoamerica, display of wealth is viewed with direct hostility. In turn, poverty is praised and resignation in the face of poverty accorded high value.[32] We have seen how much surplus wealth is destroyed or redistributed through participation in the communal religious cult. In Java, there are similar pressures to redistribute wealth: "every prosperous person has to share his wealth right and left; every windfall must be distributed without delay. The village community cannot easily tolerate economic differences but is apt to act as a leveler in this respect, regarding the individual as part of the community."[33] Surplus wealth thus tends to be siphoned off, rather than to be directed towards the purchase of new goods.[34]

It is further necessary to point out that closed corporate peasant communities in both areas are socially and culturally isolated from the larger society in which they exist. The nature of this isolation will be discussed below. This general isolation of the peasant community from the larger society is, however, reinforced by the parochial, localocentric attitudes of the community. In Mesoamerica, each community tends to maintain a relatively autonomous economic, social, linguistic, and politico-religious system, as well as a set of relatively exclusive customs and practices.[35] In Gillin's words, "the Indian universe is spatially limited and its horizon typically does not extend beyond the limits of the local community or region."[36] In Central Java, similarly, each community is a separate sociocultural universe.[37] Such localocentrism is a form of "ignorance [which] performs specifiable functions in social structure and action."[38] It serves to exclude cultural alternatives by limiting the "incentives on the part of individuals of the groups in social interaction to learn the ways of their neighbors, for learning is the psychological crux of acculturation."[39] In Mesoamerica, such exclusion of cultural alternatives[40] is strongest in the area of the *costumbres,* those religious and social features of the community which—in terms of this paper—help to maintain its closed and corporate character.[41] In Java, similarly, communities show a tendency to "preserve a balance by averting and fighting every deviation from the traditional pattern.... When the villager seeks economic contact with western society, he does not enjoy the support of his community. Quite the contrary. By so doing he steps outside the bounds of the community, isolates himself from it, loses its moral support and is thrown on his own resources."[42]

Peasant communities in both areas thus show certain similarities. Both maintain a measure of communal jurisdiction over land. Both restrict their membership, maintain a religious system, enforce mechanisms which ensure the redistribution or destruction of surplus wealth, and uphold barriers against the entry of goods and ideas produced outside the community.[43] These resemblances also mark their differences from other kinds of peasant communities. They form a contrast, for instance, with the "open" peasant communities of Latin America where communal jurisdiction over land is absent, membership is unrestricted, and wealth is not redistributed.[44] They also contrast with the peasant communities of a society like pre-British Uganda where access to scarce land was not an issue, and where local groups consisted of client families, united in temporary allegiance to a common chief by hopes of favors, bounty, and booty in war, yet able to change their residence and to better their life chances through changes in loyalties when these were not forthcoming.[45] Differences also appear when the corporate communities discussed in this paper are compared with the peasant communities of China. In China, free buying and selling of land has been present from early times. Communities are not endogamous and rarely closed to outsiders, even where a single stratified "clan" or *tsu* held sway. Constant circulation of local landowners into the imperial bureaucracy and of officials into local communities where they acquired land prevented the formation of closed communities. Moreover, state controls maintained through control of large-scale water works heavily curtailed the autonomy of the local group. In such a society, relations between individual villagers and individual government officials offered more security and promise than relations among the villagers themselves.[46] Peasants may thus be found organized into many kinds of communities; only some, however, live in closed corporate bodies of the kind described here.

These casual contrasts afford another insight. In each case, the kind of peasant community appears to respond to forces which lie within the larger society to which the community belongs rather than within the boundaries of the community itself. The "open" peasant communities of Latin America "arose in response to the rising demand for cash crops which accompanied the development of capitalism in Europe."[47] Pre-British Uganda was characterized by political instability at the top, considerable personal mobility, and frequent shifts in personal allegiances, all of which found expression in the character of its local groups. Similarly, efforts to understand the peasant community in China purely in its own terms would be foredoomed to failure. These considerations suggest that the causes for the development of closed corporate communities in Mesoamerica and Central Java may derive from the characteristics of the larger societies which gave rise to them.

Historically, the closed corporate peasant configuration in Mesoamerica is a creature of the Spanish Conquest. Authorities differ as to the characteristics of the pre-Hispanic community in the area,[48] but there is general recognition that thoroughgoing changes divide the post-Hispanic community from its preconquest predecessor.[49] In part, the new configuration was the result of serious social and cultural crises which destroyed more than three-quarters of the Indian population, and robbed it of its land and water supply.[50] Population losses and flight prompted colonial measures leading to large-scale resettlement and concentration of population.[51] The new Indian communities were given rights to land as local groups, not kinship-wise;[52] political authority was placed in the hands of new local office holders and made elective;[53] tribute and labor services were placed on a new basis;[54] and "the rapid growth of Indian *cofradías* (sodalities) after the late sixteenth century gave to parishioners a series of organized and stable associations with which personal and communal identification might readily be made."[55] In Java, similarly, corporate peasant communities did not take shape "until after the coming of the Dutch, when for the first time the village as a territorial unit became a moral organism with its own government and its own land at the disposal of its inhabitants."[56] At the time of the Dutch conquest, there was still "an abundance of waste" in Java;[57] slash-and-burn farming was carried on quite generally; population densities averaged only 33.9 persons per km^2.[58] The dosed corporate peasant community in Central Java thus represents an attempt to concentrate both population and tenure rights. "Over the greater part of Java it was only on the introduction of land revenue from 1813 on-wards that villages were reduced to uniformity and their lands bound up into a closed unit, and during this process there were numerous references to the splitting and amalgamation of villages, and to the promotion of hamlets to the status of independent villages."[59]

In the two areas, then, the closed corporate peasant community is a child of conquest; but this need not always be so. The corporate community of pre-1861 Russia, the *mir,* was the product of internal colonization, rather than of foreign domination imposed by force of arms.[60] The corporate peasant community is not an offspring of conquest as such, but rather of the dualization of society into a dominant entrepreneurial sector and a dominated sector of native peasants. This dualization may take place in peaceful as well as in war-like circumstances, and in metropolitan as well as in colonial countries.[61]

Both in Mesoamerica and Central Java, the conquerors occupied the land and proceeded to organize labor to produce crops and goods for sale in newly established markets. The native peasantry did not command the requisite culturally developed skills and resources to participate in the development of large-scale enterprises for profit. In both areas, therefore, the peasantry was forced to supply labor to the new enterprises, but barred from direct participation in the resultant returns. In both areas, moreover, the conquerors also seized control of large-scale trade, and deprived the native population of direct access to sources of wealth acquired through trade, such as they had commanded in the preconquest past.[62]

Yet in both areas, the peasantry—forced to work on colonist enterprises—did not become converted into a permanent labor force. The part-time laborer continued to draw the larger share of his subsistence from his own efforts on the land. From the point of view of the entrepreneurial sector, the peasant sector remained primarily a labor reserve where labor could maintain itself at no cost to the enterprises. This served to maintain the importance of land in peasant life. At the same time, and in both areas, land in the hands of the peasantry had to be limited in amount, or the peasantry would not have pos-sessed sufficient incentive to offer its labor to the entrepreneurial sector. It is significant in this regard that the relation between peasant and entrepre-neur was not "feudal." No economic, political, or legal tie bound a particular peasant to a particular colonist. In the absence of such personal, face-to-face bonds, only changes in the general conditions underlying the entire peasant economy could assure the entrepreneurs of a sufficient seasonal supplement to their small number of resident laborers. This was accomplished in Meso-america in the course of the enforced settlement of the Indian population in nucleated communities during the last decades of the 16th century and the first decade of the 17th. By restricting the amount of land in the hands of each Indian community to six and one-half square miles, the Crown obtained land for the settlement of Spanish colonists.[63] A similar process of limiting the land frontier of the native population was introduced in Java. If access to land thus remained important to the peasantry, land itself became a scarce resource and subject to intense competition, especially when the peasant population began to grow in numbers.

With possibilities for accumulation limited to money wages obtained in part-time employment and to occasional sales of agricultural produce or products of home crafts at low prices, peasant agriculture remained needs dependent on the expenditure of labor, a labor furnished by growing numbers of people living off a limited or decreasing amount of land. The technology of the peasantry thus remained labor intensive when compared with the capital-intensive and equipment-intensive colonist enterprises. Peasant technology is often described as "backward" or "tradition bound," in disregard of many items such as secondhand Singer sewing machines, steel needles, iron pots, nails, tin cans, factory-woven goods, aniline dyes and paints, etc. which may be found in the peasant inventory. It is backward only because the peasant is a captive of the labor-intensive technology with which he must operate. He must always weigh the adoption of a new good against the balance of his resources. This balance includes not only financial or technical resources, but also "resources in people" to whom he must maintain access by maintaining proper cultural behavior. These human relations he could only disregard at the price of sharply increasing life risks. The labor-intensive technology in turn limits the amounts and kinds of technological change and capitalization which he can afford, as well as his consumption and his needs.

The social and economic dualization of postconquest Mesoamerica and Java was also accompanied in both areas by dualization in the administra-tive sphere. By placing the native communities under the direct jurisdiction of a special corps of officials responsible to the home government rather than to officials set up by the colonists, the home government attempted to maintain control over the native population and to deny this control to the colonists. By granting relative autonomy to the native communities, the home government could at one and the same time ensure the maintenance of cultural barriers against colonist encroachment, while avoiding the huge cost of direct administration. Thus, in Mesoamerica, the Crown insisted on the spatial separation of native peasants and colonists,[64] and furthered the organization of the native population into nucleated communities with their own relatively autonomous government. It charged these native authori-ties with the right and duty to collect tribute, organize corvée labor and to

exercise formal and informal sanctions in the maintenance of peace and order.[65] In Java, the government relied from the beginning on the cooperation
of the autonomous communities, by making use of the traditional channels
of intermediate chieftainship. Administrative "contact with village society
was limited to a minimum."[66] After a period characterized by emphasis on
individualism and distrust of native communalism during the second half of
the 19th century, the Dutch administration reverted to reliance on the closed
corporate peasant community at the beginning of the 20th century.[67]

Once the dualized system of administration began to operate, however,
the colonists themselves found that they could often use it to their own advantage. In Central Java the sugar industry has preferred to rent land in block
from native villages, and to draw on the total supply of labor in the village,
rather than to make deals with individual villagers. Since sugar can be rotated
with rice, such rental agreements have usually specified that sugar cultivation by the colonist enterprise could be followed by food production on the
same land by native peasants in an orderly rotational cycle. Thus "the sugar
cultivation of the estates and the rice and other cultivations of the population are, as it were, coordinated in one large-scale agricultural enterprise,
the management of which is practically in the hands of the sugar factory."[68]
In the last years before World War II, the total area of land rented from native corporate communities did not exceed 100,000 hectares or 3 percent
of irrigated rice land. In boom years it might have been 6 percent. But sugar
production was concentrated in Central Java, and there covered a large part of
the arable area.[69] I have argued elsewhere that a somewhat similar symbiotic
relation between corporate peasant community and colonist enterprise can
be discovered in Mesoamerica. There even the voracious haciendas reached
a point in their growth where absorption of corporate peasant communities
into the estates put too great a strain on the control mechanisms at their
disposal, and where they found systematic relations with such communities
on their borders beneficial and useful.[70]

Within the native sector, administrative charges in both areas were thus
placed largely on the community as a whole, and only secondarily on the
individual. This was especially true of tribute payments and labor services.
In Central Java the demands on land-holders became so great

> that land-holding was no longer a privilege but a burden which occupants tried
> to share with others. . . . Again, in many parts of Java, the liability to service on
> public works was confined by custom to land-holders; and, as officials wished
> to increase the number of hands available for public works, and the people
> themselves wished to distribute and reduce the burden of service on such
> works, it was to the interest of both officials and land-holders that the occupa-
> tion of land should be widely shared. This encouraged communal possession
> and obliterated hereditary social distinctions.[71]

In Mesoamerica also, tribute and labor charges were imposed on the whole
community during the 16th and 17th centuries. Only around the beginning

of the 18th century were they charged to individuals.[72] The constant decrease
of the Indian population until the mid-17th century, the flight of Indians into
remote refuge areas, the exodus of Indians to the northern periphery of
Mesoamerica and to permanent settlements on colonist enterprises all left
the fixed tribute payments and corvée charges in the hands of the remnant
population. It is reasonable to suppose that these economic pressures accelerated tendencies towards greater egalitarianism and leveling, in Mesoamerica
as in Java. It is possible that the disappearance of status distinctions between
nobles and commoners and the rise of religious sodalities as dispensers of
wealth in religious ceremonial were in part consequences of this leveling
tendency.

It is my contention that the closed corporate peasant community in both
areas represents a response to these several characteristics of the larger society. Relegation of the peasantry to the status of part-time laborers, providing for their own subsistence on scarce land, together with the imposition
of charges levied and enforced by semiautonomous local authorities, tends
to define the common life situation which confronts the peasantry of both
societies. The closed corporate peasant community is an attempt to come
to grips with this situation. Its internal function, as opposed to its external
function in the social, economic, and political web of the dualized society,
is to equalize the life chances and life risks of its members.

The life risks of a peasantry are raised by any threat to its basic source of
livelihood, the land, and to the produce which is raised on that land. These
threats come both from within and without the community. Natural population increase within the community would serve to decrease the amount of
land available to members of the community, as would unrestricted purchase
and hoarding of land by individual community members. Thus, as long as
possible, closed corporate peasant communities will tend to push off surplus
population into newly formed daughter villages. More importantly, however,
they will strive to force comembers to redistribute or to destroy any pool of
accumulated wealth which could potentially be used to alter the land tenure
balance in favor of a few individual families or individuals. Purchase of goods
produced outside the peasant sector of society and their ostentatious display
also rank as major social threats, since they are prima facie evidence of an unwillingness to continue to redistribute and destroy such accumulated surplus.
They are indications of an unwillingness to share the life risks of fellow villagers according to traditional cultural patterns. Among most peasant groups,
as indeed among most social groups anywhere, social relations represent a
sort of long-term life insurance. The extension of goods and services at any
given moment is expected to yield results in the future, in the form of help
in case of threat. Departure from the customary distribution of risks, here
signaled by a departure from the accepted disposal of surpluses, is a cause
for immediate concern for the corporately organized peasantry, and for its
immediate opposition. Similarly, unrestricted immigration and unrestricted
purchase of land by outsiders would both serve to decrease the amount of

land available to community members, as it would endanger the pattern of distribution of risks developed by community members over time. Hence the maintenance of strong defenses against the threatening outsider. It must be emphasized that these defenses are required, because the closed corporate community is situated within a dualized capitalist society. They are neither simple "survivals," nor the results of "culture lag," nor due to some putative tendency to conservatism said to be characteristic of all culture. They do not illustrate the "contemporaneousness of the noncontemporaneous." They exist, because their functions *are* contemporaneous.

This is not to say that their defensive functions are ultimately adequate to the challenge. The disappearance of closed corporate peasant communities where they have existed in the past, and the lessening number of surviving communities of this type, testify to the proposition that in the long run they are incapable of preventing change. Internal population surpluses can be pushed off into daughter villages only as long as new land is available. Retained within the boundaries of the community, they exercise ever-increasing pressure on its capacity to serve the interests of its members. The corporate community may then be caught in a curious dilemma: it can maintain its integrity only if it can sponsor the emigration and urbanization or proletarianization of its sons. If the entrepreneurial sector is unable to accept these newcomers, these truly "marginal" men will come to represent a double threat: a threat to their home community into which they introduce new ways and needs; and a threat to the peace of the nonpeasant sector which they may undermine with demands for social and economic justice, often defended with the desperation of men who have but little to lose.

Secondly, while the closed corporate peasant community operates to diminish inequalities of risks, it can never eliminate them completely. Individual member families may suffer losses of crops, livestock, or other assets through accident or mismanagement. Some member families may be exceedingly fertile and have many mouths to feed, while others are infertile and able to get along with little. Individuals whose life risks are suddenly increased due to the play of some such factor must seek the aid of others who can help them. Some of these risks can be met through the culturally standardized social relations of mutual aid and support; some, however, will strain these relations beyond their capacity. Individuals may then in desperation seek aid from members of their community or from outsiders whose aid is tinged with self-interest. It would seem that even the most efficient prestige economy cannot be counted on to dispose of all surplus wealth in the community. Pools of such wealth tend to survive in the hands of local figures, such as political leaders, or nobles, or usurers, or storekeepers. Such individuals are often exempt from the everyday controls of the local community, because they occupy a privileged position within the economic or political apparatus of the larger society; or they are people who are willing to pay the price of social ostracism for the rewards of a pursuit of profit and power. Such individuals offer the needy peasant a chance to reduce his risks momentarily through loans or favors. In turn, the peasant in becoming their client, strengthens the degree of relative autonomy and immunity which they enjoy in the community. Such internal alliances must weaken communal defenses to a point where the corporate organization comes to represent but a hollow shell, or is swept aside entirely.[73]

Notes

1. This paper represents an effort to contribute to the aims and methods of the Project for Research on Cross-Cultural Regularities, directed by Julian Steward at the University of Illinois. The writer was Research Associate of the Project from 1954-55. He is grateful for comments and suggestions to Julian Steward, Robert Murphy, and Charles Erasmus, as well as to those friends of the Project who heard a reading of a first draft of this paper at the Symposium on Cross-Cultural Regularities, held at the University of Illinois on June 16th, 1955.

2. For a definition of Mesoamerica in culture area terms, see Kirchhoff, 1952, pp. 17-30. In this paper, the term is used as shorthand for Mexican and Guatemalan communities which conform to the configuration discussed. See Wolf, 1955, pp. 456-461.

3. Central Java is a region of rice-growing nucleated villages with a tendency to communal land tenure. It was also the main center of commercial sugar and indigo production which promoted communal tenure and dense populations. Western Java is characterized by cattle-breeding rather than by agriculture; Eastern Java is occupied by small hamlets, scattered among individually held rice fields (Furnivall, 1939, p. 386). Central Java is used as shorthand for Javanese communities which conform to the configuration discussed.

4. Wolf, 1955, pp. 453-454.

5. Boeke, 1953, p. 65.

6. S'Jacob, 1951, p. 144.

7. Haar, 1948, p. 85; Oei, 1948, pp. 24-25.

8. Haar, 1948, p. 85.

9. Haar, 1948, p. 119; S'Jacob, 1951, p. 143.

10. Boeke, 1953, p. 31; Haar, 1948, p. 97.

11. Haar, 1948, p. 113.

12. McBride, 1923, pp. 133, 135.

13. Tannenbaum, 1929, pp. 30-37.

14. Simpson, 1937, p. 31.

15. González Navarro, 1954, p. 129.

16. Aguirre and Pozas, 1954, pp. 192-198; Carrasco, 1951, pp. 101-102; Tax, 1952, p. 61.

17. Aguirre, 1952a, p. 149; Carrasco, 1951, p. 102; Carrasco, 1952, p. 17; Lewis, 1951, p. 124; Tax, 1953, pp. 68-69; Wagley, 1941, p. 65.

18. Tax, 1952, p. 60.

19. Haar, 1948, pp. 51, 71; Lekkerkerker, 1938, p. 568; Guiteras, 1952, pp. 99-100; Redfield and Tax, 1952, p. 33.

20. Haar, 1948, p. 155; Redfield and Tax, 1952, p. 31.

21. S'Jacob, 1951, p. 140.

22. Haar, 1948, pp. 24, 28; Kattenburg, 1951, p. 16; Ploegsma, 1936, p. 4; Supatmo, 1943, p. 9.

23. Haar, 1948, pp. 91-92.

24. Ibid.

25. I should like to express a guess that further field work might reverse this statement. It is possible, for instance, that the cemetery plays a much greater symbolic role in Mesoamerican life than is generally suspected. The Mazatec of the Papaloapan River valley, about to be resettled, took great care to transfer the bones of their dead from their old to their new villages (Pozas, personal communication). The annual feast of the dead may have more communal function than is generally assumed.

26. Camara, 1952; Redfield and Tax, 1952, pp. 36-38.

27. Boeke, 1953, p. 46.

28. Geertz, 1956, pp. 138-140; Landon, 1949, pp. 156-158; Supatmo, 1943, p. 9.

29. Vandenbosch, 1942, p. 27.

30. Aguirre, 1952a, pp. 234-242; Camara, 1952, pp. 155-157.

31. Re Java, see Boeke, 1953, pp. 48, 75; Lekkerkerker, 1938, pp. 728-729; Ploegsma, 1936, p. 24. Re Mesoamerica, see Foster, 1948, p. 154; Pozas, 1952, pp. 326-338; Whetten, 1948, pp. 357-360. Whetten's account is a summary of a manuscript by B. Malinowski and Julio de la Fuente, entitled "The Economics of a Mexican Market System," which unfortunately has never been published.

32. See e.g., Carrasco, 1952, pp. 47, 48; Lewis, 1951, p. 54; Tumin, 1950, p. 198; Tumin, 1952, pp. 85-94.

33. Boeke, 1953, p. 34. See also Geertz, 1956, p. 141.

34. See Kroef, 1956, p. 124.

35. Redfield and Tax, 1952, p. 31; Tax, 1941, p. 29.

36. Gillin, 1952, p. 197.

37. Ploegsma, 1936, p. 5.

38. Moore and Tumin, 1949, p. 788.

39. Hallowell, 1955, p. 319.

40. Linton, 1936, pp. 282-283; Moore and Tumin, 1949, p. 791.

41. Beals, 1952, pp. 229-232. See also Beals, 1946, p. 211.

42. Boeke, 1953, p. 29, p. 51.

43. Communities in both areas are also characterized by a tendency to nuclear rather than extended family organization, and by a tendency to divide access to land equally among the filial generation (Haar, 1948, p. 71; Kattenburg, 1951, p. 10; Redfield and Tax, 1952, p. 33; Aguirre and Pozas, 1954, pp. 181-182). I have not discussed these similarities in this paper, because I feel that closed corporate community organization can coexist with various kinds of families and various systems of inheritance, as long as these do not imply loss of land to outsiders. This will be the case, for instance, even where we have extended families or lineages, as long as only sons inherit rights to land and residence after marriage remains patrilocal.

44. Wolf, 1955, pp. 461-466.

45. Roscoe, 1911, pp. 13, 269.

46. See e.g., Fei, 1953; Fried, 1953; Fukutake, 1951; Hu, 1948, p. 91; Wittfogel, 1935; Wittfogel, 1938; Yang, 1945, pp. 132-142.

47. Wolf, 1955, p. 462.

48. For a recent statement of conflicting views, see Monzón, 1949.

49. For a masterly exposition of these changes, see Gibson, 1955.
50. E.g. Wolf and Palerm, 1955, pp. 277-278.
51. Zavala and Miranda, 1954, pp. 39-41.
52. Idem, pp. 70-74.
53. Idem, p. 80; Aguirre, 1952b; Gibson, 1955, pp. 588-591.
54. Zavala and Miranda, 1954, pp. 85-88; Miranda, 1952.
55. Gibson, 1955, p. 600.
56. Furnivall, 1939, p. 13.
57. Idem, p. 12.
58. Klaveren, 1953, p. 152.
59. Furnivall, 1939, p. 11.
60. See e.g., Sïmkhovitsch, 1898, pp. 46-81.
61. The concept of a "dual" structure of colonial societies has been advanced by Boeke, 1953. It is not necessary to subscribe to all parts of the author's theory, nor to his predictions regarding the future, to appreciate the utility of his concept in the analysis of social and cultural systems.
62. For Java, see Furnivall, 1939, pp. 43-44; Kolff, 1929, p. 111; Leur, 1955, p. 92; Schrieke, 1955, pp. 3-79; for Mesoamerica, see Gibson, 1955, pp. 586-587.
63. Zavala and Miranda, 1954, p. 73.
64. Zavala and Miranda, 1954, pp. 38-39.
65. Aguirre, 1952b, p. 291; Chávez Orozco, 1943, p. 8; Gibson, 1955, p. 590; Zavala and Miranda, 1954, p. 82.
66. Kroef, 1953, p. 201. See also Furnivall, 1939, pp. 118, 126, 217.
67. Furnivall, 1939, pp. 182-187, 294-295.
68. Kolff, 1929, p. 111. See also Haar, 1948, p. 85; Kolff, 1929, pp. 122-124; Pieters, 1951, p. 130; S'Jacob, 1951, pp. 144-145.
69. Pieters, 1951, p. 131.
70. Wolf, 1956.
71. Furnivall, 1939, pp. 140-141.
72. Zavala and Miranda, 1954, p. 85.
73. Wolf, 1956.

References

Aguirre Beltrán, Gonzalo. 1952a. "Problemas de la población indígena de la cuenca del Tepalcatepec." Memorias del Instituto Nacional Indigenista no. 3.
———. 1952b. "El gobierno indígena en México y el proceso de aculturación." *America Indígena* 12, pp. 271-297.
Aguirre Beltrán, Gonzalo, and Ricardo Pozas Arciniegas. 1954. "Instituciones indígenas en el México actual." In Caso et al., *Métodos y resultados de la política indigenista en México,* pp. 171-272, Memorias del Instituto Nacional Indigenista no. 6.
Beals, Ralph. 1946. *Cherán: A Sierra Tarascan Village.* Smithsonian Institute of Social Anthropology, Publication 2.
———. 1952. "Notes on Acculturation." In Tax, ed., *Heritage of Conquest,* pp. 225-231. Glencoe: Free Press.
Boeke, J. H. 1953. *Economics and Economic Policy of Dual Societies as Exemplified by Indonesia.* New York: Institute of Pacific Relations.

Cámara Barbachano, Fernando. 1952. "Religious and Political Organization." In Tax, ed., *Heritage of Conquest,* pp. 142-164. Glencoe: Free Press.

Carrasco, Pedro. 1951. "Las culturas indígenas de Oaxaca, México." *American Indígena* 11, pp. 99-114.

———. 1952. *Tarascan Folk Religion: An Analysis of Economic, Social and Religious Interactions.* Middle American Research Institute, Publication 17.

Chávez Orozco, Luis. 1943. *Las instituciones democráticas de los indígenas Mexicanos en la época colonial.* México, D.F.: Ediciones del Instituto Indigenista Interamericano.

Fei, Hsiao-tung. 1953. *China's Gentry.* Chicago: University of Chicago Press.

Foster, George M. 1948. "The Folk Economy of Rural Mexico with Special Reference to Marketing." *Journal of Marketing* 12, pp. 153-162.

Fried, Morton H. 1953. *Fabric of Chinese Society.* New York: Praeger.

Fukutake, Tadashi. 1951. *Chugoku Noson Shakai no Kozo* [Structure of Chinese Rural Society]. Tokyo: Yūhikaku Publishing.

Furnivall, J. S. 1939. *Netherlands India: A Study of Plural Economy.* Cambridge: Cambridge University Press.

Geertz, Clifford. 1956. "Religious Belief and Economic Behavior in a Central Javanese Town." *Economic Development and Cultural Change* 4, pp. 134-158.

Gibson, Charles. 1955. "The Transformation of the Indian Community in New Spain 1500-1810." *Journal of World History* 2, pp. 581-607.

Gillin, John. 1952. "Ethos and Cultural Aspects of Personality." In Tax, ed., *Heritage of Conquest,* pp. 193-212. Glencoe: Free Press.

González Navarro, Moisés. 1954. "Instituciones indígenas en México Independiente." In Caso et al., *Métodos y resultados de la política indigenista en México,* pp. 113-169, Memorias del Institute Nacional Indigenista no. 6.

Guiteras Holmes, Calixta. 1952. "Social Organization." In Tax, ed., *Heritage of Conquest,* pp. 97-108. Glencoe: Free Press.

Haar, B. ter. 1948. *Adatlaw in Indonesia.* New York: Institute of Pacific Relations.

Hallowell, A. Irving. 1955. *Culture and Experience.* Philadelphia: University of Pennsylvania Press.

Hu, Hsien Chin. 1948. *The Common Descent Group in China and Its Functions.* Viking Fund Publications in Anthropology no. 10.

Kattenburg, Paul. 1951. *A Central Javanese Village in 1950.* Cornell University Department of Far Eastern Studies, Data Paper 2.

Kirchhoff, Paul. 1952. "Mesoamerica." In Tax, ed., *Heritage of Conquest,* pp. 17-30. Glencoe: Free Press.

Klaveren, J. J. Van. 1953. *The Dutch Colonial System in the East Indies.* Rotterdam: Drukkerij Benedictus.

Kolff, G. H. Van der. 1929. "European Influence on Native Agriculture." In Schrieke, ed., *The Effect of Western Influence on Native Civilizations in the Malay Archipelago,* pp. 103-125. Batavia: Kolff.

Kroef, Justus M. van der. 1953. "Collectivism in Indonesian Society." *Social Research* 20, pp. 193-209.

———. 1956. "Economic Development in Indonesia: Some Social and Cultural Implications." *Economic Development and Cultural Change* 4, pp. 116-133.

Landon, Kenneth Perry. 1949. *Southeast Asia: Crossroad of Religions.* Chicago: University of Chicago Press.

Lekkerkerker, Cornelis. 1938. *Land en Volk Van Java.* Groningen-Batavia: Wolters.

Leur, Jacob Cornelis Van der. 1955. *Indonesian Trade and Society: Essay in Asian Social and Economic History.* The Hague-Bandung: W. Van Hoeve.

Lewis, Oscar. 1951. *Life in a Mexican Village: Tepoztlán Revisited.* Urbana: University of Illinois Press.

Linton, Ralph. 1936. *The Study of Man.* New York: Appleton-Century.

McBride, George McCutchen. 1923. *The Land Systems of Mexico.* New York: American Geographical Society.

Miranda, Jose. 1952. *El tributo indígena en la Nueva España durante el siglo XVI.* México, D.F.: El Colegio de México.

Monzón, Arturo. 1949. *El Calpulli en la organización social de los Tenochca.* México, D.F.: Instituto de Historia.

Moore, Wilbert E., and Melvin M. Tumin. 1949. "Some Social Functions of Ignorance." *American Sociological Review* 14, pp. 787-795.

Oei, Tjong Bo. 1948. *Niederländisch-Indien: Eine Wirtschaftsstudie.* Zürich: Institut Orell Füssli A.G.

Pieters, J. M. 1951. "Land Policy in the Netherlands East Indies before the Second World War." In Afrika Instituut Leiden, org., *Land Tenure Symposium Amsterdam 1950,* pp. 116-139. Leiden: Universitaure Pers Leiden.

Ploegsma, Nicolas Dirk. 1936. *Oorspronkelijkheid en Economisch Aspect van het Dorp op Java en Madoera.* Leiden: Antiquariaat J. Ginsberg.

Pozas Arciniegas, Ricardo. 1952. "La situation économique et financière de l'Indien Américain." *Civilization* 2, pp. 309-329.

Redfield, Robert, and Sol Tax. 1952. "General Characteristics of Present-Day Meso-american Indian Society." In Tax, ed., *Heritage of Conquest,* pp. 31-39. Glencoe: Free Press.

Roscoe, John. 1911. *The Baganda.* London: Macmillan.

Schrieke, Bertram J. O. 1955. *Indonesian Sociological Studies.* The Hague: W. Van Hoeve.

Simkhovitsch, Wladimir Gr. 1898. *Die Feldgemeinschaft in Russland.* Jena: Fischer.

Simpson, Eyler N. 1937. *The Ejido: Mexico's Way Out.* Chapel Hill: University of North Carolina Press.

S'Jacob, E. H. 1951. "Observations on the Development of Landrights in Indonesia." In Afrika Instituut Leiden, org., *Land Tenure Symposium Amsterdam 1950,* pp. 140-146. Leiden: Universitaure Pers Leiden.

Supatmo, Raden. 1943. *Animistic and Religious Practices of the Javanese.* New York: East Indies Institute of America, mimeo.

Tannenbaum, Frank. 1929. *The Mexican Agrarian Revolution.* Washington, DC: Brookings Institution.

Tax, Sol. 1941. "World View and Social Relations in Guatemala." *American Anthropologist* 43, pp. 27-42.

———. 1952. "Economy and Technology." In Tax, ed., *Heritage of Conquest,* pp. 43-65. Glencoe: Free Press.

———. 1953. *Penny Capitalism: A Guatemalan Indian Economy.* Smithsonian Institution Institute of Social Anthropology, Publication 16.

Tumin, Melvin M. 1950. "The Hero and the Scapegoat in a Peasant Community." *Journal of Personality* 19, pp. 197-211.

———. 1952. *Caste in a Peasant Society.* Princeton: Princeton University Press.

Vandenbosch, A. 1942. *The Dutch East Indies.* Berkeley: University of California Press.

Wagley, Charles. 1941. *Economics of a Guatemalan Village.* Memoirs, American Anthropological Association, no. 58.

Whetten, Nathan L. 1948. *Rural Mexico.* Chicago: University of Chicago Press.

Wittfogel, Karl A. 1935. "Foundations and Stages of Chinese Economic History." *Zeitschrift für Sozialforschung* 4, pp. 26–60.

————. 1938. "Die Theorie der Orientalischen Gesellschaft." *Zeitschrift für Sozialforschung* 7, pp. 90–122.

Wolf, Eric R. 1955. "Types of Latin American Peasantry." *American Anthropologist* 57, pp. 452–471.

————. 1956. "Aspects of Group Relations in a Complex Society: Mexico." *American Anthropologist* 58, pp. 1065–1078.

Wolf, Eric R., and Angel Palerm. 1955. "Irrigation in the Old Acolhua Domain, Mexico." *Southwestern Journal of Anthropology* 11, pp. 265–281.

Yang, Martin. 1945. *A Chinese Village: Taitou, Shantung Province.* New York: Columbia University Press.

Zavala, Silvio, and José Miranda. 1954. "Instituciones indígenas en la Colonia." In Caso et al., *Métodos y resultados de la política indigenista en México,* pp. 29–169, Memorias del Institute Nacional Indigenista no. 6.

9

HOUSEHOLD TO FIRM
IN ICELAND

PEASANTS, ENTREPRENEURS,
AND COMPANIES: THE EVOLUTION
OF ICELANDIC FISHING

E. Paul Durrenberger and Gísli Pálsson

The fisheries of the world have seen spectacular developments during the last decades.[1] Fishermen and others who depend on the living resources of the sea have entered a new era. New technology has been introduced for exploiting the sea, altering the bases of social interaction. Some aspects of the modernization process have already been explored in the growing body of anthropological literature on maritime adaptations (see, for example Maiolo and Orbach [eds.] 1982, Andersen [ed.] 1979, Andersen and Wadel [eds.] 1972, Smith [ed.] 1977, Spoehr [ed.] 1980).

The modernization of the fisheries in the North Atlantic is manifested at many levels of social organization. This is especially apparent in the case of Iceland where fishing products provide the major link with the international market. The fact that fishing is the major economic activity in Iceland makes Iceland unique in Scandinavia. There are no other alternatives. In this article we shall describe the emergence and development of capitalist production in Icelandic fishing. We demonstrate that a number of factors triggered a "revolution" in the Icelandic fisheries late in the nineteenth century. The result was multiplied catch, new relations of production and new centres of activity. We also show that the relative importance of the two kinds of production units which emerged, the petty entrepreneur and the firm, has varied considerably since the beginning of this century, largely as a result of structural changes which altered the balance between capital and labor. These major structural changes can in turn be seen as responses to changing conditions in the summer fishing for herring during the 1940's and 1950's. Finally, we discuss the reasons for the persistence of the petty entrepreneur, arguing that in order to account fully for the resiliency of small-scale fishermen one has to consider the long-term strategies of the production units involved as well as seasonal fluctuations in the availability of resources.

Most of the statistical and ethnographic material used in this article relates to the village of Sandgerði, near Keflavik, on the western coast of the Reykjanes peninsula of Iceland. We use this material as an example of processes that affected all of Iceland.

The village of Sandgerði and the surrounding area form one political and administrative unit—the Miðnes commune. The population of the village was 1153 in 1981. Only a small fraction of the population of the commune lives outside of the fishing village and most of the people participate in the fishing industry.

When the first census was taken in 1703 seven households formed a cluster which was called *Sandgerðishverfi*—the hamlet at Sandgerði. The amount of cultivable land on the peninsula is limited. Households tended to form clusters around small bays where open rowing boats could be safely taken ashore. Until the beginning of this century the landowners and tenants at Sandgerði fished nearby waters in such boats. Cod was then, and still is, the main species exploited during the winter season.

The first motorboat came to Sandgerði in 1907. In the 20's the number of boats operating from the locality increased at a fast rate. Earlier, fisherman and workers often left the locality when the winter season was over. With the development of the fishing industry the village at Sandgerði was founded. In the 50's and 60's the fishing industry changed radically. Boats became larger and harbor facilities and processing plants were improved. Reduced seasonal fluctuations in fishing and fish processing further encouraged the permanent residence of fishermen and workers.

At present, only part of the catch landed at Sandgerði is processed locally. The rest is transported to other areas. Most of the fish caught during the winter season is frozen, salted or dried.

During the 1981 winter season, 46 "local" vessels were stationed at Sandgerði. The term "local boats" is used by the fishermen to refer to those which regularly land their catches in Sandgerði. Of the local vessels 40 fish with either longlines or gill nets. Usually these boats use longlines from the beginning of the winter season in January until February or March. Then the gill nets are taken aboard, because by that time cod are expected to turn their attention from bait to natural prey. The nets are used for the rest of the season which ends at the beginning of May. The boats that follow this pattern are called "seasonal boats" and usually land their catches day by day. There are also two stern trawlers and four smaller trawling vessels which stay out for several days at a time.

From earliest times, the winter season has been the most important part of the fishing year. Fishermen and the general public speak of it as "the season," (*vertíðin*). The contrast between the different seasons has been lessened in recent years, partly because of the introduction of stern trawlers which minimize seasonal fluctuations in catch, and partly because of the management regulations imposed by the State. Nevertheless, the seasonal idiom is still highly significant. During recent years approximately 70 percent of the annual catch has been caught in the winter season from January until May.

From Household Production to Capitalism

Iceland was under Danish rule from the 13th Century until 1918 when it got home rule or 1944 when it got full independence. The earliest systematic data available on traditional household production is that given in the census in 1703 (*Manntal 1703, Jarðabók Árna Magnússonar og Páls Vídalíns*). Magnússon's (1935-36) description of the Gullbringu-County in southwest Iceland from the late eighteenth century is also informative. There were thirty people (seven household units) in the Sangerði-hamlet in 1703. The land (approximately 9 hectares) was owned by the family on the main farm, Sandgerði. The six tenant households paid their rent in fish, butter and services.

The growing season in Iceland has been too short for any major crop but grass during the past six hundred years or more. Agriculture has therefore centered on sheep and dairy production. The sea provided an important source of income. Kristjánsson observes (1980: 441) that "it seems to have been evident already in the 10th century that when the sea failed to yield the means of subsistence, the result was famine." Due to the limited grazing areas on the barren southwest coast this applied even more to the producers at Sandgerði, than to many other parts of the country.

Boats could only be taken safely ashore on a narrow stretch of land. Most often the landowner owned the fishing boats, but from time to time tenants rowed on their own boats. Usually the landowner or one of his sons was in control during fishing operations. In addition to him (the "foreman"— *formaður*) the crew included tenants and laborers. From 1783 to 1894 law required landless people to work for landowners for one year at a time. Magnússon's account (1935–36) indicates that in the late eighteenth century approximately 60 percent of the local catch during the winter season was exported from Iceland.

For a number of reasons peasants did not accumulate capital. Given the low level of technological development, the periodic worsening of climate reduced the size of livestock holdings and the number of opportunities for making fishing trips, leading to chronic and absolute scarcities of food. When surpluses could be produced, they were siphoned off through the relations of mercantile colonialism. From 1602 to 1787 Danish merchants monopolized the trade with Icelanders. Able to produce but a part of their means of production and subsistence, the peasants had to buy many foreign goods. Icelanders imported timber and handlines as well as grain. These goods could only be obtained by selling fish to colonial merchants. During most of the colonial era the right to trade with Icelanders was sold to the highest bidders at auctions in Copenhagen. Each producer was compelled to sell his products to one particular merchant who determined the terms of trade in his district.

Fishing returns were proportional to inputs of labor. Sustaining labor required working the land for livestock production. Availability of land thus limited the size of the labor force and put a ceiling on fishing production.

Moreover, accumulation was limited by landlord-tenant relations. The tenancy laws prevented entrepreneurial activity. It was unlawful to employ landless people for daily wages. Law required every landless person to form an annual contract with a landowner. Early in the fifteenth century small fishing villages emerged where foreign fishermen, mainly English and German, had established permanent bases of operation. These new centres were a potential attraction to laborers from the countryside. This was against the interests of the landowners. Soon they managed to ban all foreign permanent fishing operations from Icelandic harbors (Porsteinsson 1970). In 1783 the tenancy laws were enacted. Thereby the landowners gained increased control over landless people (approximately a quarter of the population). The legally enforced labor service contracts (*vistarband*) gave institutional form to patron-client relationships.

During the centuries the technical and ecological constraints on household production have varied considerably. The terms of trade have also varied through time, depending on market conditions and colonial relations. Around the middle of the 18th century two-oar boats were replacing larger ones. One commentator (Magnússon 1935–36) argues that this was due to the peasants' "stubborn individualism" and their "inability to rule and obey" (p. 158). Danish law from 1758 actually required Icelandic fishermen to use larger boats which were supposed to be safer and more economical. Presumably the purpose of the law was also to increase the production and export of fish. The proportion of small boats seems to have increased because of changes in colonial relations and not because of some psychological disposition (see Ólafsson 1942: 445). The import of timber declined due to strengthened colonial ties, and as timber was scarce larger boats were not replaced by new ones in the long run.

During the struggle for independence late in the nineteenth century Icelandic nationalists encouraged peasants to increase production and acquire new technology and knowledge. Peasants were regarded as ignorant and conservative. The main leader of the nationalist revival addressed fishermen in a pamphlet which provided practical information on fishing gear and boat technology. "It's about time," he said, "that you use all your power to participate in the progress which the land and the ocean invite" (Sigurðsson 1859: 4–5). Such efforts encouraged innovation which increased the productivity of labor, but the main impetus for the structural changes in the economy lay elsewhere.

With the relaxation of Danish trade monopolies in 1787 local capital accumulation became possible. Icelandic merchants replaced the Danish ones and invested in boats and fishing gear. In the nineteenth century new markets for

Icelandic saltfish were developed, especially in Spain and England. Fishing villages grew up along with the emergence of capitalist relations of production. As the labor market developed the patron-client bond between landowners and landless workers weakened until it was finally abolished in 1894.

At the beginning of this century several attempts were made to establish fishing firms in Iceland. Local merchants often formed share holding companies to pool Danish and Icelandic capital. One of these companies, "The Icelandic-Faroes Company" rented the bay at Sandgerði from the landowner in 1908 and had several motor boats fishing from there. Being near the rich fishing grounds off the southwest coast, Sandgerði attracted several investors. The Icelandic-Faroes Company, however, went bankrupt. The reason, according to the Icelandic manager of the company (Þórðarson 1946: 123), was that the Danish crews were inexperienced. The boat engines often failed and could not be repaired locally, and the price of fish was low. An Icelandic merchant bought the station at Sandgerði and continued to improve harbor facilities. The merchant hired local laborers to fish on their boats and process the catch. In 1913 and 1914 two merchants from Akranes in West Iceland rented the fishing stations at Sandgerði. In 1918 each of them bought his share of the land. In subsequent decades they built up large fishing firms employing several hundred people during the winter season.

In 1916 the merchants owned between them approximately 10 boats, either on their own or together with local foremen (Hagalín 1964, II: 52). At that time approximately 40 boats were stationed at Sandgerði. During the winter season in 1919 approximately 80 guest boats in addition to the boats regularly stationed at Sandgerði used the services of the merchant (Guðmundsson 1981: 35). As the productivity of fishing greatly increased with the introduction of motor boats and freezing facilities for bait, agriculture became relatively less attractive as a source of income to the local peasantry. From 1932 to 1944 the number of cattle and sheep declined from 70 to 38. Fishing became a full-time occupation. The owners of the fishing stations seem to have encouraged fishermen to acquire their own boats. If the number of fishermen-owned boats declined, the entrepreneurs enlarged their own fleet to ensure a steady source of raw material (Hagalín 1964, II: 187, 195).

Foremen who owned shares in boats together with the entrepreneurs sometimes managed to buy out the merchants' shares and establish full ownership after a few years of fishing. Their sons often became crew members while the women of their households worked in washing and drying the catch. The catch had to be sold to the entrepreneurs who owned the wharves. Occasionally fishermen complained about the monopoly of the processors. In 1917 two fishermen wrote to the editor of the journal of the Icelandic Fisheries Association (Fiskifélag Islands) criticizing the monopoly (*Ægir* 1917 [6]: 77–80). If fishermen sold their catch elsewhere the processors refused to supply them with bait or grant them access to the wharves.

During the Second World War there were four significant changes that influenced the modernization of the fishing industry. Foreign fishing in Icelandic waters decreased and the stocks were able to recover. This reduction of foreign fishing resulted in good catches for Icelandic fishermen during the war and the recovery of the stocks insured good catches for some years into the future (Próun Sjávarútvegs: 30). There were good prices for fish during the War and the immediate post war period which insured that the fishing success was translated into income (Tomasson 1980: 37). During the War the British and the Americans occupied Iceland to prevent a German invasion. They provided many jobs and opportunities for entrepreneurs (see Tomasson 1980: 37). Perhaps the major development was full independence in 1944 and the formation of a coalition government which lasted until 1947. Parties of the left and the right were united in the common cause of modernization—development of the fishing fleet, improvement of the harbors, building processing plants, and full employment. This government was known as the *Nýsköpunarstjórn* or the Modernization Government. It offered development loans to the communes (*hreppur*) which have acted as administrative units in Iceland for centuries. The condition was that the community own the harbor. In Sandgerði the merchants' monopoly was abolished in 1946 when the commune bought the wharves. Since then access to the harbor has been open. For various reasons the merchants sold the wharves to the commune. Fishermen and the local population in general disliked the merchants' monopoly. Major reconstruction of the harbor and wharves was necessary for the expansion of the fishing industry. This required too large an investment for the merchants. The reconstruction, which enabled larger boats to use the harbor and to land their catches independent of tides, was beyond the financial capacity of the owners, and the necessary capital had to come from the state.

The improved harbor enabled larger boats to land their catches and to stay in port in bad weather. Seasonal fluctuations in the distribution of landings were reduced. This was an essential condition for the profitable operation and expansion of the freezing plants established in the 1930's and the 1940's. The population of Sandgerði grew rapidly as permanent jobs became increasingly available. In 1940 the population was 316, but by 1960 it was 718, an increase of 127 percent.

Capital, Labor, Cod and Herring

The relative importance of the petty entrepreneur and the firm in capitalist fishing has varied since the beginning of this century. It was not possible to locate reliable data on patterns of ownership for the earlier years, but it seems that initially (from 1913 to 1916) the merchants owned a substantial part of the Sandgerði fleet. From 1916 to 1943 there seems to have been a gradual increase in fisherman ownership. Table 9.1 shows the percentages of the winter fleet at Sandgerði owned by fishermen and absentee investors, mainly owners of fishing plants, from 1943 to 1981. (The figures for the earlier years are estimates based on both folk accounts and *Íslenskt Sjómannaalmanak*, Icelandic Seamen's Almanac.)

Table 9.1 Boat Ownership and Size by Years (excluding trawlers)

Year		1943	1948	1952	1962	1971	1981
Fisherman-							
Owned	% of Boats	95.7	90.0	81.2	68.7	73.1	63.8
Boats	% of Tonnage	96.0	91.9	76.2	62.6	63.8	46.7
Absentee	% of Boats	4.3	10.0	18.8	31.3	26.9	32.6
Ownership	% of Tonnage	4.0	8.1	23.8	37.4	36.2	53.3
Total No. of Boats		23	20	16	16	26	46
Total Tonnage		546	743	635	784	2718	3115
Mean Tonnage		23.7	37.2	39.7	49.0	104.5	67.7

The proportion of fisherman-owned boats declined rapidly from 1943 to 1962, but after that it remained fairly stable. If one considers the importance of fisherman-owned boats in terms of tonnage, there is little change from 1962 to 1971, but a sharp decline over the last decade. The composition of the whole Icelandic fleet shows a similar pattern. In 1925 boats under 20 tons, most of which were fisherman-owned, made up 71.4 percent of the fishing fleet. This proportion remained relatively constant until 1941 when it began to decline.

Path analysis of data on net and line fishing for several seasons of cod fishing from Sandgerði provides us with some indications of structural changes that were going on in the Icelandic fishing industry. We used the size of the boat (tons of carrying capacity) as a measure of capital and the number of fishing trips as a measure of labor. In line and net fishing for cod, the trips are not usually more than a day long. There is some variability in crew sizes, but the number of trips is a good measure of labor inputs for both types of fishing. We constructed a set of path models using the uncorrelated size of boats and number of trips as exogenous or independent variables and the catch of demersal fish as the dependent variable. We computed the path coefficients to assess the strength of the relationship between each independent variable and catch of demersal fish. The stronger the path coefficient, the more important the independent variable in determining the dependent variable. The residual is a measure of the variance in the dependent variable caused by all variables not considered as part of the system, everything except the size of boats and number of fishing trips. Table 9.2 shows the path coefficients from boat size and number of trips to catch and the residuals for the years 1943, 1948, 1952, 1957, 1962, 1971, 1979, 1980 and 1981. Clearly, boat size is an increasingly important determinant of catch in later years, and the number of trips is a strong, but decreasingly important determinant.

The greater importance of tonnage (i.e., equipment carrying capacity) of the boats is an indication of the increasing concentrations of capital that they represent. To measure changes in the relative importance of capital and labor over the years one would have, ideally, to examine the extent to which equipment cost and man-days spent in fishing (i.e., crew size multiplied by

Table 9.2 Path Coefficients from Trips and Tons to Demersal Catch

Year	1943	1948	1952	1957	1962	1971	1979	1980	1981
Trips	.93	.94	.89	.88	.77	.76	.56	.41	.53
Tons	.13	.09	.05	.19	.29	.44	.66	.72	.64
Residual	.28	.35	.47	.40	.42	.51	.33	.32	.39
Unexplained Variance (%)	8	12	22	16	18	26	11	10	15

number of trips) explain variance in catches. Such data are not available for the years in question. However, other data do give indications of alterations in the proportions of capital and labor. The value of assets in the whole Icelandic fleet increased by 133 percent from 1962 to 1974 (at constant prices). At the same time the labor input has increased much less, by only 13 percent from 1965 to 1974. From 1966 to 1980 the average number of fishermen increased by 23 percent (see *Statistical Abstract of Iceland* 1974: 32–33, 75; *Útvegur* 1980 [1]: 21).

What determined this progression whereby tonnage and capital became more important than trips and labor? One might think that this was a result of changes in the traditional winter fishing for demersal species. This is not the case. As the following analysis demonstrates, the increased importance of capital was a consequence of technological development in the pelagic fisheries for herring in the 1940s and 1950s.

Prior to the sudden decline in the herring catch in the late 1960's a large part of the Icelandic fleet fished for herring off the north coast during the summer. The seasonal herring fishery in Iceland, based on the feeding migrations of the Icelandic-Norwegian stock, dates back to the last decades of the nineteenth century. Fishing for herring with active gear, purse seine or ring net, developed in three major steps: the two-dory method (*herpinót*), the one-dory method, and the power block.

Through the 40's until 1950 a few pairs of small boats (between 1 and 24 pairs of boats with mean sizes of 22 to 33 tons) fished for herring. This practice declined steadily through the 40's as the practice of two motor boats sharing the same seine was found uneconomic in the offshore fishery. The two-dory method was used mainly in inshore waters until 1944 when the herring fishery started to develop into an offshore fishery. Before that, from 1904, each fishing boat was accompanied by two 30 foot long dories that were used to encircle surfacing schools of herring with the net (*herpinót*). The dories carrying the net were rowed by hand until the late 40's when small engines were installed in them. Shooting, pursing, and hauling were also manual operations. A net boss (*bassi*) was required to make quick decisions independent of the main vessel during the casting operation. Herring travel in schools which are highly unpredictable and evasive, except when spawning when the schools are very compact and do not react to fishing gear. When the casting was done from the main vessel with the one-dory system in the late 40's the boat owner could dispense with the boss as the skipper himself was in charge of the casting.

Around 1945 the migration and behavior pattern of herring of the north coast of Iceland changed. The fishery almost collapsed since the herring no longer entered inshore waters and good schools were seldom close to the coast. Low catches encouraged skippers to experiment with a more flexible one-dory system. In 1944 some of the smaller boats experimented with the ring net (*hringnót*), and the one-dory system. It was not until 1950, however, that more boats (128) used ring nets than the *herpinót* (88). In 1962 all boats used ring nets and the *herpinót* was no longer used (*Ægir* 1962: 327).

With the ring net, a single dory carrying the net is towed behind the boat and encircles the herring with the net. This method had three major advantages. First, it increased the speed of the casting operation since it was done by one boat. This proved important in competition among ships. Second, the pursing by the motorboat was much easier than manual pursing. Third, since one dory was used, the ring net required smaller crews—ten or eleven instead of eighteen. The speed of casting allowed experimentation with sonar-guided casting (see Gíslason 1971).

The changeover to the one-dory system and sonar-guided shooting required larger and more flexible boats. The power block was introduced in 1959. The hauling was done with an engine and the net was taken aboard the main vessel making the dory unnecessary. At the same time the seines could be enlarged to fish at greater depths. This was very important during the last years of the herring boom of the mid-1960s when the Norwegian-Icelandic herring went deeper almost 20 meters per year (see Porsteinsson 1980: 148). But keeping the larger seines aboard and hauling increased weight with the power block required larger boats.

In the early stages of experimentation with power blocks in Iceland, at least one small boat was sunk trying to draw a net too full of herring. This graphically demonstrated that the minimal size of boats required for the power block seining was much larger than that required for the one-dory method.

The larger boats introduced in the 1940's as a consequence of changes in the summer herring fishing techniques required better harbors, especially for the cod fishing during the winter. Larger boats reduced the seasonal fluctuations in supplies to the processing plants. This was a necessary precondition for the development of freezing plants. The increasing size of boats in the fishing fleet as a whole was a consequence of innovation in the herring fishing and responses to changing patterns of herring behavior. The changes in herring fishing made larger boats available for cod fishing and changed the balance of forces of production from labor being more important to capital becoming more important.

Even though these changes did not originate in the winter fishing for cod they had important consequences for the demersal fishery in the long run. If someone wanted to fish for herring, he had to get a larger boat, accumulate more capital. Once a person owned a larger boat, he had to keep it in production as much as possible, and therefore, fish for cod during the winter. Also, the process of accumulation and concentration of capital became faster due to the share system in fishing (Löfgren 1972). The rewards of fishing are divided for each fisherman, the skipper and for the boat owner(s). Larger boat sizes and innovations in deck technology led to higher catches of cod per unit of labor input. As a result "boat shares" (the proportion calculated to cover investment and maintenance) increased. Proportionately more of the rewards went to the owners of capital. Absentee ownership of boats increased and the capital intensive freezing sector developed.

Many of the fishermen from Sandgerði participated in the summer fishing of herring off the north and east coast in the 50's and 60's. The fishermen's accounts of the herring years are highly nostalgic. Then, they say, tension and excitement was "extreme." These years are frequently referred to as the "herring adventure" (*síldarævintýri*), which underlines the extreme uncertainties involved. Fishing was regarded as a lottery. The total catches of each season were seen to be highly unpredictable. The performance of any one boat in relation to the rest of the fleet was also seen to be highly uncertain (see Durrenberger and Pálsson 1983). Cod fishing, on the other hand, is consistent and relatively dependable. Those who fished for herring covered their bets by also fishing cod. The technological requirements of herring fishing resulted in capital becoming more important in the demersal fishery, which led to more concentration of capital, whether or not the herring fishing was successful. If herring fishing were successful, then there was even more capital concentration.

In a sense, cod fishing subsidized herring fishing and allowed people to "play the herring lottery" as Gíslason (1971) calls it. Boat owners could count on income from cod fishing since it is relatively stable. For the odd numbered years from 1925 through 1973 the mean cod catch per year was 326.27 thousand metric tons with a standard deviation of 84.54. The mean catch of herring for the same years was 159.34 with a standard deviation of 168.05. To make these variances comparable, we can compute the coefficient of variation, the standard deviation divided by the mean. For cod the coefficient of variation is .26, for herring it is 1.05, four times as variable. The extreme variance in herring catches cannot be attributd to technological changes. The highest catch per boat was in 1945, even greater than during the boom years of the early 1960s. We suggest the fluctuations in herring catch are largely due to the extreme flexibility of herring behavior. The fishing industry has simply tried to keep abreast of behavioral changes by developing new techniques (offshore fishing in larger boats, the one-dory system) and technologies (deeper seines, the power block).

The Persistence of the Petty Entrepreneur

Despite the increase in boat size, demanded by changing circumstances in the herring fishery, the proportion of boats under 20 ton has remained relatively constant. In 1957 the proportion for the whole fleet was 35 percent. It remained virtually identical until 1968 when the under 20 ton boats began to account for a larger proportion of the fleet again. In 1973 they accounted for 38 percent and in 1978 for 39 percent. One may wonder why the petty entrepreneurs, the owners of these small boats, are still important for the fishing industry? This is even more surprising if one keeps in mind that conflicts of interest may occur between independent small-boat owners and large processing companies with vessels of their own. In some cases the large companies have refused to buy the catches of small boats.

Generally however this does *not* apply. As long as sufficient labor is available to the large companies to man their boats, they continue to encourage independent skipper ownership. After the boom in the summer fishing for herring, processing plants received large supplies of cod during the winter season but little of any species during the summer. This seasonal fluctuation of raw materials was not economical for the processors. They have responded in several ways. By encouraging independent ownership of boats they have slightly reduced seasonal fluctuations. The small boats account for a relatively large proportion of the fleet's fishing during the summer.

It seems that one of the reasons for the predominance of small boats during the summer is that their owners are prepared to tolerate more risk than company owners. Fishing is relatively unprofitable during the summer and the owners of large boats often take the opportunity and have their vessels repaired and serviced for the following winter. Meanwhile the plants need raw material. The companies "offload" the risk onto petty entrepreneurs who are prepared to take them, acting as a kind of economic shock absorber—if anyone is going to go bankrupt or accept loss of income it is the entrepreneur (and his friends and relatives) rather than the company. The processing companies have further encouraged the exploitation of other summer species such as shrimp and lobster, for which small boats are most useful.

The reasons why the petty entrepreneurs tend to tolerate more risk than the company owners relate to the different nature of the two kinds of production units. The capitalist firm is very responsive to changes in the relative profitability of fishing and processing. If the profitability of fishing goes down, the company is likely to transfer capital to processing facilities. To ensure a steady supply of fish, company owners may hire a boat from time to time. One Sandgerði firm hired two boats during the winter and summer seasons of 1981. For a household production unit it is enough to survive the year and hope for better luck next year (see Wadel 1973). The skipper-owner, unlike the company directors, tries to reinvest in boat and gear even though the economic climate worsens or the returns fail to make ends meet. The skipper-owners may limit personal consumption as well as obtain support from government funds or local processors, in the hope that the situation will improve. Many of them form share holding companies, listing family members or other relatives as share holders to prevent total loss of property in case of bankruptcy. Unlike absentee owners, skipper-owners continue to reinvest when fishing ceases to be profitable, but unlike the peasant fishermen of earlier centuries they do accumulate capital when it is possible to increase returns.

In one important respect the petty entrepreneur shares the characteristics of the fishing peasant. In both types of production family members pool their resources, capital and labor. The family budget is closely tied to that of the boat even though the latter is kept separate on paper to comply with tax laws. Sometimes the whole nuclear family, and some neighbouring kinsmen as well, are engaged in production related to one boat. The wife of the skipper-owner has an important role to play. She takes most of the responsibility for running the household while the husband is working irregular hours and for socializing the children and keeping regular contacts with neighbours, friends and relatives. She may also bait lines and prepare nets. She may work in a freezing plant leaving her young children, if any, in the care of her mother or mother-in-law. During school vacations, older children often work in the freezing plant as well. The wife's earnings may be an important source of additional income, especially if the boat hasn't been doing well.

In pooling available resources the skipper-owner safeguards himself against the vulnerability of the business. Market conditions fluctuate, the productivity of fishing differs from one season to another and the need for labor varies with seasons and fishing gear.[2] One of the barriers to converting a small family business into a company is precisely the difficulty in responding to such fluctuations, while at the same time responding to the demands of the labor market. Skippers who own boats do not have to pay salaries every week. To keep his labor the absentee owner, on the other hand, has to conform to the formal demands of labor unions for immediate payments.

Data on crew organization indicate a relationship between boat size and frequency of immediate kinship ties. Crew organization was recorded for 29 Sandgerði crews (see Pálsson 1982). All but one of the boats in the smallest category had a crew with one or more father-son or brother-brother relationships (see Table 9.3). In the medium category this applied to five out of six crews. On the largest boats these relationships occurred in only 7 out oi 17 crews. These figures are even more significant if one keeps in mind that the bigger the boat the larger the crew and, therefore, the greater the probability of kinship relations occurring. As Table 9.3 shows, the proportion of father-son or brother-brother relations to the total number of possible ties varies significantly with boat size. Only these first-degree relations were recorded, but there is reason to expect that an analysis of other kinship ties would show a similar pattern. The extent to which the petty entrepreneur is able to draw upon the labor of the domestic unit varies with its composition and its stage in the development cycle. The skipper-owners who are in the most vulnerable position are those who have no sons or whose sons are still too young to join them. This is the case for at least two of the eleven boats which are owned by fishermen resident in Sandgerði. These are small boats, of 11 and 12 tons. On one of these, the owner fishes on his own, despite the

Table 9.3 Boat Size and Frequency of Kinship Ties

Size Category (t)	Tot. No. of Boats	No. of Boats in Sample	No. of Boats with One or More F/S or B/B Rel.	Crew Size		Mean Prop. of F/S or B/B Rel. to No. of Possible Ties	
				mean	s.d.	mean	s.d.
10–16	16	6	5	2.8	1.47	0.55	0.50
21–47	10	6	5	6.3	1.96	0.07	0.06
53–203	18	17	7	7.8	1.59	0.03	0.04
	44	29	17				

difficulties involved. In exceptional cases the wife of the fisherman may join him on fishing trips.

If the skipper-owner has one or more sons interested in fishing he may expand his business and buy a larger boat. Two local skipper-owners were joined by sons still belonging to their parental domestic unit, and one of them, who had recently bought a boat of approximately 30 tons, was occasionally joined by a son-in-law as well.

As the sons of the skipper-owner grow older they are likely to take over the enterprise. In four out of the eleven cases mentioned above, the sons (all of them in their twenties) had recently taken over. Two of them still belonged to their parental domestic unit. The fathers, in their late fifties or early sixties, became shore-based "managers." Three of these boats are fairly large, from 75 to 124 tons, while the fourth is 14 tons.

If the skipper-owner has several children he may sell the boat when he quits fishing, but more often the boat remains the property of the family. Sometimes a shareholding company is formed at this stage. Sons and daughters have equal shares. Later, one or more of the sons may buy the daughters out.

Brothers often pool their resources but their cooperation is often limited to a few years. In one case five brothers who jointly owned a boat split up after several years of fishing, Three of them bought the two others out, and the latter in turn bought their own boat. As brothers establish their own families, their resources and commitments become different and they are likely to have conflicting opinions in matters of investment and maintenance. Also, during fishing trips the symmetrical relations between crewmen who are not only brothers, but also co-owners of the boat, tend to be incompatible with the authority relations between the skipper and deckhands.

While the petty entrepreneur may make profit as long as labor and financial support are available and fishing is going well, the uncertainties of fishing often pose a threat to expansion. During the "herring years" some fishermen were lucky and became rich in one season. Now the purchase of a boat demands big loans and long-term financial commitments. Even though neighbours are prepared to go on working for several weeks without getting the shares to which they are entitled, relations with kinsmen and friends can withstand time lags in reciprocation for only a limited time. Crew members, whether relatives or not, are unlikely to join a skipper-owner the following season if they have been "treated badly" during the present one. In recent years several skipper-owners, faced with their commitments to crew members and creditors and with the uncertainties of fishing, have lost their boats, through bankruptcy or forced sales. Detailed information on the financing and profitability of boats is not available. Inquiries into such matters are naturally regarded with suspicion.

Comparative Remarks

Several authors indicate that industrialization of fishing occurs relatively slowly (see Andersen [ed.] 1979: 16). Faris argues (1977: 246) that due to the nature of the resource base they exploit, peasant fishermen "lack the same possibilities that peasant agriculturalists have." He implies (see p. 246) that since peasant fishermen cannot invest labor in promoting the growth and reproduction of living resources, prior to their extraction, potential entrepreneurs are faced with "a somewhat unique" investment problem. In this sense fishing may be like mining. But even though fishing involves no fixed investment in the primary resource base, it is difficult to see why a successful peasant fisherman should not be able to achieve further growth in output through increasing his investment in boats and equipment if he wanted to. This is indeed what happened in the case of the landowner at Sandgerði late in the 19th century. He had several decked sailing boats built for him. He was noted for his efforts and known as Sveinbjörn "The Rich." His son took over the land and the boats, but having lost both of his sons to the sea, the landowner sold the "landing rights" to outside entrepreneurs.

Löfgren argues (1982), in his comparative article on fishing adaptations in the "Atlantic Fringe," that the transformation of peasant society during the period of 1750–1900 was the result of demographic and social changes whereby the numbers of landless people continued to grow. For the "new proletarians" of agrarian capitalism, he argues, fishing became an important alternative. He also suggests (p. 154) that Iceland underwent "the same process" as coastal regions in Scandinavia but somewhat later. It is true that fishing was quite an important source of subsistence for landless people in Iceland. But this was the case for quite a long period, at least four centuries. Also, it would be wrong to assume that the real growth in maritime settlements in Iceland was the result of any developments in farming.[3] On the contrary, the agrarian system remained stagnant until capitalist production in fishing transformed the political economy of Iceland. The decisive growth in fishing occurred *despite* the attempts of the landowners to maintain a labor reserve in farming by arguing for the maintenance of the patron-client bond. As colonial relations with Denmark weakened in the late nineteenth century, traditional household production gave way to different forms of production in Icelandic fishing, by the petty entrepreneur and the capitalist firm respectively. These transitions involved fundamental changes in social relations and means of production. With the emergence of capitalist fishing, the previous ceiling on production was removed. Labor became a commodity.[4]

In our discussion of the emergence of capitalist fishing we showed that petty entrepreneurial activity sustained capitalist production in its initial phase of development. A similar point has been made for other fisheries by, for example, Breton (1977: 130) and McCay (1981). At a later stage of development the relative importance of the petty entrepreneur tends to decline. Löfgren argues (1972: 9) that in Sweden at the turn of the century labor was a more important factor of production in fishing than capital. Technological changes made capital more important and small-scale production declined. We have described the same process in Iceland.

But in some cases the petty entrepreneurs persist despite the growing importance of capital. This has been evident in Iceland during the last years. McCay argues (1981: 7) that the resiliency of small-scale fishermen is a consequence of the overexploitation of fishing stocks: "Some level of production is maintained while capital can be directed to more profitable endeavors." This may apply to some fisheries, but hardly to the Icelandic one where the living resources of the sea continue to be the main source of national income. The persistence of the small-scale producers in Iceland has more to do with the labor market, seasonal fluctuations in the availability of resources, and the nature of the production units involved. As many observers have pointed out (see for example Barnes 1954, Breton 1973, Acheson 1981, Löfgren 1982) the family crew, typical of small-scale production, is a relatively fluid and flexible unit. It is highly adaptive in risky situations. And fishing is still a risky business, for financial as well as ecological reasons.

Löfgren (1982) argues that when the herring fishery collapsed in Sweden, the number of fishermen and boats declined by half and boats went begging for buyers. This was not the response in Iceland. There were short term dislocations in many locations as fishing plants laid off workers during the summer season. The response was not to abandon fishing but to intensify the exploitation of cod and develop alternative summer fisheries such as capelin. In 1967 the herring catch fell to 118,483 tons from 482,615 in 1962. In 1968 the catch dropped even further to 30,775 tons indicating the end of the boom. Icelanders started fishing for capelin in 1963 with a catch of only 1,078 tons. The catch increased to about 125 thousand tons in 1966 and then dropped off until 1969 when it reached 170,627 tons. By 1974 it was up to 462 thousand tons. No shellfish appear in the records before 1969 when the catch is reported as only 402 tons. Afterwards, it was not less than two and a half thousand tons and some years more than twice that amount. Recently, as capelin catches have declined, attention has turned to redfish which has been increasingly important.

One does not have to look far for the reasons for this difference in response. Where there are many alternatives one selects the most advantageous one available. If one endeavor becomes unprofitable, one develops another. In Iceland, there are few alternatives to living from the sea. While we do not wish to make any claims for the uniqueness of Iceland, this ecological fact seems to make Iceland different from the rest of Scandinavia. Perhaps for this reason, one official response has been not to attempt to limit access to fishing by licensing, but to insure fair and equal access through quotas. Economic decisions are not always made according to a strictly economic calculus. The commitment to full employment and equal access has resulted in "overcapitalization" of the Icelandic fleet by strictly economic calculations. This poses a certain threat to the long-term availability of marine resources as the experiences with herring and more recently with capelin indicate. In this sense the Icelandic fleet may be too modernized. Striking the balance among the factors of long run availability of the resource, the number and type of fishing boats, and who receives what returns is a matter of an ongoing complex process of negotiation among members of the various sectors of the fishing industry and the government.

We have shown that fishing is a complex matter. It is not just getting into a boat, searching for, finding, catching, and delivering fish. Adequate analyses of fishing must take account of these facts. As Faris (1977: 236) and McCay (1981: 2) point out there has been a tendency for observers to overemphasize the process of extraction. Fishing, like any other economic activity, must be understood as an historical, economic and political process, as an evolving system.

Notes

1. Paul Durrenberger is Professor of Anthropology at the University of Iowa. His work was supported by a summer fellowship from the University of Iowa and a grant from Sïgma Xi. Gísli Pálsson is Lecturer in Anthropology at the University of Iceland. His research has been supported by the British Council, Vísindasjóður and Fiskimálasjóður. This is a collaborative paper. The order of the names signifies nothing. Statistics on the Icelandic fishing fleet were collected from *Íslenskt Sjórnannaalmanak* for the odd-numbered years from 1925 through 1975 and 1978. The statistics for herring fishing and boats were collected from *Ægir*'s herring reports.

2. An analysis of the complex interactions of the present system of fishing is provided in Durrenberger and Pálsson 1982.

3. Rich makes a similar error in a recent article on social change in Iceland (1976). He comes to the odd conclusion that "the acquisition of modern farm and manufacturing technology ... has resulted in new demographic patterns and a trend toward urbanization" (p. 17), whereas these changes should be attributed primarily to the expansion of the fishing sector.

4. Elsewhere, we have shown that all of these changes are significant for the understanding of rationalities of fishing. Each successive phase brought with it changes in ideologies of fishing (Pálsson and Durrenberger 1983).

156   E. Paul Durrenberger and Gísli Pálsson

References

Acheson, J. M. 1981. "Anthropology of Fishing." *Ann. Rev. Anthropology* 10: 275–316.
Ægir. 1917–1981. Reykjavik (Journal of the Icelandic Fisheries Association).
Andersen, Raoul, ed. 1979. *North Atlantic Maritime Cultures: Anthropological Essays on Changing Adaptations.* Paris: Mouton.
Andersen, Raoul and Cato Wadel, eds. 1972. *North Atlantic Fishermen: Anthropological Essays on Modern Fishing.* Toronto: University of Toronto Press.
Barnes, J. A. 1954. "Class and Committees in a Norwegian Island Parish." *Human Relations*, 7: 39–58.
Breton, Y. D. 1973. "A Comparative Study of Work Groups in an Eastern Canadian Peasant Fishing Community: Bilateral Kinship and Adaptive Processes." *Ethnology* 12 (4): 393–418.
――――. 1977. "The Influence of Modernization on the Modes of Production in Coastal Fishing: An Example from Venezuela." Pp. 125–137 in M. E. Smith, ed., *Those Who Live from the Sea.* St. Paul: West.
Durrenberger, Paul and Gísli Pálsson. 1982. "Policy, Processors and Boats: Fishing in Modern Iceland." *Central Issues in Anthropology* 4 (2): 31–47.
――――. 1983. "Riddles of Herring and Rhetorics of Success." *Journal of Anthropological Research* 39 (3): 323–335.
Faris, J. C. 1977. "Primitive Accumulation in Small-Scale Fishing Communities." Pp. 235–249 in M. E. Smith, ed., *Those Who Live from the Sea.* St. Paul: West.
Gíslason, Þorsteinn. 1971. "The Icelandic Technique of Sonar Guided Purse Seining." Pp. 206–217 in H. Kristjónsson, ed., *Modern Fishing Gear of the World,* vol. 3. London: Fishing News.
Gudmundsson, Gils. 1981. "Sandgerði-önnur grein." *Faxi* 2.
Hagalín, Gudmundur. 1964. *Í Fararbroddi: Ævisaga Haralds Böðvarssonar.* Hafnarfjörrur: Skuggsjá.
Íslenskt Sjómannaalmanak 1925–1961. Reykjavik: Icelandic Fisheries Association.
Jarðarbóc Árna Magnússonar and Páls Vídalíns 3. 1923–1924. Copenhagen: Hið Íslenska fræðafélag.
Kristjánsson, Lúðvik. 1980. *Íslenzkir Sjávarhættir,* I. Reykjavik: Menningarsjóður.
Löfgren, Orvar. 1982. "From Peasant Fishing to Industrial Trawling: A Comparative Discussion of Modernization Processes in Some North Atlantic Regions." Pp. 151–176 in J. R. Maiolo and M. K. Orbach, eds., *Modernization and Marine Fisheries Polity.* Ann Arbor: Ann Arbor Science.
Magnússon, Skúli. 1935–1936. "Lýsing Gullbringu- og Kjósarsýslu." Pp. 1–196 in *Landnám Ingólfs.* Reykjavik: Ingólfur. (Written around 1785).
Maiolo, J. R. and M. K. Orbach, eds. 1982. *Modernization and Marine Fisheries Policy.* Ann Arbor: Ann Arbor Science.
Manntal á Íslandi árið 1703. 1924–1947. Reykjavik: Gutenberg.
McCay, B. J. 1981. "Development Issues in Fisheries as Agrarian Systems." *Culture and Agriculture* 11: 1–8.
Ólafsson, Páll E. 1942. *Saga Íslendinga: Seytjánda öld.* Reykjavik: Menntamálaráð og þjóðvinafélag.
Pálsson, Gísli. 1982. *Representations and Reality: Cognitive Models and Social Relations Among the Fishermen of Sandgerði, Iceland.* Unpublished Ph.D. thesis. Department of Social Anthropology, University of Manchester.

Pálsson, Gísli and Paul Durrenberger. 1983. "Icelandic Foremen and Skippers: The Structure and Evolution of a Folk Model." *American Ethnologist* 10 (3): 511-527.

Porsteinsson, Björn. 1979. *Enska Öldin í Sögu Íslendinga.* Reykjavik: Mál og Menning.

Porsteinsson, Guðni. 1980. *Veiðar og Veiðarfæri.* Reykjavik: Almenna Bókafélagið.

Þórðarson, Matthías. 1946. *Litið til baka,* I and II. Reykjavik: Leiftur.

Próun Sjávarútvegs. 1975. Reykjavik: Rannsóknarráð Rikisins.

Rich, G. W. 1976. "Changing Icelandic Kinship." *Ethnology* 15: 1-20.

Sigurðsson, Jón. 1859. *Lítil Fiskibók.* Copenhagen.

Smith, M. E., ed. 1977. *Those Who Live from the Sea.* St. Paul: West.

Spoehr, Alexander, ed. 1980. *Maritime Adaptations: Essays on Contemporary Fishing Communities.* Pittsburgh: University of Pittsburgh Press.

Statistical Abstract of Iceland 1971. Reykjavik: Hagstofa Islands.

Tomasson, R. F. 1980. *Iceland: The First New Society.* Reykjavik: Iceland Review.

Útvegur. 1980. Reykjavik: The Icelandic Fisheries Association.

Wadel, Cato. 1973. *Capital Management under Extreme Uncertainty: A Study of Norwegian Fishermen Entrepreneurs.* Tromsö, mimeo.

10

THE DEVELOPMENT OF UNDERDEVELOPMENT

Andre Gunder Frank

I

We cannot hope to formulate adequate development theory and policy for the majority of the world's population who suffer from underdevelopment without first learning how their past economic and social history gave rise to their present underdevelopment. Yet most historians study only the developed metropolitan countries and pay scant attention to the colonial and underdeveloped lands. For this reason most of our theoretical categories and guides to development policy have been distilled exclusively from the historical experience of the European and North American advanced capitalist nations.

Since the historical experience of the colonial and underdeveloped countries has demonstrably been quite different, available theory therefore fails to reflect the past of the underdeveloped part of the world entirely, and reflects the past of the world as a whole only in part. More important, our ignorance of the underdeveloped countries' history leads us to assume that their past and indeed their present resemble earlier stages of the history of the now developed countries. This ignorance and this assumption lead us into serious misconceptions about contemporary underdevelopment and development. Further, most studies of development and underdevelopment fail to take account of the economic and other relations between the metropolis and its economic colonies throughout the history of the worldwide expansion and development of the mercantilist and capitalist system. Consequently, most of our theory fails to explain the structure and development of the capitalist system as a whole and to account for its simultaneous generation

158

of underdevelopment in some of its parts and of economic development in others.

It is generally held that economic development occurs in a succession of capitalist stages and that today's underdeveloped countries are still in a stage, sometimes depicted as an original stage of history, through which the now developed countries passed long ago. Yet even a modest acquaintance with history shows that underdevelopment is not original or traditional and that neither the past nor the present of the underdeveloped countries resembles in any important respect the past of the now developed countries. The now developed countries were never *under*developed, though they may have been *un*developed. It is also widely believed that the contemporary underdevelopment of a country can be understood as the product or reflection solely of its own economic, political, social, and cultural characteristics or structure. Yet historical research demonstrates that contemporary underdevelopment is in large part the historical product of past and continuing economic and other relations between the satellite underdeveloped and the now developed metropolitan countries. Furthermore, these relations are an essential part of the structure and development of the capitalist system on a world scale as a whole. A related and also largely erroneous view is that the development of these underdeveloped countries and, within them of their most underdeveloped domestic areas, must and will be generated or stimulated by diffusing capital, institutions, values, etc., to them from the international and national capitalist metropoles. Historical perspective based on the underdeveloped countries' past experience suggests that on the contrary in the underdeveloped countries economic development can now occur only independently of most of these relations of diffusion.

Evident inequalities of income and differences in culture have led many observers to see "dual" societies and economies in the underdeveloped countries. Each of the two parts is supposed to have a history of its own, a structure, and a contemporary dynamic largely independent of the other. Supposedly, only one part of the economy and society has been importantly affected by intimate economic relations with the "outside" capitalist world; and that part, it is held, became modern, capitalist, and relatively developed precisely because of this contact. The other part is widely regarded as variously isolated, subsistence based, feudal, or precapitalist, and therefore more underdeveloped.

I believe on the contrary that the entire "dual society" thesis is false and that the policy recommendations to which it leads will, if acted upon, serve only to intensify and perpetuate the very conditions of underdevelopment they are supposedly designed to remedy.

A mounting body of evidence suggests, and I am confident that future historical research will confirm, that the expansion of the capitalist system over the past centuries effectively and entirely penetrated even the apparently most isolated sectors of the underdeveloped world. Therefore, the economic, political, social, and cultural institutions and relations we now observe there are the products of the historical development of the capitalist system no less than are the seemingly more modern or capitalist features of the national metropoles of these underdeveloped countries. Analogously to the relations between development and underdevelopment on the international level, the contemporary underdeveloped institutions of the so-called backward or feudal domestic areas of an underdeveloped country are no less the product of the single historical process of capitalist development than are the so-called capitalist institutions of the supposedly more progressive areas. In this paper I should like to sketch the kinds of evidence which support this thesis and at the same time indicate lines along which further study and research could fruitfully proceed.

II

The Secretary General of the Latin American Center for Research in the Social Sciences writes in that Center's journal: "The privileged position of the city has its origin in the colonial period. It was founded by the Conqueror to serve the same ends that it still serves today; to incorporate the indigenous population into the economy brought and developed by that Conqueror and his descendants. The regional city was an instrument of conquest and is still today an instrument of domination."[1] The Instituto Nacional Indigenista (National Indian Institute) of Mexico confirms this observation when it notes that "the mestizo population, in fact, always lives in a city, a center of an intercultural region, which acts as the metropolis of a zone of indigenous population and which maintains with the underdeveloped communities an intimate relation which links the center with the satellite communities."[2] The Institute goes on to point out that "between the mestizos who live in the nuclear city of the region and the Indians who live in the peasant hinterland there is in reality a closer economic and social interdependence than might at first glance appear" and that the provincial metropoles "by being centers of intercourse are also centers of exploitation."[3]

Thus these metropolis-satellite relations are not limited to the imperial or international level but penetrate and structure the very economic, political, and social life of the Latin American colonies and countries. Just as the colonial and national capital and its export sector become the satellite of the Iberian (and later of other) metropoles of the world economic system, this satellite immediately becomes a colonial and then a national metropolis with respect to the productive sectors and population of the interior. Furthermore, the provincial capitals, which thus are themselves satellites of the national metropolis—and through the latter of the world metropolis—are in turn provincial centers around which their own local satellites orbit. Thus, a whole chain of constellations of metropoles and satellites relates all parts of the whole system from its metropolitan center in Europe or the United States to the farthest outpost in the Latin American countryside.

When we examine this metropolis-satellite structure, we find that each of the satellites, including now underdeveloped Spain and Portugal, serves as an instrument to suck capital or economic surplus out of its own satellites and to channel part of this surplus to the world metropolis of which all are satellites. Moreover, each national and local metropolis serves to impose and maintain the monopolistic structure and exploitative relationship of this system (as the Instituto Nacional Indigenista of Mexico calls it) as long as it serves the interests of the metropoles which take advantage of this global, national, and local structure to promote their own development and the enrichment of their ruling classes.

These are the principal and still surviving structural characteristics which were implanted in Latin America by the Conquest. Beyond examining the establishment of this colonial structure in its historical context, the proposed approach calls for study of the development—and underdevelopment—of these metropoles and satellites of Latin America throughout the following and still continuing historical process. In this way we can understand why there were and still are tendencies in the Latin American and world capitalist structure which seem to lead to the development of the metropolis and the underdevelopment of the satellite and why, particularly, the satellized national, regional, and local metropoles in Latin America find that their economic development is at best a limited or underdeveloped development.

III

That present underdevelopment of Latin America is the result of its centuries-long participation in the process of world capitalist development, I believe I have shown in my case studies of the economic and social histories of Chile and Brazil.[4] My study of Chilean history suggests that the Conquest incorporated this country fully into the expansion and development of the world mercantile and later industrial capitalist system but that it also introduced the monopolistic metropolis-satellite structure and development of capitalism into the Chilean domestic economy and society itself. This structure then penetrated and permeated all of Chile very quickly. Since that time and in the course of world and Chilean history during the epochs of colonialism, free trade, imperialism, and the present, Chile has become increasingly marked by the economic, social, and political structure of satellite underdevelopment. This development of underdevelopment continues today, both in Chile's still increasing satellization by the world metropolis and through the ever more acute polarization of Chile's domestic economy.

The history of Brazil is perhaps the clearest case of both national and regional development of underdevelopment. The expansion of the world economy since the beginning of the sixteenth century successively converted the Northeast, the Minas Gerais interior, the North, and the Center-South (Rio de Janeiro, São Paulo, and Paraná) into export economies and incorporated them into the structure and development of the world capitalist system. Each of these regions experienced what may have appeared as economic development during the period of its respective golden age. But it was a satellite development which was neither self-generating nor self-perpetuating. As the market or the productivity of the first three regions declined, foreign and domestic economic interest in them waned; and they were left to develop the underdevelopment they live today. In the fourth region, the coffee economy experienced a similar though not yet quite as serious fate (though the development of a synthetic coffee substitute promises to deal it a mortal blow in the not too distant future). All of this historical evidence contradicts the generally accepted theses that Latin America suffers from a dual society or from the survival of feudal institutions and that these are important obstacles to its economic development.

IV

During the First World War, however, and even more during the Great Depression and the Second World War, São Paulo began to build up an industrial establishment which is the largest in Latin America today. The question arises whether this industrial development did or can break Brazil out of the cycle of satellite development and underdevelopment which has characterized its other regions and national history within the capitalist system so far. I believe that the answer is no. Domestically the evidence so far is fairly clear. The development industry in São Paulo has not brought greater riches to the other regions of Brazil. Instead, it converted them into internal colonial satellites, decapitalized them further, and consolidated or even deepened their underdevelopment. There is little evidence to suggest that this process is likely to be reversed in the foreseeable future except insofar as the provincial poor migrate and become the poor of the metropolitan cities. Externally, the evidence is that although the initial development of São Paulo's industry was relatively autonomous it is being increasingly satellized by the world capitalist metropolis and its future development possibilities are increasingly restricted.[5] This development, my studies lead me to believe, also appears destined to limited or underdeveloped development as long as it takes place in the present economic, political, and social framework.

We must conclude, in short, that underdevelopment is not due to the survival of archaic institutions and the existence of capital shortage in regions that have remained isolated from the stream of world history. On the contrary, underdevelopment was and still is generated by the very same historical process which also generated economic development: the development of capitalism itself. This view, I am glad to say, is gaining adherents among students of Latin America and is proving its worth in shedding new light on the problems of the area and in affording a better perspective for the formulation of theory and policy.[6]

V

The same historical and structural approach can also lead to better development theory and policy by generating a series of hypotheses about development and underdevelopment such as those I am testing in my current research. The hypotheses are derived from the empirical observation and theoretical assumption that within this world-embracing metropolis-satellite structure the metropoles tend to develop and the satellites to underdevelop. The first hypothesis has already been mentioned above: that in contrast to the development of the world metropolis which is no one's satellite, the development of the national and other subordinate metropoles is limited by their satellite status. It is perhaps more difficult to test this hypothesis than the following ones because part of its confirmation depends on the test of the other hypotheses. Nonetheless, this hypothesis appears to be generally confirmed by the nonautonomous and unsatisfactory economic and especially industrial development of Latin America's national metropoles, as documented in the studies already cited. The most important and at the same time most confirmatory examples are the metropolitan regions of Buenos Aires and São Paulo whose growth only began in the nineteenth century, was therefore largely untrammelled by any colonial heritage, but was and remains a satellite development largely dependent on the outside metropolis, first of Britain and then of the United States.

A second hypothesis is that the satellites experience their greatest economic development and especially their most classically capitalist industrial development if and when their ties to their metropolis are weakest. This hypothesis is almost diametrically opposed to the generally accepted thesis that development in the underdeveloped countries follows from the greatest degree of contact with and diffusion from the metropolitan developed countries. This hypothesis seems to be confirmed by two kinds of relative isolation that Latin America has experienced in the course of its history. One is the temporary isolation caused by the crises of war or depression in the world metropolis. Apart from minor ones, five periods of such major crises stand out and seem to confirm the hypothesis. These are: the European (and especially Spanish) Depression of the seventeenth century, the Napoleonic Wars, the First World War, the Depression of the 1930s, and the Second World War. It is clearly established and generally recognized that the most important recent industrial development—especially of Argentina, Brazil, and Mexico, but also of other countries such as Chile—has taken place precisely during the periods of the two World Wars and the intervening Depression. Thanks to the consequent loosening of trade and investment ties during these periods, the satellites initiated marked autonomous industrialization and growth. Historical research demonstrates that the same thing happened in Latin America during Europe's seventeenth-century depression. Manufacturing grew in the Latin American countries, and several of them such as Chile became exporters of manufactured goods. The Napoleonic Wars gave rise to independence

164 Andre Gunder Frank

movements in Latin America, and these should perhaps also be interpreted as confirming the development hypothesis in part.

The other kind of isolation which tends to confirm the second hypothesis is the geographic and economic isolation of regions which at one time were relatively weakly tied to and poorly integrated into the mercantilist and capitalist system. My preliminary research suggests that in Latin America it was these regions which initiated and experienced the most promising self-generating economic development of the classical industrial capitalist type. The most important regional cases probably are Tucumán and Asunción, as well as other cities such as Mendoza and Rosario, in the interior of Argentina and Paraguay during the end of the eighteenth and the beginning of the nineteenth centuries. Seventeenth and eighteenth century São Paulo, long before coffee was grown there, is another example. Perhaps Antioquia in Colombia and Puebla and Querétaro in Mexico are other examples. In its own way, Chile was also an example since, before the sea route around the Horn was opened, this country was relatively isolated at the end of the long voyage from Europe via Panama. All of these regions became manufacturing centers and even exporters, usually of textiles, during the periods preceding their effective incorporation as satellites into the colonial, national, and world capitalist system.

Internationally, of course, the classic case of industrialization through nonparticipation as a satellite in the capitalist world system is obviously that of Japan after the Meiji Restoration. Why, one may ask, was resource-poor but unsatellized Japan able to industrialize so quickly at the end of the century while resource-rich Latin American countries and Russia were not able to do so and the latter was easily beaten by Japan in the War of 1904 after the same forty years of development efforts? The second hypothesis suggests that the fundamental reason is that Japan was not satellized either during the Tokugawa or the Meiji period and therefore did not have its development structurally limited as did the countries which were so satellized.

VI

A corollary of the second hypothesis is that when the metropolis recovers from its crisis and reestablishes the trade and investment ties which fully reincorporate the satellites into the system, or when the metropolis expands to incorporate previously isolated regions into the worldwide system, the previous development and industrialization of these regions are choked off or channelled into directions which are not self-perpetuating and promising. This happened after each of the five crises cited above. The renewed expansion of trade and the spread of economic liberalism in the eighteenth and nineteenth centuries choked off and reversed the manufacturing development which Latin America had experienced during the seventeenth century, and in some places at the beginning of the nineteenth. After the First World War, the new national industry of Brazil suffered serious consequences from American economic invasion. The increase in the growth rate of Gross National Product and particularly of industrialization throughout Latin America was again reversed and industry became increasingly satellized after the Second World War and especially after the post–Korean War recovery and expansion of the metropolis. Far from having become more developed since then, industrial sectors of Brazil and most conspicuously of Argentina have become structurally more and more underdeveloped and less and less able to generate continued industrialization and/or sustain development of the economy. This process, from which India also suffers, is reflected in a whole gamut of balance-of-payments, inflationary, and other economic and political difficulties, and promises to yield to no solution short of far-reaching structural change.

Our hypothesis suggests that fundamentally the same process occurred even more dramatically with the incorporation into the system of previously unsatellized regions. The expansion of Buenos Aires as a satellite of Great Britain and the introduction of free trade in the interest of the ruling groups of both metropoles destroyed the manufacturing and much of the remainder of the economic base of the previously relatively prosperous interior almost entirely. Manufacturing was destroyed by foreign competition, lands were taken and concentrated into latifundia by the rapaciously growing export economy, intraregional distribution of income became much more unequal, and the previously developing regions became simple satellites of Buenos Aires and through it of London. The provincial centers did not yield to satellization without a struggle. This metropolis-satellite conflict was much of the cause of the long political and armed struggle between the Unitarists in Buenos Aires and the Federalists in the provinces, and it may be said to have been the sole important cause of the War of the Triple Alliance in which Buenos Aires, Montevideo, and Rio de Janeiro, encouraged and helped by London, destroyed not only the autonomously developing economy of Paraguay but killed off nearly all of its population which was unwilling to give in. Though this is no doubt the most spectacular example which tends to confirm the hypothesis, I believe that historical research on the satellization of previously relatively independent yeoman farming and incipient manufacturing regions such as the Caribbean islands will confirm it further.[7] These regions did not have a chance against the forces of expanding and developing capitalism, and their own development had to be sacrificed to that of others. The economy and industry of Argentina, Brazil, and other countries which have experienced the effects of metropolitan recovery since the Second World War are today suffering much the same fate, if fortunately still in lesser degree.

VII

A third major hypothesis derived from the metropolis-satellite structure is that the regions which are the most underdeveloped and feudal-seeming today are the ones which had the closest ties to the metropolis in the past. They are the regions which were the greatest exporters of primary products to and the biggest sources of capital for the world metropolis and which were abandoned by the metropolis when for one reason or another business fell off. This hypothesis also contradicts the generally held thesis that the source of a region's underdevelopment is its isolation and its precapitalist institutions.

This hypothesis seems to be amply confirmed by the former supersatellite development and present ultra-underdevelopment of the once sugar-exporting West Indies, Northeastern Brazil, the ex-mining districts of Minas Gerais in Brazil, highland Peru, and Bolivia, and the central Mexican states of Guanajuato, Zacatecas, and others whose names were made world famous centuries ago by their silver. There surely are no major regions in Latin America which are today more cursed by underdevelopment and poverty; yet all of these regions, like Bengal in India, once provided the life blood of mercantile and industrial capitalist development—in the metropolis. These regions' participation in the development of the world capitalist system gave them, already in their golden age, the typical structure of underdevelopment of a capitalist export economy. When the market for their sugar or the wealth of their mines disappeared and the metropolis abandoned them to their own devices, the already existing economic, political, and social structure of these regions prohibited autonomous generation of economic development and left them no alternative but to turn in upon themselves and to degenerate into the ultra-underdevelopment we find there today.

VIII

These considerations suggest two further and related hypotheses. One is that the latifundium, irrespective of whether it appears as a plantation or a hacienda today, was typically born as a commercial enterprise which created for itself the institutions which permitted it to respond to increased demand in the world or national market by expanding the amount of its land, capital, and labor and to increase the supply of its products. The fifth hypothesis is that the latifundia which appear isolated, subsistence-based, and semifeudal today saw the demand for their products or their productive capacity decline and that they are to be found principally in the above-named former agricultural and mining export regions whose economic activity declined in general. These two hypotheses run counter to the notions of most people, and even to the opinions of some historians and other students of the subject, according to whom the historical roots and socioeconomic causes of Latin American latifundia and agrarian institutions are to be found in the transfer of feudal institutions from Europe and/or in economic depression.

The evidence to test these hypotheses is not open to easy general inspection and requires detailed analyses of many cases. Nonetheless, some important confirmatory evidence is available. The growth of the latifundium in nineteenth-century Argentina and Cuba is a clear case in support of the fourth hypothesis and can in no way be attributed to the transfer of feudal institutions during colonial times. The same is evidently the case of the post-revolutionary and contemporary resurgence of latifundia particularly in the North of Mexico, which produce for the American market, and of similar ones on the coast of Peru and the new coffee regions of Brazil. The conversion of previously yeoman-farming Caribbean islands, such as Barbados, into sugar-exporting economies at various times between the seventeenth and twentieth centuries and the resulting rise of the latifundia in these islands would seem to confirm the fourth hypothesis as well. In Chile, the rise of the latifundium and the creation of the institutions of servitude which later came to be called feudal occurred in the eighteenth century and have been conclusively shown to be the result of and response to the opening of a market for Chilean wheat in Lima.[8] Even the growth and consolidation of the latifundium in seventeenth-century Mexico—which most expert students have attributed to a depression of the economy caused by the decline of mining and a shortage of Indian labor and to a consequent turning in upon itself and ruralization of the economy—occurred at a time when urban population and demand were growing, food shortages became acute, food prices sky-rocketed, and the profitability of other economic activities such as mining and foreign trade declined.[9] All of these and other factors rendered hacienda agriculture more profitable. Thus, even this case would seem to confirm the hypothesis that the growth of the latifundium and its feudal-seeming conditions of servitude in Latin America has always been and still is the commercial response to increased demand and that it does not represent the transfer or survival of alien institutions that have remained beyond the reach of capitalist development. The emergence of latifundia, which today really are more or less (though not entirely) isolated, might then be attributed to the causes advanced in the fifth hypothesis—i.e., the decline of previously profitable agricultural enterprises whose capital was, and whose currently produced economic surplus still is, transferred elsewhere by owners and merchants who frequently are the same persons or families. Testing this hypothesis requires still more detailed analysis, some of which I have undertaken in a study on Brazilian agriculture.[10]

IX

All of these hypotheses and studies suggest that the global extension and unity of the capitalist system, its monopoly structure and uneven development throughout its history, and the resulting persistence of commercial rather than industrial capitalism in the underdeveloped world (including its most industrially advanced countries) deserve much more attention in the study of economic development and cultural change than they have hitherto received. Though science and truth know no national boundaries, it is probably new generations of scientists from the underdeveloped countries themselves who most need to, and best can, devote the necessary attention to these problems and clarify the process of underdevelopment and development. It is their people who in the last analysis face the task of changing this no longer acceptable process and eliminating this miserable reality.

They will not be able to accomplish these goals by importing sterile stereotypes from the metropolis which do not correspond to their satellite economic reality and do not respond to their liberating political needs. To change their reality they must understand it. For this reason, I hope that better confirmation of these hypotheses and further pursuit of the proposed historical, holistic, and structural approach may help the people of the underdeveloped countries to understand the causes and eliminate the reality of their development of underdevelopment and their underdevelopment of development.

Notes

1. *América Latina,* Año 6, no. 4 (October–December 1963), p. 8.

2. Instituto Nacional Indigenista, *Los centros coordinadores indigenistas,* Mexico, 1962, p. 34.

3. Ibid., pp. 33–34, 88.

4. "Capitalist Development and Underdevelopment in Chile" and "Capitalist Development and Underdevelopment in Brazil" in *Capitalism and Underdevelopment in Latin America* (New York: Monthly Review Press).

5. Also see, "The Growth and Decline of Import Substitution," *Economic Bulletin for Latin America* 9, no. 1 (March 1964); and Celso Furtado, *Dialectica do Desenvolvimiento* (Rio de Janeiro: Fundo de Cultura, 1964).

6. Others who use a similar approach though their ideologies do not permit them to derive the logically following conclusions, are Aníbal Pinto S.C., *Chile: Un caso de desarrollo frustrado* (Santiago, Editorial Universitaria, 1957); Celso Furtado, *A formaçao económica do Brasil* (Rio de Janeiro, Fundo de Cultura, 1959; recently translated into English and published under the title *The Economic Growth of Brazil* [Berkeley: University of California Press]); and Caio Prado Junior, *Historia Económica do Brasil,* 7th ed. (São Paulo: Editora Brasiliense, 1962).

7. See for instance Ramón Guerra y Sánchez, *Azúcar y Población en las Antillas,* 2nd ed. (Havana 1942), also published as *Sugar and Society in the Caribbean* (New Haven: Yale University Press, 1964).

8. Mario Góngora, *Origen de los "inquilinos" de Chile central* (Santiago: Editorial Universitaria, 1960); Jean Borde and Mario Góngora, *Evolución de la propiedad rural en el Valle del Puango* (Santiago: Instituto de Sociología de la Universidad de Chile); Sergio Sepúlveda, *El trigo chileno en el mercado mundial* (Santiago: Editorial Universitario, 1959).

9. Woodrow Borah makes depression the centerpiece of his explanation in "New Spain's Century of Depression," *Ibero-Americana* 35 (1951). François Chevalier speaks of turning in upon itself in the most authoritative study of the subject, "La formación de los grandes latifundios en México," *Problemas Agrícolas e Industriales de México* 8, no. 1 (1956) (translated from the French and recently published by the University of California Press). The data which provide the basis for my contrary interpretation are supplied by these authors themselves. This problem is discussed

in my "Con qué modo de producción convierte la gallina maíz en huevos de oro?" *El Gallo Ilustrado,* Suplemento de *El Día* 175 and 179, October 31 and November 28, 1965; and it is further analyzed in a study of Mexican agriculture under preparation by the author.

10. "Capitalism and the Myth of Feudalism in Brazilian Agriculture," in *Capitalism and Underdevelopment in Latin America,* cited in footnote 4 above.

V

Power and Culture

11

LEAF OF PARADISE OR AID TO TERRORISM?

CULTURAL CONSTRUCTIONS OF A DRUG CALLED KHAT

Lisa L. Gezon

Have you ever heard of khat? Some people in Europe, Israel, and the United States take it in a pill form as a rave drug. People throughout the rest of the world chew the young leaves of this bushy plant for their mild amphetamine effect. It can be like speed or a heavy dose of caffeine if you chew significant quantities. It is popular with people in or from the Horn of Africa and Yemen.

You might recognize the reference to drug-crazed terrorists from the movie *Blackhawk Down* or more recently to drug-chewing and drug-trafficking Somali pirates who hijack ships and invest the ransom money in smuggling khat (Hassan 2008). It is illegal in some countries, such as the United States and France, and not in others, such as Great Britain. In Somalia, Kenya, and even Yemen people contest its legal status, and common people may not even be aware whether it's legal or not. That's the way it is in Madagascar.

The French controlled Madagascar from 1896 until 1960, and Diego Suarez was an important port and military base. During the French colonial era, Yemeni dock workers brought khat with them to Diego Suarez, or Antsiranana, in the far north of Madagascar. This migration of Yemenis to Madagascar probably coincided with the development of the port in the city of Aden in Yemen after the end of World War I, when thousands of men migrated to Aden from arid, marginal agricultural areas to find work (Wier 1985: 19). They took khat with them, and those that settled in Madagascar planted it in kitchen gardens. The first to grow it commercially, according to interviews, were the Creoles—white farmers of French descent who came over from Ile de la Réunion around the turn of the century—who established small planta-tions on Amber Mountain about twenty miles inland. When the French were forced to leave the country in the mid-1970s amid a socialist revolution, they either sold or abandoned the khat farms.

Why are some substances illegal and not others? Is it a rational, scientific process of identifying chemical compounds and then assigning substances into categories based on how dangerous they are? If you are reading Paul Dur-renberger and Suzan Erem's *Anthropology Unbound* (2007), you probably already realize that things are not always as they seem and that cultural codes, jockey-ing for status, and greed shape what happens on the ground. If you suspect that it is the same with drugs, you're right. It is at least somewhat arbitrary that some stimulating substances are labeled as "drugs" and made illegal (say, cocaine or khat) or controlled as a pharmaceutical (such as Ritalin), whereas others are considered a respectable pastime (coffee or vodka, for example). If it were just a question of being dangerous, tobacco would be illegal.

Medical Anthropology

One common differentiation between drugs is how "dangerous" they are. So what makes a substance dangerous? What do we even mean by dangerous? There are three factors: physiological effects, cultural contexts, and cultural codes. First, as to physiological effects, Erich Goode (1998) notes that drug substances cannot be evaluated in a vacuum, isolated from all social and cul-tural contexts of use. Drug action, he writes, refers to the chemical reactions of a substance. The physiological effects of a drug depend on the "route of administration," which may be needle, pill, tea, smoking, and so on. The ef-fects also depend on any kind of mixing with other drugs, food, and drink.

Second, medical anthropologists point out that in addition to the phar-maceutical properties, cultural contexts such as the person, the setting, the norms, and, importantly, the placebo effect shape a drug's effects. A placebo is a neutral substance that can have a physical effect if a person believes it will. Cultural norms, therefore, are important not only in shaping *interpreta-tions* of objectively identifiable chemical substances, but also in structuring the actual effects. But remember that many of the physical effects of the substances cannot be mitigated by wishful thinking. No amount of thinking you won't get drunk after consuming several drinks in an hour will reduce the amount of alcohol in your bloodstream! Nor will such thinking restore your judgment while driving.

Linda Bennett and Paul Cook (1996: 242) argue that the distance "between acceptable usage . . . and dysfunctional-pathological usage is extremely com-plicated." This means that in one cultural context, drug use may be socially disruptive and in another, it is not. They note that in Jamaica, although a study showed no correlation in work productivity between those who consume cannabis and those who do not, cannabis has a reputation for making people "lazy." The same is true for khat, which, ironically, is a stimulant. What this tells us is that the study of drugs cannot end in a laboratory. The study of drugs is not purely a medical question, but a social question. We are a bit further along in answering our question about what makes a substance an illegal drug.

So, if identifying chemical properties is not enough, what do we need to know to understand drugs in a society? We need to start with good ethnographic studies of the contexts of substance use on the ground. This may tell us that middle-class Jamaicans consider cannabis to be socially disruptive but many working-class Jamaicans do not. It's the same for khat. We may learn when, where, and with whom people smoke marijuana or chew khat, as well as how they say they feel when they consume either substance. As important as all that is, it is not the whole story, however. Consumption of any substance takes place within broader political and economic systems.

This is where critical medical anthropology (or CMA) comes in. A CMA perspective compels us to ask larger questions about the context of drug use and to go beyond the local to put drug use into context. Critical medical anthropologists Merrill Singer and Hans Baer (2007: 33) define a critical understanding as one that pays attention to "the 'vertical links' that connect the social group of interest to the larger regional, national, and global human society." CMA focuses on systems of power, both horizontally within communities and vertically—that is, on how class, race, and gender structure unequal access to health care and exposure to health risks. CMA also recognizes that perceptions of health (and of what is "good for you" and "bad for you") exist in a field of competing perceptions, where the ones held by the ruling class are more powerful than others and will more likely be translated into action. This is sometimes known as hegemony, which Durrenberger and Erem (2007: 113) define as "the predominant power of one class—especially the power to control the content of the cultural code."

So we ask not only about how drugs, or psychotropic ("acting on the mind") substances, make people feel, but also about the political and economic contexts within which "drugs" exist and come into being. To be able to interpret statements about drug-crazed terrorists chewing khat in Somalia, we need lots of information. Most obviously, we need a basic ethnography of consumption. Being anthropologists, we know we also need to look into the social relationships between people involved in any way with khat—be they chewers, sellers, family members, or even policymakers who are often less visible locally. We also realize that how people say khat makes them feel is shaped by cultural codes and perceptions of what khat is, and these may vary, depending on how khat fits into local cultural codes and political economies of various places.

Political Ecology

Because it costs labor and money to produce and acquire drugs, we can understand them in ecological and economic contexts. We can also go beyond their consumption to understand their production and distribution and how they affect local communities.

So we need to dig even further to explore the economic base and political context of khat. Political ecology does about the same thing as critical medical anthropology, only with a specific focus on the environment. Like CMA, political ecology focuses on unequal social relations, cultural politics, and relationships between local and broader dynamics. We place studies of local human ecological interactions within broader political and economic contexts to understand not just what farmers know of farming practices, for example, but also why their opportunity to farm is being threatened by land tenure changes, population increase stemming from migration of people escaping poverty in other places, conservation efforts, or lower commodity prices. Remember Roy Rappaport's study in chapter 6 in Durrenberger and Erem (2007)? Although his study of local ecological systems is brilliant, he was criticized for focusing too narrowly on local ecologies without taking into consideration broader political and economic dynamics (Gezon 1999; Peet and Watts 1996), such as colonial rule and the impact of the plantation economy. CMA and political ecology combine in making connections between drugs and the environments they are based on—the land and water used to grow them.

In this chapter, I explore the cultural, political, and economic contexts of khat in Madagascar to analyze how and why it is labeled as a drug and what this means for local people in terms of their livelihoods and consumption habits. To understand the local context, I discuss on-the-ground ethnographic information. To connect these local people to the broader system, I discuss what other scholars have written about khat in other cultural settings, about the process of labeling substances drugs, and about how other drugs compare with khat. I connect local with global processes to understand the material conditions under which a substance is likely to be considered an illegal drug. We already know that a drug is declared illegal not just because it is "bad for you," but also because it is tied in particular ways to class difference and power.

Local Contexts: Commodity Chains of Khat

Perceptions of khat consumption tend to follow class lines, with the working poor supporting the khat trade and the middle and upper classes treating it with disdain. Remember that class is about more than income. Cultural codes also define the ways people differentiate themselves from others along class lines. Orientation toward Western economic development models is central to the cultural code of the ruling class because class members have to articulate with international bureaucrats and others who "speak that language." Many, including middle-class professionals, share it. In the logic of this cultural code, which stereotypes local male youth as perpetually seeking fast money, chewing khat seems to *cause* low economic growth, not merely correlate with it.

How can we study complicated systems to understand the place of drugs etically, apart from peoples' cultural codes and perceptions? Durrenberger and Erem (2007: 243) point out that ethnography—the observation of people in their daily lives—is critical to this process. It is, as they say, "one leg of the stool" that also depends on comparison and investigation of systems that exist beyond the local level. These systems are not easy to study with ethnography because observable phenomena are often located far from the core sites of our ethnographies and may not even have an easily identifiable place to study—how does one study a government or the International Monetary Fund or corporate capital flows, for example? Studying larger systems involves creative ethnography. It also requires, as Durrenberger and Erem (2007) point out, reaching beyond observation to read archival materials, reports, and relevant analyses by other scholars.

We can use a commodity chain analysis (Bernstein 1996; Ribot 1998), an approach that examines khat from the ground to the consumer. Such an analysis sees the three major economic processes—production, distribution, and consumption—as a chain of interconnected events. This enables us to understand how rural places are connected to wider consumer markets. Commodity chain analyses trace grapes and green beans from peasant farmers' fields to American and European tables. The market for Malagasy khat is mainly local, so it is possible to study much of the commodity chain ethnographically, but even then we cannot focus on a single site. When I studied khat, I visited farm fields in several different villages that grow khat. I found where people gathered to send khat to urban markets, and I visited two cities to observe khat sales and consumption.

Production

The bushy khat plant grows well in the cool temperatures of the Amber Mountain region in northern Madagascar, and its growing local popularity has meant a significant increase in revenues for farmers during the last ten to fifteen years. Wherever khat is grown throughout the world, it tends to be cultivated by smallholders (most farming under two hectares) and distributed through small-scale traders (Carrier 2005; Gebissa 2004; Kennedy 1987). This is also the case in Madagascar. A well-maintained khat field must be weeded about once a year, but other than that, the labor input is minimal (it is somewhat higher for farmers who irrigate), so it is a good investment for a household with available land. Farmers tend to begin harvesting four to five years after planting, and then the new growth on the ends of the branches is removed once or twice a week, because people chew only the tenderest leaves.

In the dry season, if farmers do not irrigate, they often do not have enough khat to send to market. Those who do irrigate earn two or three times the income of those who don't. Those who do not irrigate do not tend to rely on khat as their sole crop, but also plant rice for subsistence and fruits or vegetables for cash. Khat, like many drug crops, has a relatively high value per unit of weight vis-à-vis other cash crops, which makes it attractive to farmers—especially to those who can irrigate.

Many households supply all the labor from planting to weeding to harvesting (and sometimes even to selling wholesale). Some of the larger landowners take on a live-in worker to help with khat and other farm labor. Usually, these are young male migrant workers who have come from the south and live with a landowning family for a few years before they move on. Absentee landowners hire people to watch their fields for them. Smallholder households with little labor available sell to traders, and traders harvest as well. This extra work ensures that the traders get the best-quality khat—and it gives them free access to eat khat as they work!

Distribution

Some farmers carry their khat directly to markets in the nearby city of Diego Suarez (population around eighty thousand) or the smaller city of Ambilobe. Those who take their khat to Diego Suarez live primarily in or around the town of Joffreville, to the northwest of the Amber Mountain National Park. These khat wholesalers take public transportation for the forty-five-minute ride to the city, where they fan out to sell to street vendors stationed throughout the city, often grouped by where the khat is from. Some wholesalers go directly to the airport, where they send khat to cities throughout the country. They used to make clandestine arrangements with airport workers instead of paying for this service. When I visited in 2007, however, the airline had established a system of payment by weight. Shipments tended to be small-scale, not weighing more than twenty kilograms. As khat becomes a more central part of the local economy, authorities are beginning to find ways of taxing it as freight rather than as a drug.

A business partner (often a family member) of the Diego-side khat trader meets the airplane at its destination to pick up the khat. The partners either split profits or buy the khat outright and assume any risks involved in trying to sell it. Nadia, a particularly successful khat trader living in Joffreville, had her business partner deposit the payment into her bank account up front. By the way, people tend to associate women with trading, and there seem to be more women than men traders. In terms of local emic perceptions, the ideal woman trader is married to a man who stays on the farm to work while she makes frequent runs to the city to sell their khat and possibly buy and sell that of others to earn extra money. Nadia fits that profile. Less successful traders reported that their partners were unreliable, often not paying for the khat at all.

Khat fuels Diego's street economy. Dotted along well-traveled streets are sellers and chewers, and people stop to shop and chat. People in one part of town told me that sometimes when the khat arrives, there is such a large crowd gathered around that the gathering could be mistaken for a funeral or some other large ritual by those who did not know better.

Several profiles illustrate the diversity of sellers. The sellers may have family ties to the khat growers, or they may have landed in the business by chance. One man grew up in a khat-growing region (in the southern zone near Antsalaka) and buys his khat from family members, but he has lived in the city doing a variety of jobs. He sold khat for a long time, then took a job as a gas station attendant, and now sells khat again. He says that he doesn't make nearly the money now that he did before, partly because he lost all his regular clients and partly because the khat economy has changed. Another family has a well-organized division of labor among the father and his adult children, enabling them to cover all functions in the commodity chain, including the selling of khat on the street.

The oldest and most productive establishment on Amber Mountain today is owned by a family that bought land from a Creole family and that identifies as a mix of Yemeni, Malagasy, and Creole descent. This family is reputed to be one of the oldest khat-growing families on the mountain and to have the highest-quality khat in Joffreville. This family owns the tallest khat bushes I saw (claimed to be forty years old), and its irrigated fields enable the family to produce high-quality khat during the dry season. Family members did not tell me directly about earnings, but they use costly technology (pipe irrigation) and own cars, a rare luxury.

Those who have been selling for a long time complain that, despite the rise in the number of chewers, several factors have made it harder to make a living from khat now. They cite increased competition from other sellers as well as workplace policies that increasingly forbid khat chewing on the job, making the demand lower per person for some categories of chewers.

Consumption

Until the early 1990s, consumption was mainly by those of Arab descent, referred to locally as "Arabs," who were Muslims and drank cold water or tea to quench their thirst while chewing. People would often chew khat in groups over a span of several hours in the afternoon and spit out the leaves when they were done. They would chew it from once to several times a week, and they would chew it more often during Ramadan in order to stay awake later at night. When people of Arab origin were asked why they chewed it, often they said merely that it was the custom of Arabs. Others mentioned the welcome feeling of alertness it provided, and some mentioned the enjoyment of chewing khat together with friends.

Gradually, more and more non-"Arabs" began chewing it. Many concur that the taxi drivers were among the first, using it to stay awake at night. Many Malagasy chew khat by themselves, and this is not stigmatized as it is in Yemen, where there is great social pressure to chew in groups. It is mainly men who chew khat, with moderate acceptance of women who chew it. Many of those who chew are not practicing Muslims and drink beer after spitting out their wad of khat in order to "kill the effect" (*mamono ny dosy*) of the stimulant. Two categories of men are likely to chew khat: workers with stable incomes who chew on days off or at work if permitted to help their concentration, and young men, often stigmatized as *barbo,* or shiftless youth in search of distraction. The barbo are often involved in the informal economy in one way or another, often with the stated goal of making enough money to purchase more khat. Some are students, and few have stable employment.

The barbo are in a highly suspicious and vilified category, especially by those who have received more Western education, who are not originally from that region of the country, and who are more Western oriented in general. Many of these more middle- to upper-class Malagasy people don't know how the barbo earn their money to buy khat and suspect them of stealing. Ethnographic interviews reveal that this is not common, however. More importantly, barbo are suspected of being a barrier to economic development because of their perceived unwillingness to take on a steady job. My study revealed that it is more likely that there are just not enough jobs to absorb the available labor.

Background of Khat

The ultimate origins of the khat plant are unknown, but there are different versions. John Kennedy (1987: 60–62), an anthropologist who did seminal research on the cultural and medical aspects of khat, notes that it is reasonable to assume that it was initially introduced to Ethiopia in the eleventh century, where it was first used recreationally. Although most writers accept that khat came to Yemen from Ethiopia, Kennedy proposes that there is some evidence that it went in the opposite direction. In any case, he notes that by the twelfth century in both places khat was probably in limited recreational use, but became widespread by the fourteenth century.

Chewing khat has been an important social ritual in Yemen for hundreds of years, mostly among men, but also among women. We have evidence that khat has been an important part of religious life in Yemen at least since the sixteenth century. Sufi mystics wrote poetry about it, embracing khat as a divine gift because it facilitates a sense of union with God (Wier 1985). For example, Mark Wagner (2005: 24), a scholar of comparative literature, quotes from a poem dated 1699: "Whenever I wanted my sight to rise to the sky, to existence, [khat] served as my stairs, [Allowing me] to cross the stars is one of its merits" (second bracket in original).

Khat chewing also has a long tradition in Ethiopia and Somalia. It is mainly produced in the Hererge highlands in eastern Ethiopia, which borders northern Somali (Gebissa 2004: 36–37). Apparently they liked their khat in Ethiopia just as much as in Yemen. Historian Ezekiel Gebissa (2004: 76) quotes the British explorer Richard Burton writing on khat in 1853: "[It is] Food for the Pious, and literati remark that it has the singular properties of enlivening the imagination, clearing the ideas, cheering the heart, diminishing sleep, and taking the place of food." Khat use expanded in Ethiopia as the Oromo pastoralists became sedentary farmers and began converting to Islam. Gebissa (2004: 52) writes: "By 1910 khat-chewing had become a widespread practice among the Islamized Oromo, among whom the leaf quickly attained social, cultural and religious importance.... Non-Muslims, however, considered khat-chewing to be a sign of conversion to the Islamic faith."

Khat continues to have religious significance. Today, in Ethiopia and Somalia, people consume khat to celebrate marriages, births, and other religious ceremonies (Brooke 1960). Though some Somali Muslim orders forbid khat, others advocate using it to facilitate prayer and meditation. Even though some may associate chewing khat with Islam in Yemen, Ethiopia, and Somalia, it is not generally recognized as an acceptable Islamic practice. Khat chewing is, in fact, considered improper by most Muslim authorities throughout the Arabian Peninsula. There have been many bans on khat, some by Islamic leaders, some by the colonial governments, and some by contemporary governments that see khat as a socially disruptive drug.

Another major production zone is in Kenya, especially in a mountain range to the northeast of Mount Kenya, where it is farmed by subgroups of Bantu-speaking Meru (Carrier 2005b). Anthropologist Neil Carrier (2005a) reports that production and consumption in Kenya are deeply rooted in some Meru cultural practices. The oldest trees (which people claim to be hundreds of years old) provide a symbolic association with ancestors and form an important part of cultural identity. Khat is also used in many ceremonies, including marriage negotiations and circumcisions (Carrier 2005a: 208–209; 2005b: 540). Carrier (2005a: 210) found evidence that chewing khat was strongly associated with male elders and that there were strong prohibitions against chewing among the youth.

Even though khat is a culturally integrated indigenous crop, it has also become increasingly popular among Kenyan women and youth in rural and urban areas. Carrier (2005a: 210) argues that khat has become central to a youth ethos and helps "forge an identity as young, modern and Meru." The situation is similar in Madagascar, where the fastest-growing market for khat is among the Malagasy youth, especially young men. Khat is also an economically important international cash crop exported primarily to Somalia and controlled by Somali traders (Carrier 2005b).

Understanding the history and current situation of khat sets the stage for understanding the context for khat's position within Malagasy society: how it got there, what it means symbolically to those who chew and are familiar with its history and current use, and how current trends of popularity—and vilification—articulate with other global dynamics. Khat reveals another set of nodes in this complex system of governmental regulation.

Khat as a Drug

As you read this discussion of local and international perceptions of khat's effects, think carefully about medical science and public health and what kind of relationship they may have with foreign policy or other nonmedical goals and with cultural codes. Think about the hegemony of the statements made by powerful international and national organizations.

Global Classifications

According to medical terminology popularized in part by the World Health Organization (WHO) in the 1950s, khat is not a physically addicting drug. In fact, very few drugs are technically physically addicting according to their classification (Goode 1998). Opiates (for example, opium, heroin, and codeine) and alcohol are considered physically addicting because of the way they operate on the body's chemistry and produce distinctive "withdrawal" symptoms of chills, fever, vomiting, and so on. Under these criteria, even cocaine is not considered physically addictive, though it is considered one of the most psychologically addicting drugs. This manner of placing crack cocaine and caffeine into the same category of "psychologically, [but not physically] addicting" substances means that we cannot decide how dangerous a drug is to individuals and society in a laboratory. Such a determination requires a great deal of analysis and social judgment—and leaves a lot of room for the powerful to impose their interpretation on the rest. The WHO is powerful in this context, because individual nations throughout the world, including the United States, look to this organization to define acceptable and unacceptable pharmaceutical use. WHO drug studies are highly respected and virtually unquestioned.

The WHO categorizes psychotropic substances into "schedules" according, first and foremost, to their medical usefulness and second, to their "abuse risk" and potential for causing dependency. Although few laboratory studies of khat have been done (World Health Organization 2003), and ethnographic studies show it is only mildly psychologically addicting, someone (or more likely, some committee) at the WHO decided that khat's chemical components place it into two different schedules. When it is fresh, it contains cathinone, which has been determined to be a Schedule I drug, marking it as having the highest risk and abuse potential of all the categories. Schedule I substances are "drugs with a high abuse risk" and no recognized safe medical use (http://www.tsbp.state.tx.us/consumer/broch2.htm). Other drugs in this category include certain narcotics (including opium and heroine), LSD, and methamphetamine.

Within twenty-four to forty-eight hours after the plant is picked, the cathinone in khat breaks down into cathine, which is a Schedule IV drug, defined as having low abuse potential, currently accepted medical use, with some risk of low-level dependence. Other drugs in this category are Valium, Xanax, and

Ambien. For comparison, coca leaves, crack, and cocaine belong in Schedule II: "drugs with a high abuse risk, but also have safe and accepted medical uses in the United States. These drugs can cause severe psychological or physical dependence" (http://www.tsbp.state.tx.us/consumer/broch2.htm).

This classification has been ratified by the United Nations in what are called conventions. The first, passed in 1961, was called the Single Convention on Narcotic Drugs, 1961 (http://www.unodc.org/pdf/convention_1961_en.pdf). The word "single" referred to the fact that the document established an international agreement on how to classify drugs. Individual nations, then, have adopted them, as is evident on the Web sites I pasted in the previous paragraph, which refer to the U.S. Drug Enforcement Agency's adoption of these schedules, which, again, were developed by the WHO and ratified by the United Nations. This is all rather complicated and ultimately obscures the origin of the decision about how to classify substances. So many layers of official formality make it hard to critically examine the system based on evidence, even when, as in the case of khat, policymakers admit that there have not actually been enough studies to reliably place it in a schedule (World Health Organization 2003). The questions get buried in bureaucratese.

In the end, this placement of cathinone as a Schedule I drug makes it illegal in the United States and many other countries, including France. This label of illegality has a concrete effect on the lives of Malagasy (and any other khat-involved) people. Even though khat is legal in Madagascar, the government of Madagascar receives millions of dollars in funding from the United States and other lenders. Its leaders cannot afford to upset these powerful funders by embracing a substance they find deplorable. People in Madagascar feel the hegemony of the WHO indirectly because they must please lenders who accept WHO pronouncements. The official position on khat in Madagascar makes sense only in this global context. The ruling class in Madagascar must answer to actors in the global capitalist system. Remember that these schedules must be viewed as cultural documents with the power to relegate any substance deemed problematic to the realm of the pathological, subject to control within an institutionalized biomedical framework.

User Experiences and Local Perceptions

As Durrenberger and Erem (2007) note, anthropologists tack back and forth between ethnography and understandings of broader systems. Let's get back to the local scene and tie together some of these strands. Recall that any evaluation of recreational drugs and their dangers must consider a drug's biological and chemical effects, the kinds of experiences users have with the drug, and the contexts in which they consume it.

Local producers, traders, and users in Madagascar consider khat's effects gentle compared with those of other drugs, including alcohol and marijuana. People in the khat network (consumers, producers, traders) scoff at the idea that the drug could ever qualify as anything other than a "mild drug." Khat users cross-culturally describe its effects in some similar ways, noting its ability to increase concentration either on one's thoughts, on one's job, or on the conversations one is having. In Madagascar, chewers reported finding it an enjoyable way to kill time. They say they like the feeling it gives them of being concentrated on their thoughts (*concentré*) and of having the opportunity to share conversation with companions. Khat chewers say that it motivates them in their jobs, opens up thoughtful conversations on politics and current events, and also allows them to think about how to make more money or otherwise improve their individual lives. During interviews in March 2005, when rice was so expensive, many said that they still bought khat to chew because it enabled them to get rid of their worries and strategize solutions to their problems.

Shelagh Wier's (1985) description of the khat experience in Yemen fits with my observations in Madagascar and corroborates what others have written about it in other contexts (Carrier 2005a). Wier notes that Yemenis stop using khat when they go overseas, without any negative consequences beyond a mild craving. When John Kennedy and his colleagues studied khat use in Yemen, they found that it did not produce a heavy dependence (Kennedy, Fairbanks, and Teague 1980; Kennedy et al. 1983). Culturally, however, khat chewing is a deeply embedded social ritual in the lives of chewers in Yemen and Somalia, and people go to great lengths to make sure they have enough khat to chew, daily for many. Despite the fear some have of khat in Madagascar, heavy chewers that I talked with claimed that they missed it and even craved it when they did not chew, but that they did not experience any physical withdrawal symptoms and continued to meet social obligations. Many weekend chewers and other light users do not talk about craving it.

Whether khat is or ought to be classified as a hard drug (*drogue dure*) or a mild drug (*drogue douce*) is a common subject of conversation among people in the city of Diego Suarez, both within the khat production-distribution-consumption network and among professionals. Opinion tends to fall predictably along two lines. Those in the khat network argued that it is not a hard drug and is no worse than caffeine. Many professionals I spoke with, including a psychiatrist, a psychiatric nurse, and a judge, tended to believe that it is, or should be, classified as a hard drug. Those in the psychiatric profession claimed that it made people "crazy." An inspection of a psychiatric hospital (a twelve-bed establishment with seven patients at the time of my visit) revealed that five out of seven of the patients were there for drug-related reasons. According to the judge, khat made people lazy and led to petty crimes, such as theft.

Although professionals are not technically a part of the ruling class, their positions respond to the cultural codes of the ruling class, sometimes contesting them, but often informing and reinforcing them, as do these professional opinions of khat. Medical doctors, however, refrained from such a dichotomous judgment and admitted that they did not really have enough evidence to say. Based on their practice, they could not directly link any particular ailments with khat. They wished they had the resources to conduct better studies. Certain others, particularly practicing Christians and well-educated people far removed socially from khat-chewing environments, admitted they were not sure but would not be surprised if it were a hard drug.

The confusion of the Malagasy as to whether khat is a "hard" (presumably a Schedule I or II drug) or a mild drug is justified based on the dual WHO classification of cathinone and cathine. But this confusion is also justified based on a discrepancy between international discourse on the drug and its observed characteristics. To read about khat in Yemen or to observe khat use in Madagascar, one would scarcely believe that khat could qualify for such a radical placement in the WHO classification.

The schedules have many weaknesses, but a significant one is that they are not sensitive to context-dependent factors, such as route of administration. Consumed as khat is in Madagascar, Yemen, and East Africa, chewed over a period of two to five hours, the release of its active ingredient is necessarily slow relative to other routes of administration—and hence the effects less intense than if khat were consumed in pill form, for example, as it has been marketed in Israel and the West (as a rave drug).

Shifting Western Perceptions of Khat

Western opinions of khat have shifted since the beginning of Western contact with khat-chewing areas of the world. As Wier (1985) notes, early accounts tend to be either descriptive or laudatory of khat's effects. Neibuhr, who was the leader of a Danish expedition to Yemen in 1763, compared khat chewing to the taking of snuff. A Frenchman who visited Yemen in 1837, for example, wrote that he "ended up getting great pleasure from its gentle stimulation and the vivid dreams which followed" (quoted in Wier 1985: 55). It was only in the early twentieth century that Western accounts of khat more or less uniformly condemned it as a moral and economic vice to which the Yemeni were pathetically and unhealthfully addicted. One account referred to khat as "the most debilitating, time-wasting scourge of Yemen" (quoted in Wier 1985: 58). In 1922 one traveler described the social setting of the small, enclosed, smoky room in which people chewed khat as "disgusting." Another referred to the act of chewing as "filthy." Wier notes that much of the disapproval stemmed from an ethnocentric lack of ability to appreciate the aesthetic qualities of Yemeni life. The early twentieth century was a time of political and economic expansion of the United States and Europe in the Near East, and they had little incentive to appreciate the aesthetic qualities of a social pastime that they perceived to stand in the way of capitalist expansion.

Since then, opinion has diverged, with some emphasizing khat's mild effects (Kennedy et al. 1980) and others condemning it on nonmedical grounds. According to a recent WHO Expert Committee on Drug Dependence, for example, the effects of khat are not well-known, but it is "believed to be dependence-producing" (World Health Organization 2003: 18). The committee nevertheless felt confident enough to write that khat is "associated with a variety of social and economic problems affecting the consumers and their families" (World Health Organization 2003: 18).

It is clear that evaluations of khat vary tremendously. Observers have identified it as everything from an Arabian delicacy and an enjoyable, mildly stimulating social ritual to a scourge that wrecks individual lives and causes social havoc. This vast range of opinion makes it clear that cultural factors play a significant role in khat's evaluation.

Analysis

We are back to the original question: How do some substances become social taboos (and in some instances illegal) and not others? Obviously, there are many factors involved, including localized experiences with the substance, the history of its use, and the relationship between it and its users, on the one hand, and the ruling class, on the other. Thus far, it seems that a substance is more likely to be socially acceptable at local levels if it has a long history of use, is culturally integrated, and is incorporated into socially acceptable forms of practice, such as engaging in ceremonies, passing the time with others, or stimulating job performance. A substance's level of acceptance at broader levels is harder to define easily. A substance is likely to be socially acceptable if the practice of its use is shared across classes—as in coffee or alcohol in the United States. In some cases, however, drug use is so emotionally charged, so lucrative, and also so socially destructive that there is widespread disagreement among the ruling class. Coca-derived products are an example: In practice, cocaine is a ruling-class drug, whereas crack is a (sub)working-class drug (though many people in each class do not condone its use). At the policy level, even though many in the ruling class support eradication at all levels of coca production, distribution, and consumption, some have actively promoted it (Chien, Conners, and Fox 2000). In general, it seems fair to say that drug use tends to be acceptable to those who use it and/or make money off of it and not to anyone else.

Local people and scientists alike have found khat's effects to be of a mild stimulant, comparable with caffeine, for example. Overall, local communities of users, traders, and producers in Madagascar like it a great deal, even if they do recognize some negative aspects, including consumers' drain on household budgets, questions about health effects, and concerns about youth getting distracted from education. So why is it illegal in some places? Why does the U.S. government, for example, bother to prosecute people for possessing or selling khat? If you read newspaper reports, you learn that emic explanations from the point of view of detractors contend that it has strong psychological effects that make it socially dangerous. One spokesperson for the Drug Enforcement Agency said: "It is the same drug used by young kids who go out and shoot people in Africa, Iraq and Afghanistan. It is something that gives you a heightened sense of invincibility, and when you look at those effects, you could take out the word 'khat' and put in 'heroin' or 'cocaine'" (http://www.latimes.com/news/nationworld/nation/la-na-khat3-2009jan03,0,863585.story).

A small dose of critical thinking suggests that the drug itself is not caus-ing the conflicts in "Africa." Perhaps khat is threatening, not because of its chemical properties, but because it is the stimulant of choice of people many Americans consider enemies and is associated with terrorism and other ag-gressive and antagonistic behavior. Even before the recent association of khat with Somali terrorism and unrest in Africa, khat in Somalia and Djibouti had long been a symbol of resistance against foreign intrusion (Cassanelli 1988; Green 1999). So fear of difference partially explains ruling-class reactions against khat.

What else might be going on? Another piece of the puzzle may be po-litical and economic in a self-intensifying loop. In short, khat's economic marginality fuels its illegality (or dislike of it in Madagascar, where it is not technically illegal), which in turn fuels its economic marginality. Basically, khat is not part of the formal, regulated global capitalist economy because it is not formally traded. Either it is illegal and part of a black market economy, or in several countries where it is grown (and legal), including Madagascar and Yemen, the primary market for it is local. Therefore, it does not generate export earnings for the country. In other words, khat does not provide a country with a way to earn hard currency or to increase its gross domestic product. Khat is economically marginal. Despite the considerable revenues it provides to small-scale farmers in producing countries, khat does not fit into formal economic development plans and is therefore discouraged or ignored.

Kenya and Ethiopia export khat to Somalia, Europe, and the United States. But khat is illegal in some of those countries, and so its trade is not formally regulated. Furthermore, the people who control its export to those countries are, by definition, outlaws and so are threatening not only because they deal in drugs but also because they do not follow the law. The use of khat becomes self-intensifying this way: It became illegal because of a perceived social and health threat. Because it is illegal, traders must deal clandestinely, angering authorities and reinforcing the vehemence with which it is declared illegal.

The implications of this illegal status and the cultural codes that support it reach down to the level of small-scale producers, traders, and consumers in places such as Madagascar. As an agricultural practice, khat production has been invisible to those planning economic development and agricultural extension services. As a result, people involved in this khat commodity chain live with insecurity, for they do not know when or if it may become illegal in light of national or international pressure.

This analysis has shown how cultural codes and material conditions are interrelated and mutually dependent. Ideas about psychotropic substances vary dramatically and are not tied directly to any objective physiological ef-fects. For anthropologists, this makes these substances interesting to study.

Such investigation reveals the deeply engrained and holistic connections between biology and culture. Attitudes toward these substances tell a lot about people: their history, what is important to them, what their goals are, who has access to resources, and who does not.

References

Bennett, Linda, and Paul W. Cook Jr. 1996. "Alcohol and Drug Studies." In *Medical Anthropology: Contemporary Theory and Method,* edited by C. F. Sargent and T. M. Johnson. Westport, CT: Greenwood, 235-251.

Bernstein, Henry. 1996. "The Political Economy of the Maize Filière." *Journal of Peasant Studies* 23, no. 2: 120-145.

Brooke, Clarke. 1960. "Khat (*Catha edulis*): Its Production and Trade in the Middle East." *Geographical Journal* 126, no. 1: 52-59.

Carrier, Neil. 2005a. "'Miraa Is Cool': The Cultural Importance of Miraa (Khat) for Tigania and Igembe Youth in Kenya." *Journal of African Cultural Studies* 17, no. 2: 201-218.

——. 2005b. "The Need for Speed: Contrasting Timeframes in the Social Life of Kenyan Miraa." *Africa* 75, no. 4: 539-558.

Cassanelli, Lee V. 1988. "Qat: Changes in the Production and Consumption of a Quasilegal Commodity in Northeast Africa." In *The Social Life of Things: Commodities in Cultural Perspective,* edited by A. Appadurai. Cambridge: Cambridge University Press, 236-257.

Chien, Arnold, Margaret Conners, and Kenneth Fox. 2000. "The Drug War in Perspective." In *Dying for Growth: Global Inequality and the Health of the Poor,* edited by J. Y. Kim, J. V. Millen, A. Irwin, and J. Greshman. Monroe, ME: Common Courage Press, 293-327.

Durrenberger, E. Paul, and Suzan Erem. 2007. *Anthropology Unbound: A Field Guide to the Twenty-First Century.* Boulder, CO: Paradigm Publishers.

Gebissa, Ezekiel. 2004. *Leaf of Allah: Khat and Agricultural Transformation.* Athens: Ohio University Press.

Gezon, Lisa. 1999. "Of Shrimps and Spirit Possession: Toward a Political Ecology of Resource Management in Northern Madagascar." *American Anthropologist* 101, no. 1: 1-10.

Goode, Erich. 1998. *Drugs in American Society.* New York: McGraw-Hill.

Green, R. H. 1999. "Khatt and the Realities of Somalis: Historic, Social, Household, Political, and Economic." *Review of African Political Economy* 79: 33-49.

Kennedy, John G. 1987. *The Flower of Paradise: The Institutionalized Use of the Drug Qat in North Yemen.* Norwell, MA: Kluwer.

Kennedy, John G., Linda A. Fairbanks, and Teague. 1980. "Qat Use in Northern Yemen and the Problem of Addiction: A Study in Medical Anthropology." *Culture, Medicine, and Psychiatry* 4, no. 4: 311-344.

Kennedy, John G., et al. 1983. "A Medical Evaluation of the Use of Qat in North Yemen." *Social Science and Medicine* 17, no. 12: 783-793.

Peet, Richard, and Michael Watts. 1996. *Liberation Ecologies: Environment, Development, and Social Movements.* New York: Routledge.

Ribot, Jesse C. 1998. "Theorizing Access: Forest Profits along Senegal's Charcoal Commodity Chain." *Development and Change* 29: 307-341.

Singer, Merrill, and Hans Baer. 2007. *Introducing Medical Anthropology: A Discipline in Action.* Lanham, MD: Rowman and Littlefield.

Wagner, Mark. 2005. "The Debate between Coffee and Qat in Yemeni Literature." *Middle Eastern Literatures* 8, no. 2: 121–149.

Wier, Shelagh. 1985. *Qat in Yemen: Consumption and Social Change.* London: British Museum.

World Health Organization. 2003. "WHO Expert Committee on Drug Dependence." In *WHO Technical Report Series.* Geneva: World Health Organization.

12

BORDERING CULTURE
THE U.S.-MEXICO CASE

Josiah Heyman and Howard Campbell

Imagine a man and a woman warmly hugging on a street corner in downtown El Paso, Texas. Is this a joyful greeting or the expression of a passionate romance? Knowing the cultural code of Latin Americans, we can understand correctly that it is a sign of friendship. In the frontier between the United States and Mexico, however, both the performance and the interpretation of this act are ambiguous, because the cultural frame of reference could be either Latin American or North American. We would need to understand exactly who these two people are and how they relate to each other to make sense of this border example.

We often pigeonhole the concept of culture as belonging to a "people" (often, a euphemism for nationality or ethnicity, or both). We refer to Mexican culture, or American culture, as we did in the opening example. Sometimes this assumption works, and sometimes it blinds us to other ways we can be cultural beings. There are cultures of women and men, older and younger generations, social classes, occupational groups—not just nations or nationlike ethnic groups. There are important cultural codes for how different people relate to each other—workers and supervisors, say, or elders and youth. Culture can be a relation of difference as well as a relation of similarity.

Because we associate cultures with single nations (or nationlike ethnic groups), we tend to think of culture as internally uniform; it covers all members in about the same way. We also tend to think of it as externally bounded. People are almost all the same, and then suddenly at a boundary, one culture comes to a stop and a new culture takes over. There is no way of conceiving crossing, blending, mixing. We can call this the "thing" view of culture; the fancy term is that it is "reified."

189

This thing view does not work very well at the U.S.-Mexico border (henceforth, "the border"). (Useful background readings about the border include Anderson and Gerber 2008; Ganster and Lorey 2008; Martinez 1994; and Wood 2008.) Yet the word "culture" was helpful when we analyzed the complicated possibilities of a border example: the warm embrace on a downtown street. It pointed to different codes of how people act and ways people can interpret those actions. So how can we make better use of culture rather than tossing it aside? We might see culture as a useful *word* for thinking, a verbal pointer, rather than a solid thing. It points to the specific uses of general human capacities for learned ideas and behavior in particular relationships and settings. The setting may be a nation, but it may also be an activity (such as a certain way of working and making money—an occupational culture) shared across national boundaries. The relationship may be a way people from two different countries coordinate their ideas and behaviors to successfully work with each other.

Let's make this more concrete. The United States is a centralized political unit, a "state"; Mexico is likewise. This much is certain. They are also, in some ways, great masses of people with somewhat similar ways of life and thinking—two different national cultures—though we have not explained how they got that way or how they continue to change. It is easy to slap labels on these things: U.S. culture in this box, Mexican culture in that (especially if the box is a bounded territory). It is likewise easy to see these cultures as contrasting: Mexicans celebrate Día de los Muertos (Day of the Dead); Americans, Halloween. And it is awfully tempting to see these countries as opposed: the United States as ultramodern, Mexico as quaintly traditional, or some other set of misleading stereotypes.

In such a view, cultural material and cultural carriers (the people themselves) seeping over from Mexico into the United States risk contaminating the orderliness and uniformity of the American cultural "thing," and vice versa. The border is important in this view, but in one way only: as an outer defense against disorder and dilution. The border is what defines and protects everything inside of it. We can easily imagine the politics of this view of the border in both countries. It is a politics of suspicion, a politics of exclusion, a politics of rejecting people (unless they instantly assimilate to the new place), and a politics of walling off the border—which is literally happening right now. In some cases, too, there is a politics of pity, imagining Mexico simplistically as a place of endless poverty and an object of charity, in mere contrast instead of intricate connection to the privilege of the United States. The border in this way of thinking is simplified into a symbol of fear and defense against such fear, and there is no space for understanding the people and places of the actual U.S.-Mexico borderlands (see Heyman 2008).

South of the border, U.S. and Mexican engineers converse in English about fine measures of quality, playing vital roles in the world economy. North of the border, store clerks spend much of their workday helping shoppers in Spanish (some, but not all, visiting from Mexico), but turn quickly if needed to English for a shopper just arrived in El Paso from Michigan. And two locals rapidly jump back and forth between both languages—speaking the hybrid called "Spanglish" (Stavans 2003)—occasionally laughing at a particularly well-turned phrase. Border cultures occur within relationships and transactions, often mix and blend, and sometimes produce wonderful bursts of creativity. At the same time, border settings sometimes involve conflict and separation, and a fair assessment of border cultures takes note of national and other distinctions. Being open to the topic of border cultures involves an attitude of confidence in one's own culture and willingness to see how it shares and interacts with other cultures, even when relations become complicated or difficult, a perspective suited to the social and political challenges of the contemporary North American continent and indeed of the world as a whole.

Borders pose a specific challenge to the "thing" view of culture. One "culture-thing" at borders hybridizes with other supposedly solid "culture-things." Indeed, cultures are not things at all, but complex webs of interactions, including social relations and political power. The word "culture" can aim us in a useful direction. It says, "Don't get stuck looking for nationally defined units when they really are mirages, appearing on the horizon but never achieving palpable solidity. Instead, look for connections and disconnections within and across nations and other units" (Wolf 2001: 308). This is not just a lesson about borders. In fact, it is also a lesson for understanding culture and relating to other people in many different settings. (For more on border cultures and their lessons for cultures generally, see Donnan and Wilson 1999; Heyman 2001.)

The everyday culture at the border is set within vast flows of corporate investment, commodities, mobile working people, and governmental policies and actions (Heyman 1991). The operations of capitalism and state power, crucial in all places, are displayed in obvious ways at seams between political and economic spaces such as borders. The U.S.-Mexico border is the largest boundary in the world between a prosperous country and a relatively poor one (though both nations are highly unequal class societies, with much wealth in Mexico and considerable poverty in the United States). Such powerful forces undergird the issues that border residents confront every day.

Important Issues at the Border

The maquiladoras are manufacturing plants owned by U.S., Canadian, Mexican, and Asian corporations, large numbers of which are found along the Mexican side of the border (a dated but still fundamental ethnography is Fernández-Kelly 1983). There, working people—especially young women and men—earn low wages, even by their own standards (ranging from $40 to $80 a week), assembling products to be purchased by consumers in richer lands. An American might struggle to buy a $400 new washing machine assembled in Ciudad Juárez, Mexico, but it is at least within the realm of possibility; a

Mexican worker can hardly aspire to that sum (she might settle for a cheaper, used machine imported from the United States). This global economic arrangement—subassemblies brought from China or the United States, bolted together by Mexican youth sweating for low wages, and then exported to Europe and the United States to be sold at prices commensurate with the higher purchasing power in those places—illustrates a fundamental principle of the border: Wealth and poverty join there in a *relationship of the unity of opposites*. Another descriptive phrase is "combined and uneven development," which grounds a panoply of flows back and forth across the borders.

The U.S.-Mexico drug trade dramatically illustrates how borders connect and divide individuals and socioeconomic groups (Campbell 2009). Mexico is a major producer of marijuana, heroin, and methamphetamine consumed in the United States. Mexican drug cartels (large illegal businesses comparable in size to small corporations) also handle most of the cocaine produced in South America that is transported across the border into U.S. cities. Because of low labor costs, these drugs are cheap and easy to produce in Latin America. Their monetary value increases by a magnitude of ten or more once they cross the border. Without the huge U.S. demand for recreational and narcotic drugs, the Mexican cartels would not exist. Likewise, if Mexican drug-trafficking organizations did not exist, there would be far fewer illegal drugs in the United States. Consequently, the United States' drug problem is Mexico's and vice versa.

In border communities this drama is played out every day as smugglers employ increasingly creative methods to conceal and transport tons of cocaine and pot through mountains, rivers, and deserts and across international bridges. Simultaneously, numerous U.S. law enforcement agencies, including the Border Patrol and Drug Enforcement Agency, mobilize agents to prevent smuggling. In recent years, thousands of Mexicans have been brutally murdered as cartels fight with rival cartels for control of the lucrative smuggling routes through Tijuana/San Diego, El Paso/Juárez, Laredo/Nuevo Laredo, and elsewhere. A small number of powerful drug traffickers make huge fortunes through the multibillion-dollar illegal drug trade, whereas others simply obtain dangerous low-paying jobs and consumers benefit from lower prices for drugs that ultimately may do them great harm.

Tourism and daily business on the border are fueled by the comparative economic advantage of buying or selling specific products on one side of the border rather than the other. Every day thousands of Mexican shoppers flood the streets and shopping malls of U.S. border cities in search of bargains on food, clothing, tools, toys, and other basic items. In fact, a major portion of the retail sector in American border cities is targeted at the Mexican consumer, especially the small buyer whose household budget is quite limited and who can save substantial amounts just by crossing the border for regular purchases. Residents of the U.S. border communities cross into Mexico in much smaller numbers (due to current border drug violence and U.S. immigration restrictions) to buy cheap generic and brand-name medicines, tortillas and other Mexican food items, beer and tequila, and more. They also take advantage of cut-rate dental and medical treatments, auto repairs, and other services that are less expensive on the Mexican side. Additionally, folkloric tourism to markets, plazas, bullrings, bars, and nightclubs attracts crowds of Americans and others who enjoy the way the border allows one to quickly pass from one culture to another.

The border is known for undocumented immigration to the United States. Even though clearly true, this image misses important points and also raises questions about how and why such unauthorized migration takes place (for more information, see Massey, Durand, and Malone 2002). Most immigrants in the United States are legal (temporary residents, permanent residents, or naturalized citizens), although the proportion of undocumented residents has grown in recent years. People arrive through various routes (e.g., airports) and become unauthorized immigrants in various ways (e.g., overstaying visas), not just hiking across the deserts and ridges of the southern border. Despite stereotypes, by no means are all people of Mexican origin immigrants, let alone undocumented, and not all immigrants are Mexican. In fact, most border crossings are done legally, at the official ports of entry, by people commuting back and forth for work, family visits, shopping, school, and so forth; and many such crossers are U.S. citizens who live in Mexico, and vice versa. (The ratio of legal to unauthorized crossings at the border is approximately 100 to 1.)

Mexican migration to the United States is varied, particularly in the U.S. borderlands, where many rich and educated Mexicans maintain residences. Nevertheless, the core of Mexico-U.S. migration involves hardworking poor people. People come to the United States because, directly and indirectly, prosperous North Americans seek their labor in services, construction, agriculture, food processing, and light manufacturing. They leave Mexico because of stagnation in small farming and ranching areas (while big farming for exports to the United States booms), stunted educational opportunities, and pervasive corruption and unfairness in everyday life. The North American Free Trade Agreement intensifies these driving forces. Many migrants, though not all, are "illegalized" (their socially encouraged and rather unavoidable decision to move treated as a violation of law) because the United States allocates not nearly enough legal visas for the number of people from Mexico that it employs.

Because migrants who cannot get visas are economically encouraged yet legally and politically discouraged, to move northward they must cross the border in the face of eighteen thousand Border Patrol officers, extensive electronic and airborne surveillance, increasingly lengthy sections of steel walls, and so forth. Migrants do this at considerable risk to their lives—more than four hundred people a year die crossing the border—and largely through hiring smugglers, creating one of North America's few growth industries. Interestingly, migrants tell interviewers that these laws, patrols, sensors, walls, dangers, and smugglers do not deter them from entering the United States (Fuentes, Esperence et al. 2007), although slumps in U.S. job markets do. Border law enforcement has been distinctly ineffective.

Enormous government agencies, including force-wielding organizations such as the military and various federal police units (Border Patrol, Customs, Drug Enforcement Administration, military-civilian surveillance centers, etc.), are highly important features of border life. Indeed, borders are privileged places for recognizing the penetration of the state into society and culture. The border itself is a product of centralized government; nonstate societies have much looser territorial forms. Furthermore, the more tightly the boundary is governed, the more moving people and goods across the border matters. For example, there is little incentive to smuggle, or to catch smugglers, when there are few effective differences in laws and taxes across boundaries. There clearly has been a trend toward increasingly extensive and expensive U.S. government enforcement of border rules across the twentieth and now twenty-first centuries, and the Mexican government is not far behind; yet this period has also seen the expansion of income, sophistication, and violence in illegal and informal economies at the border. It appears that law evasion and law enforcement reinforce each other in an endless spiral of coercion (Andreas 2001; also see Dunn 1996; Nevins 2002).

If we want to understand what the border is like in everyday life, we might envision that individuals, households, and personal networks bounce and ricochet among these forces, sometimes taking advantage of opportunities they present and always having to cope with their effects (see Vélez-Ibáñez 1996). To illustrate how these big issues shape everyday border culture, then, we offer four ethnographic case studies.

Colonias: Poor People's Suburbs

Colonias (as they are called in the United States) and *colonias populares* (the term in Mexico) illustrate perfectly how people creatively cope with inequity (Campbell and Heyman 2007). Colonias are residential areas where people purchase or lease a lot (or sometimes, in Mexico, just squat) and build their own house. They do not have preplanned and installed urban services, such as water, sewage, electricity, paved streets, and sanitation and police services. Often, through these enduring efforts, residents finally obtain some or all of these services, and colonias can become quite pleasant places to live. Because houses are installed or self-built, or built with the services of small entrepreneurs, and because the community strives for many years to gain services that subdivision dwellers encounter from day one, the colonias are an outstanding example of the creative quality of border society and culture.

Colonias occur because people want to own their own home and their own small plot of land. However, they have low incomes because of the exploitative character of the North American production system at the border (maquiladoras, as discussed, or mass production farmwork). Or they earn money in the informal economy, working off the books in (say) construction, meaning that they have no bureaucratic record of their income. Having little or no formal credit, they have little or no chance of getting a mortgage from a regular bank. Hence, they cannot borrow the large amount needed to buy a corporately made house in a fully serviced development, even if they had the downpayment to start with. Rather, landlords make money from subdividing and selling undeveloped land on the far edges of border cities and towns (and other farming and food processing areas) to such people, sometimes on reasonable terms and at other times in quite unfair and manipulative fashions. The colonia dweller then places a house, initially a small and rudimentary affair, on the lot, digs a primitive pit latrine, and purchases water by the barrel. Gradually, over time, the house is expanded, upgraded, or replaced, an interesting cultural process.

Colonia residents on both sides of the border have to fend for themselves with little government help or external sources of support. On the Mexican side, colonias are often formed by groups of people who invade or squat on public land and then have to defend their homes by force from their political enemies or the goon squads sent to evict them by angry landlords. Colonia occupants may establish their own local grassroots political organizations that essentially govern at the local level and negotiate with official authorities. U.S. colonia land is usually purchased from private sellers, often at usurious rates; therefore U.S. colonia residents confront somewhat less hostile political circumstances than their Mexican counterparts. Yet American colonia residents must also start a community from scratch with minimal government assistance. As a result of these conditions, there is a self-selection process such that colonias are generally occupied by those willing to make great sacrifices to own a home and land and create a neighborhood.

Colonia residents construct their own streets, water and sewage lines, and other facilities. In Mexico electricity may be stolen from municipal power poles through a series of ingenious "hot-wired" electrical lines known as *diablitos* (little devils). Mexican colonia residents also build their own homes out of the discarded materials from factories and wealthier consumers, such as wooden pallets, cardboard, tires, and scrap wood, as well as with building supplies they purchase, including sand, cement, and brick. The result is a creative "vernacular architecture" that wealthier outsiders may disdain but residents view with pride and a sense of ownership.

The independent, self-reliant ethos of *colonos* (colonia residents) carries over into their employment lives. Mexican-side colonia males work in maquiladoras, the construction industry, various types of labor on the U.S. side (often accessed clandestinely), and self-generated jobs in the informal economy (drug and other kinds of smuggling; street sales of food, watches, and other items; manufacture of arts and crafts; begging; etc.). Women also labor in the maquiladora industry and as maids in U.S. cities, prostitutes in border brothels, and street sellers of myriad items. On the U.S. side, employment is better paid but equally fluid and poorly paid—an example being contract janitors in public and private office buildings.

Because colonias are new communities composed of settlers with a fluid, dynamic approach to survival, the patterns and habits they adopt may not fit preestablished, formalized cultural categories. Hence, lacking preexisting Catholic parish churches, many colonia residents join the aggressively expanding Protestant churches in large numbers. In other respects their emerging lifestyles may embody less traditional ways, including joining opposition political parties, consuming a mix of American and Mexican products, and participating in transnational youth subcultures.

Cultural Blending at the Frontier: Border-Crossing Strategies

The border creates a pervasive set of differences right next to each other. On one side (Mexico), avocados are cheaper and more plentiful, on the other side (the United States), scarcer and more expensive, because U.S. government rules severely restrict the importation of avocados. Of course, borderites smuggle avocados from Mexico to the United States, and U.S. Customs officials sporadically try to catch and fine them. The example can be multiplied by a thousand, with some of these disparities being rather large and important. And each time there is a disparity, someone will cross to the other side to take advantage of it.

The uses of cross-border differences go beyond economic matters. They also involve playing with social relationships and symbolic meanings. Mexico is relaxed, bright, tropical, a place for pleasure and tourism (according to one set of stereotyped meanings, of course); the United States is advanced, modern, a showcase of new trends and exciting consumer goods (an equally simplistic stereotype). Millions of visiting trips annually are made at the border just on the basis of accessing such meanings. Families likewise spread across the two nations—a home place with grandparents in Mexico, a striving young couple in the United States, with differences bridged by international visits every weekend.

In such a situation, individuals sometimes deploy binational strategies, using dual cultural codes, one for each setting, or create novel hybrids of the two. Felipe Jácquez (a pseudonym), for example, grew up in Ciudad Juárez, Mexico. He learned fluent English as a kid by watching American television programs (easily accessed by border residents) and accompanying his parents on shopping and social trips to El Paso, Texas, the adjacent border city. As a youth, he struggled to find his niche in Mexican society. He was not accepted into an elite college preparatory high school in Mexico, so he decided to cross the border and join the U.S. Army, which offered a generous signing bonus, college-level educational benefits, and a steady income. Jácquez eventually left the military, but in the process he perfected his English, traveled the United States, and gained computer skills. Today he works for a multinational communications firm, with offices in Juárez and El Paso, which allows him to maximize his knowledge of both U.S. and Mexican customs.

Jácquez maintains a house on the Mexican side, easily acquired with no downpayment and low monthly payments, and a small apartment in El Paso. Although he is a dual citizen of Mexico and the United States, Felipe prefers Mexican food and social life, yet buys mainly American consumer goods and is paid in dollars. His young son is growing up bilingual and effortlessly switches back and forth, both linguistically and culturally, which is to say that he can function equally well within Mexican or American society. Such lives and identities are not easily compartmentalized, because they entail mixture and combination, rather than strict separation. Many people on the border thus live in both the United States and Mexico simultaneously and often cross the international line several times in one day.

"Don" Chepe, as we knew him (Don and Doña are terms of honor, often used for older people, and Chepe is a nickname—we never knew his given name), is another case of an individual who used the border as a resource, although it could also be said that the border "used" him. Don Chepe grew up in Santa Barbara, a small mining town in southern Chihuahua, Mexico. The only business in town was a major American-owned silver mine. Don Chepe worked his entire adult life in the mine until his lungs filled up with dust and he was forced to retire. Yet Don Chepe did not know what to do besides work. In retirement, he moved to Juárez to join his daughter. On the border he learned that laborers could earn five times as much or more in the United States than in Mexico. He then joined the veritable army of men who cross the border every day with *pasaportes locales* (border-crossing cards valid for short shopping or social visits, not employment) to work in the yards of wealthy El Pasoans (women likewise cross to clean houses and mind children).

Don Chepe, perennially dressed to the "T" in northern Mexican male fashion—worn, pointed leather cowboy boots; a red bandanna; a *cinto piteado* (*ixtle* fiber belt); and a battered cowboy hat—became a fixture in the Kern Place neighborhood adjacent to the University of Texas at El Paso. The professors and other upper-middle-class residents of the neighborhood, as well as the Mexican maids who worked in their homes, loved Don Chepe's swaggering style, his colloquial Spanish, and his Old World courtliness. In turn, he kept their lawns, yards, and rock walls immaculate. His wages were low by American standards but high compared with the prevailing rates for Mexican laborers. Sadly, Don Chepe died one day while walking back to Juárez after a full day's work in the El Paso sun. His lungs finally filled up and stopped his heart. He passed on at the top of the Paso del Norte International Bridge, directly underneath the flags of the United States and Mexico.

Cultural Blending at the Frontier: Creative Results

Border cuisine and language offer two flavorful examples of cultural blending (Campbell 2005; on cultural hybridization generally, see García Canclini 1995). Restaurants in this region often mix Mexican and American food items on their menus. Hybrid foods include "Mexican-style" bright red hot dogs (*winnies*) smothered with *chile con carne* served on a hamburger bun and then slathered with green *jalapeño salsa*; brisket with *chile con queso* sauce; "Chico's Tacos"—tacos made of cooked ground hamburger meat hand-rolled, fried in corn tortillas, served in a deep pool of slightly spicy tomato sauce, and then coated with grated American Velveeta cheese and soaked with hot green salsa—sold by a legendary El Paso restaurant of the same name; *hamburguesas* (hamburgers sold in Mexico that contain slices of avocado, ham, chile peppers, salsa, and other items seldom encountered on an "American" hamburger); hot dogs wrapped in slices of bacon (a common late-night food sold from carts on the Mexican side); and *burritos* featuring hundreds of different kinds of ingredients. On the U.S. side of the border, there is a booming business of fast-food restaurants and food stores selling a wide range of Mexican foods, including even the most exotic or obscure items. These largely Mexican products are retailed through slick American-style outlets that are otherwise identical to a McDonald's restaurant or a Safeway grocery store. Likewise, on the Mexican side of the border, one can find almost any American food, though these foods are sold in stores and restaurants whose architecture, atmosphere, and clientele are distinctly Mexican.

Language is perhaps the richest source of border cultural mixing. People who speak both Spanish and English as native languages—the typical situation on the U.S. side and somewhat frequent in border Mexico—typically engage in code-switching, linguistic behavior that includes (1) speaking both English and Spanish in the same sentence, (2) coining and using words that are a mix of both languages, (3) applying the grammatical rules of one language to the other, and (4) pronouncing words in one language according to the pronunciation rules of the other. The extent of border linguistic creativity is virtually limitless. Examples include

1. The mixing of grammatically distinct units in one statement: "I was talking to *ese* guy *a las* seven." "Come here *mi'ja*, give me your *mano*, *saludale a tu* grandfather." "My *panza* is hurting because I ate too much *carne, muy rapido y ahora me siento mal.*"
2. English nouns borrowed into Spanish: *troka* (truck), *marketa* (market, store), *la pompa* (pump), *yonke* (junkyard), *keki* (cake), *chopping* (shopping).
3. English verbs borrowed into Spanish and given Spanish verb forms: *qüitear* (to quit), *chutear* (to shoot), *monkear* (to monkey around), *over-holear* (to overhaul). In these constructions, a Spanglish infinitive verb is formed from an English verb root combined with the Spanish infinitive suffix *ear*.
4. Changes in pronunciation between the two languages: *Alameda*, a Spanish word for a park pronounced by English speakers as Alameeda; the English word "sorry" pronounced Spanish style with a rolling double-r pronunciation (usually done jokingly).

Cultural Boundary-Drawing and Nationalism

The border certainly creates cultural mixing, but it also encourages distinctions of identity on the basis of nationality, concepts of "my side versus their side" (Vila 2000). An example of this not only shows how strong national identification emerges in the borderlands, but also suggests ways that state institutions shape cultural identity and practices throughout society, including its interiors. Luis Antonio "Tony" Guerra is a strongly patriotic American, currently a Border Patrol officer and formerly an enlisted soldier in the U.S. Army, although he also is a lifelong borderlander who inveterately mixes Spanish and English. Guerra's father first worked in the United States without documents, mainly as a migratory farm laborer. Eventually, he settled in southern Arizona after becoming a permanent agricultural worker, operating machinery in a seed mill. His employer petitioned for his legal immigration, an option that is no longer possible for low-skill workers. Guerra's mother moved from Mexico after her husband's legalization. Guerra's older siblings were born in Mexico, but he was born in the United States and thus is a U.S. citizen by birth.

Guerra went to school in a small U.S. town, where he did moderately well. There, he learned to speak and read English, as well as learn lessons in patriotic U.S. history and civics. Although he visited Mexico often as a child, where his parents' relatives still lived, he always wanted to be "like the Americans," perceiving his family's circumstances to be humiliating in their poverty and uncertainty (although he also felt pride in his parents' endurance and hard work). Driven by these desires, he joined the army, where he served eight years and traveled far from the small-town borderlands. When his father became ill, however, he returned home, taking a few community college courses, struggling with low wages in the chronically depressed border economy, and eventually landing a job in the rapidly expanding Border Patrol.

Although Guerra told one of us that he would not like to be seen as a racially discriminatory officer—"to catch Europeans, blond people"—in reality, "all the people we arrest here are Hispanics" (he noted, however, that in recent years some non-Mexicans, such as Brazilians, had been arrested crossing through Mexico). He no longer visits Mexico, because he perceives that country as different from the visits of his childhood, as dirty and dangerous now, and his job as a Border Patrol officer is important in keeping the "bad people" from coming into the United States. Admittedly, most people still come to work "honestly," Tony noted, but "there needs to be some respect for American laws." Through the various institutions of the U.S. state, such as schools and the military; through his own drive to become included in mainstream America (as he perceived it from a marginal position); and through his adaptation to the realities of his job enforcing current immigration and drug laws, Guerra cannot be dismissed as naively forgetting his ethnic essence, as if he acquires one just by genetic inheritance, nor can he be embraced for magically recognizing it. (For more on U.S. immigration officers of Mexican origin, see Heyman 2002; and for a vivid ethnography of the work of the Border Patrol, see Maril 2004.)

What Can We Learn from the Border?

The U.S.-Mexico border offers lessons to us all, even if we live far from international boundaries. In this age of air transportation and electronic communication, borderlike social and cultural phenomena appear throughout society, not only in large cities such as New York, Los Angeles, London, and Mexico City, but also in small cities and towns throughout the world. The worldwide "new migration" since 1945 (in the United States, mainly since 1965) reinforces the continuing emergence of these phenomena. People are brought into interactions that may initially provoke stereotyping and tension, but also spark curiosity and change and in the long run result in creative new social and cultural blends.

Even these important observations understate the value of the border example for understanding the social and cultural world around us. Because complex and unequal societies—the sorts of societies that assuredly all readers of this book inhabit—involve interactions among people of differentiated backgrounds and resources, there is *always* something of the border situation confronting all of us. On the one hand, groupings of people with relatively similar cultural practices and a unified identity as a nation or ethnic group do not occur naturally; rather, they occur through the work of dominant institutions such as militaries and schools, as well as through demands by previously stigmatized people for incorporation and recognition. We saw just such processes at work in the life of Tony Guerra. On the other hand, cultures are not fixed, bounded "things" but rather works in progress, constantly being fashioned by sharing, exchange, struggle, vision, and creativity. Such change takes place within webs of unequal power, admittedly, so that it is not just a matter of free choice. Nevertheless, the inventive possibilities of culture are real and meaningful and are worth exploring and cultivating.

References

Anderson, Joan B., and James Gerber. 2008. *Fifty Years of Change on the U.S.-Mexico Border: Growth, Development, and Quality of Life.* Austin: University of Texas Press.
Andreas, Peter. 2001. *Border Games: Policing the U.S.-Mexico Divide.* Ithaca, NY: Cornell University Press.
Campbell, Howard. 2005. "Chicano Lite: Mexican-American Consumer Culture on the Border." *Journal of Consumer Culture* 5: 207-233.
———. 2009. *Drug War Zone: Voices from the U.S.-Mexico Border.* Austin: University of Texas Press.
Campbell, Howard, and Josiah McC. Heyman. 2007. "Slantwise: Beyond Domination and Resistance on the Border." *Journal of Contemporary Ethnography* 36: 3-30.

Donnan, Hastings, and Thomas M. Wilson. 1999. *Borders: Frontiers of Identity, Nation, and State.* Oxford, UK: Berg.

Dunn, Timothy J. 1996. *The Militarization of the U.S.-Mexico Border, 1978–1992: Low-Intensity Conflict Doctrine Comes Home.* Austin: Center for Mexican American Studies Books, University of Texas at Austin, 1996.

Fernández-Kelly, María Patricia. 1983. *For We Are Sold, I and My People: Women and Industry in Mexico's Frontier.* Albany: State University of New York Press.

Fuentes, Jezmin, Henry L'Esperance, Raúl Pérez, and Caitlin White. 2007. "Impacts of U.S. Immigration Policies on Migration Behavior." In *Impacts of Border Enforcement on Mexican Migration: The View from Sending Communities,* edited by Wayne A. Cornelius and Jessa M. Lewis. La Jolla, CA: Center for Comparative Immigration Studies, 53–73.

Ganster, Paul, and David E. Lorey. 2008. *The U.S.-Mexican Border into the Twenty-First Century.* Lanham, MD: Rowman and Littlefield.

García Canclini, Néstor. 1995. *Hybrid Cultures: Strategies for Entering and Leaving Modernity.* Minneapolis: University of Minnesota Press.

Heyman, Josiah McC. 1991. *Life and Labor on the Border: Working People of Northeastern Sonora, Mexico 1886–1986.* Tucson: University of Arizona Press.

———. 2001. "On U.S.-Mexico Border Culture." *Journal of the West* 40, no. 2: 50–59.

———. 2002. "U.S. Immigration Officers of Mexican Ancestry as Mexican Americans, Citizens, and Immigration Police." *Current Anthropology* 43: 479–507.

———. 2008. "Constructing a Virtual Wall: Race and Citizenship in U.S.-Mexico Border Policing." *Journal of the Southwest* 50: 305–334.

Maril, Robert Lee. 2004. *Patrolling Chaos: The U.S. Border Patrol in Deep South Texas.* Lubbock: Texas Tech University Press.

Martínez, Oscar J. 1994. *Border People: Life and Society in the U.S.-Mexico Borderlands.* Tucson: University of Arizona Press.

Massey, Douglas S., Jorge Durand, and Nolan J. Malone. 2002. *Beyond Smoke and Mirrors: Mexican Immigration in an Era of Economic Integration.* New York: Russell Sage Foundation.

Nevins, Joseph. 2002. *Operation Gatekeeper: The Rise of the "Illegal Alien" and the Making of the U.S.-Mexico Boundary.* New York: Routledge.

Stavans, Ilan. 2003. *Spanglish: The Making of a New American Language.* New York: Rayo.

Vélez-Ibañez, Carlos G. 1996. *Border Visions: Mexican Cultures of the Southwest United States.* Tucson: University of Arizona Press.

Vila, Pablo. 2000. *Crossing Borders, Reinforcing Borders: Social Categories, Metaphors, and Narrative Identities on the U.S.-Mexico Frontier.* Austin: University of Texas Press.

Wolf, Eric R. 2001. "Culture: Panacea or Problem?" In *Pathways of Power: Building an Anthropology of the Modern World,* edited by Eric R. Wolf with Sydel Silverman. Berkeley and Los Angeles: University of California Press, 307–319.

Wood, Andrew G. 2008. *The Borderlands: An Encyclopedia of Culture and Politics on the U.S.-Mexico Divide.* Westport, CT: Greenwood.

13

WEALTH UNBOUND
CORPORATE CAPITALISM AND THE
TRANSFORMATION OF U.S. CULTURE

Dimitra Doukas

Fear goes a long way toward controlling others in the contests for great wealth and power that punctuate human history, but great numbers of people will not work or soldier with enthusiasm and peak effectiveness out of fear alone—to give their full cooperation, they must *believe*. Besides, maintaining fear is expensive. The apparatus of force is expensive: soldiers, armament, vehicles, camping gear for thousands, tons of food and fuel. So all parties who have maintained power over others for any length of time have discovered the expedient of ideology—giving 'em something to believe in.

This is a lesson of *Envisioning Power* (1999), the great Eric Wolf's last book. Wolf examined the connections between ideas and power across three radically different societies, a chiefdom, an archaic agrarian state, and a modern industrial state. In each case a people under pressure embraced the "cosmic and frenzied ideologies" (Schneider 1999: 398) of desperate leaders. These are extreme cases, Wolf admitted, but because they are extreme, they are visible to us as researchers—they leave a lot of data in their wake (Wolf 1999: 16-17). Ideology, he found, is a necessary element of what he called "structural power," the power to specify the "direction and distribution of energy flows," that is, crucially, to direct the labor of others (Wolf 1999: 5-6, 275). (Even if it appears that wealth is the source of power, the power to *act* on a large scale will require the coordinated services of others.)

The seminal German sociologist Max Weber nailed it neatly. The problem, the challenge for would-be elites, is converting *power* to *authority* (Weber 1947 [1919]). Power (*Macht*, or might), for Weber, boils down to the plain ability, by whatever means, to force one's will on others. Authority is different.

202

Authority is *legitimate*. It became a legitimate part of a people's belief system by way of social instruments such as laws, compacts, treaties, and consensual agreements. So to endure for any length of time, power must try to create legitimacy for itself, to establish itself as a "proper" authority. If it can do this, it has achieved some measure of *hegemony*, in Antonio Gramsci's useful sense (1976). Gramsci was pointing to the cultural or ideological side of legitimized power—public acceptance of a power elite's bid for legitimacy, its "spin," we might say, on the legitimacy of its dominance.

In the United States, for example, we accept the power of the president and the police because we accept their claim to the authority of the Constitution and its democratic due process. Our acceptance rests on a structure of belief that has become hegemonic, the kind of thing "everybody knows" (cf. Certeau 1985): for instance, that the Constitution is a good system of government and the president is duly elected. These ideas are intertwined with other truisms that everybody knows, such as "It's a jungle out there," "Economic growth is a rising tide that lifts all boats," and "Everybody has a price."

This chapter argues that much of our "everybody knows" has been hegemonic for barely a century—your great-grandparents would not have recognized it. In the United States today we live in the ideological product of a party of elites whose giant corporations came into existence in the late 1900s and faced exactly the challenge of converting power to authority. This they did in the classic way: by mounting a campaign for a new "frenzied" ideology. I came to this conclusion after years of immersion in the popular press of the nineteenth-century United States and a great deal of ethnographic and historical research. What became disturbingly clear as the data lined up is that, on the eve of corporate power, U.S. political and economic ideology was radically different from—and adamantly hostile to—the new corporate elites. The U.S. culture of the *precorporate* era and the U.S. culture of the *corporate* era (our own) are diametrically opposed and so near each other in time as to preclude a gradual development of the second out of the first. I have used the privilege of conducting anthropological research to find out about this cultural transformation (Durrenberger and Doukas 2008; Doukas 1993, 1997, 2003).

With a couple of cautions in mind, Table 13.1 can serve to introduce the problem and set up the historical data. No effort to boil down the complex stew of cultural differences can avoid oversimplification. For one thing, clearly there are "survivals" or remnants of the precorporate ideology still afloat in U.S. culture,[1] though not in the limelight and not as a reigning logic of public decisionmaking. Likewise, cultural minorities have transmitted elements of the corporate ideology for centuries—what Andrew Carnegie (1889b, 1900a) influentially called "the gospel of wealth." Following Carnegie's lead, I call the precorporate ideology "the gospel of work" for what will be obvious reasons.

The gospel of work was an ideology of self-empowerment through hard work. It was shared across classes at least to the degree of paying lip service

Table 13.1

Gospel of WORK	Gospel of WEALTH
live "by the sweat of your brow"	money makes money
monopoly is corrupt	corner the market!
no central banking(!)	strong central banking
no "wage slavery"	a vast (low) waged workforce
frugality as a moral principle	consumerism
labor produces prosperity	capital produces prosperity

to a set of ideals, but often more than that. People of the early United States spoke of it in religious terms, as God's command that humankind must "earn their bread by *the sweat of their brow*" (Genesis 3:19; Lazerow 1995). Work of any kind was dignified, almost sacred, in this view. Not working was morally wrong. Not working and accumulating wealth off the work of others was blasphemous—"worshipping Mammon." Chief among these "parasites"—yes, they used this word even way back in the 1700s—were capitalists, people who made money from money, who produced nothing, who lived by preying on others (Fink 1983; Lazerow 1994; Doukas 2003).

The image of community in the gospel of work was an Adam Smithian world of thriving local economies in which the butcher, the baker, and the candlestick maker plied their trades in their own little shops and exchanged the goods they produced with each other and nearby farmers. This was the economic world in which Smith suggested that supply and demand naturally adjust to each other, as if by an "invisible hand" (1982 [1776]). But as Smith warned, along with many others before him,[2] nothing destroys the natural balance of supply and demand faster than *monopoly,* control of essential goods by a few hands, control complete enough to force up the "natural price" (Smith 1982: 164, 230, 232, 240).

And the last place that nineteenth-century Americans wanted to see monopoly was in money itself. Bankers could perform a social service in this ideology, as in Adam Smith's model, but *central banks* were an abomination, a *money monopoly* that could tyrannize the whole society. The politically feisty public of the nineteenth-century United States pulled down three attempts to establish a central bank. The third time, led by President Andrew Jackson in the 1830s, seemed to be the final one—it held until the rather stealthy foundation of the Federal Reserve in 1913 (Jackson 1949 [1832]; Livingston 1986).

The political-economic ideal of the gospel of work was *independence,* in this public's sense, not being dependent, being free.[3] Slaves were dependent, the image of dependency (Roediger 1991)—they lived and worked at the whim of another. Working for wages was too close for comfort to the dependent condition of slavery. As Americans of the time saw it, a person might work for wages as a youth and off and on into adult life, but what people worked *for* was to achieve and maintain their independence, their own access to a farm, shop, mine, well, woodlot, garden, or other productive resources. "Wage slavery" was more or less permanent wage work, work for another that did not pay well enough to buy one's freedom and get out of it, to, as we still say, "work for myself." Wage slavery was undignified.

The virtue of *frugality* lodged at the root of the gospel of work, in its historical opposition to aristocratic luxury, though surely most people enjoyed their little treats when they could. Frugality was a matter of group identity. It was also good practical advice in the rough settlements that Europeans carved out of the American woods and plains. "Waste not, want not" was the watchword of household management and business success (Weber 1976 [1904]; Horowitz 1992).

Last but not least, the gospel of work embeds a labor theory of value. Centrally, as Americans then saw the matter, *labor produces prosperity.* Of course, a person needs land and energy and materials and so forth to produce wealth, but these remain inanimate without the living hand of labor (Lincoln 1953 [1861]; George 1979 [1879]). In a nutshell, hard work was the center of this ideology, the foundation of collective prosperity and collective religion, both at home and in people's view of the society as a whole.

Now to be sure, not everybody who worked hard did achieve independence. Anthracite coal mining, for example, was a great livelihood for a couple of generations (Wallace 1987), until it came under the control of the "coal trust." The road to independence was blocked, by definition, for the enslaved and "conquered" peoples of this land, and it remained rugged for their free descendants, as it did for women who lacked adequate masculine support. Victorian literature abounds with desperate women and children, widows scrambling to feed youngsters, youngsters having to fend for themselves before they can defend themselves. Nevertheless, many people did work hard and achieve their modest success, enough people that it seemed to others to be attainable. The gospel of work was the road to independence, the alluring ideal of the real (as in historically genuine, original) "American dream" (Doukas 2003: 151-153).

Step down this list again, and it will be clear that not a single item is congenial to the practice of corporate capitalism. Capitalists do not earn their bread by the sweat of their brows. Monopoly, "cornering the market," was the royal road to the conquest of corporate empires. Central banking is key to the whole enterprise—it partakes in the coercive force of the state to back the capitalists' wealth tokens. "Wage slavery" has to be a permanent status for many—the corporate production system needs millions of laborers. Frugality has to be discredited—the system needs large numbers of lusty consumers. And in the late nineteenth century, nothing seemed to rankle the early corporate elites more than the pivotal proposition that labor produced wealth and prosperity. No, they insisted, capital, not labor, was the real producer of wealth and social prosperity—and they, its owners, were the chosen custodians of the nation's resources.

The Trusts and the Centralization of Production

The rise of corporate power is the greatest story *never* told in U.S. history. Looked at from a bird's-eye view, it wasn't an especially sudden economic transformation. It took about thirty years for the "trusts," the disreputable ancestors of today's giant corporations, to construct their power base, that is, to *centralize* production in all the key industrial sectors of the economy.[4]

"Centralize" is a neutral-sounding word under which lie a lot of arm-twisting and dirty tricks. The process meant taking over, taking control of, thousands of thriving local and regional enterprises, mines, mills, and factories and attaching them as subsidiaries to business empires of national scope. Centralization is the process whereby ownership passes from many hands to few. It makes enemies. From the point of view of the townsfolk, the capture by outsiders of productive resources they thought were theirs was a sudden transformation. Unexpectedly, the town was run by a new crew, with headquarters in a distant city. This abrupt transformation happened to relatively small-scale, independently owned enterprises across the industrialized landscape.

What is the time frame for this transformation? We could use 1871 as a possible start date for a period of accelerated daring and aggressiveness among U.S. capitalists (not, as noted, a beloved or respected occupational group). We can see corporations being formed before then in some productive sectors, in railroads and other capital-intensive infrastructure projects, and in massive textile developments—that is, generally in enterprises that relied heavily on credit. Bankers liked incorporated debtors (the easier to take them to court if they defaulted). But most enterprises in the nineteenth-century United States were unincorporated (most were kin-based partnerships [Licht 1995]), and much of the reason for that was a serious reluctance in all of the United States (plural) to grant corporate charters (Horwitz 1992). Corporations, in the gospel of work, were legalized monopolies, a social abomination.

In 1871 two transformative figures boldly subverted state laws, at the same time, in the same way, on opposite sides of Pennsylvania. On the eastern side, resident of the Reading Railroad Franklin Gowan launched a program to evade a Pennsylvania law that prohibited railroads from owning anthracite coal mines. The railroads ran on anthracite coal then. The spirit of the law was antimonopoly. Gowan guided through the state legislature a dummy corporation with fictitious owners, called Laurel Run Improvement Company, which then quietly purchased a large fraction of the anthracite reserves. On the western side, president of Standard Oil John D. Rockefeller evaded another antimonopoly law to pool the stock of supposedly competing companies and make a price-fixing deal with the railroad monopoly (under Tom Scott, Carnegie's mentor). Rockefeller called his dummy corporation South Improvement Company and proceeded to gobble up the remainder of his competition (Lloyd 1894; Tarbell 1966 [1902]; Wallace 1987).

The coincidence of names and strategies is either uncanny or historically significant, probably the latter. From the 1870s through the rest of the nineteenth century, circles of capitalists pooled their wealth and surreptitiously, illegally, pieced together their economic empires out of thriving local enterprises. A targeted enterprise could go willingly or unwillingly, but resistance was futile in the face of the fabulous pools of wealth that the capitalist juggernaut could muster. The historical process of industrial centralization in the United States, in other words, was accomplished in acts of power that resorted to illegitimate means. The trusts had achieved wealth and power but had not been able to convert that into legitimate authority (Livingston 1987).

We'll return to the coal trusts in a moment. First, I offer an up-close, ethnographic example of how this played out on the ground in the 1800s.

The Valley

For more than a decade, I pursued a major ethnographic and historical research project to get a close-range view of what corporate centralization meant on the ground. The project was sited in central New York State among a string of small manufacturing towns that have lined the Erie Canal since the 1820s. I focused on what was, for most of the nineteenth century, the economic backbone of the region, the enterprises of E. Remington and Sons in Ilion, the most bustling of four small industrial towns that locals refer to collectively as "the Valley."

In their heyday, two sides of the Remington enterprises faced each other across the canal. The Agricultural Works produced everything that the modern farmer of the nineteenth-century United States would wish to use, from pitchforks to plows and reapers. Across from it, the Armory originally produced gun barrels, and eventually guns and shot, and countless other metal objects, from knives to fire engines to iron bridges.

The Armory had its bread-and-butter hunting guns, but its big-time fortunes rose and fell on the tides of war. Such was the family's good judgment that when peace broke out, the Remingtons would redirect the work to other product lines and keep the shops open, albeit with fewer workers. They are still remembered fondly for this in the Valley. By the 1870s the Remingtons were courting inventors for new products and found a winner, the typewriter, though it was slow to reach commercial viability. The "QWERTY" keyboard we all know and love was invented at Remington Typewriter as an ingenious solution to a stubborn technical problem.

The Valley was gospel of wealth all the way in those days. How did residents square that with working at the Remington factories? Didn't that make them wage slaves? Actually, no. Workers at the Remington enterprises did not hold "jobs" in our sense of the term. The Remingtons contracted to skilled specialists who ran relatively autonomous shops of their own, on the Remington campus, using the Remington infrastructure. The contractors of each shop brought in the men and women that they needed to fulfill their contracts (women mostly specialized in delicate engraving). The contractors got paid when they sold their shop's product back to the Remingtons. The workers got paid by how much of that product they produced. We might see that as a "job," but, structurally, these contractors were much more independent. Within the bounds of cooperation, they could set their own hours and work as much or as little as they needed to.

A big contract meant work at the shops for a lot of people. A gap between contracts emptied the shops. And that meant that it was time to work on other subsistence strategies, expand the garden, take a hunting trip, or practice some other useful employment. In the prosperous Valley, working for the Remingtons was part of a household's diversified strategy for achieving and maintaining independence; that work was not wage slavery. With a range of subsistence resources and skills, these people did not have to depend solely on the wage for their subsistence.

The Remingtons, three generations of them, were paragons of the gospel of work who prided themselves on their artisan skills and their local roots in grandfather's blacksmith shop. The family wished the artisans who worked with them and the community they lived in to see them as producers of wealth, not capitalists (Doukas 2003). Now realistically, they owned the place, and for a period they even ran a bank on Main Street. The Remingtons' adherence to gospel-of-work values may have been something of a fiction, but it was ideologically potent. They directed the labor of thousands, who accepted the direction of "mechanics" like themselves. The family legitimated its authority with the gospel of work.

All this changed in the late 1880s when E. Remington and Sons was divided and conquered by two protocorporate cartels, the "gun trust"—later discovered to be led by Oliver Winchester of Winchester Arms—and the "typewriter trust," an organization so secretive that for seven years the Valley believed that the company had been bought by two local men. Local elites organized valiantly to save the Armory from trust conquest in a protracted and unsuccessful struggle that left a churning wake of bitterness in the Valley. (See Doukas 2003 for all the details.)

At first the new bosses shamelessly threw their weight around in the stunned little towns. Within a couple of years, both the new Remington Typewriter and the new Remington Arms threatened to close their doors and leave the Valley *if* they were not given "inducements" and concessions from the community, including tax breaks and direct cash infusions (Doukas 2003). The trusts had "cornered" the community. Under trust management, a new spirit of "efficiency" ruled the factory floor with an iron hand. New managers took control of the varied workplaces, wresting them from the senior skilled workers who had always run them. The managers tried to dictate every detail of work processes.[5] No Remington shop had ever experienced "labor problems." Under trust management, strikes and impromptu walkouts became common as the workforce fought a losing battle against the loss of its independence.

Local archives reveal an intensifying animosity between the trusts and the towns in those early years of corporate domination.[6] Local elites were not on the trusts' side. One answer was the founding of a new organization, the Ilion Board of Trade, by a couple of corporate managers from the Armory and the Typewriter and a couple of procorporate local elites. The idea was to persuade the people who "mattered" that the trusts would advance their interests, too. From 1897 to 1910, 150 or so men met over sumptuous banquet tables, where corporate supporters made speeches long into the night to persuade the invited locals that their views were obsolete and misguided. Local newspapers printed the speeches in full.[7]

It was a new world, they said; give up your old ways. It was only natural, they said, that social institutions "evolve" from simple to complex—and it was time for another great evolutionary leap! Thus, we have to "stand by" our "combination" (a synonym for trust). In the oblique words of a protrust clergyman (lightly edited by the author), This is "the era of Federation," of "combination of industries." Now we can see that "the unit owes by its very integrity a duty to the aggregation of units—to stand by them in the statement of totality." *"There is a mighty change,"* he thundered, as he described a great general "law of combinations" that operates also in religious, educational, and commercial life to form a few giant organizations from many small ones.[8]

The president of a nearby university said, in his own elaborate way, that the trusts were humankind's evolutionary destiny: "If I were to tell you my creed I would say that this great movement fits the niche in this closing century as did the improvements of the last century the niche in their time. It is impossible for us to keep up with the thought of our minds without the massing of labor and this combination of money forces. I will have a greater college and the working man will have better wages for these trusts."[9]

This is not Charles Darwin's evolution. It is Herbert Spencer's. Spencer, a younger colleague of Darwin, actually coined the term "evolution," as well as its motto: "survival of the fittest" (Wiltshire 1978). Spencer's great vision was a social "law" of inexorable moral and material progress—he called it "evolution"—that scooted some toward perfection and left others behind, a law that could produce the desired effect only if governments let nature take its course and weed out the "unfit" (Spencer 1882). It took "steel baron" and devotee Andrew Carnegie to invest Spencer's libertarianism with the full sweep of so-called social Darwinism, a synthesis that made converts of the new corporate rich right and left (Hofstadter 1955 [1944]). At last, in a culture where capitalists were hated parasites, social Darwinism let them be the leading edge of evolution.

Carnegie drew out the implications. Clearly, it would be wasteful to pay high wages because the poor backward workers would only spend more on debauchery (partying), promiscuous charity coddled the "unfit" to the detriment of "the race," and labor unions were "unfit" organizations (Carnegie 1889a, 1889b, 1900a, 1900b). Not only that, but capital was purely benevolent. The "concentration of capital," he said, "is an evolution from the heterogeneous to the homogeneous, and is clearly another step in the upward path of development.... Through the operation of this law [evolution] the home of the laboring man of our day boasts luxuries which even in the palaces of monarchs ... were unknown" (Carnegie 1900b: 89). Evolution was the ideology that corporate capitalism turned to for legitimation in order to turn its raw power into authority.

As the procorporate propagandists spun the message in Ilion, capital became the very mark of evolutionary superiority, almost magically potent. It was capital that was responsible for all the progress of this "titanic new age." In a community where success was synonymous with hard work by the sweat of one's brow, a new corporate manager bluntly told his Board of Trade audience: "Let me say that the success of those two industries [Armory and Typewriter] is due to the energy and push of the men who furnish the capital."[10] This was a direct affront to the reigning belief system.

According to an honored guest, the lieutenant governor of New York (and probable member of the typewriter trust), capital not only produced goods—it also produced *citizens.* He addressed the assembled banqueters: "You are not only making guns, typewriters and bicycles here, but through the instrumentality of Mr. Seamans [local member of the typewriter trust] you are manufacturing first class intelligent citizens."[11]

Membership in the Board of Trade fluctuated from year to year. (The newspaper accounts provided lists of attendees.) At first, its meetings were well attended by the artisan elites, elder skilled workers, and old Remington contractors, all pillars of the community. This group's attendance quickly dwindled during the board's first couple of years, which we can take as a sign of resistance. Banquet speakers complained about this resistance in the most unflattering terms. "Every progressive movement always meets much opposition on the part of the *dead weights....* The ignorant, self-satisfied, contented spirit is in every village, and has to be overcome." A new corporate manager at the former Armory advised circumventing politics: "If the citizens of Ilion wish to see their village progress they must accomplish it through this board; *it cannot be done by politics.*"[12] Why did the artisans leave the Board of Trade? They were sacrificed on the altar of the trusts. Their skills and leadership were devalued; their status in the community was demoted. They were in the way of the trusts installing a new command hierarchy and establishing new relations of production.[13]

The local response to this frenzied ideology of evolutionary progress took a few years to make its way to the protected venue of the Board of Trade. When it did, it hit with a rebellious bang. The rebels were having none of the new social Darwinist babble. And the senior skilled workers were back at the banquet tables.

"Why are politicians corrupt?" a respected judge prodded the banqueters— "because *Big Business* has made them so!" The "apostles of Big Business," he went on, "by tortuous paths and devious methods have wrested great fortunes *unearned* from producer, wage earner, and consumer alike, these are the real blots upon civilization, the real curse to the rising generation, in whose breasts they generate the desire of emulation and the spirit of *trampling down* all humans who stand in their way!" "A moderate sized corporation is a benefit," said another speaker that night, an attorney from nearby Utica, but "it is the monster of power and strength which is a menace to our existence as a free people. . . . *Such a corporate life should be killed,* its debts paid, stockholders paid par value and the rest of the assets forfeited to the state."[14]

Brave words. If this meeting represented an organizational coup, it was short-lived. Three years later, corporate supporters were again in control, and it was the Board of Trade whose organizational life was killed. From its ashes, in 1914, arose the new, nationally "federated" Chamber of Commerce, and no more gospel-of-work talk would be heard in this venue. Not coincidentally, this was the year of the first big strike in Ilion, by the Aligners at the Typewriter, the downwardly mobile craft elite.

One more "apostle of Big Business" can stand in for many who trekked to central New York in this period. Here is Governor Frank Lowden of Illinois—son-in-law of railroad car "baron" George Pullman and contender with Warren Harding for the Republican presidential nomination—in Ilion in 1923 for the half-century anniversary of Remington Typewriter. (Harding himself was a featured speaker for the Armory's centennial in 1916.)

> Scientific discovery and mechanical inventions have so changed the world that today the working man lives in greater comfort than the king of a few centuries ago. This is a great achievement. . . . Without capital we would sink back into barbarism from which the race painfully has emerged. . . . Mankind would still be living a nomadic life. . . . There are those who speak of the nationalization of wealth as something new. It is the oldest thing in the history of the world. The savage tribes in every land and clime have been communists.[15]

He grabbed that line about the working man and the king from Carnegie.[16] Here capital is more than just the provider of prosperity; it is the civilizing grace of the human race, the very *cause* of evolutionary advance. Opposition to corporate capitalism, by implication, is a clear sign of evolutionary "backwardness." Here's the ideological kernel of the corporate capitalist persuasion.

The Great Coal Strike of 1902

From the Valley we can see the corporate cultural campaign at the grassroots, as it entered the life of a small factory town. From the Great Coal Strike of 1902, down the Susquehanna from the Remington shops, we can see the same culture clash shouted through a national megaphone. Even without all the details (they can be found in Doukas 1997), this strike can reveal the extent to which the United States was torn apart by the problem of the trusts and the scope of the trusts' program for ideological change. It serves as a second and more sharply defined example of the corporate cultural campaign.

By the turn of the twentieth century, exposés of the trusts' crimes against competitors, workers, and communities were selling like hotcakes, from

Henry D. Lloyd's punctilious *Wealth against Commonwealth* (Lloyd 1894; Destler 1944) to courageous original "muckraking" such as Ida Tarbell's *History of Standard Oil* and David Graham Phillips's *Treason of the Senate*, both serialized in the most popular magazines of the day (Tarbell 1966; Phillips 1964 [1906]). As the power of the trusts increased, the resistance to them only sharpened.

With a clear case of trust/corporate abuse on their hands, union leaders began strategizing for a strike of unprecedented proportions. They raised massive support from across the country by promoting the strike as a major fight for democracy against the "tyranny" of the trusts. The coal trust, for its part, seized the moment to teach the public some hard social Darwinist "truths."

The *United Mine Workers Journal* (*UMJ*), ideological organ of the strikers (published in a dozen languages), bristled with gospel-of-work antimonopolism. On every page, in letters from miner-correspondents, in excerpts from newspapers across the country, and (unexpectedly) in thousands of poems, the question was not whether or not the fruits of industry had been misdirected by the trusts—that seemed obvious enough—but how the strikers could save themselves from wage slavery.

For the correspondents of the *UMJ* in this period, the central problem was precisely the allocation of labor, as Wolf proposed, most specifically keeping the coal trust from foreclosing on the miners' independence. Anthracite miners, like Remington artisans, had not traditionally held jobs. Certified miners, the "zenith of possibility" in the mines, as the young union president testified,[17] ran the underground workplaces, hiring and training aspiring miners, buying their own tools and supplies, and selling the coal they produced back to the company.

Certified miners, like aspiring certified miners, and like free laborers all over the country, did not expect to work under a boss like a "wage slave," and unions of the time tried to prevent that through the organization of labor. "The lesson for this holiday," a union organizer told a Fourth of July crowd in 1902, "is that the workingman" must stand united "until the Declaration of Independence is read in a land and to a people which is free not only politically but also economically, where no man has to beg his fellowman's leave to earn a living for himself and his family" (*UMJ*, July 10, 1902, 1). Abraham Lincoln said forty years ago, a middle-class labor activist reported to the *UMJ*, that "there is no such thing in this country as a man being confined to the condition of a hired laborer for life." When the few are able to monopolize "the storehouse of nature," Lincoln argued, they also monopolize "natural opportunities" (*UMJ*, August 27, 1902, 3).

The monopolizers made their conquests in the anthracite coalfields by stealth, under the veil of Franklin Gowan's Laurel Run Improvement Company (mentioned previously). The region was rich in coal-bearing deposits, the largest anthracite deposits in the world. Anthracite is the hardest, densest coal, and it burns hottest and cleanest. By the last quarter of the nineteenth century, it was the fuel of choice in many cities, both for domestic use and for powering the steam engines of factories (e.g., the Remington's) and trains. Gowan got away with this theft, and five other railroads followed his lead, competing for coal-bearing lands, all illegally. By 1900 they had ceased to compete—they were all bound together in a trust under the iron rule of banker J. P. Morgan.

The Great Coal Strike of 1902 started in the spring. The United Mine Workers (UMW) had organized 150,000 anthracite miners of more than a dozen different linguistic and religious communities (Cornell 1957). The coal trust responded by refusing to negotiate. The strike moved on into the summer, when the livin' was relatively easy in the forested hills of the anthracite region. But as fall drew near, a wave of panic rippled through the big eastern cities. How were people going to heat their homes? The press was staunchly sympathetic to the miners. Contributions of cash and food poured in from across the country, allowing the strike to continue until the trust caved in.

But it did not, surely under J. P. Morgan's instruction. As the air chilled, experienced politicians were seriously afraid of open rebellion—then U.S. president Theodore Roosevelt, fearing a "social war," made a secret plan with the army chief of staff to take over the coal mines and the railroads that depended on them, by force if necessary, and *nationalize* them (Cornell 1957: 174, 211).

At this juncture the secretary of war arranged a secret meeting with Morgan aboard the latter's yacht to make a deal. If Morgan would bring the mine owners to the table, any table, the administration would accept his conditions. These were stringent, a special commission and an arbitration hearing (not a court of law), all to be conducted in such a way as to deny the existence of both the trust and the union—oh, and the arbitration hearing was to be announced to the press as the mine owners' idea.[18]

The hearings of the Anthracite Coal Strike Commission commenced immediately, in front of standing-room-only crowds, a large proportion of them reporters from all over the country. It went on for six months, as miner after miner took the stand to testify to the trust's abuses, and some thirty pseudo-separate coal companies denounced the union and pled that they were treating the miners as well as they could.

The trust's vindication rested largely on the shoulders of Morgan's hand-picked head of the coal trust, George Baer, attorney and railroad "baron" in his own right. Baer argued evolution, delivering the words of the master, Herbert Spencer, on the unfitness of labor unions. Progress, he argued, was "the powerful stimulus which individual liberty gives to individual initiative"—unions retarded liberty. "Herbert Spencer, in his last book says, 'Those who, joining a trade union, surrender their freedom to make engagements on their own terms, ... have no adequate sense of that fundamental right which every man possesses to make the best of himself." What was a union, Baer sneered, but a "crude democracy where by a majority vote my rights and privileges are to be fixed?"[19]

In the end, the Coal Strike Commission agreed with the trust. Evolution had passed these poor miners by. It was unfortunate that the "evolution to greater combinations" had disrupted the face-to-face labor relations of the past, the commissioners lamented in their *Report to the President* (1903: 38), but the mine owners should recognize that organizing labor would civilize it. Without unions, the commissioners argued, these poor laborers, who had so little "opportunity to upbuild their higher being," would be prey to "incendiary appeals to prejudice or passion" (1903: 62–63). (I think they were referring to socialism.) And anyway, the commissioners added, the very geography of the anthracite coalfields made them a "natural monopoly" (1903: 17, 23). In the end, the commissioners denied every one of the miners' demands (Doukas 1997).

Conclusions

The question of the relative value of labor versus capital was fought out for more than a generation after the troubling events of the Remington takeover and the Great Coal Strike of 1902. Today, the relative privilege of capital over labor is infused in the laws of the land and accepted, if often grudgingly, among the populace. We *believe* that capital has the right to profit, money makes money, corporations are necessary to civilized life, centralized production over far-flung international supply lines is efficient, lifelong wage labor is normal and necessary, central banks are normal and necessary, consuming more is living better, and the more capital there is, the more prosperous a society is.

We believe, we cooperate, *and* we doubt. We believe and we don't believe. We expect others to believe. We feel pressured to act as if we believe even if we're not sure. When presidential candidate Barack Obama said that we wanted "an economy that rewards work" (Obama 2008), we wanted to believe that, too, and instinctively sensed its radicalism—the United States is a capitalist society. But something of the gospel of work lingers on in the culture, despite Herculean efforts to dislodge it. Paul Durrenberger and I have spotted figments of it in our research (Durrenberger and Doukas 2008).

The next phase of the corporate cultural campaign acknowledged its emotional force by trying to co-opt the gospel of work. After a rough beginning, the corporate elites got smart, placing a large capital investment in mass media,[20] an ideology propagator of unprecedented efficiency (cf. Ginsburg, Abu-Lughod, and Larkin 2003). Historian Roland Marchand's *Creating the Corporate Soul* takes the story of corporate legitimation into the early twentieth century and the next phase of the corporate quest for authority, when the sophistication and media savvy of the public relations "industry" were brought to bear on the corporate "crisis of legitimacy" (Marchand 1998: 3).

Railroads identified their "souls," in full-page, full-color ads, with "bringing life" to mythic small towns (Marchand 1998: 1). The telephone monopoly identified itself with small-town neighborliness. Huge consumer products corporations identified with the tiny shops and artisan values of their supposed founders. H. J. Heinz Company went so far as to have the original house where the founding father made his first jar of preserves floated down the Allegheny River by barge and enshrined at its giant Pittsburgh factory (Marchand 1998: 34–35).

The corporate campaign for legitimacy minimized the disturbing scale of corporate centralization by identifying with the imagery of the gospel of work—little, self-sufficient communities where nobody was poor or rich, where humble artisan geniuses in humble settings made the inventions that changed the world. In this period the public relations agency of Remington Arms (then a subsidiary of DuPont) told exactly this story of founder Eliphalet Remington (Doukas 2003). The corporate campaign appropriated the "look" but hollowed out the substance, the ideal of independence.

Wolf was right. In the corporate cultural revolution, ideas and power converged around allocating the labor of others. For corporate purposes most workers would have to accept lifelong dependency on capitalist employers—this was a revolution "from above" in the organization of labor. In an arcane new discourse, corporate capitalists sought the legitimate authority to do this in terms of the productivity and civilizing force of capital. The corporate campaigners used the substantial means at their disposal to promote the cold conclusions of social Darwinism, declaring a new age, discrediting "sentimental" connections to the past as backward tradition. Most of all, just as Wolf found (1999: 275), the gospel of wealth rationalized a division of the population into the advanced and the backward, the fit and the unfit, the few destined to lead and the many destined to do the work.

Notes

1. To be conscientiously explicit, what I mean by U.S. culture here is the whole complex of circulating ideas, ideals, expectations, concepts, and so forth, that are available to members of the society and used by them/us every day of our lives. The whole is multicultural, multilingual, multitraditional, but *patterned* because all members of the society must intersect and interact in a common culture of shared rules and a shared sense of appropriateness just to make a living in this society. That common culture or public culture, however complex, is clearly *dominated* by the messaging of power elites—in the United States and in every modern state. Who else has the means to simultaneously message the millions? Our shared culture is not, at this time, a democratic product. We can work toward democratizing it.

2. The antimonopoly tradition in English common law had a long past before it was formalized in the turbulent mid-1600s (Coke 1648).

3. Independence is not individualism. In the practical sense, as an almanac writer of the time put it, the desired state in a healthy republic was "to live decently without acquiring wealth" (cited in Blumin 1989: 36–37). The ideal was what they called a "competence," a modest, sufficient living.

4. The legal device of the trust was pioneered by John D. Rockefeller and his attorney Samuel C. T. Dodd in 1881 to get around state laws against corporations owning other corporations (Horwitz 1992).

5. So-called scientific management sought to control every hand and eye movement (Braverman 1974).

6. I worked most extensively with the historical collection of the Ilion Free Public Library, a vast and wondrous assortment of documentary and other materials. The Herkimer County Historical Society (Herkimer, NY) and the Remington Archives (Ilion, NY) also provided important pieces of the puzzle (Doukas 2003).

7. My source of these accounts is a multivolume "scrapbook" of local notable Walter Rix at the Historical Room of the Ilion Free Public Library. Emphasis is added.

8. "Ilion Board of Trade Held Its First Annual Banquet," *Utica Daily Press*, n.d., Walter Rix Scrapbook, Ilion Free Public Library.

9. "Ilionites Enjoy a Banquet: Board of Trade's Annual Dinner," *Utica Daily Press*, n.d., Walter Rix Scrapbook, Ilion Free Public Library.

10. Ibid.

11. "Ilion Board of Trade Held Its First Annual Banquet."

12. "Ilionites Enjoy a Banquet: Board of Trade's Annual Dinner."

13. When the "producers of wealth" controlled the workplace, Karl Marx (1976) called it a "formal subsumption" of labor by capital—capital formally owned the enterprise but just sat on top of a preexisting organization of labor. He opposed that to a "real subsumption" of labor by capital in which capital controlled the flow of work and workers.

14. "Ilion Board of Trade Dinner: Annual Banquet Last Evening," *Utica Daily Press*, February 18, 1911, Walter Rix Scrapbook, Ilion Free Public Library.

15. "Scholes Ended Drudgery Says Gov. F. Lowden," *Observer Dispatch* (Utica, NY), September 12, 1923, Walter Rix Scrapbook.

16. Lowden's argument was anthropological, following closely the reigning synthesis of Lewis Henry Morgan (1877) but "spun" to promote a concentration of wealth of which Morgan would have disapproved (Trautmann 1987).

17. John Mitchell, *Proceedings of the Anthracite Coal Strike Commission*, 12, Library of Congress, Washington, DC.

18. These and other conditions, it was later discovered, were laid out in the notorious *Corsair* letter, literally dictated by Morgan aboard his yacht, the *Corsair* (copy held in the J. P. Morgan Library, New York City).

19. Anthracite Coal Strike Commission, *Proceedings of the Anthracite Coal Strike Commission*, 9782, 9793, and 9793.

20. They started early. Railroad baron Jay Gould bought a small telegraph company in 1874 and conquered Western Union in 1881 to form a telegraph monopoly. His company controlled the transmission of messages along the railroad and from town to town, the stock market "ticker tape" of the day, and the Associated Press news feed to the most influential newspapers in the country (Starr 2004: 180-182).

References

Anthracite Coal Strike Commission. 1902-1903. *Proceedings of the Anthracite Coal Strike Commission.* Microfilmed transcript, Clarence Darrow Collection, Box 2, Manuscript Division, Library of Congress, Washington, DC.
———. 1903. *Report to the President of the Anthracite Coal Strike Commission.* Washington, DC: U.S. Government Printing Office.

Blumin, Stuart M. 1989. *The Emergence of the Middle Class: Social Experience in an American City, 1760–1900.* Cambridge: Cambridge University Press.

Braverman, Harry. 1974. *Labor and Monopoly Capitalism: The Degradation of Work in the Twentieth Century.* New York: Monthly Review Press.

Carnegie, Andrew. 1889a. "The Best Fields for Philanthropy." *North American Review* 397: 682–698.

———. 1889b. "Wealth." *North American Review* 391: 653–664.

———. 1900a. "The Gospel of Wealth." In *The Gospel of Wealth and Other Timely Essays.* New York: Century, 1–19.

———. 1900b. "Popular Illusions about the Trusts." In *The Gospel of Wealth and Other Timely Essays.* New York: Century, 85–103.

Certeau, Michel de. 1985. "What We Do When We Believe." In *On Signs,* edited by Marshall Blonsky. Baltimore, MD: Johns Hopkins University Press.

Coke, Edward. 1648. "Against Monopolies, Propounders, and Projectors." In *The Third Part of the Institutes of the Laws of England: Concerning High Treason, and Other Pleas of the Crown, and Criminall Causes.* London: M. Flesher.

Cornell, Robert J. 1957. *The Anthracite Coal Strike of 1902.* Washington, DC: Catholic University of America.

Destler, Chester McArthur. 1944. "Wealth against Commonwealth, 1894 and 1944." *American History Review* 50, no 1: 49–72.

Doukas, Dimitra. 1993. "The Great Coal Strike of 1902: Historical Ethnography of an American Hegemonic Crisis." Paper presented at the ninety-second annual meeting, American Anthropological Association, Washington, DC.

———. 1997. "Corporate Capitalism on Trial: The Hearings of the Anthracite Coal Strike Commission, 1902-1903." *Identities* 3, no. 3: 371–401.

———. 2003. *Worked Over: The Corporate Sabotage of an American Community.* Ithaca, NY: Cornell University Press.

Durrenberger, E. Paul, and Dimitra Doukas. 2008. "Gospel of Wealth, Gospel of Work: Counterhegemony in the U.S. Working Class." *American Anthropologist* 110, no. 2: 214–224.

Fink, Leon. 1983. *Workingmen's Democracy: The Knights of Labor and American Politics.* Urbana: University of Illinois Press.

George, Henry. 1979 [1879]. *Progress and Poverty: An Inquiry into the Cause of Industrial Depressions and of Increase of Want with Increase of Wealth.* New York: Robert Schalkenbach Foundation.

Ginsburg, Faye D., Lila Abu-Lughod, and Brian Larkin. 2003. "Introduction." In *Media Worlds: Anthropology on a New Terrain.* Berkeley: University of California Press, 1–36.

Gramsci, Antonio. 1976. *Selections from the Prison Notebooks.* Translated by Quintin Hoare and Geoffrey Nowell Smith. New York: International.

Hofstadter, Richard. 1955 [1944]. *Social Darwinism in American Thought.* Boston: Beacon Press.

Horowitz, Daniel. 1992. *The Morality of Spending: Attitudes toward the Consumer Society in America, 1875–1940.* Chicago: Ivan R. Dee.

Horwitz, Morton J. 1992. *The Transformation of American Law, 1870–1960: The Crisis of Legal Orthodoxy.* New York: Oxford University Press.

Jackson, Andrew. 1949 [1832]. "Veto Message." In *Jackson versus Biddle: The Struggle for the Second Bank of the United States.* Boston: D. C. Heath.

Lazerow, Jama. 1995. *Religion and the Working Class in Antebellum America.* Washington, DC: Smithsonian Institution Press.

Licht, Walter. 1995. *Industrializing America: The Nineteenth Century*. Baltimore, MD: Johns Hopkins University Press.

Lincoln, Abraham. 1953 [1861]. "Annual Message to Congress, December 3, 1861." In *The Collected Works of Abraham Lincoln*, vol. 5, edited by Roy P. Basler. New Brunswick, NJ: Rutgers University Press, 35–53.

Livingston, James. 1986. *Origins of the Federal Reserve System: Money, Class, and Corporate Capitalism, 1890–1913*. Ithaca, NY: Cornell University Press.

———. 1987. "The Social Analysis of Economic History and Theory: Conjectures on Late-Nineteenth-Century American Development." *American Historical Review* 92: 69–95.

Lloyd, Henry Demarest. 1894. *Wealth against Commonwealth*. New York: Harper.

Marchand, Roland. 1998. *Creating the Corporate Soul: The Rise of Public Relations and Corporate Imagery in American Big Business*. Berkeley and Los Angeles: University of California Press.

Marx, Karl. 1976. *Capital,* vol. 1. Harmondsworth, UK: Pelican.

Obama, Barack. 2008. "Remarks of Senator Barack Obama" (as prepared for delivery), St. Louis, MO, October 18, 2008, http://www.demconwatchblog.com/2008/10/barack-obama-speech-from-st-louis-mo.html (accessed October 31, 2008).

Phillips, David Graham. 1964 [1906]. *The Treason of the Senate*. Chicago: Quadrangle.

Roediger, David. 1991. *The Wages of Whiteness*. London: Verso.

Schneider, Jane C. 1999. "Eric Wolf, 1923–1999." *American Anthropologist* 101: 395–399.

Smith, Adam. 1982 [1776]. *An Inquiry into the Nature and Causes of the Wealth of Nations*. Harmondsworth, UK: Penguin.

Spencer, Herbert. 1882. *First Principles of a New System of Philosophy*. New York: D. Appleton.

Starr, Paul. 2004. *The Creation of the Media: Political Origins of Modern Communications*. New York: Basic Books.

Tarbell, Ida. 1966 [1904]. *The History of Standard Oil,* edited by David Chalmers. New York: Harper and Row.

Trautmann, Thomas R. 1987. *Lewis Henry Morgan and the Invention of Kinship*. Berkeley and Los Angeles: University of California Press.

Wallace, Anthony F. C. 1987. *St. Claire, a Nineteenth-Century Coal Town's Experience with a Disaster-Prone Industry*. Ithaca, NY: Cornell University Press.

Weber, Max. 1947 [1919]. "Politics as a Vocation." In *From Max Weber: Essays in Sociology,* edited by H. H. Gerth and C. Wright Mills. Oxford: Oxford University Press, 77–128.

———. 1976 [1904]. *The Protestant Ethic and the Spirit of Capitalism,* edited by Talcott Parsons. New York: Scribner's.

Wiltshire, David. 1978. *The Social and Political Thought of Herbert Spencer*. London: Oxford University Press.

Wolf, Eric R. 1999. *Envisioning Power: Ideologies of Dominance and Crisis*. Berkeley and Los Angeles: University of California Press.

VI

Global Processes and Local Systems

14

HOUSEHOLDS AND GENDER RELATIONS IN ECONOMIC DEVELOPMENT

A Central Anatolian Village

Emine Onaran İncirlioğlu

This chapter is about the economic changes in a relatively small Central Anatolian village, Sakaltutan, in the province of Kayseri, Turkey, and about gender relations in that village.[1] What does economy have to do with gender relations? If economy is about the production, distribution, and consumption of goods and services, and gender relations are basically relations between women and men, how do we bring together gender and economy? Here, by describing Sakaltutan's economy, I want to show, on the one hand, the development of this village and, on the other hand, the complexity of gendered division of labor and the intimate relationship between gender relations and economic development.

Economic development in rural Turkey has taken diverse forms depending on various factors (see, for example, Keyder 1983). Several social science scholars who studied "rural transformation" focused on and argued for different "paths" of change. What they meant by "rural transformation" was the transformation of "traditional" agricultural systems into capitalism or into systems that coexisted with capitalism in various ways. The discussion has been going on for at least one hundred years on the ways in which capitalism has influenced agricultural structures, especially in countries where peasantry is widespread. In the literature on peasant studies, there are contrasting views concerning peasantry and its future. These views, however, acknowledge that change is uneven and that different processes coexist. Thus, we may observe different paths of transformation in different villages in different regions in Turkey, and we may also witness variation in different households in the same village.

Even though macro theoretical approaches do provide us with a broad perspective, only long-term ethnographic fieldwork can give a picture of how economic change is experienced in daily life by "real people"—men and women. And this is how we can link the study of economic change and gender relations.

About the Research

In 1949–1951, British anthropologist Paul Stirling conducted anthropological fieldwork in two Central Anatolian villages in the Kayseri province: Sakaltutan and Elbaşı. Then in 1971 and 1986, he went back to restudy the same villages in order to observe the changes over time (Stirling 1965, 1976). I collaborated with Stirling during this last phase of the research, because he had realized that teaming up with a woman anthropologist who spoke Turkish as her native language would probably yield more reliable and valid information. During and after our fieldwork, I came to realize the value of teamwork and particularly appreciated the role of the researcher in ethnography (İncirlioğlu 1994). Who we are is important in what we see and what we make out of what we see. After our collaboration, and after Stirling died in 1998, I remained in contact with these villages and especially with my friends in Sakaltutan, on which this chapter focuses. Although the formal research itself ended in the 1990s, I maintained my relations with my Sakaltutan friends, visited them, and frequently spoke with them on the telephone.

The *units of analysis* in the study were both households and individuals. Households are important to look into because there are differences between them depending on their composition and size, as well as on the land they own or have access to. The operations within the households are important as well, which is why individual members merit study. Who does what in the household—that is, the division of labor by age and gender—would go unnoticed if households were the only units of analysis.

A Tripartite Economic Structure

In 1986 when I went to Sakaltutan for the first time, the economy had three constituents, or ingredients, that were more or less equally important for village households. As an agricultural village, farming, by definition, was the most noteworthy activity. The second income-generating activity within the village was women's carpet weaving. Men's construction work and other wage labor during migration constituted the third source of income. Depending on the resources and the composition of households, the distribution of these economic activities varied from household to household.

Agriculture

Agriculture defines life in the village in spite of its decreased importance as an income source in many households. Stages in the agricultural process (for example, plowing, weeding, and harvesting) are landmarks in the life cycles and life courses of the villagers. Someone's birth, death, or wedding is marked by the agricultural activities that were going on at the time it took place. Agriculture constitutes the frame of reference in villagers' lives. Almost all adults in Sakaltutan have farming skills, whether they are parts of landed households or not, and whether agriculture is a source of income for their households or not. The agricultural cycle provides the villages with their "tempo and rhythm," as Paul Magnarella (1979: 89) stated in describing the Georgian village of Hayriye. However, there have been a number of changes in agriculture since the 1950s; these have influenced agricultural production, decreased the importance of agriculture as an income source in many households, and necessitated nonagricultural activities.

Intensification of agriculture in Sakaltutan had three components: mechanization, the introduction of agricultural inputs including fertilizers and pesticides, and crop change. On the one hand, intensification of agriculture increased short-term productivity, shortened the plowing and harvesting periods, and decreased the amount of human labor required in these processes (which traditionally required men's labor). On the other hand, it drastically increased the total cash need of agriculture—ranging from chemicals to diesel—making villagers more vulnerable to poor harvests. Because reliance on weather conditions did not change and "dry cereal agriculture" still dominated agriculture, many villagers had more to lose in a bad harvest, and they believed that farming was not worth the labor anymore.

These changes had major impacts on gender division of labor. In some villages, mechanization changed the gender division of agricultural labor and relieved women from fieldwork (that is, cereal agriculture), transferring women's tasks to men. Introduction of new, labor-intensive cash crops in Sakaltutan, however, increased women's workload in agriculture.

In Sakaltutan, gender division of agricultural labor depends, by and large, on the tools used. Men use tractors and scythes; women use sickles, hoes, and adzes for weeding and do other jobs done by hand with no tools. However, exceptions are not strongly sanctioned, and in most cases people explain a particular division of labor by either household composition or personal choice.

The entrance of agricultural wage labor in the village was an important change since the 1950s, but it is limited to a very short term during the harvesting period. The extra labor that is required in most households during the weeding and harvesting periods, mostly female labor, is recruited through social links within the villages. This "informal exchange-labor" takes different forms of "paying." The most common form is the *öndüç* system, defined as "we go and pull up the beans in my field today and do the same in yours tomorrow." General reciprocity is a second form, which does not involve a predetermined, prenegotiated value in exchange for the labor but is calculated in the long run by the villagers involved. Similarly, in-kind payment is not prenegotiated but is left open in a wider understanding of general reciprocity. Labor recruitment in its different forms of informal exchange (and even the recruitment of wage labor in many situations) is based on either reciprocity or in-kind payments. These highly complicated relations are impossible to understand in purely economic terms. Reciprocity and calculation are distinctive characteristics of labor recruitment, and negotiations for payment include the integration of an Islamic discourse of *günah*, "sin," and *sevap*, "good deed."

Male outmigration accompanied an increase in landless single-family households, which in turn influenced livestock raising in Sakaltutan. In order to make sheep raising profitable, households needed to cultivate cereal in order to produce cheap hay for animal feed. Also, because raising large flocks of sheep requires the labor of several girls or women in the household, many Sakaltutan households gave up sheep. They continued to be responsible for tending cows—milking, feeding, watering, and grooming the animals; cleaning the barn; and collecting the droppings, as well as producing yogurt, cheese, and butter. It was women's job to decide whether they would sell or use the milk, to actually sell it to the milk trader or the dairy, to collect the money, and to purchase household goods in return for the milk or by advance credit. Men did not interfere with the income from milk sales; women kept the money and decided where to spend it. However, dairy production was not a profitable business. In most households, all women spent the milk money to "try to patch the needs of the household." Since the 1950s, the shift from work oxen and local cows to European stall-fed milk cows in many households increased women's daily chores, at the same time as it provided more income. Although European cows yielded twice or more milk than local cows did, they were far more expensive to purchase and to maintain; women's gains from cow milk were negligible.

Men benefited from village-level changes in the intensification of agriculture more than women did. In decisionmaking at the household level, however, if the household has options, women's interests are recognized and considered. One good example is women in Sakaltutan giving up sheep raising, a labor-intensive activity. Another example is the preference for garbanzo beans, a relatively less labor-intensive crop than lentils, in many Sakaltutan households. Although Sakaltutan villagers recognize that growing lentils is more advantageous in terms of its impact on the soil, its price, and its yields, in a number of households garbanzo beans, not lentils, were produced in order to decrease women's labor.

To supplement agriculture, carpet weaving developed as a village-based nonagricultural income source, an exclusively women's task. Male outmigration to supplement and subsidize agriculture, if not to replace it in most Sakaltutan households, also impacted gender relations.

Carpet Weaving

Although the history of carpet weaving in the Kayseri province spans more than one thousand years, in the early 1950s it was virtually unknown in Sakaltutan. By 1986, carpet weaving had become quite widespread. This does not mean, however, that women's paid work did not contribute to the household before the entrance of carpet weaving. In 1950, women in most households used to weave rugs (*kilim*); in fact, rug weaving was the only source of cash income for many households, which corresponds to today's labor migration in Sakaltutan.

Carpet weaving was part of the state's five-year development plan, which recognized it as an important rural income source that could contribute to foreign exchange. Almost all of the silk and about 40 percent of the wool hand-woven carpets in the Kayseri region were produced for export. The public sector, however, had been negligible in carpet production. Instead, private carpet-manufacturing companies developed, and especially in the Kayseri region the home-based "putting-out" system, some form of subcontracting characterized the relations of production among rural weavers. Workshop production did not develop, because the legal requirements of the state, such as workplace safety, insurance, and social security, did not fit the economic interests of the merchant-manufacturers. They were not interested in making large investments for women who were not reliable long-term workers. Women could leave wage work anytime as soon as their income was not needed in the household, as the dominant ideology defined men, not women, as the "breadwinners."

In 1950, rug-weaving households in Sakaltutan were independent. They owned their means of production: the loom, yarn, comb, and scissors. Even though weavers had control over the production process (i.e., decided what, how, and when to weave), household men exercised control over the product (i.e., they took the rug to the market and sold it). When carpets replaced rugs, independent weavers became a kind of "contract laborer," providing wage labor for private carpet manufacturer-merchants. In weaving households, men lost control over the product. Women's control over the production process decreased, too.

By 1986, carpet weaving was an important source of commercialization in Sakaltutan, although its relative importance changed from household to household depending on the household composition. Predominantly wool carpets were woven, although some other villages in the Kayseri province had shifted to silk carpet weaving in the early 1980s. This difference has different consequences in terms of the production process, production relations, and the weaving earnings of households.

Silk carpet weavers in the few households had to work full time (longer daily weaving hours all year round), they were supervised more carefully by the carpet merchants and their employees, and their total annual earnings were much higher than part-time wool carpet weavers. It is true that as weavers in the putting-out system (as opposed to workshop weavers, for example), women exercise some control over the time allocation of the weaving process. However, full-time weavers who work for more than ten hours a day do work as if they were workshop weavers. In Sakaltutan, where carpet weaving has a shorter history and wool carpet weaving is predominant, women's weaving time is more flexible and shorter. Women take less weaving time daily, and they weave only half of the year, the other half working in agriculture. However, this does not mean that they have control over the production process. The patriarchal authority structure in the household and the dependence on extrahousehold weavers in the "weave-sharing" system help institute regular weaving hours. Flexibility in daily weaving time allocation does not help women either because of their domestic responsibilities.

A household's structure and composition have considerable influence on the weaving process. The organization of weaving, the number of weavers working on the same loom, the volume of weaving, the size of the carpet to be woven, and even the choice to weave silk or wool carpets are determined by the household demographic structure. The number of women and girls in the household determine the weaving capacity. As daughters grow, the weavers increase; as older women die, previous weavers may take up their house tasks and quit weaving; as daughters marry and leave the household and brides have children, the number of weavers in a household decreases. Although most carpets are woven in groups, there are women with young children and other household responsibilities who weave small carpets individually, because they cannot be depended upon as partners. Because the weaving process involves unpaid family labor, too, in addition to the number of actual weavers in the household, other members influence the volume of production. Hence, the organization of weaving depends on the household size and composition and the particular stage of the household "domestic cycle."

The household weaving decision itself, however, depends on the necessity of women's participation in wage earning for household subsistence. The gender ideology in Sakaltutan, as in many other places in the world, defines men as the primary wage earners. If men's cash income is adequate for the subsistence of the household, women are more than eager to withdraw from wage labor. This is why young women stop weaving when their husbands start commuting to various towns to take part in seasonal construction work and as soon as they begin sending remittances to the village. Another important factor that determines whether women in a household will weave or not is the amount of land and animals that household has. Likewise, most weavers stop weaving during the agricultural season. Even in villages where full-time, yearlong weaving is widespread, if the household needs women's agricultural labor temporarily, they do not weave in the summer; when sons leave the village to do their military service or to migrate for work, daughters may stop weaving in the summer, though rarely.

Women's attitudes toward weaving vary. Whereas some find weaving to be a painful activity over which they have no control, some others enjoy both the company of other women and girls and the actual process of weaving and seeing a finished product, and they prefer weaving over other household chores. I have observed in Sakaltutan, however, as in some other villages, that even the ones who enjoy weaving see it as a temporary activity and prefer not to continue weaving after marriage or as soon as their husbands secure a job with adequate income. Clearly, women's preferences are not relevant to whether they weave or not, however, if the household has no other options. The change in a few Sakaltutan households from part-time wool carpet weaving to yearlong wool or silk weaving indicates that economic conditions (the absence or inadequacy of land and of nonagricultural income sources) in combination with the appropriate household composition (a number of women in the household) determine the presence and nature of weaving in the household.

Considering both the gender ideology and the lack of benefits women derive from weaving, there seem to be three interrelated factors that explain women's negative attitudes toward carpet weaving: (1) their lack of control over the weaving process and product; (2) the strikingly low pay of their labor both in comparison with men's wage labor and in light of the fact that they are skilled workers, mastering the art in a long training period; and (3) the dominant ideology, which associates women with domestic work and men with paid work.

By 2009, I was not surprised to learn that virtually no carpet weaving was left in Sakaltutan households. Now, men's income was adequate to supplement or replace agricultural income. However, in other Kayseri villages with more agricultural land per capita, fewer men migrated to towns as wage laborers and women's village-based carpet weaving continued to be the sole nonagricultural source of income.

Construction Work and Migration

The most significant source of income for most Sakaltutan households has long been men's construction work during labor migration. Almost 50 percent of the men age fifteen and older had migration experiences in 1949–1950. After that, village men's "stability" further decreased. By 1986, almost 87 percent of men in Sakaltutan had experienced migration. More than 80 percent of Sakaltutan households had had at least one man in international migration. Construction work and labor migration continued to be significant in the 2000s.

Temporary labor migration, sometimes called "pendular" labor migration and sometimes called "male outmigration," includes international migration.

Availability of land per capita in various Central Anatolian villages has influenced men's wage labor through internal and international migration. In Sakaltutan, where land is relatively scarce in comparison with other villages, agriculture is either replaced or subsidized to a great extent through male labor migration. Several international labor migrants not only subsidize agriculture by transferring remittances but also accumulate and make investments in the village, thereby channeling their surplus from nonagricultural activities into agriculture.

Men's pendular labor migration to Turkish towns and construction work is influenced by and influences gender relations in at least four ways. First, finding construction jobs requires a large network that utilizes matrilateral and affinal kin in addition to the readily available patrilateral relatives, which in turn increases the importance of links through women. Second, pendular labor migrants in towns are often accommodated in households that have previously migrated from their villages; this increase in the number of "temporary" household members increases women's workload in the "host" households. Third, depending on how long these male migrants stay in towns, their absence from their village households has an impact on the women and children who are left behind. Fourth, the earnings in urban wage labor change the household economy. The extent of agricultural occupation in a household, the yields in a particular year, and the household demography determine men's wage labor (i.e., whether men will have construction skills, the duration of their pendular migrations, and the continuity of migration). Like women, men from landed households withdraw from wage labor if they do not have any children.

International labor migration from the villages had a more profound impact on households and gender relations, both qualitatively and quantitatively. Labor migration to Germany started in the early 1960s, following the national trend in accordance with the first five-year development plan. After the oil boom in the 1970s, international migration was directed toward the oil-rich countries of the Middle East, particularly Libya and Saudi Arabia. Beginning in the 1990s, when Turkish construction companies started to go into the newly established states of the former Soviet Union, Sakaltutan men found themselves in "Russia."

Income from international remittances is by far the largest contribution to the household. Village households with international remittances not only are better off but are also the only ones that can accumulate beyond subsistence. This, however, does not mean that all international migration is profitable. It is both expensive and risky, and numerous unsuccessful attempts to work abroad have considerable costs for the household, especially for the women who lose their gold (marriage "security") in the process.

In Sakaltutan, many women take full responsibility for farming and household decisionmaking in the absence of men. The most important factors influencing the impact of male outmigration on a woman's status are the structure and composition of the household she belongs to. In multifamily households, senior women who already have more decisionmaking power usually gain more authority in the absence of their husbands and sons. Young women who live with their husband's parents experience the least amount of autonomy because they cannot exercise much control over their labor. Young women who live with their young children, if they have any, enjoy a traditionally "premature" authority and autonomy. As a category, they exercise more control over their lives; yet the woman's age, origin (whether she is a native of the village she is married into), children (whether she has any, their ages, and their sexes), literacy, and personality make a difference in this autonomy. Being the only adult woman in a single-family household, however, does not guarantee her power in household decisionmaking. There may be friction between the woman and her husband's relatives who are not a part of the household but who make the decisions concerning her household anyway. Moreover, because most men handle their finances themselves or send the bulk of the remittances to other men for investment, village women receive only what is adequate for the daily reproduction of the household and are not in a position to make significant financial decisions, do major purchasing, or handle household management. Migrant women who are based in cities, however, exercise more control over the remittances their husbands send.

Husband-wife relationships changed as a consequence of changes in both household structure and men's labor migration. First, with changes in the household authority structure, gender hierarchy was emphasized more than generational hierarchy. Young men who were subordinate to their fathers and elder brothers in the multifamily household became heads of their household once they had access to wages. Young women who had a variety of relations (some subordinate, some dominant, and some reciprocal) with other men and women in the multifamily households found themselves in only one, subordinate relationship: the one with their husbands. Second, in the absence of her husband's seniors, a young wife had more possibilities for influence in household decisions. Depending on individual characteristics, women could now gain power and authority in the household at a much earlier stage in their life cycle. Third, the change in the ideology of fertility among young village women left behind by migrant husbands was seen in a decrease in childbirths and an increased use of birth control. Reliance on men's wage labor and scarcity of land seemed to be important factors in this change. Although the quantitative data to support this observation are not analyzed, I can safely argue that in villages where agriculture and village-based production were more significant for the household economy, young women in 1986 had more children than in Sakaltutan, where most women who remained in the village when their husbands became migrant workers verbalized their desire to have fewer children. Fourth, men's wage labor made it possible for women to quit carpet weaving willingly and redefined women as consumers of men's income and reproducers (which was not in question for women who worked in agriculture, but was probably an ideal for the ones who wove carpets).

The use and investment of remittances indicate the path of rural transformation. Whereas for many households migrant wage labor perpetuated rural-based small production, for some it opened paths for capitalist transformation and for others urban-based petty commodity production or trade.

Gender, Marriage, and Work

The stated general norm in Sakaltutan for gender decisionmaking arenas is that women are responsible for internal affairs and men for external affairs. However, because women have always worked in agriculture, this norm does not correspond to a strict gender division of labor; "internal" and "external" affairs have fuzzy boundaries. In some villages where women have withdrawn from cereal agriculture and are involved in full-time carpet weaving, the gender division of labor comes closer to reflecting a public (male) versus private (female) dichotomization. Nevertheless, depending on the household composition, there were numerous exceptions in Sakaltutan. Only among some households with male outmigration, women withdrew their labor from agriculture; in most cases, however, women continued to do farmwork, whether they belonged to wealthy or poor households. In fact, wealthy households with large landholdings required their women's labor more than did poorer ones.

In one Kayseri village in the summer of 1986, an old man whom I thought of as a "peasant philosopher" used to visit and spend long hours having deep conversations with us. One late night during one of those philosophy sessions, he asked me what I thought marriage was about. I was used to posing questions, not answering them; I must have mumbled something about love. He immediately took time to answer his own question: "Marriage is all about producing crops and generations; search for love elsewhere!" This peasant philosopher was saying in his own words that *kinship* and *marriage* were about *production* and *reproduction*. During my long stay in the villages, I witnessed and heard of several love stories behind marriages, but marriages were always about "producing crops and generations." Marriage decisions always involved explicit discussions on household economy.

In the 1980s, the increased importance of weaving in village households and women's negative attitude toward it had two major impacts on marriage. The first impact was on the girls' age at marriage. As the villagers themselves reported, more girls were married at later ages because of their contributions in their fathers' household. The second impact of weaving on marriage was related to spouse selection. Many girls (and their families) preferred marrying boys with nonagricultural occupations, preferably in towns, in order not to have to continue weaving in their husband's house. Likewise, girls preferred to marry into households with no animals and little farmwork (see İncirlioğlu 1993a).

Permanent household migration from villages to towns and big cities is not within the scope of this chapter, as it is the "exit option" from the rural economy. However, it is important as far as gender relations are concerned. Like pendular labor migrations, permanent household migrations from Sakaltutan increased. By 1986, about one-half of the households that were patrilineal descendants of the 1950 households were living outside the villages.

Most village women and the young in general are interested in rural-to-urban household migration, and they explicitly associate this preference with the "balance of power" in intrahousehold relations—that is, relations between both the husband and wife and the junior and senior families. The most significant change in gender relations through household migration is observed in women's work. From villages to towns, women shift from directly productive and paid work (agriculture and carpet weaving) to unpaid domestic work. Almost all women prefer this shift, and it is an important factor in women's (1) input in the household decision to migrate and (2) spouse selection. The "cleanliness" of city life, which is connected to the ease of domestic work there, is attractive to most women. Nevertheless, there are some recent migrants to the city as well as some return migrants in the village who show a clear preference for the villages. This negative attitude toward urban household migration is closely linked with awareness of, and participation in, the urban class structure in a disadvantaged position.

Conclusions

One general conclusion from this discussion is the *holistic nature of anthropology* and the interconnectedness of various subjects that may seem unrelated at first glance. The three aspects of the village economy are interwoven, and the key to our understanding of economic development in Sakaltutan is the intimate link between the village economy and the changes in kinship relations and marriage patterns (Stirling and İncirlioğlu 1996). The household is the major unit of production, and in turn, household formation, household composition, and household structure are all linked with how kinship works in the village. To give one example, if the household is landless or does not have access to land, the household size tends to be smaller, consisting of a "nuclear" single family of parents and unmarried children. Those with relatively large landholdings, however, tend to be larger multifamily households with parents and married sons with children and grandchildren. Likewise, gender relations, because they are an integral part of economic life, are essential to look into if we want to better understand the village economy.

Another conclusion is a *warning against generalizations*. Even in one small village like Sakaltutan, one can observe diversity in the gendered economic system, depending on household size and composition. Comparison among different villages will yield yet more variation, and generalizations about Turkish women will prove futile.

Turkish women gained their rights, including suffrage, during the 1920s as part of the modernization process initiated by the state. Turkish women had the right to vote before many European women obtained equal rights before law. Women were not granted the right to vote in France until 1944 and in Switzerland until 1960. In such an advanced legal position, however, all women in Turkey do not benefit from these rights equally. Whereas in towns and cities access to education is easier for girls, village girls have a harder time going to school and *practicing* the equality that is legally granted to them. In any case, gender ideologies are persistent in both towns and villages.

A final conclusion is that nations are not *bound* to their particular histories; histories and ideologies merge as people come into contact in various ways. In Sakaltutan several interrelated changes happened simultaneously: Women withdrew from direct production, remittances from international migration increased, and a gender ideology was imported that was foreign to village women prior to men's outmigration and contacts with the capitalist world. These changes combined to redefine women's femininity and to create the necessary consumption for that. Hence, the increased consumption in the households of many young international migrants now includes the purchase not only of durable household goods but also of women's clothing. "Feminine" possessions (such as nylon stockings and synthetic lingerie in hot colors) brought back by men to their wives are a good indication of the change in women's identity. Now, women have less value for their households and husbands as hardworking farmers or gainful carpet weavers. Hence, the meaning of "being a woman" in the villages has begun to change, as it has in towns.

Note

1. Parts of this chapter are taken from my Ph.D. dissertation (İncirlioğlu 1993b).

References

İncirlioğlu, Emine. 1993a. "Changing Marriage Patterns, Gender Relations, and Rural Transformation in Anatolia." In *Culture and Economy,* edited by Paul Stirling. London: Eothen Press, 115–125.

———. 1993b. "Gender Relations in Rural Transformation: Two Central Anatolian Villages." Ph.D. diss., Department of Anthropology, University of Florida, Gainesville.

———. 1994. "Negotiating Ethnographic Reality: Team Fieldwork in Turkey." In *When History Accelerates: Essays on Rapid Social Change, Complexity, and Creativity,* edited by Chris M. Hann. London: Athlone Press, 255–275.

———. 1999. "Images of Village Women in Turkey: Models and Anomalies." In *Deconstructing Images of "the Turkish Woman,"* edited by Zehra Arat. New York: St. Martin's Press, 199–223.

Keyder, Çağdar. 1983. "Paths of Rural Transformation in Turkey." *Journal of Peasant Studies* 11, no 1: 34-49.

Magnarella, Paul. 1979. *The Peasant Venture: Tradition, Migration, and Change among Georgian Peasants in Turkey.* Cambridge, MA: Schenkman.

Stirling, Paul. 1965. *Turkish Village.* London: Weidenfeld and Nicolson.

———. 1976. "Cause, Knowledge, and Change: Turkish Village Revisited." In *Aspects of Modern Turkey,* edited by William M. Hale. London: Bowker.

Stirling, Paul, and Emine Onaran İncirlioğlu. 1996. "Choosing Spouses: Villagers, Migrants, Kinship, and Time." In *Turkish Families in Transition,* edited by Gabriele Rasuly-Paleczek. Berlin: Peter Lang, pp. 61-82.

15

ECONOMISTS' BLIND SPOTS
FIELD STORIES OF THE INFORMAL
ECONOMY AMONG MEXICAN
IMMIGRANTS IN SILICON VALLEY

Christian Zlolniski

Widely used today by social scientists and government officials, the concept of
the informal economy is one of the central contributions of anthropology to
the social sciences. The term was originally coined by British anthropologist
Keith Hart in 1973. Hart was studying employment and labor markets in the
urban economy of Accra, Ghana, when he noticed through his ethnographic
fieldwork an interesting paradox: Although according to official statistics the
unemployment rate was rather high, a large segment of the people statistically
defined as idle or unemployed were indeed actively engaged in a myriad of
small but dynamic economic activities that were not captured by government
figures about employment and income (Hart 1973). He proposed the concept
of the informal sector to denote all such income-generating activities that
occurred outside the perusal of the state and that enabled many people and
families, especially the urban poor, to survive. Hart's goal was not to invent a
fancy theoretical concept, but simply to describe and capture a dimension of
economy in Accra that, although crucial for a large segment of its population,
seemed to be beyond what economists using classic employment definitions
and devices to measure it were able to capture. Ethnographically grounded
fieldwork allowed him to see that there was much more to the urban economy
that economists were ready to admit.

Hart's concept turned out to be a seminal one and was rapidly adopted by
the International Labour Organization (ILO), an influential UN agency that
formulates standards for labor and social conditions, especially in developing

233

countries, and by many social scientists and government officials studying employment in these countries. The idea that there was a large segment of the economy that was not reflected in official statistics was especially welcome for developing countries, as it explained how many people made a living, often as self-employed workers, in the context of high structural unemployment and stagnant national economies.

But why were so many workers in developing countries employed in the informal sector? At first, many scholars subscribed to the premises of modernization theory, according to which informal economic activities were traditional, "backward," precapitalist forms of work that would disappear as developing countries emulated the path of economic development and progress of Western industrialized countries. With time, however, it became increasingly clear that the informal economy was not a temporary phenomenon but rather a persistent and even growing dimension of the economies in developing countries. For example, in many Latin American countries the informal sector not only persisted but also expanded at a rapid pace during the 1980s, just at a time when the national governments were implementing economic policies recommended by the United States and international organizations to stir capitalist economic development (Roberts 1994; Fortuna and Prates 1989).

Yet the significance of Keith Hart's seminal concept of the informal economy was not limited to developing countries in Africa, Latin America, or Asia. As anthropologists and other social scientists would soon reveal, the informal economy was also an important but underrated and understudied dimension of the national economies in Western industrialized countries. The "discovery" of the informal economy in the midst of some of the most advanced capitalist countries was a blow to the orthodox doctrine of neoclassic economists. After all, informal economic activities were supposed to correspond to precapitalist modes of production in Third World countries and have no or little room in technologically advanced economies such as that of the United States. But a series of case studies conducted in the 1980s and 1990s proved otherwise, showing that, in the midst of neoliberal economic policies that decreased workers' protections by the state to make employment more "flexible," many workers were forced out of their formal sector work and into informal employment (Portes, Castells, and Benton 1989).

The growth of the informal economy in the United States sparked considerable scholarly attention as well as interest by government officials preoccupied with losing the taxes associated with this sector. It soon became evident that informal economic activities were particularly common in large cities with large immigrant populations. Sociologist Alejandro Portes, for example, argued that the arrival of thousands of illegal immigrant workers in the United States fueled the labor exploitation of immigrant labor by firms operating in the informal economy under subcontracting arrangements with large companies in the formal sector (cited in Martínez Veiga 1989: 48). From this angle, the informal economy was defined as the set of all income-generating activities that are neither taxed nor controlled by the state and for which there is a parallel set of activities in the formal economy regulated by state laws (Castells and Portes 1989: 12). Empirical studies showed that informal economic activities were particularly common in immigrant and minority urban neighborhoods (see Sassen 1994; Raijman 2001), especially in Mexican and other Latino immigrant communities (Stepick 1989; Fernández-Kelly and García 1989; López-Garza 2001; Staudt 1998; Moore and Pinderhughes 1993; Zlolniski 2006).

Different theories have been proposed to explain the expansion of the informal economy in the United States. Scholars influenced by modernization theory reduce informal activities to a set of survival strategies by immigrant workers with low education and poor occupational skills who cannot find employment in the formal sector. An approach influenced by a neo-Marxist perspective maintains that the informal economy is the outcome of structural changes in today's capitalist economy that seek to reduce labor costs and enhance labor flexibility, causing old forms of exploitation to reemerge, such as sweatshops, industrial homework, and subcontracting (Castells and Portes 1989). Saskia Sassen, for example, distinguishes two components in the informal economy in immigrant neighborhoods in New York. The first consists of hidden industrial activities in which immigrants are employed as a source of cheap labor to reduce production costs (i.e., garment, footwear, and construction industries) (1989: 71). The second component is the "neighborhood subeconomy," which consists of goods and services that satisfy the consumption needs of low-income immigrants whenever these goods are not produced in the formal sector or when they are sold at a price beyond the immigrants' reach (e.g., low-cost furniture or family day care) (Sassen 1994: 2296).

Another theoretical approach combines the insights of the neo-Marxist model with a perspective that underscores the skills and social capital of immigrant workers to explain the diversity and dynamism of the informal economy in immigrant communities (Wilson 2005; Cross 1998; Zlolniski 2006; Dohan 2003). This approach seeks to explain not only the structural factors that fuel the growth of the informal economy, but also how workers themselves respond to these factors by developing their own informal income-generating activities as self-employed workers and petty informal entrepreneurs, in the process shaping the contours of the informal sector from below.

But what kind of informal activities can be found in cities with a high concentration of immigrant workers? Are undocumented immigrants employed in the informal sector because they cannot find jobs in the mainstream economy? Is employment in the informal economy a stepping stone for better-paid and more stable jobs in the formal sector? And what do all those activities reveal about the nature of the mainstream capitalist economy in advanced industrialized countries such as the United States? One of the beauties of doing ethnographic fieldwork is that it allows the anthropologist to arrive in the field with some theoretical assumptions in mind and then examine, scrutinize, and critically modify them in light of the empirical findings on the ground.

With this spirit, in the rest of this chapter I address these questions by discussing the cases of two Mexican immigrants who work in the informal economy in the city of San Jose, California. These cases are part of a larger study I conducted among undocumented Mexican immigrant workers in Silicon Valley in Northern California who are employed in low-paid jobs in both the formal and informal sectors (Zlolniski 2006). I describe the nature, internal organization, and economic rationale that underlie the occupations and decisionmaking rationale of these two immigrant workers and how their occupations fit with the mainstream economy in the city.

Víctor: An Ambulant Cheese Merchant

Street vendors—one of the stereotypical and most visible images of the informal economy in immigrant communities in the United States—usually evoke the idea of self-employed workers or people employed in locally run businesses who cannot find work in regular jobs in the mainstream economy. The case of Víctor, an itinerant merchant selling Mexican-style cheese, shows the limitations of this view. Born in Mexico City in 1974, Víctor is a slender and talkative young immigrant whom I met in San Jose on a Saturday when he usually worked in the city. He works for a small but highly structured business in the informal economy that spans well beyond the geographical boundaries of any immigrant neighborhood in San Jose, or the whole city for that matter.

The youngest of nine siblings, Víctor started working at the age of seven in a series of casual occupations, such as seller of bus fares, shoe cleaner, and popsicle vendor, to help his parents make ends meet. In 1984 his oldest brother migrated to Los Angeles, and two years afterward two of his sisters followed him to work as seamstresses in a garment factory in this city. In 1992, guided by a sense of adventure, Víctor decided to join his siblings in Los Angeles in search of better work opportunities. Arriving in Los Angeles as an undocumented immigrant, he first started working as a street vendor of strawberries for a small merchant from Mexico City he met through his sisters. When the strawberry season ended, he started selling cheese in the streets for a local merchant. A few months later, a family relative of this merchant offered him the opportunity to join a team of itinerant street vendors that sells Mexican fresh ranchero-style cheese—a popular item among Mexican immigrants from rural areas—outside Los Angeles. Young and equipped with a sense of initiative, Víctor accepted the offer and started traveling in different towns and cities throughout California.

Business Organization and Work Routine

As an ambulant vendor, Víctor is on the road four days a week and travels several hundred miles a week to visit numerous rural towns and cities with a large Mexican immigrant population. His weekly schedule starts on Thursdays in Lompoc, a small rural town in Southern California, where he and his team-mates sell cheese in the morning. In the afternoon, they go to Santa Maria, a town located about 160 miles north of Los Angeles, where almost half of the population is made up of Mexican farmworkers. In the late evening they drive to Salinas, where they spend the night in the van. Friday morning they sell in Salinas, and in the afternoon they continue to Watsonville, where they work until dusk. At night they drive back to Salinas to sleep in a motel, and on Saturday morning they travel to San Jose, the largest city by far in their itinerary, where they work all day long. In the late evening they continue to Fresno, another town with a large farmworker population, where they spend the night in the van to work Sunday. At night they drive back to Los Angeles, where they arrive early in the morning on Monday. All and all, in a weekly trip that lasts more than four days, Víctor and his teammates manage to sell their merchandise in dozens of different Mexican immigrant neighborhoods dispersed across hundreds of miles in several towns and cities north of Los Angeles, revealing the true geographical scope of some of the businesses in the informal sector.

The business is well organized and had been running for many years before Víctor joined it. It first started operating in the mid-1980s, when the merchant for whom the driver of Víctor's van originally worked decided to try selling his products beyond the confines of Los Angeles due to the intense competi-tion from other street vendors. By the time I met Víctor, the van driver, who is also his boss, was working for a cheese merchant who owns two vans and employs eight vendors, four per van. The third van is owned by Hector's driver, who works as a semi-independent merchant selling cheese from that producer in exchange for a commission and maintenance expenses for his van. Víctor's team is composed of five other vendors, in addition to the van driver. All vendors are men, four immigrants from Mexico City and one from Guatemala with several years of experience in the trade. As the vendor with the least experience in the group, Víctor has fewer customers and therefore generates less profit, as the ones with more time and experience in the busi-ness have more clients and generate more revenues. Vendors are paid on commission, a percentage of the sales they make, with the rest of the profit distributed between the van driver and the cheese-maker. The van driver is responsible for coordinating with all the vendors to take them to the differ-ent neighborhoods where they sell, for refilling their merchandise, and for searching for new areas and routes for the business.

The success and viability of this business critically depend on the careful organization and coordination among the team members. In San Jose, for example, I had the opportunity to shadow Víctor at work on several occa-sions to learn about his job. As the most profitable of the towns he visits every week, he works from 11:00 in the morning to 8:30 in the evening, with only short breaks. He divides his schedule in four different parts, each one in a different neighborhood and lasting about two hours, during which he is going door to door to sell his merchandise. He sells only in apartment buildings where working-class Mexican immigrants usually live; their high population density makes them favorite targets for all sorts of street vendors. He has an excellent mental map of each street and apartment building on his route, remembering where his customers live. According to him, sales are best in the afternoons because that is when his clients are most likely to be home after spending the morning running errands or attending to family business. On any given Saturday in San Jose, he estimates that about 35 percent of his regular clients are not home; of those who are, around 75 percent buy cheese from him. While he is working, the driver coordinates with and takes the other vendors to the different neighborhoods of their respective vending routes. Normally, the meeting points between the driver and the vendors are grocery stores where they can drink a soda, use the restroom and refresh before the next segment in their route, and get change they can use later with their clients.

Víctor carries the cheese and other products in a cooler. When it is full and heavy, he carries it on his shoulder, and when it gets lighter after a few sales, he carries it by hand. Every time he meets with his boss, he replenishes the merchandise in the cooler, which he stuffs with forty pieces: twenty-five cheese units, which he sells at $2.50 apiece; nine creams, also at $2.50 per unit; two cottage cheese units at $3 apiece; and two chorizos at $3 each. The most popular item by far is the fresh cheese; a distant second is the cream his clients use when they prepare tacos and other food items. Ranch cottage cheese sells less but has the comparative advantage that it is hard to find in regular food markets. Chorizo was the last item introduced shortly before I first met him and was still on trial. Inside the cooler and on top of the merchandise, Víctor carries a sample cheese from which he cuts pieces that he offers his potential clients to taste. As a calculated strategy, he often offers samples to children because they are likely to ask their parents to buy goodies for them. Every time he refills his merchandise, his boss carefully counts and records in a notebook the number and types of pieces Víctor sold in the previous leg so that the former can get his commission at the end of the day.

Víctor's job demands considerable physical strength, as he has to walk all day long from apartment to apartment, going up and down stairs, and carrying a rather heavy cooler. This is especially hard in the summer when temperatures usually are in the nineties in places like Fresno. And because workers get paid on a commission basis, they have to work fast and knock on as many doors as possible to optimize sales. Sometimes Víctor's most regular clients would invite him in to have a glass of water or beer, an opportunity he uses to go to the restroom, refresh, and take a short break. Reflecting about his work, he feels the hardest part is knocking on doors of many people he does not know. As he puts it, "Sometimes I feel bad because people would shut the door in your face and you feel ashamed to keep knocking on more doors." Regardless of how tired and shameful he might feel, he tries keeping a clean appearance, being polite and smiling every time he steps into somebody's apartment to sell cheese. Although his customers usually pay him cash, some use checks, and still others pay with food stamps. Whenever this is the case, he hands the stamps to his boss, who is in charge of exchanging them for cash after returning in Los Angeles, a transaction that takes place in the informal sector.

Sales, Income, and Subjective Evaluation

Being an ambulant cheese merchant is a harsh and risky occupation, as sales go up and down on a regular basis depending on a number of factors beyond vendors' control. First, sales vary according to the season. In winter they go down when many of his clients, especially farmworkers, go back to their home communities in Mexico; during the harvest, when rural communities are full of activity, sales go up. Sales also vary according to the time of the month. By the end of the month, Víctor has noticed that sales tend to decline as people start saving to pay the rent and other expenses and have less disposable income for nonessentials. Competition from other vendors also has an effect on sales, and Víctor feels that there are now more cheese merchants in the towns he visits as compared with when he first started working in this trade, which has brought his sales down. Another negative impact on his sales is supermarkets that now stock some of the items that had been sold exclusively in the informal sector.

Despite street vending being a strenuous job, Víctor considers it a good alternative to low-paid jobs in the formal economy. His income is comparable to that of other immigrant workers I met in San Jose who were employed in low-skilled jobs in the formal economy. Víctor's vending itinerary, sales, and income in an average week are summarized in Table 15.1. He earns $.80 for each unit of fresh cheese or cream he sells, and in a regular week he sells about 270 units between the two products, the majority of them cheese. This provides him with an income of about $215 a week. The most profitable of all the locations on his route are San Jose and Watsonville, because of their sheer size and high concentration of Mexican immigrant population; the least profitable are Lompoc and Santa Maria, where he sells only a few dozen pieces. As previously mentioned, sales vary and go up and down. In San Jose, for example, Víctor considers a bad day whenever he sells fewer than 100 units of fresh cheese; a good day is when he sells 150 units or more. On Mondays, after coming back from the trip, he takes the day off, and on Tuesdays and Wednesdays he usually works helping his brother, who owns a car shop, and makes about $35.

Like many other ambulant vendors who represent the most vulnerable link in a business chain in the informal sector, Víctor is directly affected by many of the factors that determine sales in the business. First, he is responsible for recruiting his own customers and maintaining their loyalty. However, selling in apartment buildings where there is a high turnover, he loses clients on a regular basis because they move without a trace or to places far away from his regular vending route. To counteract this turnover effect, he tries recruiting

Table 15.1 Víctor's Vending Route and Sales

Day of the Week	Town	Units Sold	Income Generated	Income Earned
Thursday	Lompoc	12	$ 30.0	$ 9.60
	Santa Maria	13	$ 32.5	$ 10.40
Friday	Salinas	25	$ 62.5	$ 20.00
	Watsonville	45	$112.5	$ 36.00
Saturday	San Jose	130	$325.0	$104.00
Sunday	Fresno	43	$107.5	$ 35.00
Total 4 days	**6 towns**	**268 pieces**	**$670.0**	**$215.00**

new customers every week. Another risk factor is when for any reason—raw materials, manufacturing, preservation, storage, handling, transportation— the cheese or the other products he sells go bad before the expiration date. Whenever this happens, the business takes a hit and he loses the trust of many of his clients. As he explained to me, this occurred several weeks before I met him, and as a result his boss decided to stop working with the former cheese producer and found a different one. In the meantime, Víctor had to invest considerable time apologizing to his regular customers, giving them free cheese units to earn back their trust, and recruiting new clients to make up for those who stopped buying from him.

Another risk factor is associated with the low-income profile of his regular customers. As in other informal businesses that target Latino immigrant workers and families, selling on credit is a common strategy he uses to attract and maintain his customers. Such a strategy backfires when clients fail to pay him either because they cannot do so or because they move out to live somewhere else. According to the business rules, each vendor has to pay a percentage of the income from the units sold at the end of the day regardless of whether clients paid for them, so that whenever a client fails to pay, Víctor takes the loss. Thus in any given week, he might sell about $25 on credit, and he estimates that between this and previous weeks, his customers owe him between $40 and $50.

An even bigger risk associated with Víctor's work is being detained by the police for selling without a license. In his first year of work he was detained three times: The first two times he was given a fine; the third time the police confiscated his merchandise. With experience and with the goal of minimizing the likelihood of being identified by the police in case of detention, Víctor decided to go to work without any type of documentation, either real or fake. Combined, all these risks have a negative impact on Víctor's sales and place him in a rather vulnerable position; at the same time, his boss and the business as such are more isolated and protected from these calamities. Even though many of these risk factors are not all that different from those in similar businesses in the formal sector, the fact that this is an unlicensed business places Víctor and the other vendors in a rather precarious position.

Despite vending being a strenuous and risky job, Víctor prefers it over more tedious low-wage occupations in the formal sector. He values not having to work under the scrutiny of a supervisor and having money in his pockets every day he works rather than waiting to being paid every two weeks, as is the case in most jobs in the mainstream economy. He also considers it an advantage not having to rely on fake documents to go to work, as many other undocumented immigrants have to obtain false Social Security cards to work in the formal sector. More importantly, he values that in a four-day week of intense work, he can earn the same money as working five days a week in a full-time job in the formal sector. Even though street vending is not a good job, as he acknowledges, it is a good alternative to low-paid jobs in the formal sector where many of his friends work and, as he puts it, has the advantage "that nobody bosses me around."

Víctor's case illustrates the true geographical scope of some businesses in the informal economy in Latino immigrant communities throughout California. The extent of these informal businesses challenges the reduction of immigrants' informal activities to the category of neighborhood subeconomy, understood as a set of small-scale, locally run occupations in immigrant communities. In addition, the high degree of internal organization that characterizes this business shows that activities in the informal economy often have a complex organizational structure similar to that of enterprises in the formal sector, critically depending on such an elaborated structure for their normal functioning (Peattie 1980: 24).

Víctor's job also illustrates the dynamic interplay between structural and personal factors for the development of businesses in the informal economy. The existence of a large consumer market for affordable fresh cheese among the low-income Mexican immigrant population in numerous rural and urban communities in California explains the successful development of this ambulant vending business. At the same time, the previous experience that vendors like Víctor have in the informal economy in places such as Mexico City represents an important source of skills—the know-how—that facilitates their entrance and success in street vending jobs in the United States, a set of skills often overlooked by structurally oriented theories of the informal economy. If structural factors explain the conditions under which informal economic activities emerge and thrive in large cities in the United States, immigrant workers' agency, including their cultural capital, helps explain the initiative, creativity, and ingenuity needed to take advantage of such structural opportunities.

Finally, working in the informal sector cannot be reduced to an economic decision alone, as it also has important, although subtle, political connotations. To Víctor, working as a cheese vendor represents not only an alternative to low-skilled jobs in the formal sector, but also a form of resistance to the harsh working conditions and discipline that prevail in these jobs. Despite his erratic income, this job offers him more autonomy, less labor control, and similar or higher income than for low-skilled jobs in the formal sector. The erosion of wages and labor protections of many blue-collar occupations in the formal economy is thus an important incentive for workers like him to choose employment in the informal sector and avoid jobs with strict methods of labor control that do not pay much more than more flexible occupations in the informal sector.

Gustavo: A Dentist in the Informal Sector

The informal economy in Latino immigrant communities often evokes images of unskilled workers employed as street vendors, day laborers, construction peons, nannies, and the like. Yet there is more to the informal economy in immigrant neighborhoods than meets the eye of the casual observer. This is the case of Gustavo, a young Mexican immigrant with a professional dentistry degree from Mexico who worked as an informal dentist in San Jose. Born in Aguililla, Michoacán, in 1963, Gustavo's parents first migrated to San Jose in the late 1950s, while he and an older brother remained in Mexico, where they were raised by their grandparents with the remittances their parents sent home. In the summers, they came to San Jose to visit their parents, learned English, and became familiar with life in the United States. Upon finishing school, Gustavo decided to pursue a degree in general dentistry in a public university in Mexico, and in 1986 he graduated as a dentist and married Antonieta, also a student.

While studying at the university, Gustavo and his wife had planned to open a dental clinic in Morelia upon graduation, but when the time finally came, they realized they did not have enough capital to carry out their plan. It was then that they decided to move temporarily to San Jose, where they could work and save money to buy the equipment they needed to set up a dental office in Mexico. With the support of his parents, Gustavo convinced his reluctant wife to leave Morelia and try their luck in San Jose in 1987.

Providing Dental Care to Immigrants

I first met Gustavo through one of his brothers, who had been a good friend of mine for several years. At that point, I had already established a close relationship with his family, which greatly facilitated my access to Gustavo and his work. As he explained to me, his initiation as an informal dentist in the United States was the outcome of fortuitous events rather than of a preconceived plan. During his first year in San Jose, he worked mostly in low-skilled jobs with no relation to his professional training, the most stable of which was a job as a painter in home remodeling projects. Soon afterward he realized that, even though he could not work as a dentist in California, he could obtain a license as a dental assistant and make more money than he received from manual labor. In 1988, while he continued working as a painter, he started taking courses in a private school to prepare for his certification as a dental assistant; he passed his exam at the end of that year. Shortly after, he quit his construction job and started work as a dental assistant in a private clinic in San Jose for $8.50 an hour, a job that was better paid and less strenuous than his previous job.

In the meantime, when a number of Gustavo's family friends, acquaintances, and neighbors learned he was a dentist, they started asking him to do, as he put it, "simple dental jobs" such as cleanings, fillings, and tooth extractions. Reluctant at first, he gradually started to do them in his spare time at home for free or for a small fee. Soon afterward more people started calling or coming to see him at home for dental work. At this point, he realized that he could work on his own if he chose to. After discussing it with his wife, who offered to help him, he decided to set up his own clinic at home and began working part time in the evenings to earn extra income after coming home from his formal job as a dental assistant. In 1990, with some money he had saved and an additional $3,000 borrowed from his father, Gustavo bought the minimal equipment and tools he needed and opened his own clinic at home. The business prospered so rapidly, with new clients contacting him, that within a few months he was able to repay his father and buy new equipment. To avoid health and legal risks, Gustavo usually performed relatively simple dental jobs such as fillings, extractions, cleanings, crowns, and simple orthodontic treatment.

Gustavo's dental clinic consisted of three small rooms divided by curtains hanging from the ceiling. In what used to be the garage of his parents' house, which he remodeled with the help of his brother, there was no sign that would indicate there was an informal dental clinic in Gustavo's house. In fact, I only learned about it through his brother. The first of the three rooms was what he called his "laboratory," where he kept the instruments and material he needed, such as false teeth, crowns, and paste for fillings. Next to it was the main room, where he treated his patients. Occupying only about forty-three square feet, it had a dentist's chair placed in the middle of the room, a mobile lamp attached to a wall, a tray with dental instruments, a recycled spittoon, and a crucifix hanging on the wall. The third room was what Gustavo called his "office," where he stored the files of his patients. In this room there were a filing cabinet, a bookcase with dentistry books and magazines, and a phone and answering machine to make appointments with his clients.

Most of Gustavo's patients were low-income immigrants employed as electronic assemblers, gardeners, janitors, construction workers, domestic workers, and the like. The majority did not have dental insurance, others could not afford to pay the fee increases in their dental insurance, and still others were workers who had lost their insurance after changing jobs or being laid off. Regardless of why they could not go to a licensed dental office, most of Gustavo's patients came to him for emergencies such as toothaches, broken teeth, or tooth infections. The heavy demand for his work was evident in the fact that, less than three years after he first started working on his own, he had to stop taking new patients because he was constantly booked solid with his 175 regular patients.

Gustavo's fees were considerably lower than those charged in regular dental clinics, which explains the popularity of his underground clinic. On average, he charged about one-third of what licensed dentists charged for the same treatments, and, of course, he did not pay insurance fees. He also offered a flexible payment policy, extending credit to his patients without demanding big downpayments or regular monthly installments, a strategy that suited low-income patients. To protect himself and leave no record of financial transactions, he asked his patients to pay him in cash.

Income, Risks, and Subjective Evaluation

Gustavo's under-the-table earnings were considerably lower than what dentists earned in the formal sector, but considerably higher than what Mexican immigrants earned in low-skilled occupations in the formal or informal sector. By 1993, working in his office in the evenings and on weekends, he was making an average of $1,500 a month, although there were months when he made close to $2,000, especially if he took new patients. Out of these earnings, he had to pay the expenses generated by his business, including materials used for dental work and disposable instruments as well as phone and utility bills. He reinvested much of the profit generated by his business, buying new dental equipment, which he planned to take back to Mexico upon his return. In addition, Gustavo earned about $1,300 a month working full time as a dental assistant in a licensed clinic. Although this formal job was less profitable than his business, he preferred to keep the job because it provided him with a steady income each month, something he could not always count on in his informal clinic. Commenting on the comparative advantages of both jobs and the economic rationale behind combining the two, he explained: "When I was only working full time [as a dental assistant], I was making a thousand dollars [per month] for eight hours a day, but working at home in my own practice I made the same amount [per month] in just two hours [per day]! By working only fifteen hours [per week] here, I make the same as working forty hours in my regular job, and without anybody telling me what to do or yelling at me."

Like most other informal occupations, however, Gustavo's underground business practice involved important financial and legal risks. Because, as Sudhir Venkatesh argues (2006), work in the informal sector is unregulated, workers cannot go to the authorities for help or for enforcement of their contracts. Gustavo's case illustrates this point. First, the flexible payment policy that allowed him to keep his low-income clients was often one of his principal problems. Because he had no written contracts with his patients, many of them, after completing their treatment, failed to fully pay for it. He estimated that, at any given point, about 50 percent of his patients either were behind in the payment schedule they verbally agreed on or simply avoided paying him and did not come back after he had completed his work.

Second, a more serious risk that Gustavo took was that he could be denounced to government authorities, an important reason he often cited in our conversations for not pursuing his debtors with more determination. To make malpractice suits and any other legal problems less likely, he provided only a limited range of dental services, even though he had the training and skills to do more complicated and financially rewarding work. He carefully checked the personal background of his clients, found out who referred them, and, if he sensed a potential risk, turned them down, giving some credible excuse. Aware of the importance Latino immigrants usually place on trusting their family physicians and dentists, Gustavo always tried to establish a good rapport with his patients:

> I only treat Latinos because we are used to doing businesses under the table, and we are not afraid of it. All my patients are Latinos, except for an Irish man from San Francisco who came here recommended by my brother Samuel.... Besides, we Latinos look for a doctor we can trust and we can relate to. Here, American doctors only care about the technical aspect, [and] they do not offer the human touch that Latino patients look for. But not all Latino patients are trustworthy, so I have to be very careful and avoid those that look untrustworthy, who might cause me trouble.

In 1995, five years after he started working as an informal dentist in San Jose, Gustavo's fears materialized when he received an official letter from state authorities stating they were informed he was operating "an illegal dental practice." The letter stated that if he continued, he would be fined, have his dental assistant's license suspended, and face criminal prosecution. To avoid further problems, Gustavo decided to dismantle his office immediately. He sold off dental equipment that could not be taken back to Mexico, discontinued receiving patients at home, and informed all the clients that he could no longer treat them.

In spite of the financial setback, Gustavo continued with his plans to go back to Mexico. He estimated that by 1996, with the income generated by his job as a dental assistant and his own dental practice, he had invested about $25,000 in building the new house in Mexico where he and his wife planned to set up their own dental clinic when they returned. In addition, he had spent a considerable amount of money in medical equipment and instruments to take back home. With the lower cost of living in Mexico, he and his wife expected to raise their living standard to a level they regarded as commensurate with their professional status, a scenario he preferred over living as an undocumented immigrant in the United States, where his professional degree was not recognized.

In 1998, after more than ten years in Silicon Valley, Gustavo, Antonieta, and their two children returned to Mexico. Their departure came as a surprise to me. I had believed that, like many other immigrants who first come with the intention of staying temporarily and who end up settling down, they would stay longer. In the end, Gustavo's choice was to practice his profession as a licensed dentist in Mexico rather than in the informal sector in the United States. He preferred to openly develop his career in the formal sector in Mexico, which would not require him to renounce his hard-won degree.

Gustavo's case shows the limitations of conceiving the informal economy solely as a set of unskilled activities by immigrants with little education or human capital. It illustrates the situation of a small but important group of professional immigrants who work in the informal sector because their formal degrees are not recognized in the United States. Although many of these professional workers are employed in unskilled jobs with no relation to their training, the informal economy provided Gustavo an opportunity to put his skills to work and a better option than working in the sort of low-paid jobs that most undocumented immigrants in Silicon Valley accept. With little access to credit and capital markets in Mexico, Gustavo found that the informal economy offered an avenue for building savings at a rate that he could not have duplicated by working solely in the formal sector as a dental assistant. Rather than merely supplementing low wages earned in the formal economy, Gustavo's self-employment as an informal dentist helped him to accumulate capital to open his own dental office in Mexico's formal sector.

But Gustavo's informal dental office was not merely the result of these factors and his personal determination to accumulate savings. The lack of access to basic dental care for many Latino immigrant workers because of their low wages and lack of insurance was an equally, if not more relevant, factor. This was the structural context that allowed him to work as a dentist in the informal economy in the first place. In a country that lacks a universal health care system, there is a big structural incentive for the proliferation of doctors, dentists, and other health-related practitioners working in the informal economy that caters to immigrant communities. In fact, the concentration of working poor immigrants in particular urban neighborhoods and communities generates a demand not only for goods at low prices, but also for professional workers and services at more affordable costs than in the formal sector.

Conclusion

The concept of the informal economy demonstrates the power of ethnography to reveal economic trends otherwise not captured by economics and other disciplines that rely on top-down surveys and other aggregate research methods and techniques. The discovery of the informal sector in developing countries enabled social scientists to acknowledge the existence of informal economic activities at the heart of advanced industrialized countries such as the United States, dispelling the myth that this sector belonged to "backward" economies where a capitalist market economy had not fully developed.

Neoliberal economic policies that withdraw labor protections for workers employed in the formal sector under the rule of economic efficiency have only spurred the growth of the informal economy in the United States. The variety, heterogeneity, and complexity of informal economic activities found in Mexican and other Latino immigrant communities defy their conceptualization as simple survival strategies by immigrant workers excluded from the formal sector. More often, Mexican immigrants use income generated by work in the informal economy to supplement wages from low-paid jobs in the formal sector; still others use the informal economy as an alternative to unstable, unpleasant, and poorly paid jobs in the formal economy. The apparent paradox of petty informal economic activities in the midst of an advanced capitalist economy cannot be explained as a result of a lack of integration of Latino immigrants into the local economy. Rather, it is immigrants' employment in low-wage occupations in the formal economy as janitors, gardeners, construction laborers, and the like that is the central force behind the proliferation of informal activities in the communities where they live, as the low wages preclude workers from access to goods and services that they cannot afford in the mainstream economy.

The informal sector constitutes a bonus to the formal economy not only by subsidizing the costs associated with the subsistence and reproduction of labor, but also by serving as an unofficial welfare and unemployment safety valve when workers are laid off. The informal sector cannot then be conceptualized as a transitory employment stage for immigrants and other low-paid workers before they move to better-paid jobs in the formal economy. As Ubaldo Martínez Veiga (1989) astutely indicates, a transition from employment in the informal to employment in the formal economy is the exception rather than the rule, whereas a transition from employment in the formal to employment in the informal sector is rather common in industrialized countries, especially during times of economic slowdown and unemployment.

The case studies here also illustrate the importance of considering immigrants' agency and motivations in any examination of informal economic activities. As Sassen (1994) correctly points out, the informal economy in immigrant communities cannot be explained as a product of cultural practices immigrants bring with them. Yet we cannot ignore the skills and experience that immigrants such as Gustavo and Víctor do bring. These work skills and social capital are often essential ingredients of the informal businesses in which they engage, as well as the source of the creative strategies they often develop to confront the numerous legal and economic risks involved in their jobs. These factors play an important role in explaining the initiative, creativity, and ability necessary to seize business and market opportunities in the informal economy created by structural factors. Anthropologists using reliable ethnographic methods are in a privileged position to explain how macro forces interact with people's agency at the local level to generate different patterns of informal economic activities in societies with different political and cultural contexts.

References

Castells, Manuel, and Alejandro Portes. 1989. "World Underneath: The Origins, Dynamics, and Effects of the Informal Economy." In *The Informal Economy: Studies in Advanced and Less Developed Countries,* edited by Alejandro Portes, Manuel Castells, and Lauren Benton. Baltimore, MD: Johns Hopkins University Press, 11–37.

Cross, John C. 1998. *Informal Politics: Street Vendors and the State in Mexico.* Palo Alto, CA: Stanford University Press.

Dohan, Daniel. 2003. *The Price of Poverty: Money, Work, and Culture in the Mexican American Barrio.* Berkeley and Los Angeles: University of California Press.

Fernández-Kelly, P., and Anna M. García. 1989. "Informalization at the Core: Hispanic Women, Homework, and the Advanced Capitalist State." In *The Informal Economy: Studies in Advanced and Less Developed Countries,* edited by Alejandro Portes, Manuel Castells, and Lauren Benton. Baltimore, MD: Johns Hopkins University Press, 247–264.

Fortuna, Juan Carlos, and Suzana Prates. 1989. "Informal Sector versus Informalized Labor Relations in Uruguay." In *The Informal Economy: Studies in Advanced and Less Developed Countries,* edited by Alejandro Portes, Manuel Castells, and Lauren Benton. Baltimore, MD: Johns Hopkins University Press, 78–94.

Hart, Keith. 1973. "Informal Income Opportunities and Urban Employment in Ghana." *Journal of Modern African Studies* 11, no. 1: 61–89.

López-Garza, Marta. 2001. "A Study of the Informal Economy and Latina/o Immigrants in Greater Los Angeles." In *Asian and Latino Immigrants in a Restructuring Economy: The Metamorphosis of Southern California,* edited by Marta López-Garza and David Diaz. Palo Alto, CA: Stanford University Press, 141–168.

Martínez Veiga, Ubaldo. 1989. "El Otro Desempleo: La Economía Sumergida" (The Other Unemployment: Underground Economy). *Cuadernos de Antropología* 10 (Anthropos, Spain).

Moore, Joan, and Raquel Pinderhughes. 1993. "Introduction" to *In the Barrios: Latinos and the Underclass Debate.* New York: Russell Sage Foundation, xi–xxxix.

Peattie, Lisa R. 1980. "Anthropological Perspectives on the Concepts of Dualism, the Informal Sector, and Marginality in Developing Urban Economies." *International Regional Science Review* 5: 1–31.

Portes, Alejandro, Manuel Castells, and Lauren Benton, eds. 1989. *The Informal Economy: Studies in Advanced and Less Developed Countries.* Baltimore, MD: Johns Hopkins University Press.

Raijman, Rebeca. 2001. "Mexican Immigrants and Informal Self-Employment in Chicago." *Human Organization* 60, no. 1: 47–55.

Roberts, Bryan. 1994. "Informal Economy and Family Strategies." *International Journal of Urban and Regional Research* 18, no. 1: 6–23.

Sassen, Saskia. 1989. "New York City's Informal Economy." In *The Informal Economy: Studies in Advanced and Less Developed Countries,* edited by Alejandro Portes, Manuel Castells, and Lauren Benton. Baltimore, MD: Johns Hopkins University Press, 60–77.

———. 1994. "The Informal Economy: Between New Developments and Old Regulations." *Yale Law Journal* 103: 2289–2304.

Staudt, Kathleen. 1998. *Free Trade? Informal Economies at the U.S.-Mexico Border.* Philadelphia: Temple University Press.

Stepick, Alex. 1989. "Miami's Two Informal Sectors." In *The Informal Economy: Studies in Advanced and Less Developed Countries,* edited by Alejandro Portes, Manuel Castells, and Lauren Benton. Baltimore, MD: Johns Hopkins University Press, 111–131.

Venkatesh, Sudhir A. 2006. *Off the Books: The Underground Economy of the Urban Poor.* Cambridge, MA: Harvard University Press.

Wilson, Tamar Diana. 2005. *Subsidizing Capitalism: Brickmakers on the U.S.-Mexican Border.* Albany: State University of New York Press.

Zlolniski, Christian. 2006. *Janitors, Street Vendors, and Activists: The Lives of Mexican Immigrants in Silicon Valley.* Berkeley and Los Angeles: University of California Press.

16

WATER, THE OTHER NAME OF LIFE

SOUTH ASIAN PERSPECTIVES

Azizur R. Molla

If we look at the crossroads of culture and health, we can establish a connection between people's emic cultural codes and the etic consequences of their actions. Sometimes the connection is costly. In Bangladeshi villages people believe that evil power causes disease and holy words can get rid of the evil power. Some villagers go to religious healers to get treated. The healers may ask them to bring a glass or a bottle of water. The healer then whispers some holy words and blows on the water. The idea is that if the patient drinks the water, the evil power will leave the body and the patient will be cured. If we see this practice from a scientific point of view, we can argue that even if the water is safe to begin with, blowing onto it may bring germs into the water that makes it less safe to drink. But from the point of view of the cultural code of the village people, the water with holy words has the power to remove the evil that is causing the disease. So what is useful from one point of view may be harmful from another. People rely on such healing methods for three reasons: (1) They believe that this kind of treatment has benefits, (2) they lack access to modern medicine because of finances or transportation, or (3) they lack knowledge about the scientific worldview.

If we want to establish the relationship between cultural codes and health, we have to understand the relationships among cultural codes, actions, and consequences.[1] We can understand the cultural codes by talking to people, but we can understand the etic consequences of their actions only if we understand a number of facts about their etic worlds. To understand the health of the rural people of my homeland of Bangladesh, I worked with a team of researchers on a large project to do both of these things.

The task of understanding how the environment affects health is great for even a single village, but for a whole country with the population of Bangladesh, it is truly daunting. We couldn't talk to each person or even one from each village. But because the issue was important, we had to be sure that our study could provide valid data upon which policymakers could rely to improve the situation.

We collected ethnographic data through ethnographic surveys, a review of related studies, and our own experience growing up in the country. We also measured various dimensions of water quality, socioeconomic factors, and access to medical care. We then used statistical methods to see how these etic factors are related to the incidence of diarrhea, malaria, and skin disease in Bangladesh. The etic variables, things we can measure, do not necessarily have meaning or causal force from the point of view of the cultural codes of the people whose health we want to understand. And their actions, predicated on their cultural codes, may not have the consequences they desire. For instance, if a person drinks blessed water, she or he may get sick from a communicable disease instead of cured.

It will be helpful to keep these questions in mind as you read this chapter:

1. How and why do Bangladeshis use polluted water?
2. Is formal education more powerful than tradition?
3. What part does religion play?
4. What would you recommend to improve the rural health of Bangladeshis and those of countries with similar conditions?

The highest priority of Bangladesh's National Water Management Plan is clean drinking water for all households to replace the dangerously polluted surface water they had been relying on. More than two decades ago, UNICEF launched a campaign to provide clean water to all communities in Bangladesh by introducing hand pumps and tube wells.

Tube wells are iron pipes that go 70 to 120 feet below the surface through sandy soils to a water source. At the top is a hand pump to raise the water, at the bottom is a filter to prevent the sand from coming in, and in between is the iron pipe to keep the hole from collapsing. Because the water runs through the iron pipes, it has a huge amount of iron in it. Often, iron particles from the pipe are visible in the water. Many people believe that the iron in the water makes the food color different if they cook with it and makes their hair sticky if they shampoo with it. Some tube wells use PVC pipes instead of iron, but we heard the same complaints about the water.

It would be financially impossible to provide a tube well and pump to each and every household, so the government decided to provide one for every ten households and ensure that each household had access to it. This campaign was supplemented through the efforts of such nongovernmental organizations (NGOs) as the Rotary and Lions clubs and individual donors.

Today in Bangladesh, tube wells with hand pumps are the main source of drinking water. Our survey showed that about 99 percent of people get drinking water from tube wells.

Just as the well campaign had reached a better than 80 percent success rate, high levels of arsenic were discovered in the groundwater in many parts of the country. Millions of people now face a dire dilemma: Surface water sources are contaminated with organic pollutants and could be a source of life-threatening diseases, whereas long-term use of tube-well water may lead to arsenicosis. This problem is as yet far from being resolved.

Our survey analyzed water from forty tube wells in eight villages and four *thanas* (subdistricts). Table 16.1 shows that all areas are not equally affected. The four villages in the northern subdistricts (Jamalpur Sadar and Modhupur) are relatively safe in terms of arsenic levels. In the south, Chandina thana is particularly badly affected, as are parts of Sonagazi thana.

Almost all of the people in the study villages (98.9 percent) obtain their drinking water from tube wells with hand pumps. It is apparent that dependence on tube wells is absolute. This, of course, makes the search for a solution to the arsenic problem even more urgent.

There are perhaps even greater health risks from drinking groundwater. According to our study's data (see Table 16.2), nearly one-half of the households use surface water for washing kitchen utensils and cooking. Yet the issue of arsenic is so ominous that it is hard to say that surface water poses a greater hazard.

Culture and Water Use

The cultural code of the people as well as their experience determines how they use water and what water they use. Villagers rarely use tube-well water for cooking, as they believe it gives food a bad color or taste. Nor do they bathe in well water because they believe it makes their hair sticky. Therefore, for cooking, bathing, and other households uses, except drinking, people use water from ponds, canals (*khaal*), rivers, ditches, wetlands/marshlands (*beel*), and rain. Bangladesh is a low-lying area with plentiful conveniently available surface water from many sources, such as streams, rivers, wetlands, and marshes. People therefore use water from ponds, ditches, canals, and/

Table 16.1 Arsenic in Groundwater of Study Area

Thana	Arsenic level μg/l
Sonagazi	3.67–6.42
Chandina	6.37–6.46
Modhupur	0.03–0.28
Jamalpur	00.0–10.96

Note: Acceptable level of arsenic is .05 as set by Bangladesh government.

Table 16.2 Place of Washing the Kitchen Utensils

Water Source	MZP	BDD	KMK	Study BSP	Village CAM	RDN	SFP	CRP	Total
Tube-well (hand pump)	6	2	9	8	52	52	56	65	250
	9.23	3.08	13.85	12.31	80.00	81.20	84.85	100.00	51.92
Pond/ river/ canal (Khaal)/ bog	59	63	56	57	13	12	9	–	269
	90.77	96.92	86.15	87.69	20.00	18.75	13.64		48.08

or rivers near their households for everything except drinking water, which they do get from wells.

Young girls, boys, women of almost all ages, housemaids, and day laborers all collect water to meet the household demand for drinking water as well as water for the kitchen and other household uses. Villagers who have tube wells or ponds usually collect their water directly from the source as needed. Others collect and store water in pottery vessels. They keep these vessels with drinking water inside the home in the dining place and other areas with household water in the kitchen. These vessels are not usually covered, so any kind of insect has easy access to the water.

Villagers consider pond water a gift from Allah (God). Use of pond water is associated with religious and social values and traditions. If there is a serious need for drinking water but it is scarce, people will drink pond water with the name of Allah: "Allah will take care"; "Nothing will happen, 'inshallah'" (Allah willing). When adults, usually mothers, wash dishes in the ponds, they sometimes dip their hands into the pond water and give it to the children that are with them. When asked about this practice, they mostly reply that they started taking water with the name of Allah, who will take care of their health with his kindness. Culturally the Muslims in the country believe that every work, like starting a new job, taking food, or drinking water, should start with the name of Allah to seek his kindness (*rahmat*); the exact word in Arabic is *Bismillaher-rahmaner-rahim,* meaning "I am starting in the name of Allah, most gracious, most merciful." It is strongly believed that anyone who starts any work with these words will get kindness from Allah and the work will be accomplished better since Allah's blessing/kindness is present. Islamic codes of conduct suggest checking any food that may have made people sick before sharing it again with others. The Prophet Muhammad instructed that if anybody got sick in taking any food item, it was the host's duty to make sure that the food was not harmful to health before offering it again and then to convey information about the food item to neighbors.

Culture and Treatment of Disease

The health culture of rural Bangladesh is characterized by traditional beliefs and practices. People believe the source of disease is evil power rather than a virus or bacteria. They also believe that personal problems like disease are tests to prove the purity of their faith (*iman*) in Allah and that it is Allah who will ultimately cure them. When a baby is born, the elders, including the mother, will start feeding blessed water and oil to the baby; they also strongly encourage all the children to wear amulets and the mothers to put a black ink dot on the forehead of the baby to get rid of evil power. Within these boundaries of religious doctrine, elders try their best to enforce the traditional treatment of a disease and ensure a person's well-being.

Traditional social customs also contribute to the health culture. In Bangladesh, for example, particularly in rural areas, pregnant women are kept in a dark room when their delivery date approaches because people think that if bad air enters the room, it may harm the expected baby. Thus, all the ventilation passages, such as windows and doors, are closed. Moreover, to get rid of any bad influences, smoke is always present in the room. Men are not usually allowed in the room, and their help in delivery is discouraged. Due to unhygienic conditions, many mothers die before and during child delivery.

Bangladeshi villagers usually go through three steps in treating disease:

1. They try the traditional (social and religious) treatments.
2. They get help from untrained health care providers, such as uncertified pharmacists.
3. They go to trained health care providers, such as a Bachelor of Medicine and Bachelor of Surgery doctor.

Initially, elders will usually suggest traditional medication: for example, juice from particular leaves or roots to cure jaundice, herbs for broken bones. Sometimes they also take the patient to a religious healer, who may prescribe blessed oil or water and an amulet containing holy words as a remedy, say, for mental problems, body aches, or indigestion.

In the second step, people go to the local pharmacists or village doctors, who prescribe certain medications based on their experience. The findings from participant observation suggest that some of these health care providers give antibiotics (which are available all over Bangladesh without prescription) quite freely for minor complaints.

In the third step, people seek modern medicine. Villagers have easy access to local family welfare visitors (FWVs) or health workers who can provide only the very basic level of treatment and refer cases to the subdistrict level. At the subdistrict level, however, people find that either there are less qualified doctors or that they are often absent and/or they have to pay to see the doctor, who is supposed to provide free treatment.

Officially, the doctors are supposed to be in their hospitals to serve the people, but in reality some of them do not actually remain on duty. People with such high levels of education do not like to live in small rural towns, so they leave and manage still to get their salaries by bribing high officials. These doctors argue that the subdistrict towns lack facilities such as good schools for their children. If these doctors were actually available, more people might get health care service. But the people who need and seek the services of these doctors are poor and cannot afford transportation costs to go to a district-level hospital in a larger town where there are more doctors. Most of these villagers usually cannot reach the tertiary care level located in the largest towns at the district or capital level.

Health care is a campaign issue in every election, and villagers look to the candidates for political commitment to the concept of better health care by qualified doctors. Regardless of who wins the elections, villagers still mostly depend on health care services provided by traditional and less qualified health care providers. Although health experts and health administrators believe that there is gradual improvement in health care services, these are not up to the level of need or expectation.

Health Care Service: Nature and Structure

In Bangladesh, there are three basic types of health care: modern medicine, ayurvedic medicine (literally referred to as "life science," a traditional healing medicine that originated in India to treat different types of disease), and homeopathic medicine. All these types of health care services are available all over the country. The latter two types are privatized ventures located both in town and in village areas, whereas the first type has a formal structure from the village level to the country's capital.

The Ministry of Health and Family Welfare (MHFW) is charged with ensuring health care service through modern medicine. The MHFW has two directorates: health and family planning. Both directorates have independent service structures that extend to the village level. Each of the directorates is run by a director general, who is a deputy secretary–level official. Under the directorate are divisional, district, thana, and union (township) offices to implement health care services. All of the tertiary care hospitals and specialized health centers are located in Dhaka, the capital city of Bangladesh. The basic health care services are provided at all four administrative levels (division, district, thana, and union) of the country.

There are six divisional health offices in the country. Each office is run by a director of health, along with specialists who provide services to district offices. The divisional offices also ensure medical and related supplies for sixty-four district health offices. The district health office is run by a deputy director of health, a civil surgeon, and specialists who provide services to thana offices.

The district office is in charge of district hospitals where outpatient care, ambulatory care, and surgery are performed. The district health official (civil surgeon) ensures medical and related supplies for the thana hospitals. The lower-ranking health office is the thana hospital; this hospital is run by the chief medical officer, and it is staffed with doctor, paramedics, laboratory assistants, technicians, and nurses. The Family Welfare Center (FWC) is the lowest-ranking and most easily accessed health care center for modern health services. On paper, the FWC should be run by a doctor, but in reality it is often run by a senior paramedic (FWV). It is staffed with an FWC, family welfare assistant, and health assistant. The FWC performs basic health care services, including prescribing some medicine. However, no surgery is done at this level. Almost all FWCs are located at the center of a union. The typical FWC serves an average of thirty-thousand residents.

The thana hospital and the FWC are the main health care service hospitals/ centers for rural dwellers. These often lack qualified health care providers and do not have enough supplies, including basic medicine, to ensure normal services. Poor rural people have limited access to thana hospitals, as they cannot afford to be absent from their daily work and also pay the bus fare to a distantly located (on average, three to six miles) hospital.

By law, the health care services of doctors and basic medicines such as paracetamol (Tylenol) from a government clinic or hospital are free. However, some government clinics and hospitals recently have started taking token fees for their services. The average distance between the FWC and a village is two to four miles, and communication is very poor. So although there are hospitals and health care service centers, rural people have limited access to them.

As mentioned earlier, although the health of rural Bangladeshis is interconnected with several socioeconomic and cultural factors, it also needs to be seen from a holistic point of view. Villagers' knowledge about environment and health is not well linked in that they remain unaware of how environmental factors such as water contamination affect health. Cultural beliefs and traditional customs—the cultural codes—are powerful forces in shaping the health behavior of rural Bangladesh.

Environmental, Social, and Health Factors

The total area of Bangladesh is 56,977 square miles, 12 nautical miles of which is territorial water (BBS 2008). People use 1.2 percent of the country's total water annually. The country consists of 13,000 square kilometers of forest, or 10 percent of the total land area. However, the annual deforestation is 1.3 percent. Per capita energy use of the country is 159 kilograms, and carbon dioxide emission per capita (in metric tons) is 0.2 (World Bank 2001).

There are 140 million people currently living in Bangladesh. About 97 percent of them have access to improved water sources. The life expectancy at birth is fifty-nine years, and the infant mortality rate is sixty-six per one thousand (Population Reference Bureau 2001). Thirty-six percent of people live below the poverty line, which is defined as 2,122 kcal of food intake per day (Ravallion and Sen 1994; Hossain and Sen 1992; Sen 1995). This can also be stated as the starvation line (World Bank 2001). So in Bangladesh, below the poverty line means below the level of starvation.

I assessed the interactions of different variables to provide a clearer picture of the impact of water quality and socioeconomic variables on the incidence of disease.

Methodology

Data Source for the Study

In 1998 the team I worked with collected data in a survey of 520 rural Bangladeshi households and supplemented the data with focus group discussions. For our etic measures, we collected samples of water and soil for laboratory testing. The purpose of the study was to examine the effects of contaminated water on the incidence of disease in eight randomly selected villages in Bangladesh.

Bangladesh is uniquely suitable for this study because it is one of the most densely populated countries in the world, a high proportion of its people live below the poverty line, and most of the areas of the country are environmentally endangered. This research examines how population density and water quality influence disease in Bangladesh.

Sampling

One of the problems of trying to study anything in a country the size of Bangladesh is how to be sure that our findings are accurate for the whole country and not just the few people we have time and energy to talk to. The best way to do that is to ensure that every household in the country has an equal chance to participate in the study, and the best way to do that is to use a random sampling method. It wasn't entirely random because we were interested only in rural people, so we ruled out the cities and suburbs. For this study we selected four rural thanas, equivalent to U.S. counties, based on population density. We selected one from each of four different agro-ecological zones of Bangladesh, of which there are thirty in total. Then from each thana we randomly selected two villages of approximately 250–300 households for a total of eight villages. Finally, we randomly selected 65 households from each village for a total of 520 households.

In addition to the household surveys, we held eight focus group discussions. We selected the sites for these by what was convenient for the villagers, usually in the center of the village. In most cases, the villagers preferred a meeting at a school or clubhouse. We tried to improve the potential for maximizing the contributions by avoiding people who might dominate the discussion or whose presence might be an obstacle for other members' participation. Finally, all members of the focus groups were equally wealthy—or poor.

Data Collection

Part of the task of coordinating such a large study is to be sure that all the participants are doing similar things. All of the investigators visited all the selected villages to observe the physical environment and other sociocultural aspects before we made any survey questionnaires to pretest. We selected one supervisor for every four interviewers and gave these supervisors a three-week-long training course. Each investigator supervised supervisors and data collectors in a pretest of the questionnaire before we finalized the questionnaire. This way we could be sure that the questions were emically relevant to each site.

During the data collection period, the supervisor traveled the study area and reported his findings to the investigators. To ensure better understanding of the data, the investigators also visited the study area several times to become familiar with village/household environments, villagers' perspectives, and villagers' health. We were meticulous about preparation—the investigators' initial visits to the study villages, the questionnaire design, and extensive training for the interviewers—because we wanted to increase the validity and reliability of the study. The project supervisor's regular visits and investigators' surprise visits to the study areas also improved the quality of the interview data.

Two investigators were moderator and note-taker for each focus group, and an interviewer recorded the discussion. Later, we prepared a report of each focus group based on the recordings and notes.

We collected groundwater samples from five different tube wells of each study village to examine arsenic levels. We collected surface water samples from five different ponds of each village and measured total coliform and fecal coliform (fc) bacteria.

Results and Discussion

Table 16.3 shows that almost one-half (47 percent) of householders were illiterate and 25 percent had completed primary education. Another 23 percent had completed secondary school, and just 5 percent had postsecondary education. More than one-half of householders were involved in agriculture: 34 percent were farmers with their own land, 15 percent had some land, and just 8 percent were landless agricultural workers. At the same time, 31 percent were involved in nonagricultural work. In addition, 13 percent were female household heads, students, or unemployed. When we defined income simply in terms of low and not so low, 79 percent of households fell into the low category, with the remaining 21 percent having a household income equal to or better than the average per capita income for Bangladesh. Again, there is variation across villages in household socioeconomic characteristics.

Table 16.3 also presents the results of cross-tabular analysis, including chi-square statistics testing for statistically significant associations of the independent with the dependent variables (disease). Looking first at the health/contamination variables, we see that those households using pond/canal water for household tasks were significantly more likely to have experienced diarrhea and skin disease than those using tube-well water.

Nobody had the indoor plumbing to which most Americans are accustomed. Instead, the toilets were located behind and outside the houses. They may have been a modern sanitary toilet with a water trap set into a cement slab, as recommended by health officials, or a more old-fashioned hanging toilet or open latrine. The type of toilet the household had turned out to have a significant relationship to diarrhea, malaria, and skin disease. Those households using the modern slab/sanitary latrines were significantly more likely to have experienced diarrhea than those using hanging or open latrines. The level of fecal coliform had a statistically significant association with each disease; households characterized by high levels of fc were more likely to have experienced diarrhea, malaria, and skin disease.

The type of health care provider did not have a statistically significant relationship to diarrhea experience. However, those households using trained providers were less likely to have experienced malaria and skin disease than those using traditional providers.

At least one of the indicators of household socioeconomic status had a statistically significant relationship to each disease. Although education and occupation were not related strongly to diarrhea, those households with higher incomes were significantly less likely to experience diarrhea. Malaria was not associated with education or income but was more likely to have been experienced by agricultural households than by nonagricultural households. Agriculture was not associated significantly with skin disease, but those households having a head with postprimary education or a higher income were *more* likely to have experienced skin disease.

We expected most of these relationships. Diarrhea is affected by both water quality and household resources. Malaria is affected by water quality, access to health care, and differential disease exposure via agricultural work. Skin disease is affected by water quality, health care, and household resources that might predispose households to use tube wells. However, it was surprising that households using the supposedly healthier latrines were more likely to report experience with malaria and skin disease. Public health experts believe that use of sanitary latrines decreases incidence of diseases. However, it appeared that in this sample, hanging and open latrines may have been better than sanitary or slab latrines.

The focus groups and ethnographic data help point to where the problem lies. The qualitative data showed that toilets reported as sanitary (in the

Table 16.3 Bivariate Association of Independent Variables with Household Experience with Disease

Independent Variables	N	Diarrhea		Chi-square
		Yes	No	
HOUSEHOLD-LEVEL CONTAMINATION				
Source of kitchen wash water	520	246 (47)	274 (53)	3.925
Pond/Canal		139 (52)	131 (48)	
Tube well		107 (43)	143 (57)	
Type of toilet used	520	246 (47)	274 (53)	1.896
Slab/Sanitary		155 (50)	158 (50)	
Hanging latrine		48 (42)	66 (58)	
Open latrine		43 (46)	50 (54)	
Level of fecal coliform (fc)	520	246 (47)	274 (53)	12.938
Low (μfc/L 3–11)		72 (38)	115 (62)	
Medium (18–52)		124 (49)	128 (51)	
High (81–360)		50 (62)	31 (38)	
MEDICAL CARE ACCESS				
Health care provider	520	246 (47)	274 (53)	1.814
Trained		27 (40)	41 (60)	
Untrained		219 (49)	233 (51)	
HOUSEHOLD SOCIO-ECONOMIC STATUS LEVEL				
Education	520	246 (47)	274 (53)	0.098
Primary or less		179 (48)	196 (52)	
More than primary		67 (46)	78 (54)	
Occupation	520	246 (47)	274 (53)	0.496
Agriculture		144 (49)	152 (51)	
Nonagriculture		102 (45)	122 (55)	
Household income	520	246 (47)	274 (53)	3.779
Low (Tk 22,000 and less)		203 (50)	207 (50)	
High (Tk 22,001–300,000)		43 (39)	67 (61)	

survey data) often were not actually sanitary. The water seal is what makes the slab latrine a sanitary latrine. Because villagers faced difficulty cleaning the narrow channel of the water seals using small pots of water, they broke the water seal to make it easier to clean, but then the pan of the slab became open and was no longer sanitary.

The results of the analysis provide only partial support for the original hypotheses. As expected, when only household-level health/contamination predictors were considered, at least one indicator had a statistically significant impact on the disease being considered. The level of fecal

| | Malaria | | | Skin Disease | |
Yes	No	Chi-square	Yes	No	Chi-square
106 (20)	414 (80)	34.506	237 (46)	283 (54)	20.902
82 (30)	188 (70)		149 (55)	121 (45)	
106 (20)	414 (80)	8.725	237 (46)	283 (54)	15.637
77 (25)	236 (75)		162 (52)	151 (48)	
15 (13)	99 (87)		48 (42)	66 (58)	
14 (15)	79 (85)		27 (29)	66 (71)	
106 (20)	414 (80)	4.797	237 (46)	283 (54)	10.194
29 (15)	158 (85)		78 (42)	109 (58)	
56 (22)	196 (78)		109 (43)	143 (57)	
21 (26)	60 (74)		50 (62)	31 (38)	
106 (20)	414 (80)	6.443	237 (46)	283 (54)	4.357
6 (9)	62 (91)		23 (34)	45 (66)	
100 (22)	352 (78)		214 (47)	238 (53)	
106 (20)	414 (80)	1.224	237 (46)	283 (54)	8.575
81 (22)	294 (78)		156 (42)	219 (58)	
25 (17)	120 (83)		81 (56)	64 (44)	
106 (20)	414 (80)	3.625	237 (46)	283 (54)	
69 (23)	227 (77)		140 (47)	156 (53)	
37 (16)	187 (84)		97 (43)	127 (57)	
106 (20)	414 (80)	2.089	237 (46)	283 (54)	4.524
89 (22)	321 (78)		177 (43)	233 (57)	
17 (16)	93 (84)		60 (55)	50 (45)	

coliform was positively related to experience with diarrhea; the use of pond water for kitchen tasks and the use of a slab or sanitary latrine were positively related to experience with malaria and with skin disease. The type of health care used had no statistically significant effect in any of the equations.

Also as expected, when socioeconomic household indicators were added to the analysis, the effects of household health/contamination indicators persisted. In other words, the health and contamination variables were stronger than the socioeconomic ones. In addition, at least one of the socioeconomic indicators also made a statistically significant contribution. Income was related negatively to diarrhea experience, suggesting that income could affect the capacity to access safe water. Having a nonagricultural occupation was related negatively to malaria experience, suggesting that those households that did not depend on agriculture had decreased exposure to standing water. Finally, all of the socioeconomic indicators were related to skin disease experience. Education and nonagricultural work were related negatively, whereas income had a positive association with skin disease. The latter finding was consistent with an expectation that those households that used tube wells more would have increased exposure to arsenic. However, in the same equation, pond water use was also positively related to skin disease, so perhaps the respondents were referring to different types of skin disease.

Ethnographic Analysis

The researchers hoped that insights from other sources would contribute to explaining the results of this study. Perhaps most importantly, the researchers explored why Bangladeshi households continued to use stagnant water for various household needs. We based our conclusions on data from the eight focus groups, one in each village, as well as on participant observation. Because of the patrilineal structure of the society in Bangladesh, most of the participants in these discussions were men. In almost every household, decisions were made by males who were usually the heads of the household and the breadwinners. The household economy was controlled by the household head. Therefore, a housewife had very little or no influence in family decisions. However, recently, educated women have been getting involved in family decisions.

This adherence to tradition was reflected in water-related behavior. Historically, the initial settlers of Bangladesh lived close to rivers, canals, lakes, and ponds. In the British era, the philanthropists, feudal *zaminders* (landlords), and the public dug ponds to ensure people's access to water close to their homes. These ponds became symbols of prestige. When researchers found high incidence of waterborne diseases, they began advocating tube wells as the source of safe water. When the first tube well was sunk in 1962 in the district of Nadia, West Bengal, people reacted by saying, "Away, away, the water from Hell is coming out!" (Meharg 2004).

The focus groups and our participant observation findings showed that the villagers believed that pond water was given by Allah and was therefore better to use for any purpose. However, they did not understand contamination or its negative effect on health. These religious beliefs might be one of the reasons for the strong adherence to traditional water usage. In addition, just when most Bangladeshis obtained access to tube wells as a source of safe water, it came out that there was arsenic poison in tube-well water. This caused many to return to or to persist in using pond water for most household tasks.

Policy Recommendations

Increase Access to Environmental Health Education

This study shows that almost one-half of those sampled were illiterate or without formal education. The MHFW has a good information, education, and communication program, but the program is not targeted to educate people about environmental degradation and the dangers of using contaminated pond water. The MHFW needs to work closely with educators to develop programs that encompass environmental health aspects so that people can become aware of the advantages of using safe water and sanitary latrines and the value of maintaining a safe physical environment.

Improve Practices of Sanitary Latrine and Personal Hygiene

A slab latrine is considered sanitary if it is installed and used in a hygienic way (to ensure that the slab is not broken or cracked and that there is no leak in the water seal to pass odors or insects that might carry germs). To keep the latrine hygienic while in use, the pan part of the slab needs to be kept clean and people need to wash their hands with soap, not just water. The health workers can organize *Uthan boithak* (a meeting at a home backyard) to share the advantages of using the slab latrine and the disadvantages of using hanging and/or open latrines. Such meetings can also be organized at elementary and high schools, at religious places such as the mosque for Muslims and the *mandir* for Hindus, and at youth clubs to encourage mass awareness of the advantages of using sanitary latrines and the disadvantages of using hanging and open latrines.

Maintain Safe Water Resources Such as Pond Water

Historically, people used pond water according to their cultural codes as expressed in their level of education, religious and other beliefs, and village culture. Culturally, they always preferred pond water for cooking, bathing, and fish cultivation, because it is Allah-given. It might take time to habituate people to keeping their water resources safe and protecting them from contamination, as traditional practices are not easily changed, but it is necessary to maintain safe water for healthy lives.

Provide Access to Trained Health Care Providers

Our data suggest that seven out of ten people go to untrained medical care providers for treatment. Currently, many people suffer from diarrhea, and its prevalence will likely increase. Under these circumstances, the MHFW needs to formulate policies and undertake programs directed at increasing the number of trained health care providers. The MHFW should undertake a long-term plan to develop technical skills among the unskilled or untrained health care providers. A policy requiring certification to operate or work in a pharmacy could be implemented, for example. Through this policy, the number of trained health care providers would increase and people who use pharmacies would obtain better health care.

Adopt Development Interventions

Some local and international initiatives have been taken to purify pond water so that people have access to an alternative source of safe water. The government can encourage these initiatives by providing them with necessary funding. Caution is needed to ensure that methods used to purify pond water are safe for both the environment and the people using it.

Support Community Efforts for Healthy Environments

To make the environment healthy, certain initiatives can be taken involving local youth through their clubs to form area-based small groups that will encourage people to safeguard natural resources and take care of the environment for their own safety and welfare. For example, local governments could declare a week of cleanliness, and announce some award to the best-performing group. Elementary and high schools could initiate student-based projects to take care of the fragile environment.

Conclusion

This research demonstrates that pond water is contaminated with fecal coliform, which is contributing to incidence of disease. Slab latrines are used in an unhygienic way, and the use of hanging and open latrines contaminates the pond water. It also demonstrates that the ponds are the symbol of prestige to the villagers. They value it based on traditional beliefs and values rather than scientific knowledge. In villages we found ponds adjacent to mosques. In those ponds, the worshipers take *odhu* (washing certain parts of the body before entering the mosque). I observed that if there is a tube well and a pond close to the mosque, people still use pond water. It is logical that many people can complete their *odhu* quickly in the pond compared with at a tube well. But regardless of educational level, people use pond water for their religious as well as household use. There appears to be a strong village effect on disease incidence. However, which specific factors are making this strong impact remains to be explored. Further study with ethnographic details would be helpful in discovering these unknown factors affecting incidence of diseases such as diarrhea, malaria, and skin disease in rural Bangladesh.

Note

1. Some parts of this chapter are taken from my book *Water, Sewage, and Disease in Bangladesh: A Medical Anthropology* (New York: Edwin Mellen, 2008).

References

Bangladesh Bureau of Statistics (BBS). 2008. *Statistical Pocket Book 2008.* http://www.bbs.gov.bd/dataindex/pby/pk_book_08.pdf.

Hossain, Mahabub, and Binayak Sen. 1992. "Rural Poverty in Bangladesh: Trends and Determinants." *Asian Development Review* 10: 1-34.

Meharg, Andrew. 2004. Available as "Hellish water," on http://www.spectroscopynow.com/coi/cda/detail.cda?id=12636&type=Feature&chId=1&page=1.

Molla, Azizur R. 1996. *Health and Family Planning Program in Bangladesh: Successes and Challenges—A Reference Manual.* Dhaka, Bangladesh. BRAC Printers. Printed by Pathfinder International/Bangladesh with funding from the U.S. Agency for International Development.

———. 2008. *Water, Sewage, and Disease in Bangladesh: A Medical Anthropology.* New York: Edwin Mellen.

Population Reference Bureau. 2001. World Population Data Sheet. PRB, Washington, DC.

Ravallion, Martin, and Binayak Sen, 1994. "When Method Matters: Towards a Resolution of the Debate over Bangladesh's Poverty Measures." Policy Research Working Paper. Washington, DC: World Bank.

Sen, Binayak. 1995. *Recent Trends in Poverty and Its Dynamics, Experiences with Economic Reform: A Review of Bangladesh's Development.* Dhaka, Bangladesh: Centre for Policy Dialogue and UPL.

World Bank. 2001. *World Bank Atlas.* Washington, DC: World Bank.

17

THIS LITTLE PIGGY WENT TO MARKET

THE SOCIAL, CULTURAL, AND ECONOMIC EFFECTS OF CHANGING SYSTEMS OF SWINE PRODUCTION IN IOWA

Barbara J. Dilly

I-80 connects New York with California. If you've driven any part of that distance in the corn country of the Midwest, you've probably driven through at least a few minutes of a harsh, pungent, acrid, almost choking smell. People driving through Utah, North Carolina, and the northern parts of Texas as well as many other areas of rural America experience the same thing. It's more than a smell. It's almost solid, and the closer to the source you get, the more solid the sensation becomes. That smell is the tip of the iceberg of a big problem with industrial pollution that poses particular political challenges to the social and physical environments of rural America.

That smell is from pigs. Biologist Laura Jackson (1998: 105) reports that one adult hog generates eight times as much solid waste per day as a human. Her studies show that even minor increases in the nitrogen from manure in the environment can threaten species survival through contamination of soil and water. A few pigs can't make that big a stink. But if you keep several thousand pigs in a large enclosed building and feed them as much corn and soybean protein as they can eat every day for six months from the time they weigh 3 pounds until they grow to a butchering weight of 280 pounds, they make a lot of ... manure, to be polite about it. People in "the industry," the livestock industry that is, call it "nutrient." The jump from "poop" to "nutrient" might puzzle a reasonable person. They call it nutrient because if properly used, it can help plants grow. But if you put too much on any piece of land,

266

it's bad for plants. It is also bad for groundwater and for human health. But the people who make the decisions to raise pigs industrially don't think about those issues and their long-term effects. They think about profits and short-term gains.

So the industrial approach makes sense at one level. You grow corn and feed it to pigs and use their manure to fertilize the next crop of corn. It sounds sustainable. It can be if you are a farmer and keep the pigs in balance with the corn. The trouble comes when you have more pigs than corn because then there's more "nutrient" than the land or crops can use. The system is out of balance. If you're a corporation that sells pork, you want to produce as many pounds of pork as you can in as short a time as you can as cheaply as you can. The manure isn't nutrient in this system; it's industrial waste. You dispose of it any way you can. You spray it on any land you can get permission to spray it on as a way to get rid of it.

What you smelled when you were driving down I-80 or I-35 in Iowa going in any direction was that nutrient. You were able to drive out of it. What happens to people who live close to these places? They can't just drive away. And it's not just smell. When you have that many swine that close together, it's an incubator for diseases. But you can reduce the vulnerability of your pigs by feeding them large doses of antibiotics with their corn and soy protein. They excrete most of it. Then it gets into the water, along with whatever disease agents the pigs may be harboring. That water eventually gets to people and becomes a problem.

Some people organize to pressure the government to control water and air quality because they affect the health of everyone. These environmentalists become part of a political process. The corporations hire lobbyists and make campaign contributions to politicians and are deeply involved in political processes as well. Finally, all citizens can vote, and if they don't like what their representatives are doing, they can throw them out. It could be a town or city, a county, a state, or the whole country. There may be all kinds of other governmental units in between, such as water districts, sewage districts, and zoning commissions, that define drainage systems and roads, for example. All of these units are funded by taxes. If you're elected to be a county supervisor in Iowa, one of the things you have to worry about is getting enough money from taxes to run the county government. Those are taxes mainly on the agricultural production in the county.

Industrial agriculture frustrates county government processes by threatening the local tax base and generating conflicts among interest groups over resources. In March 2003, the state legislature in Iowa responded to pressures by various interest groups at local and state levels to grant counties more control over decisions to determine how big livestock confinement operations could become. Senate File 2293 focused primarily on imposing more stringent regulations on manure management plans of large swine producers, but it reflected more than the conflict between urban residents and agricultural producers over air and water quality. It recognized increasing conflicts between corporate agribusiness confinement operations and local family farmers over access to markets, higher land prices, and overproduction.

Elected and appointed county-level officials were in conflict with the legal authority of the state over the powers of county supervisors. Conservationists were in conflict with agribusiness over the future of habitat for wildlife and soil fertility. Federal environmental agencies and agricultural programs differed on how to protect environmental resources. Different local, state, and national groups were seeking to protect their own interests. All had their own data to justify their points of view.

The transformation of hog production in Iowa from family farms into corporate industry gives us a laboratory for seeing how social, cultural, economic, and political systems interact together. Our laboratory is four different counties with different social, economic, political, and environmental contexts that affected how county supervisors viewed corporate agribusiness and small family farm swine production systems.

Rural county officials in Iowa want to protect and expand their tax base by stabilizing and developing agricultural production. The requirements for manure management specified in the new law called the Master Matrix plan gave local officials more control over stricter rules, but the officials do not set up standards that are impossible to meet. From a local perspective, the manure management issue is not so much about meeting environmental standards as it is about defining the tax rules and how these encourage and benefit larger corporate interests.

It works this way: To get a large-scale confinement permit from a county board of supervisors, a corporation has to demonstrate that it can successfully coordinate manure applications over a large area of farmland. This encourages the corporation to get more land. But if the corporation follows the state policies for manure management and builds a manure pit, or "lagoon," it earns a tax break, and that encourages it to build more pits and expand confinement units. This expansion requires the kind of capital that few individual farmers can raise. With the tax benefits in their pockets, corporations can pay higher rents or prices for more land than family farmers can.

You often hear people talk about markets, and if you listen to the radio any morning in any farm state, you hear farm market reports that tell you the price of pigs, cattle, and other agricultural commodities that morning. These prices can change over the course of the day. Economics operates on the assumption that everyone participates in markets on the same basis and that everyone has all the same information. The radio broadcasts help with that, but today there is no *free* market for pigs because corporations that butcher and package the meat from the pigs contract with large corporate swine producers to buy all of their hogs before they are even big enough to kill. There's no room for small farmers in this system. They can't just drive up to a processor or local auction lot with a pickup load of hogs to sell when they need to pay the mortgage. With no place to sell hogs, small operators have been squeezed out, and that enables larger corporate interests to acquire access to more land, which makes it easier for them to expand hog confinement operations because they can coordinate the spreading of more manure over a larger area. The system reinforces and intensifies itself. No self-intensifying system is sustainable.

Because Iowa's tax policies, decided by state political processes, favor large corporate agriculture over small-scale family farms, large-scale hog confinement operations have become a threat to environmental sustainability and social justice (see O'Riordan 2005). The maximization of economic gain through large corporate hog confinements is not consistent with long-term public good because it's flooding Iowa and other swine-producing areas with industrial waste. Increasing application of hog manure threatens water quality and soil fertility balances. This is a result of corporate political power and the political weakness of farmers. We can conclude that the power inequities between small-scale farmers and corporate agriculture threaten the local ecosystem and the well-being of rural farming communities for the long term.

These issues can be examined through the perspective of political economy, which focuses on the relationship between politics and economics in understanding how people make a living (see Gezon, Paulson, and Watts 2003). In Iowa, the conflicts between the state legislature and local county decisionmakers about resource management reveal differences in power between counties in which industrial agriculture operations contribute greatly to the local economy and those in which family farming still defines the local economy. The political ecology perspective helps us examine how people make economic decisions about environmental resources through their representative political processes at the state and county levels—and whether those actually work in favor of the people. This perspective also reveals the imbalances of power. It helps us examine environmental conflicts at local levels in the context of state-level political power mechanisms (see Bassett and Zimmerer 2003). To understand local environmental realities, we need to place them in historical and political contexts (see Wainwright 2005).

Historical and Political Contexts at State and Local Levels

The Iowa legislature relies heavily on the agricultural sector for tax revenue. Cheerleaders for industrial swine production say the state must retain the state's leadership in pork production because it's central to the state's agricultural heritage. The corporate model seeks to increase profitability by producing more hogs per unit of land, labor, and feed and acquiring more land for dispersal of the inevitable hog manure. Small family farms seek to survive with smaller numbers of hogs per unit of land and less manure. Iowa's current environmental regulations and tax policies encourage greater hog production in large-scale confinement operations and do not protect farmers. Local governments try to encourage and protect the interests of both family farming and corporate agribusiness, but they must enact the policies and laws that favor agribusiness strategies because these are the people who have all the power in the state legislature. There is little local governments can do to protect family farming at the local level, even when that's the kind of farming most people are doing.

Pork production in Iowa was well and good when family farms were producing pigs and could envision the balanced system of corn and nutrients, but there were a number of developments outside of Iowa that moved it toward corporate swine production. One was a massive reorientation of meatpacking beginning in the 1980s when there was a big strike in Austin, Minnesota. Meatpacking was good work, with a union that protected wages and benefits. Meat plant workers could buy houses, cars, and boats and send their kids to college. During the recession of the 1980s, some meatpackers declared bankruptcy, which allowed them to keep operating *and* to cut wages and benefits to workers by about one-half. When Hormel insisted on a 23 percent wage cut, the workers went on strike. There were riots, and the governor called out the National Guard. The union local continued the strike and was thrown out of its international, the United Food and Commercial Workers. After ten months, Hormel started processing meat again and the union had been busted.

At the same time, Iowa Beef Processing (IBP) was experimenting with a new method of disassembling animal carcasses. Instead of producing large cuts of meat to send to butchers in local grocery stores, IBP began cutting animals into small pieces and wrapping them for final sale, packaging the small packages into boxes, and shipping the boxes to grocery stores, which then didn't need to pay butchers. IBP made what had been a high-paying craft into a low-paying factory job. Not many midwesterners would put up with the low pay and dangerous conditions. Anthropologist Deborah Fink worked in one such factory and wrote an ethnographic description, *Cutting into the Meatpacking Line* (Fink 1998). The meatpackers began to import workers from Mexico and other lands, wherever they could find people willing to do the dangerous work for low wages. This created problems for the surrounding communities. Where would these immigrant workers go when they were sick or injured on the job? Where would their kids go to school? Where would they live? Anthropologists Donald Stull (1994), David Griffith (2005), and Mark Gray (1995a, 1995b) have written about these processes in their work on the effects of meatpacking on rural communities.

The 1980s weren't kind to farmers. The agricultural economy was changing as a result of global market forces. The price of corn dropped, and so the Iowa legislature thought that increasing swine production with local corn for feed would boost the corn market and raise the price. But farm decision-making is more complicated than just feeding local corn to local hogs on the production side of things. There are also the issues of access to markets and control over the processing side of the industry. At the same time, many small meatpacking plants throughout the state closed because they couldn't compete with IBP's lower prices.

Meanwhile, in North Carolina, Wendall Murphy, a former schoolteacher, was experimenting with raising swine the same way he'd seen people raising chickens in large buildings. Working with agricultural scientists at North Carolina State University (and serving on its board of regents), he developed the method of importing corn and soybeans from the Midwest; mixing hog feed with antibiotics; timing the birth, weaning, and fattening of the pigs just right; standardizing the genetics so that there was a uniform carcass; and contracting deals with Smithfield packing, which had come to North Carolina to escape environmental regulation in other states. Iowans watched in amazement and envy as North Carolina climbed in the ranks of swine producers.

In response to these perceived successes in corporate swine production, Iowa and the federal government offered tax incentives to meatpackers and communities to provide business management skills through community colleges and to educate immigrant workers to read and write in English and offered corporate agriculture legal protection against lawsuits in hopes that these actions would bring outside capital to the state, create new jobs, and boost the agricultural economy. Additional tax benefits came in the form of a five-year depreciation schedule that allowed producers to deduct the cost of a livestock confinement building from taxable income. This program achieved the desired effect of promoting the expansion of the corporate swine industry in Iowa, but it also caused fiscal shortfalls for some local governments that lost tax revenues. This is one example of how decisions made at the state level can have unintended negative consequences at local levels. It is often only through ethnographic observation and anthropological analysis of structures and systems that the full effects of policy decisions on local cultures are revealed and understood. For instance, no one looking at the economic models or just reading the bottom line figured in the health care, education, and social costs of poor immigrants living in Iowa (and Kansas) communities. It took ethnographic fieldwork to see and understand these problems.

The larger farm crisis of the 1980s accelerated the steady decline in Iowa's rural population from 41.1 percent in 1980 to 38.9 percent in 2002 as farmers, following the advice of Iowa State University agricultural economists, borrowed money to expand production but found that they couldn't keep up with their debts and lost their land (State Data Center of Iowa 2006). This decline in population was also accompanied by a steady consolidation of landholdings in a process agricultural economists call "cannibalism": The surviving farmers (or corporations) buy up the farms of those who fail. The loss of population from the countryside and the land consolidation process were necessary for the expansion of swine facilities. These facilities were typically placed away from farm home sites and required access to a large number of acres for spreading of the concentrated manure that accumulated in the pits beneath the confinement units.

Due to the economic crisis of the 1980s, many family farmers were already getting out of hog production. These farmers didn't just produce swine. They might also grow corn and soybeans, sell some beans and corn, and feed some to the hogs in a mixed operation. But as industrial meatpackers took over and started looking for producers who could keep them supplied with endless semitrailer loads of swine and made contracts with anyone who could, the market for pigs dried up. The auction lots and small meat processors went out of business, except for those that could get along with the seasonal processing of deer that hunters brought them.

Agricultural experts from Iowa State University and North Carolina State University argued that larger production units vertically integrated with feed processors that sold them the corn and slaughterhouses that packaged and marketed the meat could make a profit if they were supported by tax and cheap labor policies. These experts produced very neat-looking and optimistic economic models based on what they said was sound science. They convinced the state legislature to create such a climate to guarantee a market for Iowa corn and to increase capital revenues in the state. They argued that this was the only way to save pork production in the state of Iowa.

This is one place to see the politics of the process because the governor of Iowa in the 1990s, a Republican named Terry Branstad, had a special fund to give to the dean of agriculture at Iowa State University for research. He could then use the money to hire people who would produce the "science" that would make it seem necessary and inevitable for swine production to be industrialized. At the same time, the biggest contributor to the governor's political campaign fund was also the largest industrial swine producer in Iowa. The fix was in at all points (see Thu and Durrenberger 1998).

Increased pork production from large operations drove prices even lower, and the surviving farmers could no longer compete. In addition, the local markets were increasingly closed to them as the large packers would accept only hogs contracted from large operations. As smaller farmers lost this important piece of their production revenue, their operations became more reliant on grain prices, which made them even more vulnerable to unstable markets. In lean years, vertical integrators were more likely to be able to rent or buy ground from these smaller operations on terms not favorable to family farmers. Large corporate operations were able to control land use, all phases of hog production, processing of pork, and wholesaling of the packaged meat.

Several social scientists began to examine this process. John Ikerd (1998), professor of agricultural economics at the University of Missouri, found that the new agribusinesses did not replace as many local people and jobs as they displaced. Local residents also expressed concern that hog confinement operation odors seemed to drive people away, thereby lowering the values of rural residences. Corporate employees, at least those involved in the management process, didn't live in the rural areas where their operations were established. They didn't participate in local schools and churches or support local businesses. And even though many local farmers got involved in the new industries either by producing swine on contract with one of the firms or by working as laborers, they rarely received any share of the profits. Some local farmers did benefit from the expansion of corporate hog production. They learned from the big corporations how to dodge their debts—they set up limited liability corporations that separated their pork production business interests from their personal economic situations. If the pork production business failed, and it often did, they would not be personally liable for unpaid bills.

The state legislature noted, with satisfaction, that pork production in Iowa was increasing. Local communities expressed dissatisfaction as they noticed that odors were increasing and that the social fabric of rural communities was unraveling. Experts from Iowa State University traveled the state and explained that these were not problems but opportunities. Swine didn't smell that bad. It was the smell of money, they said, and swine poop was a cheap source of organic fertilizer.

Local communities sought to control the expansion of the swine production operations, first complaining to county supervisors and calling for the exclusion of outside corporate interests. Even though there was no legal way to do this, some locals resisted selling their land to outsiders for the construction of large confinement operations. In response, corporate operations appeared under the names of local farmers who were financially backed by outside investors. Still other operations emerged following the corporate model. Local construction or electrical companies would form limited liability partnerships with local feed processors and local farmers to create their own confinement operations. They argued that the only way they could compete with the larger corporations and stay in business was to adopt the corporate strategy of minimizing risk and maximizing tax advantages. Their more traditional small-scale farmer neighbors argued that this also allowed larger operations to gain more access to land, thereby furthering inequality.

The expansion of corporate production units also transformed local rural economies. Those counties that had previously relied on local businesses to support the local tax base lost more than they gained from the growth of corporate swine production. Small businesses, like small-scale family farmers, could not leverage capital to reduce risks and avoid taxes. Like local auction lots and small meat processors, local feed mills were also in trouble. They continued to pay more than their fair share of the local tax bill. County auditors noted that the taxes paid on new hog confinement buildings did not compensate for the loss of taxes generated from traditional agricultural properties and small businesses prior to the corporate economy. This was not an issue in the counties where diverse urban industrial sectors compensated for the loss of the traditional rural economy sector. But rural counties with little or no urban growth saw their tax base seriously eroded, just the opposite of what the optimistic "scientific" models had promised.

Rural community taxpayers and tax managers grew increasingly concerned that the growth of corporate agribusiness and the decline of family farms threatened the local economy and tax base because of inequities generated by the political process at the state level. The increase of swine production did not result in the increase of profits, and in the case of corporate production, profits were taken to urban places, often outside the state, and not plowed back into the local rural economy (Thu and Durrenberger 1998: 7). Local residents were also alarmed that the large corporate operations polluted the environment, which threatened property values as well as residential and recreational quality of life. Declining property values further strained the economic base and resulted in higher burdens of taxation on remaining residents, causing more inequality.

Local rural governments incurred increasing costs and resource degradation from corporate expansion. Manure spills polluted local streams and wells draining into underground aquifers (Iowa Department of Natural Resources 2006b). In addition, millions of gallons of water were pumped each day from underground water systems into corporate facilities (Thu and Durrenberger 1998). County roads required constant upgrading and maintenance as large trucks hauled cement and construction materials, feed to hogs, and hogs to meat-processing plants. Employees and rural residents suffered health problems from dust and gases (Thu and Durrenberger 1998), and animal diseases spread rapidly (Donahue 1998).

Gathering Ethnographic Data to Understand Historical Processes and Make Comparisons

To understand the conflicts among groups of people as a result of public policies, we have first of all to understand each group's interests in the processes. We also must figure out what each group does in the process and how much power it has. For instance, in Iowa, we have to understand the role of Iowa State University in the whole process. Family farmers, agribusiness operators, rural residents, and county elected and appointed officials are the primary actors in Iowa's system of swine production.

In this study, I examined the tax records available to the public at county assessor's offices in four counties. I reviewed environmental regulatory agency policies and programs from the Department of Natural Resources and the Natural Resources Conservation Service. I also engaged in semistructured interviews with federal agency officials at the Department of Natural Resources, the Conservation Reserve Program (CRP), the Farm Service Agency (FSA), and the Natural Resources Conservation Service (NRCS) offices at regional and county levels. I also engaged in ten semistructured interviews with elected and appointed county supervisors, auditors, assessors, engineers, and staff persons. I interviewed seven local family farmers and one regional contractor involved in a limited liability partnership operation and one small-town city attorney. I engaged in participant observation as a member of a family farm operation and a small rural community residential property owner. I observed a small-town city council meeting and participated in the discussion of the threats to small towns by hog confinements. I also examined two newspaper articles reviewing the conflicts between local residents and outside corporations in two of the counties.

I also looked at public records of building permits and manure management plans compiled by county assessors, auditors, and engineers. Information available to the public on Web sites reveals the policies that define feeding operation requirements. The Department of Natural Resources posts maps that include the number and type of animal feeding operations in the state as well as the environmental features they can affect. This includes groundwater vulnerability, aquifers, drainage wells, sinkholes, and watersheds. The maps also include areas of manure spillage, impaired watersheds, fish kills, and livestock burial grounds.

A wide variety of public databases collected at federal, state, and local levels are currently available. At this point, however, much of it is collected to serve the needs of specific agencies and is not interactive with other agencies or offices. Many federal and state agencies, however, do provide county-level databases in their programs. These include the NRCS, CRP, and FSA. The Iowa State University Extension program also provides county-level data and manure management literature and identifies county historical trends that provide quantitative data on rural population, Hispanic immigrants as corporate agribusiness laborers, the rates of decline in the number of farms, the increase in farm size, the rates of change in the numbers of farms selling hogs and pigs, the total number of hogs and pigs sold, the percentage of market share and percentage of total market value for hogs and pigs, the percentage of change in farm earnings, and the percentage of change of the market value of agricultural products in the local economy. The State Data Center of Iowa and the Office of Social and Economic Trend Analysis at Iowa State University also provide demographic and farm production data for quantitative analysis.

Iowa State University Extension data report that Iowa experienced a steady decline in the number of farms producing hogs since 1969. During this time, agricultural production was concentrated in fewer larger operations. Despite conventional wisdom that farm operations needed to get bigger in order to survive, these operations were not more profitable. The percentage of earnings from these farms declined in the total economy from 1987 to 1997. Except where corporate integrated swine production was concentrated, there was a shift away from farming to off-farm jobs. Between 1990 and 2000, the statewide share of agricultural earnings from farms dropped from 6 percent to 4.2 percent. And even though hog production increased and profits were generated by large corporate entities, pork production in Iowa did not "save" the agricultural economy or rural communities from agricultural market instability.

Differences That Matter

The ways in which counties experienced the effects of the transformation of swine production varied greatly. Comparisons of four counties illustrate the relationships generated between state-level political and economic forces and local social, cultural, and biospheric realities. These relationships can be examined in some detail through the comparison of the family farmer and corporate agribusiness groups. My interviews of county supervisors, engineers, assessors, and auditors revealed that these local decisionmakers saw a difference between these two political interest groups because they represented different production strategies, social patterns, and cultural values. Even though the two subcultures do differ significantly, members of both groups share a common goal of engaging in surplus production for the global marketplace.

Family farmers engaged in face-to-face interaction with family and kin, neighbors, and members of the local community. The family farmer is horizontally integrated in a system of local cultural institutions of value and practice. Farming is the activity that forms identities centered in a family and a moral community in which individuals take pride in honesty and integrity in business dealings. Family farmers participate in community institutions such as schools, churches, service clubs, and Main Street businesses.

Family farmers personally own most of their land, livestock, equipment, and home. They use diverse resources to adapt to changing natural environments and markets. They borrow money, buy goods and services, sell their products, and pay taxes locally but also make sophisticated decisions based on knowledge of complex local and global realities. They govern their economic activity by social rules and cultural norms that value physical labor, thrift, calculated risk-taking, individual innovation, efficiency, social responsibility, and stewardship of natural resources. Family farmers are concerned about environmental resource protection as productive resources for themselves and future generations. They are also protective of their recreational resources, such as hunting, fishing, boating, and other forms of nature enjoyment.

But in the last twenty years, from the late 1980s to 2008, the transformation of agricultural production from diversified family operations to specialized family operations to highly specialized corporate agribusiness transformed social relations. Corporate agribusiness managers are less likely to participate in local community institutions or to want to retire in the area. Many are also not from the area. They have less investment in the quality-of-life issues associated with the local environment. But corporate managers greatly value the rights of private property ownership enjoyed by rural residents; these rights guarantee these managers the freedom to use the environment for economic gain in any way they can get away with under the law for their exclusive benefit. According to anthropologist Daniel Bates (1998: 38), this freedom "significantly alters an individual's ties to the group." Corporate agribusiness managers do not have time for "neighboring." Their identities are based on their corporate roles as business managers and as urban consumers.

In contrast to family farmers, corporate industrial agribusiness managers do not typically own land, labor, or the capital associated with their businesses. Their investments in the production process are protected from personal loss or lawsuit through a limited liability partnership legal arrangement that separates their private property from their business operations. They draw salaries and share profits from the corporation, which is taxed separately from their individual income. Even if they draw handsome salaries, the business can show a loss for tax purposes.

Corporate agribusinesses are vertically integrated using outside businesses as a source of financing, purchasing supplies, and marketing commodities. They borrow money externally and produce for exterior markets. The corporate agribusiness manager buys little from local businesses and hence does not contribute to local sales tax revenue. Economic decisions are based on enhancing profits in terms of short-term bottom-line calculations, not local social or cultural norms that stabilize local communities.

The differences characterized here reflect different interests in the environment, social interaction, and economic stability in rural communities. They reflect decisionmaking challenges at county levels regarding local tax structures. The state did not consider local dynamics when formulating policy that influenced the development of corporate agribusiness swine production in Iowa. Even the 2003 development of the Master Matrix plan for local environmental regulation of manure management does not give local decisionmakers effective legal power to prohibit large-scale confinement operations. Ethnographic evidence does show, however, that local social norms, cultural values, and political processes have been effective in slowing down the rate of advancement of corporate swine operations in two counties in this study where family farming is still the dominant mode of agricultural production.

Results of the Study

Marshall County is the home of the Swift and Company meatpacking plant and one town with more than twenty-five hundred people. Supervisors work to protect the economic opportunities of local family farmers and large corporations. There is a concern that one large family agribusiness corporation has expanded its landholdings and swine production in the area over the last twenty years through vertical integration with outsiders. But because this operation is still locally owned and supports local businesses and the local tax base, supervisors are reluctant to limit the corporation's expansion. Nevertheless, local officials recognize the threats to the local tax base by the encroachment of corporations. Local business activity and local profits do decline as corporations extract profits from the area. Feed sales went down 11.2 percent and cash livestock sales went down 21 percent from 1980 to 2002.

But it still is the case that the growth in the urban industrial economy as a result of the packing plant appears to compensate for the loss in the percentage of farm earnings in sustaining the local tax base. Also, the decline in the rural population is compensated for by Hispanic immigrants who work in the packing plant.[1] The problem of undocumented workers and raids by immigration authorities threatens the stability of the local economy, however. Nevertheless, local officials feel the packing plant does contribute to the local economy and hence the local tax base. Nor are they concerned with environmental problems. Marshall County has few acres and little water vulnerable to pollution from contamination due to manure spills. There are few drainage wells and aquifer areas and no significant wetlands or streams. Even though aquatic life is threatened in public wildlife areas, there are only 792 such acres in Marshall County.[2]

The dynamics of Hardin County are different. It has two towns with populations of more than twenty-five hundred and is the home of Iowa Select headquarters and the Christensen Farms regional offices and its swine production sites. Hardin County is connected to the Swift and Company packing plant in Marshall County by a major rail service. It has so many corporate hog confinement units that the manure management plans fill a room-size vault in the basement of the county courthouse. No staff, however, monitors spills or leaks. This is the job of the regional Department of Natural Resources, which is too understaffed to do the job. Even though there are laws that define penalties when violations are discovered, they are not always collected or discovered. Local governments have no power over these matters.

The expansion of corporate agribusiness in Hardin County is credited with the increase in swine production in Iowa. The largest and second largest Iowa-based swine producers are located there, where they own feed mills, a swine genetics company, a nutrition-and-research program, an agricultural builders' division, and management information systems. The total number of swine sold, the market value of swine, and farm earnings have increased substantially in Hardin County. From 1980 to 2002, hog farmers almost tripled the amount of feed they purchased and cash livestock receipts were up 28 percent.[3] The successes of Hardin County agribusiness represent the aims of the Iowa legislature when it promoted industrial swine production in the 1980s. Farm earnings increased by 40 percent during the late 1980s and early 1990s.

The success of these operations also correlates with a higher-than-average decrease in the number of farms and the rural population in Hardin County. The size of farm operations is much larger than state averages. This also correlates with an overall decline in the entire population of the county by 13 percent from the mid-1980s to the mid-2000s. And even though corporate operations have provided urban industrial growth, the entire county is more dependent on one revenue-producing industry that does not circulate much of its profits locally. Hardin County officials are not concerned about the tax base, nor are they concerned about the environment, despite high nitrogen and phosphorus inputs from manure. There are no large vulnerable groundwater areas, no wetlands, few woodland acres, and only 119 acres of public wildlife management areas.

In contrast, Bremer County has one town with more than twenty-five hundred people and rail service to a Tyson packing plant in Waterloo. Its urban community contributes greatly to the local economy by diversifying the economic base. Small-scale manufacturing, a college, and a full range of medical services support a growing urban center that provides shopping for the entire region. But in 2000 the rural population was still 67.2 percent of the population. The strongly German family farming culture persists, with efficient small-scale family farms smaller than the state average and farm earnings continuing to increase. There are a growing number of family farm and local agribusiness swine confinement operations formed through limited liability partnerships in the county, but they are small by comparison with those in Marshall County. And even though feed purchases went down slightly from 1980 to 2002, cash livestock receipts went up 3 percent. And even though 33.6 percent of farms producing hogs and pigs had one thousand or more animals, the preservation of the rural landscape for a large number of residential sites is one of the main reasons that large integrators haven't penetrated Bremer County. Another reason is that farmers can earn additional income working at urban jobs, which are more attractive than swine operations.

Another important factor is the existence and enforcement of a local zoning law that supervisors applied to frustrate the application process for confinement building permits. In July 2006, however, they were threatened with a lawsuit over the legality of the ordinance when applied to agricultural areas. The supervisors were forced to back down, but they are still slow to act on confinement permit requests. They argue that large-scale operations, both agricultural and commercial, threaten the local tax base. Furthermore, Bremer County officials are very aware of the vulnerability of the natural environment. The water supply can be contaminated through agricultural drainage wells and aquifers. Flooding is common in the area, leaching pollutants into the 677.8 acres of wetlands and 2,518 acres of public wildlife areas bisected or bordered by six rivers and streams.

In comparison, Butler County has no towns with more than twenty-five hundred people and is therefore considered 100 percent rural. The population declines steadily, but its rate of family farm decline is one of the lowest in the state. The average farm size is 44 acres smaller than the state average of 343 acres. Farm earnings increased 7 percent from 1990 to 2002, and feed purchases were up slightly from 1980 to 2002. Both family farm and corporate operations produce pigs, but cash livestock receipts were down and the percentage of farms with hogs and pigs was only 10 percent in 2002, with only 29.3 percent of them feeding one thousand or more hogs and pigs.

Most Butler County farmers are German, and they value the sense of community they sustain. The construction of livestock confinement operations is attractive to some as a means by which they can incorporate their sons into the family farm with the aid of external financing. This is not always an attractive option for the sons, however, who perceive industrial livestock operation work to be a class below large-scale grain farming. Grain farming still provides more stable incomes and maximum flexibility for scheduling vacations. Also, family members do not like to live near confinement operations. Nevertheless, almost no family farmer involved in pork production owns or operates all phases of swine production on his property even if he is the primary investor and source of labor. Furthermore, he almost always has one or more partners who helped finance the construction of the operation or who provided feed and additional services. Individual farmers are contracted by Iowa Select, Heartland, Kairos, and local corporate operations that control access to markets. Their operations are facilitated by two rail lines, one of which is connected to a major grain buyer and swine confinement operations.

The expansion of corporate-driven industrial swine production in Butler County is slowed by the smaller size of landholdings. This frustrates the manure application management. Landowners also tend to live in rural residences and are reluctant to sign agreements to allow the spreading of concentrated manure on their property. Furthermore, neighbors of confinement operations are socially and politically active in their resistance to manure application. Butler County residents also value their environmental recreational amenities. They have a large number of acres in woodlands, wetlands (780.8), grasslands, streams, rivers, wildlife management areas (4,380), and prairie preserves.[4] The county has two rivers and many streams as well as vulnerable groundwater supplies. Many farmers also have their own private hunting preserves and are actively involved in conservation programs and organizations.

Butler County residents are socially, economically, and politically conservative. They see capitalization and incorporation with outsiders in order to expand operations as "risky business." They also see it as "bad neighboring." In 2006, some local farmers formed an informal coalition with nonfarm residents to fight the expansion of hog and pig confinements in the county. They published the names of local people aligned with outside investors and appeared at public meetings to express their outrage. They also joined efforts with local decisionmakers who argued that political decisions made at the state level that affected the local economies of rural counties were unfair.

Public Policy Discussions

We can understand the effects of state policy decisions on local economies only by carefully examining local processes. What benefits some people may hurt others; what benefits one part of the system may hurt another. In this study, the most rural two counties are much more vulnerable to groundwater and wildlife habitat contamination. The U.S. Geological Survey (2001) reported that nitrate and phosphorus levels in the streams in Butler and Bremer counties frequently exceeded drinking standards in 2001. The soils in this area are more rolling and experience erosion with heavy rains and melting snow, which contribute to the pollution of rivers and streams. The rivers in these two counties also flood regularly. These same two counties are also more vulnerable to local tax base erosion. Clearly, the state legislature's encouragement of global market mechanisms is insensitive to local conditions. Anthropologists approach these problems holistically. We argue that the ratios of swine/human populations in specific counties need to be considered in terms of the total balance in the biosphere.

Tax policies typically shift the short- and long-term responsibilities of environmental protection away from corporations and onto the general public. Most public policy discussions of these issues are driven by only a few interest groups. In a democracy, everyone can and should participate. But it takes a lot of work to educate citizens about these processes, and most aren't interested unless issues directly impact them. And corporations have allies that help them to hide the realities of what they are doing. In Iowa, Iowa State University has been their ally.

The smell of concentrated hog manure in Iowa got the attention of a lot of people. But getting organized and forming coalitions to promote a broader understanding of environmental and economic consequences of large-scale corporate agribusiness takes time and energy. Doing so also goes against powerful ideologies—often promoted by land grant institutions and chambers of commerce—that spread myths such as "progress is always good" and "bigger is always better." These myths often run counter to the interests of small communities and individual citizens. Kendall Thu and Paul Durrenberger et al. (1998) did the research that reveals how that happens and described it in the book *Pigs, Profits, and Rural Communities.*

In order to protect the agricultural economy and the environment in rural Iowa for future generations, local officials argue that tax codes need to favor, not make vulnerable, these valued ways of life and natural resources. In order to secure support for tax revisions, people in Butler and Bremer counties have formed new alliances. In 2005, assessors and auditors from the League of Cities and Association of Counties presented a proposal to the Iowa state legislature to address tax inequities they argue resulted from the corporate-controlled industrialization of agriculture. They further argued that state legislators had abandoned their constituents by not understanding the consequences of legislation or listening to local officials when told about these consequences. The auditors asked the legislature to assess hog confinement buildings as industrial property above and beyond the agricultural land values on which they reside, but the request was rejected. The auditors and assessors next proposed that small-town businesses be given exemptions like that extended to agriculture, which is not taxed at 100 percent of productivity. The local governments were seeking to protect small-town businesses and the family farms they saw as necessary to protect and stabilize the local tax base. These local officials argue that residential farm buildings owned by family farmers should still be protected by homestead exemptions but that the agriculture credit for corporations and industrial buildings should be eliminated.

Tax code modifications require state-level decisions. Current Iowa law does not distinguish between family farmers and corporate entities in the assessment of property taxes on farmland and buildings. These tax laws, which tax the productivity of farmland and its improvements, were established long ago when farmers benefited equally from tax-funded services. But changes in production were already apparent in 1949 when T. F. Haygood (1949: 677–678) argued that policymakers needed to understand that the tax load of agriculture varied in particular local circumstances. Haygood argued, as the research in this study demonstrates, that when the agricultural economy is transformed, we need to ask whether the costs of local services are evenly distributed among the economic groups in a community or even among the individuals within each economic group. We can't answer these questions without ethnographic data.

In Butler and Bremer counties, family farmers bear a disproportionate share of property taxes when they pay at the same rate as the corporate farmer. Currently, the tax code reflects the state legislature's priorities of attracting new larger businesses, not protecting existing farmers or small businesses. Rural county governments argue that a more equitable tax code would not only encourage the revitalization of commercial property, but also reward the small-scale family farms that preserve and protect the environment. A more equitable tax code would give tax incentives for raising grass-fed hogs, for example, and not for the construction of manure pits. Furthermore, an additional tax paid for spreading concentrated pit manure would help offset the costs to the public health fund and the Department of Natural Resources in its monitoring of wildlife habitat and treatment of contaminated drinking water supplies.

Conclusion

Public policy discussions can benefit by studies of local variation in the effects of tax laws and the regulation of economic activities. Comparisons of local realities often reveal inequalities in the consequences of public policy decisions. Understanding these issues at local levels can be enhanced by anthropological methods. Defending the rights of individuals at local levels can be enhanced through ethnographic data that connect local and state processes. With anthropological insights, we can address the problems associated with threats to Iowa's local economies, biophysical environments, social institutions, and cultural values. But without local organization and effective mobilization of political power, inequalities in access to economic benefits will continue to favor corporate swine production and deterioration of the environment.

Notes

1. See U.S. Census Bureau; State Data Center of Iowa, http://www .iowadatacenter.org; Iowa State University Extension to Communities 2002.

2. See the Iowa Department of Natural Resources Web site for details.
3. See the Iowa Select Farms Web site for more details of its success story, http://www.iowaselect.com/production/index.htm.
4. See the Iowa Department of Natural Resources Web site.

References

Basset, J. J., and Karl S. Zimmerer, eds. 2003. *Political Ecology: An Integrative Approach to Geography and Environment-Development Studies.* New York: Guilford.

Bates, Daniel G. 1998. *Human Adaptive Strategies: Ecology, Culture, and Politics.* Boston: Allyn and Bacon.

Donahue, Kevin J. 1998. "The Impact of Industrial Swine Production on Human Health." In *Pigs, Profits, and Rural Communities,* edited by Kendall M. Thu and E. Paul Durrenberger. Albany: State University of New York Press, 73–83.

Fink, Deborah. 1998. *Cutting into the Meatpacking Line: Studies in Rural Culture.* Chapel Hill: University of North Carolina Press.

Gezon, Lisa L., Susan Paulson, and Michael Watts. 2003. "Locating the Political in Political Ecology: An Introduction." *Human Organization* 62, no. 3: 205–217.

Grey, Mark. 1995a. "Pork, Poultry, and Newcomers in Storm Lake, Iowa." In *Any Way You Cut It: Meatpacking and Small-Town America,* edited by Donald D. Stull, Michael Broadway, and David Griffith. Lawrence: University Press of Kansas.

———. 1995b. "Turning the Pork Industry Upside Down: Storm Lake's Hygrade Workforce and the Impact of the 1981 Plant Closure." *Annals of Iowa* 55: 1–16.

Griffith, David C. 2005. "Class Relations among Old and New Immigrants." *Journal of Latino–Latin American Studies* 1, no. 4 (Fall 2005): 89–205.

Haygood, T. F. 1949. "Analyzing the Tax Load of Agriculture." *Journal of Farm Economics* 31: 668–678.

Ikerd, John E. 1998. "Sustainable Agriculture, Rural Economic Development, and Large-Scale Swine Production." In *Pigs, Profits, and Rural Communities,* edited by Kendall M. Thu and E. Paul Durrenberger. Albany: State University of New York Press, 157–169.

Iowa Department of Natural Resources. 2006a. "Iowa DNR Wildlife." http://www.iowadnr.com/wildlife.

———. 2006b. "Animal Feeding Operations in Iowa and Groundwater Vulnerability: Aquifers and Wells Map." http://www.iowadnr.com/water/nutrients/index.

Iowa State University Extension Service. 1999. "Agricultural Data for Decision Makers," September. http://www.extension.iastate.edu.

———. 2002. "Data for Decision Makers," September. http://www.extension.iastate.edu/communities.

Jackson, Laura 1998. "Large-Scale Swine Production and Water Quality." In *Pigs, Profits, and Rural Communities,* edited by Kendall M. Thu and E. Paul Durrenberger. Albany: State University of New York Press, 103–119.

O'Riordan, Tim. 2005. "On Justice, Sustainability, and Democracy." *Environment* 47, no. 6: 0.

State Data Center of Iowa. 2006. "General Population Characteristics—Iowa." http://www.silo.lib.ia.us/specialized-services/datacenter/index.html.

Stuhl, Donald D. 1994. "Cattle Cost Money: Beef Packing's Consequences for Workers and Communities." *High Plains Applied Anthropologist* 14: 65.

Thu, Kendall M., and E. Paul Durenberger, eds. 1998. *Pigs, Profits, and Rural Communities.* Albany: State University of New York Press.

U.S. Geological Survey. 2001. "Water Quality in Eastern Iowa Basins, Iowa, and Minnesota, 1996–1998." *USGS Circular* 1212. http://www.iowa.usgs.gov/nawqa/reports.html.

Wainwright, John. 2005. "The Geographies of Political Ecology: After Edward Said." *Environment and Planning A* 37: 1033–1043.

18

COOPERATIVES IN JAPAN
JAPAN'S WORKER COOPERATIVE MOVEMENT INTO THE TWENTY-FIRST CENTURY

Bob Marshall

The pace of Japan's economy is picking up again after more than a decade of stasis.[1] During this long period of economic stagnation, the many personnel practices favoring employees known by the rubric "lifetime employment" have been subjected to increased criticism by pro-investor, neoliberal voices. Yet other less-well-amplified voices in Japan offer an alternative criticism of, and look for opportunity in, the changing status quo as well. In the last quarter of the 20th century efforts to create worker-owned and democratically governed businesses in Japan began to emerge with the support of a wide variety of economic actors—among them labor unions and union organizers, consumer cooperatives, income-seeking housewives, the elderly, employees of small businesses, farmers and farm workers, employees of failing firms and maverick employees of large firms. And as worker owned and managed businesses have increased in size and number, their awareness of each other and their common interest in alternative ways to organize production have also grown.

As many as 30,000 people now work cooperatively in Japan, a number that has been growing steadily since the 1970s. These worker cooperatives are concentrated in the Kanto and Kansai, but can be found from Sapporo to Nagasaki. The Women's Worker Cooperatives (12,000), the Japan Workers' Cooperative Union (9000), the recently invented hybrid Senior Cooperatives (15,000 workers)—a consumer/worker cooperative of, by and for those 55 and older in Japan—and a congeries of independently founded worker cooperatives (3000 workers) from diverse backgrounds, all play major roles in this movement.

285

While a formidable array of forces has coalesced around the single idea of direct worker control of production at this moment in Japan's history, and as exciting as the prospects are for its further development, this movement toward an alternative way to organize work still has a very long way to go to match the contribution of other patterns of cooperative organization—agricultural cooperatives, credit unions, consumer cooperatives—to the Japanese economy. The growth of worker cooperation in Japan has been steady, principled and deliberate, however, not a product of desperation. Certainly I have heard no one suggest there are useful parallels to be observed between the current economic situations of Japan and Argentina, where employees have been operating, with limited governmental approval, a variety of businesses abandoned by their owners and managers in response to a collapsing national economy.

Other forms of institutionalized cooperation in Japan have a long head start and continue to enjoy greater political support than cooperation among workers. In the late 19th century, when the idea of cooperative economic organization was at its height in Europe and being introduced to Japan as part of the large-scale importation of all things Western, cooperation for consumption, credit and marketing was recognized and endorsed through legislation that was forbidden to workers, among whom cooperation was condemned as socialist. Now no longer explicitly forbidden, neither do worker cooperatives yet enjoy positive law to facilitate this way of owning and working. But for Japan's worker cooperatives to ever achieve the size and effect of more common and accepted forms of economic cooperation, it seems that more will have to change than just laws governing the organizational forms of businesses. Below I introduce and discuss Women's Worker Collectives, the Japan Workers' Cooperative Union, Senior Cooperatives and EcoTech, an independent worker cooperative.

The most commonly used phrase meaning "worker cooperative" in Japanese is *rodosha [seisan] kyodo kumiai,* "cooperative" *(kyodo kumiai)* preceded by "[production] worker." This phrase is not widely known in Japan; among insiders, it is often contracted to *rokyo,* in the way that "consumer cooperative"—*seikatsu kyodo kumiai*—is contracted to the widely used *seikyo* in daily speech. Some speakers use the English words "collective" and "cooperative," subjecting them to typical Japanization through abbreviation: "workers collective," *wakazu korekuteibu,* is shortened to *wako,* "co-op" to *koppu.* The cooperative way of organizing work is not yet as well known in Japan as the many other forms of cooperation that are part of the fabric of everyday life.

Women's Worker Cooperatives (WWCs)

Worker cooperatives offer housewives in Japan's new middle class, for whom employment prospects have always been and remain bleak, an opportunity to work part time and, by controlling the conditions of their own labor, still care for their families to their own exacting standards. Since the mid-1980s, an emerging movement from within consumer cooperation dedicated to organizing worker cooperatives among women, has attracted increasing numbers in the Tokyo-Yokohama region. As many as 12,000 women now work at women's worker cooperatives.

In December 1982, a handful of women in Kanagawa Prefecture started Ninjin, Japan's first women's worker cooperative. *Ninjin* means "carrot" in Japanese: the business began as the workforce for a consumer cooperative's produce distribution center. But these women write the name of their business by duplicating the simple two-stroke character which means "person," or "people." In colloquial American English *Ninjin* should be taken as "The People People," which is exactly how these women think of themselves. Extending Ninjin's breakthrough, women opened another fifteen co-ops over the next two years. The decade following Ninjin's founding saw 7,000 women start over 250 co-ops. The authoritative roster compiled by Workers' Collective Network Japan, the official organ of the WWC movement, lists 463 worker cooperatives in the network in February 2000.

Ninjin Website

The women owning, running and working in these worker cooperatives are overwhelmingly middle aged and middle class. Over eighty percent are between 40 and 60 years old, more than half in their forties. Their household incomes, rates of homeownership and educational accomplishments are well above national averages. These co-ops' many different business activities arise from the knowledge, skills, interests and values members developed as well-educated wives and mothers, and in consumer cooperatives. A partial list of business activities spun off from Ninjin alone includes recycling shop, cooking class, lunch restaurant, home care service, day care, culture class (*karucha kyoshitsu*), marriage counseling, hand made goods, ice cream making, soap making, welfare cooperative, bread bakery, display group, translating, printing, editing, international exchanges, video production, consumer cooperative office work, delivery service, "and so on," writes the author of this list. These co-ops practice principles of workplace democracy, ownership equality and social responsibility.

Its critics assert that this cooperative alternative to the economic status quo can only continue as long as these women remain dependent on their husbands' substantial incomes. A 1999 survey of 221 members of co-ops found more than two-thirds with spouse's annual income above $50,000; more than one-fifth were above $100,000; 15 percent did not answer the question. In 1995 more than two-thirds of co-op members reported annual household incomes above $80,000. The average income for working households in 1999 was $68,500. The common perception is that the women in worker cooperatives do not work from economic necessity, and these figures bear out that view substantially. The movement's critics frame a paradox from which we can appropriately launch analysis: why *do* these women so eagerly bite the hand—of the system, not the husband—that feeds them so well? How does it happen that these women who enjoy all the advantages available to women of the new middle class, the heart of the economic miracle, would like to change the ways Japanese, all Japanese, work?

A first approximation to an answer is not difficult to come by: this is a movement that advances on three legs: labor market constraints, tax and equal employment opportunity law, and consumer cooperatives. Each of these sets of conditions, separately necessary for the rise of Japan's WWCs, create together a widespread and growing appeal among potential members.

The frequency-by-age curve of the labor market for women in Japan has two modes, and has been commonly described as "M-shaped": women in the new middle class typically work full time for several years after graduation, "retire" to bear and raise a small number of children, and then reenter the market for part-time labor in different, usually much less attractive, occupations some years later.

Second, Japan's income tax law hits a household's "secondary income" astonishingly hard above a quite low maximum in the middle-income brackets, a phenomenon infamous as the *hyaku-man-en kabe,* the "Million Yen Wall."

Government policies designed to bolster "a breadwinner plus housewife" family system reinforce the particular ways Japan's labor market fails women.

A wife who earns in excess of one million yen loses her dependent status and has to pay her own social security taxes and health insurance. Here, one million yen arbitrarily though not unrealistically equals ten thousand U.S. dollars.

Effectively, the first $10,000 a dependent wife earns is tax exempt; but the next $7,000 to $10,000 is a dead loss, all going to taxes of one kind or another. At the low hourly wages typical of jobs available to them, middle-aged women must expect to work 20 to 25 hours per week to earn $10,000 annually. Vanishingly few jobs paying more than $20,000 are available to women over 35. The Equal Employment Opportunity Law of 1985 and the Young Childcare Leave Law of 1992 are of a piece with tax law, designed to prop up and help reproduce a family structure in which economically dependent wives continue to have substantial daylight hours to devote to the care of their rarely divorced husbands, fewer than two children, and the world's longest lived parents-in-law.

Third, almost all members of these women's worker cooperatives have long belonged to the Seikatsu Club Consumer Cooperative, internationally extolled for its motto "Stop Shopping," its social activism, and its distinctive structure of networked small groups. Seikatsu Club intentionally incubated the first several co-ops as part of its overall aim to create alternatives in Japanese society.

Unlike other consumer cooperatives, Seikatsu Club continues to develop ever greater member activism on several fronts rather than turn itself into a chain of stores. In the words of Yokota Katsumi, one of the founders of

Seikatsu Club Kanagawa, "It is not our ultimate purpose in life, as individuals, to buy safe reliable consumer goods at reasonable prices."

Seikatsu Club

Taken together, these three circumstances create a category of Japanese women predisposed toward cooperation and prepared to experiment with cooperation in its less familiar forms. Looking for appealing work once again, these women can create, with family savings they themselves manage, work opportunities where they control their own labor and schedules, as they are accustomed to doing as housewives, consumer cooperative members, and even cooperative and social activists.

Seikatsu Club Q and A

Conservatively, hundreds of thousands of Japanese women might see themselves in this specific description. In 1999 over 20 million members owned more than 650 consumer cooperatives throughout Japan. According to a 1987 survey by the Kanagawa Prefecture Consumer Cooperative League, slightly less than half of member housewives were employed, half of those remaining without work wanted it, and half of those wanting work wanted to work at their consumer cooperative. From the late 1960s to the early 1990s, the singular Seikatsu Club Consumer Cooperative itself grew to over a quarter of a million members, 95 percent of whom are women. The resources these novice entrepreneurs bring to their businesses, coupled with the advantages to them of working cooperatively, have allowed them to succeed and their movement to grow steadily from the mid-1980s through the present during successive phases of intense speculation, collapse and recession, and continuing stagnation and turmoil in Japan's market economy.

There is no question these women would not be able to enjoy the standard of living they do without their husbands' substantial incomes; but the same must be said of the contribution of their own incomes, smaller though they are in almost all cases, to their household economies.

A more complete answer to the question of why they so eagerly pursue this different way of working must next take into account the binds or contradictions as well as the opportunities working cooperatively in this context presents to these women. The prominent theme of the desirability of women's "independence" and "self-reliance" (*jichi, jiritsu*) echoes throughout the movement, and from which point of view the Million Yen Wall and other forms of gender discrimination are strongly decried. The independence most women in WWCs want, however, is independence from waged employment and from the constraints of current tax law: we cannot forget that these women's primary identity remains that of "professional housewife," not "entrepreneur." The goal of self-reliance does not lead to self-sufficiency and away from the primary activity of nurturance within their families, and by extension their communities. Independence from families or communities has not been a reason Japanese women mention for taking employment. So while many women want to work more hours in their WWC than they do, many others resist pressure from *within* their own WWC to work more hours by letting the Million Yen Wall deflect coworkers' unspoken accusations of selfishness. Whatever complex motivation each individual might feel deep inside, she will never allow her co-owners to accuse her of having gone into business "for herself."

The sharp limit on their work hours, whether they want to work only part time or not, lets these women better fulfill their obligations to family and community, obligations Seikatsu Club philosophy prominently embraces as the essence of personal life, the best of a way of life that is being destroyed by the commodification of the skills and relationships needed for daily living. Rather than themselves work more, many WWC members would prefer men to work less, and in different ways. Yet the reason surveyed co-op members overwhelmingly gave for working at all is to create *ikigai*, "a purpose in life," followed by "help out with the family budget" and "revive my experience." The popular answer among WWC members for why they are in WWCs, that they are looking for *ikigai*, must be understood within the context of WWCs as businesses rather than the volunteer organizations or non-profit-organizations (NPOs) in which younger suburban housewives have recently become active (Nakano 2005). *Ikigai* is a more general and inclusive answer than "want to help the family out with income." The two answers are not, however, mutually exclusive. It is the challenge of starting and running a business successfully that gives them a reason to get up in the morning now that their children no longer require their constant attention. *Keizaiteki jiritsu*, "economic independence," finished ahead of only "make better use of my leisure time." At this point, that some WWC members do not get the support for economic independence they hope for from other members must surprise no one, but certainly few co-op members can care to have such different desires aired openly in their own co-op. They decided to go into business together and remain committed to working together.

Japan Workers' Cooperative Union

A little smaller (9000 members in 2005) than the WWC movement, JWCU evolved its present form through the 1970s and 1980s from its origin as the Kenketsu Ippan Zennichi Jiro, the Day Laborers National Union, a casual laborers' union with its stronghold in the Kansai rather than the Kanto. Union organizers negotiated with and sometimes pressured local governments politically to find service work for its growing number of members, frequently on a basis of day labor but sometimes on a continuing basis. Growing in size on the one hand, and faced with municipal governments' cutbacks in budget allocations for these projects on the other, the union took the unusual step of transforming itself into a business owned and democratically run by its members, that would contract for work with a variety of organizations.

JWCU Home Page, May 2006

Through the 1970s they organized local groups in several prefectures and the Tokyo region that would find work and work with organizations to create work for members. These work groups took the name Jigyodan (Business Group), by which name they are still most commonly known throughout Japan.

The Japan Workers' Cooperative Union's (JWCU) origins at the edge of the trade union movement set it on a substantially different path than that of the WWCs. It is probably not accurate to say that JWCU is more politically active or involved than the league formed by the WWCs, which after all has its origins in the wing of consumer cooperation that has elected members to prefectural assemblies. But JWCU has certainly interacted more deliberately and directly, and substantially differently, with elected officials at all levels from its very start. Its main political focus at present is the passage of legislation recognizing worker-owned and managed firms as a distinct kind of economic organization different from personal ownership, partnership, and the limited liability joint stock corporation. A major campaign to pass sponsored legislation at the national level was launched in the fall of 2002, thus far without success. Perhaps when the WWC league makes a worker cooperative law a higher priority, an alliance formed for this purpose may become successful.

These homegrown experiments in the organization of work, JWCU and WWCs, are owned and run democratically by their workers, and both structure work around relatively small groups, from 10 to 50 people in a working group. But JWCU shows greater centralization in important ways: it was a union with a central staff of activists and organizers that became a worker cooperative with differentiated contracts and sources of income. WWC businesses are each independently owned by their members and started with only the encouragement of the Seikatsu Club Seikyo. These independent businesses later formed a league among themselves to foster the flow of information and political action. Consequently, friendly critics have questioned the degree of democracy in JWCU: its central organization does provide a great deal of leadership and support to local work groups whose members are usually not as knowledgeable about worker cooperation nor as committed to making it work. Members seem more to ratify and implement, rather than originate policies, which is the activity of professional staff. On the other hand, WWCs do not have a strong center at all, and their members see themselves as members of Seikatsu Club Seikyo rather than as members of any sort of organization beyond their own WWC, with which they identify as worker-owners.

Always an unusually innovative work in progress, it has never been as easy for JWCU to see itself clearly. In 1979, 36 local Jigyodan groups established a national council to provide critical analysis of, and guidance for, the organizations they had created. In their collective experience, they had no model in Japan along which lines they might develop their own organization. At this time the principle of the creation of "work for the good of the community rather than for profit" was first clearly enunciated. In 1982 the national council created a center to make propagation of their organizational practice easier by developing a "best practices" model of a work group, by establishing a stable financial base, and by opening a members' learning center to raise member skill levels.

During the early 1980s researchers at the national council discovered European cooperation, in particular the League of Italian Cooperatives and the Mondragon cooperatives of Basque Spain. In 1986 local Jigyodans decided to organize themselves as worker cooperatives; or perhaps more accurately, they realized they had been developing a membership-based organization dedicated to providing work for their members in the way a worker cooperative might. In 1991 the national council established the Japanese Institute of Cooperative Research. By 1993 the transformation was complete: each Jigyodan changed its name to "Workers' cooperative" and the Jigyodan managed by the national council became the "Workers' Cooperative Center."

These changes in name each represent a deepening understanding of the ways what had once been a labor union of the unemployed had been gradually transformed into a business owned and managed by its members as a workers' cooperative.

JWCU began as a trade union with low capital accumulation and little credit. As its earnings have grown, it has developed more capital intensive and more knowledge intensive industries. Home helper training centers are one example, and another is the development of construction cooperatives. Member cooperatives were active in the dismantling and subsequent repairs and reconstruction of Kobe following the earthquake there. After these beginnings in Kobe, JWCU opened a general office in Tokyo in 1996 for worker cooperatives in the construction industry. Still, however, about 75 percent of JWCU business is accounted for by work crews in consumer cooperative distribution centers, and hospital and park cleaning and maintenance.

Like those of the WWC network, the economic activities of the JWCU are diverse, labor intensive, and largely oriented toward low or unskilled service industries. JWCU cooperatives, however, focus especially on such activities as building, grounds and park maintenance. Through contracts with Min'iren, a group of hospitals run collectively by their member physicians in association with the Japan Communist Party, JWCU worker cooperatives provide hospitals with a variety of services such as floor and restroom cleaning, shop management, medical waste disposal, catering and food service, office and reception staffing. As well, JWCU worker cooperatives provide the labor force for many distribution centers of some of Japan's largest consumer cooperatives organized as grocery store chains.

A third important and growing source of work for JWCU members is care for the frail elderly. This care work primarily involves personal attention as home helpers, but also minor sorts of nursing as licensed by the national government. JWCU itself, with the support and collaboration of municipal governments, has opened several training courses for home helpers who would like to qualify for national licenses. A license makes it possible for the person who hires a home helper to be reimbursed by a national home care insurance program. I'll return to this issue below in the discussion of the development of "Senior Cooperatives," a JWCU initiative of the mid-1990s.

One of the most salient features of Japan's day laborers now is that they are old. Historically, day labor was work for the young and unskilled who become able to find more secure and regular employment as their skills and contacts increase. The average male day laborer in 1998, however, was 53, up from 39 in 1975. His mean age of death is 56, twenty years earlier than for the average Japanese male (Gill 2001: 163, 204). The North Tokyo Jigyodan crew, which cleans Azusawa Hospital's floors, toilets and attached clinics, checks and bundles its bed linen, launders the staff's surgical uniforms, collects and incinerates all hospital trash, comprised nine women and three men, all between the ages of 55 and 75 when I worked with them in 1994. Such patterns of mortality may account for why so many JWCU members are women; another reason doubtless is the gender associations of cleaning and care giving. Okyasu Kisaburo, at the time General Director of the Japan Institute for Cooperative Research, surveyed about 1600 JWCU members who ranged from teens to octogenarians (2002: 24). He divided his sample into "youth," "middle aged," and "seniors." Those members 40 to 59 years old are middle aged and make up half the sample. Seniors outnumber youth almost two to one. Only in the last decade have numbers of workers in their twenties become members. Cooperation among workers in Japan is not a movement of young people who in general, both as line workers and staff, join JWCU to acquire new skills and leave because they "cannot earn enough money to make a living" (Okayasu 2002: 30).

Senior Cooperatives

The first Senior Cooperative (Koreikyo) chapter was started in 1995. By 2000, more than 27,000 of Japan's seniors had joined chapters around the country. Koreikyo now has over 100,000 members and a chapter in each of Japan's 47 provinces. The Kawasaki City chapter that I got to know in 2002 has about 400 members. The current goal of the national organization is one million members. There is no mass membership organization for the elderly such as AARP in Japan yet. Koreikyo professional staff have studied AARP, however, and have invited AARP executives to Japan in recent years. They have a long-term goal of making Koreikyo such an advocate for Japan's growing elderly ranks.

As JWCU developed and grew, the union activists who made up its cadres of organizers aged. In the early 1990s Nakanishi Goshu, author and the inspirational leader of these activists, learned at age 75 that he had developed diabetes; he began dialysis. His genius let him see in his personal affliction an opportunity to help people organize themselves for self-help, and his energy and charisma brought together the people who could start Senior Cooperatives, hybrid cooperatives combining features of worker and consumer cooperatives of, by and for Japan's seniors. Koreikyo's central mission is to find ways to help seniors remain in their own homes as long as they possibly can, and it approaches the problem from both ends: how to get frail seniors the help they need to stay independent, and how to help able seniors find work that pays, through which they can stay active and add meaning to their lives by service to others. When I was invited in 1994 to attend an early organizational meeting among some union activists, JWCU members, politically active seniors and social activists at a Meiji era primary school building which had been turned into a retreat center in the hills of Western Tokyo, how little did I appreciate what these people were trying to accomplish then, and how successful their efforts would become a decade later. Although the first Senior Cooperative was started by people with a close association with JWCU (many of them were or had been JWCU staff members), and the relationship between the two organizations remains extremely close both in the movement of staff between them and in so far as there are people who are members of both cooperatives, Japan's Senior Cooperative has since grown very much larger than JWCU.

Koreikyo is a cooperative, a business run for the benefit of its members. All co-op members make a one-time purchase of a capital share in the co-op when they join (about $50 and which is returned to members when they leave the co-op). They pay an annual $30 membership fee, which includes a newsletter subscription. Members benefit from using the services their co-op provides rather than from profits on their investment. Typical of cooperatives everywhere, Koreikyo is run democratically. Members elect a board of directors and officers, and each functioning group within the local chapter sends a member to their board. What makes Koreikyo an unusual cooperative is the way it combines features of both consumer cooperatives, which are common in Japan, and worker cooperatives, which are not.

These two different kinds of cooperatives are combined by the simple method of a "pay-as-you-go" ticket system. The different prices of the co-op's services are published, and generally kept slightly below market prices. Members buy books of tickets and as they use co-op services, they turn over the appropriate number of tickets to the co-op member providing the service.

Service providers—themselves all co-op members as well—in turn redeem the tickets they've collected at the co-op office for their pay. And the co-op retains a small amount from each transaction to pay their local and national professional staff, and finance expansion.

An organization of this sort—of, by and for seniors—is necessarily more complicated than a brief description can express. One ongoing discussion concerns the appropriate mix of strictly commercial activity and the many activities sponsored by the co-op that members enjoy with each other for their own sake. And even here, distinctions are not always sharp. I met Uchida Hiroshi for the first time at the Kanagawa Koreikyo office where he had come to find a suitable activity for himself:

> We, my wife and I, became members because we appreciate the personal touch and the safety of the drivers. She has diabetes and gets dialysis twice a week. So people from the Koreikyo pick her up and drop her off. It is so much better than a taxi and it's a little cheaper too.
>
> We heard about Koreikyo from a flyer at the hospital. Now, I don't know what I can do, maybe pruning and the like, but I'd like to be more active and do something with people in the group. It is really difficult for men much more than women to become involved in something local. Everything is about work for men. But you can't just stay home all the time watching TV, you'll go *boke* (senile) in no time. So while I've lived right in this area for a long time, I really haven't been involved locally. But it's so important for people to help each other and do things together, this is really the principle behind cooperatives, whether consumer cooperatives or medical co-ops or senior co-ops. What can people do together, that's what we have to discover.

There are lots of things people do together as Koreikyo members, not all of them exactly what one might think would be part of a business. In addition to their home helper service and transportation for dialysis and other kinds of therapy, Kawasaki Koreikyo provides a variety of other services to its members, among them nursing home assistance (feeding, bed linen changing), the clothing retailoring group "ReForm," and home environment repair and renovation. But there are also many activities for members that are not strictly business services, such as touring and hobby groups (knitting, doll-making), social service group volunteer opportunities, organizations to raise funds for Koreikyo and other charitable institutions, reading and discussion circles, and newsletter publishing. In other parts of the country, chapters provide lunch and dinner cooking and home delivery, day-care centers for seniors and even three assisted living centers. The Kanagawa Koreikyo office is on the second floor of a building which has a JWCU lunch delivery kitchen (*shidashi bentoya*) on the ground floor. Several of the women members of this kitchen are also Koreikyo members; one sits on the Kanagawa Koreikyo board as well.

Koreikyo is also becoming a major educational institution. In 2000 the Japanese government instituted Long-Term Nursing Care Insurance (Kaigo Hoken), for the elderly. This insurance program's goal is broadly identical to Koreikyo's, to enable the elderly to remain in their own homes as long as they can and want to. Everyone over 40 is enrolled in this national insurance program and pays a small premium that entitles people 65 and over to such services as home helper and visiting nurse care, day care and brief stays at nursing facilities as needed, according to the judgment of a trained care plan manager.

This new nursing care insurance program made it possible for families to be reimbursed for the expense of home helper services for the first time, but only by certified home helpers, and never for care from one's own family members. Overnight an immense demand for home helper training that would lead to certification was created. Koreikyo members started programs to train and certify themselves, and then opened these programs to the general public with the support of municipal governments. The training of home helpers and the operation of home helper dispatch stations have become a major part of Koreikyo activities.

Until quite recently in Japan, daughters-in-law and daughters were the primary care givers at home to the elderly who were fortunate enough to have families to care for them. But there are many tasks seniors prefer to have someone their own age do for them, especially help bathing, dressing, hair care, and feeding. And they like to have people of their own generation to talk to at home. On the other hand, they prefer to have someone from their own family cook and shop for them, someone who already knows their tastes. Survey after survey shows widespread satisfaction with the new nursing care insurance program among family members, care givers and the elderly who make use of it.

Mrs. Yoshida (78), a member of the Koreikyo linen changing crew at NewGreen Nursing Home, handed me one end of the sheet.

> No, I don't have any children of my own; I never married. I was born in Manchuria when it was part of Japan and after my father died there near the end of the war, my mother and I were brought back to Japan. So I've had to work to support myself all my life. Without a family of my own, this chance to work here and rely on Koreikyo means a very great deal to me. I'm sure I'll need it even more in the future, so I'm really grateful it's here.

During World War II, Japan lost nearly 3.3 million men. More than 2 million women lost the opportunity to marry and raise a family. This group of women, Mrs. Yoshida among them, had cared for elderly parents in extended households in the past, and they are in need of long-term care today. But they do not have families to care for them. While recent statistics show that about half of Japan's aged continue to live with their families, extended family living will likely be less important in Japan's future than it has proven to be in the past. And like Mrs. Yoshida, more and more of Japan's seniors are finding that, with or without families of their own, Koreikyo and cooperation are rapidly becoming an important part of the solution to many of the problems aging presents them.

EcoTech

Japan's dean of worker cooperation researchers, Iwami Takahashi, gives an accounting of approximately 100 alternatively organized and operated economic enterprises in 1985 under the title "Workers Collectives" (Iwami 1985). In 1989 the Asahi Shimbun referred to "more than 300" worker cooperatives (*rodosha kyodo kumiai*) in an article about a mainstream bank employee who resigned to start an alternative press workers' cooperative.

Fifteen years after his earlier census, Iwami (2000) recognized that worker cooperatives, growing into the many hundreds, had become no longer easy to census. The bulk of these are cooperatives organized within the frameworks of JWCU or the WWC league. There are, however, several widely known independently formed worker cooperatives in Japan. Christina Turner (1995) documents the failing Paramount Shoe Company's employees' efforts to rebuild and revivify the business as a custom orthopedic shoe manufacturer through its union. Her research from the early 1980s was carried out before Paramount reorganized as a worker-owned and managed business. Here I briefly introduce one of the worker cooperatives of this origin I know best, Workers Co-op EcoTech, a designer and manufacturer of environmentally friendly technology. Like Paramount, EcoTech was able to use its employees' union to organize their workplace cooperatively and operate it democratically.

Ecotech Home Page

EcoTech's story and its president's name are relatively well known in labor, environment and progressive community activist circles throughout Japan. Yamane Masako (1991) tells the story of the emergence and separation from the Toshiba conglomerate after an eight year struggle in the courts and in the streets by the self-governing business operating under the name Tau Giken Labs, which later spun off EcoTech. The leader of this struggle and later president of EcoTech, Suzuku Ke, tells this story in his own words in an interview with Ronald Dore (1994) for the magazine *Sekai* (World) in a series on Japanese who march to different drummers. In brief, Toshiba bought the Ampex corporation, an American business with valuable tape recording technology assets, and moved production to Japan. When this technology was judged exhausted, Toshiba sought to split up the group that had been working as Toshiba-Ampex and reassign the workers. They resisted, in the streets and in the courts. After eight years operating this business autonomously while the matter was under litigation, the employees won the right to own and operate what remained of the business known as Ampex, a settlement worth several million dollars but scarcely a fortune for a business of its size and technological sophistication. Essentially they won the right to keep their jobs and become legally independent of Toshiba. The business, by then down to about forty workers, took the name Tau Giken Labs. Over a disagreement about the degree to which the business ought to remain activist, Suzuku and eight others left Tau Giken to found EcoTech with their share of the settlement. Tau Giken itself continues as a worker cooperative.

Workers Cooperative EcoTech proclaims its mission, its grand design, to become the center of an environmental products movement. (You can take a look to see one of their products available in the United States through Real

Goods, a bioactive home composter that reduces all organic waste in just a few days to water and CO_2, by aerobic and anaerobic decomposition.) They see themselves growing into the hub that draws together manufacturers, retailers, customers, monitors, university faculty members, their labs and departments, nonprofits and NGOs, local and regional governments and government agencies, and worker, consumer and producer cooperatives. And they recruit individual citizens of many backgrounds into the organizations that make up EcoTech's networks. EcoTech designs and develops environmentally friendly products and products with a connection to the environmental movement, that fit into these networks. But they don't just design and make things, they organize individuals and groups into the networks of which they too are part.

Rather than have EcoTech itself, which has only 10 full-time members, grow large, they try to spin off as many activities as possible into parts of their network. For example, EcoNet is a loose group of 25 or so small retailers who handle many of their products. The AlterNet is a network of groups of soap-from-old-cooking-oil makers who use EcoTech's soap-making machines. A network of groups in the Tokyo area monitors various toxic NOX compound emissions with EcoTech digital analyzers, and they are forming a network of groups to monitor acid rain with a parallel device.

EcoTech opened for business on September 20, 1993, with eight full-time and three part-time members. The three part-time members each have continuing responsibilities with other cooperative organizations. The firm focuses on the environment, making products that are easy on the environment, help clean it up, or are less energy demanding. Their greatest challenge, however, has no clear counterpart in U.S. ecological alchemy, the turning of used household cooking oil into soap. EcoTech came into being largely to take on this issue: in 1990 a woman deeply involved in the Seikatsu Club Seikyo's "soap movement," as it is known, called on EcoTech president Suzuku Ken, to ask if there was anything his company could do about making a washing machine that worked well with soap made from used cooking oil. When he and five others left Tau Giken to found EcoTech, they took the washing machine project with them. (Tau Giken Technical Engineering Labs remains an independent workers' cooperative.)

The soap movement is almost 30 years old now. It has woven a complex web around a complicated issue. Standard sanitary sewage treatment plants manage toilet wastes conventionally to international public health standards, but gray water, which includes water from sinks and washing machines, is discharged directly and untreated into streams, rivers, lakes, wetlands, and finally, the ocean. This gray water contains large quantities of two serious pollutants: synthetic detergents and used cooking oil. Synthetic detergent of course is a well known pollutant in the United States and is degraded in treatment facilities. In both countries phosphorous is no longer added to synthetic detergents. Used cooking oil is not treated at all either, and it goes directly into gray-water drains all over the country.

Households and restaurants cook with oil daily. The walls and ceilings of older kitchens are a rich dark brown and sticky with years of built-up oil deposits. After a few or even only a single day's use, cooks throw their cooking oil "away." Of course, there's no such place as "away." Large restaurants pay to have their used oil hauled to commercial facilities; small restaurants and housewives just wash theirs down the sink with cold water. But both detergent and oil have long lives in water and break down only slowly, finally strangling the life out of the streams, wetlands, and bays where they end up.

The deep insight of the soap movement was that something useful could be done about both pollutants at the same time and provide valuable educational, political and economic opportunities to anyone interested as well. Cooking the oil with caustic soda for a few hours, then adding soda ash and cooking some more, is how people used to make soap in the predetergent days. The housewives in the soap movement urge their neighbors to start doing so again. There are for-profit businesses that turn bulk used oils from the food product industry into soap, but there is no commercial network to collect used oil from households and family-run restaurants. Commercial enterprises aren't interested in such a labor intensive source of supply largely because the market for soap is still so small. So the soap movement organizes neighbors to collect their own used oil and turn it into soap themselves. And as with all substantial social movements, the soap movement too offers magazines and newsletters, workshops, ancillary goods and services to its members and potential members. Some of the more central *things* of the movement, though, are soap-making machines, soap powdering mills, and washing machines.

EcoTech has spliced three strands of its organization into the soap movement. First, EcoTech designs, assembles and programs portable, user-friendly soap-making machines. These soap-making machines are too expensive for individuals to buy as household appliances, but they're well within the reach of community organizations: the complete setup for the large capacity machine is about $10,000, about $3000 for the smallest. So individuals do not make soap at home, and commercially manufactured soap is widely available through consumer cooperatives. But soap making is an ideal activity for a local chapter of the soap-making branch of the environmental movement: members can spend an evening a month or even more, go around to events and places where people gather, demonstrate how to make soap and how to organize a soap-making group, and educate about what damage cooking oil does to the water supply. It all adds up to a helpful, nonconfrontational, middle-class grassroots environmental consciousness-raising movement for, especially, housewives, who are highly motivated and still have some leisure. Many WWC members and enterprises are deeply engaged in the soap movement. As well, this campaign gives even politically uninvolved housewives something to do about a serious environmental problem in an especially productive way: each person who brings some oil to a collection point sees the oil she hasn't dumped down the drain being turned into soap, and then can use that soap instead of detergent. And when she brings her oil in, she is exposed to the movement message.

EcoTech's second strand organizes networks of soap makers, teaching them how to make soap in some cases, learning more about how to make soap in others, teaching and learning how to get people moving in the same direction and help them build enduring and effective organizations. EcoTech's members have extensive, valuable experience organizing social support networks as a result of their eight-year struggle for independence from Toshiba. Their effort in these activities weaves EcoTech into the consumer co-op movement, especially Seikatsu Club Seikyo, but also prefectural consumer cooperatives.

And they also organize a network of retailers for these and other products, finding retailers who are community and environmentally minded and working with them, working them into the movement too. EcoTech is made up of an interesting and unusual mix of scientists, engineers, technicians, business people, advocates for cooperatives and community activists. Most of EcoTech's members easily fit two, and even three, of these descriptions.

Their third tie to the soap movement is the prototype washing machine they've designed to use the soap made from cooking oil. Many of this washer's features improve on those of regular washers: it's gentler on clothes, and uses about one-third less water as well. They call it the EcoDrum because while still top-loading, it revolves on a horizontal rather than vertical axis. The clothes are dropped, as it were, again and again into the soapy water, rather than twisted back and forth. The lint left in the filter after a load of wash comes from the twisting motion of the washer breaking down the fabric fibers of the clothes as it washes them, I was told and shown. The EcoDrum resulted from the visit of the woman from the soap movement to Suzuku Ken in 1990. The original horizontal drum washer is Finnish. The Brother Corporation holds contracts to manufacture the washing machines.

EcoTech also makes a digital analyzer that individuals or groups can use to monitor various toxic oxides of nitrogen, airborne pollutants created as products of combustion, especially, of internal combustion engines. These monitors are organized much like the soap makers are. EcoTech helps organize groups of monitors and holds meetings and workshops with them on how to get the most out of the analyzer, how to get reliable results, how to monitor nitrogen emissions scientifically. They make air quality maps from the reports turned in by the increasing numbers of people and groups who have gotten involved.

As with the development of the washing machine EcoDrum, air pollution movement people came to EcoTech to get help with the *thing* it needed to add credible precision to their activity. Integrated into this project from its start are a group of nationally recognized scientists specializing in air pollution issues, one of whom is the conceptual inventor of the digital analyzer. Engineers at EcoTech made the actual plans and built it.

Now the monitors' network includes EcoTech too. Each workday starts with analysis of the air sample collected over the past 24 hours on the roof of their original office building, located directly behind Shin Yokohama station. And then monitors began organizing school science classes whose students can be trained and counted on to collect reliable data. EcoTech has also designed a similar product, a handheld acid rain analyzer. The monitor goes to the collecting station, sticks the sensor into the vial of reagent and gets a digital readout of parts per million of selected airborne pollutants with the one, waterborne pollutants with the other. All this activity builds toward gathering and publicizing reliable information about the wretched quality of Japan's air and water, to pressure the government to move its support away from internal combustion engines, especially, and do more for clean electric alternatives.

Japan Institute of Cooperative Research (JICR)

The JICR (Kyodo Sogo Kenkyūjo) was founded in 1991 by the JWCU to ally with cooperative and community activists, and academic researchers, to publish the results of national and international research on cooperatives and related topics of use to the Institute's member activists and worker cooperative members. The Institute's journal *Kyodo no Hakken* (The Discovery of Cooperation) is published monthly. As an example of what it publishes, the April 2006 issue, number 165, features a series of reports prepared for a workshop to promote a workers' cooperative law for Japan. The April 2005 issue, number 153, contains articles on the workers' cooperative taxi cab business in Fukuoka, and another on its counterpart in Madison, Wisconsin. As well there are articles on how jobs change under employee management, the rights of associated workers and community renewal through social enterprises.

There is also in each issue a section reporting on relevant news from abroad. JWCU and JICR have always been oriented toward the international, especially European, cooperative movement and active participants in Interfaculty Committee Agraria (ICA)–sponsored events. Currently about 400 individual members and 50 institutional members belong.

JWCU also publishes a newspaper, "Rokyo Shimbun" (Workers' Co-op Newspaper), three times a month and a bimonthly magazine, "Shigoto no Hakken" (The Discovery of Work), for members of JWCU work cooperatives, primarily. Their content is largely devoted to the activities of worker co-op members and activity in the wider world that might affect the activity of JWCU worker co-ops.

Into the Future

Cooperatives emerge where markets fail. As Japan's economy becomes both less responsive to its workers and its manufacturing sector continues to hollow, we can expect an increasing number of workers to try, as they try in many other countries, to make a go of it under various structures supporting varying degrees of worker ownership and democratic management. At this point, the instrument most widespread in the United States through which management maintains control over worker-owners after employee buyouts of the businesses in which they work, the Employee Stock Ownership Plan (ESOP), is not available in Japan. Consequently, while employee ownership of the firms that once employed them remains quite rare in Japan, worker-owners do seem to have a strong voice in the management of those businesses where they have become owners.

Although ESOPs are not available in Japan to restructure ownership, if not management, of failing firms, neither is there yet a legal recognition in Japan of the distinctive features and advantages of worker cooperatives. Managers of businesses purchased by their employees find they must pour their new wine into bottles old and poorly shaped for their intended purpose, the control of capital by labor. The legal requirements of organizing as a joint stock corporation, through which organizational form capital has historically controlled a labor force, have proven cumbersome for worker-owners in Japan as elsewhere. There is simply no easy, legal way to organize worker cooperation in Japan yet, and this must surely be a barrier to their spread.

Another area in which legal changes may make a difference to the future of worker cooperatives in Japan is that of tax law. If the laws maintaining the "Million Yen Wall" are removed, the number of hours it will make sense for women of the new middle class to consider working may change, and this may possibly reduce their interest in forming worker cooperatives. The Diet discussed bills embodying such changes, and the newspapers predicted their imminent passage, in the fall of 2002. Nothing has come of this discussion yet, however. And in any event, I see nothing on the Equal Employment Opportunity legal horizon that is likely to change the "M-shaped" curve of female employment or the wide wage differentials between men and women of the same age and education levels. The status quo in this area strongly favors a preference among many women to start a WWC rather than take conventional employment.

At the moment, the movement toward worker cooperation is a movement of middle-aged, middle-class women, the elderly of both genders and both working and middle class, and a limited number of unusual outliers of the sort that must appear in any complex system. From this perspective, that the future will be something rather like the past, we can expect that the pool of people in Japan to whom worker cooperation holds potential interest will only continue to increase. And yet, there seems to be no connection between these existing worker cooperatives and young people whom the labor market has failed significantly since the early 1990s when compared with the experiences of their parents.

We cannot forget that starting a business requires both capital and knowledge. Once the JWCU transformed itself from a labor union into a worker-owned business, its assets and dues structure provided a foundation for capital accumulation. The housewives of the WWC league and the members of the senior cooperatives have their personal and family savings to invest, although none of their investments are large and their work capitalizes their life experience to a high degree. And the workers who restructure through their ownership the businesses that formerly employed them often have a variety of sources of capital to invest in the success of their companies. While it is true that many start-up worker cooperatives are founded on members' "sweat equity," the retention of earnings that result from members' labor, we still have to ask where young people are likely to find the capital they need to start a business and knowledge relevant to the niche they hope to exploit, to say nothing of how to organize and run a worker cooperative if they are not associated with the organizations discussed above. There are at least a few work groups composed entirely of young people in JWCU, after all. Today we live in a global era reminiscent of the classic age of plutocracy prior to the First World War, in which capital is in the driver's seat and does not spare the whip. How will growing numbers of today's young workers ever manage to control sufficient capital to do other than keep themselves alive at near-minimum wage in the growing service sector of the economy?

Women's Worker Collectives, Japan Workers' Cooperative Union and Senior Cooperatives all are expanding in their characteristic ways and have every reason to expect that they will continue to do so. They don't make much money from their businesses but they seem to make enough for their members to keep them going and for others like them to want to join or start their own similar cooperative businesses. Many of their members are seniors and much of their business activity centers on the needs of seniors. Certainly there will be no shortage of seniors to keep them going in Japan's future. Seen from this perspective, perhaps the biggest barrier to the spread of this alternative way of working among the young is simply their lack of knowledge about its possibilities. Recalling that the category "youth" reaches to age 39 in his survey, Okayasu (Okayasu 2002: 29–30) observes that while almost 70 percent of staff belong to other co-ops in addition to JWCU, only 27 percent of youth members do. And this in an organization that sedulously promotes cooperation of all kinds among JWCU members. How low must knowledge of institutionalized cooperation, and especially worker cooperation, be among Japan's young people at large?

Note

1. Field research on which this article is based was supported by grants from the Social Science Research Council and the Japan Foundation.

References

Asahi Shimbun. 1989. *Leaving the Bank for a Grassroots Company* (Ginko yamete kusanone kaisha). June 13th.

Dore, Ronald. 1994. *Conversations with Japan—Aspects of Dissatisfaction* (Nihon to no taiwa—fufuku no shoso). Tokyo: Iwanami Shoten.

Gill, Tom. 2001. *Men of Uncertainty: The Social Organization of Day Laborers in Contemporary Japan.* Albany: SUNY Press.

Iwami Takashi. 1985. *Japan's Workers Collectives: A New Way of Working Changes Society* (Nihon no wakazu korekuteibu: Atarashii hatarakikata ga shaki o kaeru.) Tokyo: Gakuyo Shobo.

———. 2000. *Let's Create Jobs and Workplaces with Cooperation: Workers Coops and Senior Coops.* (Shigoto to shokuba o kyodo de tsukuro.) Tokyo: Shakai Hyoronsha.

Nakano, Lynne Y. 2005. *Community Volunteers in Japan.* London and New York: RoutledgeCurzon.

Okyasu Kisaburo. 2002. "Views of Young Members Who Work in Workers' Cooperatives on Work, Management and Neighborhood" (Rodo kyodo kumiai ni hataraku shonen kumiai-in no shigotoken, chiku-ken, kei'ei-ken). *Kyodo Kumiai Kei'ei Kenkyū Geppo* 587, no. 8: 24–31.

Turner, Christena. 1995. *Japanese Workers in Protest: An Ethnography of Consciousness and Experience.* Berkeley: University of California Press.

Yamane Masako. 1991. *An Autonomous Production Labor Union—The Struggle of the Eight Year Long Toshiba Ampex Dispute.* (Jishu seisan roukumi—Toshiba anpekkusu sogi hachinen no tatakai.) Tokyo: Kodamasha.

VII

Where Do Individuals Fit?

19

RESPONSES TO TOURISM IN INDONESIA

Ethnic Tourism and the Renegotiation of Tradition in Tana Toraja (Sulawesi, Indonesia)

Kathleen M. Adams

In January of 1987, tourists descending from jets at the Ujung Pandang airport in South Sulawesi, Indonesia,[1] were greeted with a mimeographed announcement of an elaborate, pageantry-filled funeral ceremony to be held in the Toraja highlands for the late Ne' Ke'te'.[2] Using a smattering of anthropological terminology, the pamphlet outlined the cultural functions of Torajan funeral rituals, made reference to a Torajan origin myth, and presented a schedule of events for the ten-day funeral ritual. Hoteliers and travel agents boasted that this was the first Torajan funeral ceremony that would adhere to a definite time schedule; this time no tourists would be disappointed with the last-minute postponements so typical of Torajan rituals. Television newscasters declared that this promised to be a "truly unique Torajan event: the largest, most elaborate, and impressive funeral in several decades." As exceptional as this barrage of publicity was, the funeral (which was for my former Torajan mentor) proved to be momentous, but for very different reasons than those heralded in the media.

Since the early 1970s, tourists have been visiting the Toraja highlands in ever-increasing numbers. In 1994 alone, approximately 53,700 foreign tourists and 205,000 domestic tourists[3] journeyed to the Toraja homeland, lured

306

by guidebook accounts of Torajans' pageantry-filled funeral rituals, haunting burial cliffs, elaborate architecture, and breathtaking scenery. Touristic celebrity has precipitated a number of new issues for the Toraja, certain aspects of which have been discussed elsewhere (Adams 1984, 1993a, 1993b, 1995; Crystal 1977, 1994; Volkman 1987, 1990; Yamashita 1994). This article concerns the ways in which Torajan history and custom are being reshaped as a result of tourism development. Over the past two decades, anthropologists and historians have become increasingly concerned with processes of cultural construction and invention (cf. Wagner 1981 [1975]; Keesing and Tonkinson 1982; Hobsbawm and Ranger 1983; Linnekin 1983, 1992; Handler and Linnekin 1984; Clifford 1988; Jackson 1989; Hanson 1989; Keesing 1989; White and Lindstrom 1993). As many have stressed, in order to advance our understanding of the construction of tradition, our questions must go beyond examinations of which aspects of culture are authentic and which are invented (White 1991: 3). Closer attention must be paid to the processes whereby traditions are invented and the conditions under which custom is renegotiated. This article explores some of the microprocesses involved in the contemporary renegotiation of Toraja history and ritual practice. Whereas the majority of studies of the "invention of tradition" concern the artificial creation of ritual traditions by colonial governments or indigenous elites, the focus here is on a different sort of context in which tradition is negotiated: that of ethnic tourism. As the Toraja case suggests, encounters with foreign tourists (and a national government interested in further stimulating tourism revenues) are prompting new challenges to local forms of meaning, power, and identity. In short, ethnic tourism creates a fertile context for the reinterpretation of history and custom. Specifically, this essay explores the contemporary Torajan engagement with touristic imagery and chronicles the strategies whereby Torajans attempt to refashion this outsider imagery in order to enhance their position in the Indonesian hierarchy of ethnic groups (as well as their own local standing).

Various writers have suggested that ethnic tourism engenders "staged authenticity" and "museumification" (cf. MacCannell 1973, 1976, 1992; Cohen 1988, 1989). That is, as a tourist-hosting society undergoes economic and cultural changes through its intensifying contact with outsiders, efforts are made to stage the traditional cultural rituals and activities that are becoming increasingly rare and increasingly divorced from their original cultural significance. While the explosion of traditional Torajan architectural embellishments and family-run museums in tandem with tourism development certainly resonates with this notion of staged authenticity, the cases discussed in the following pages underscore the fact that self-conscious staging of rituals does not entail a loss of meaning for local people. Despite the fact that large-scale Torajan funerals are increasingly sculpted to address the needs and expectations of visiting tourist dignitaries, these ritual events continue to carry tremendous cultural significance for Torajan participants. As Crick (1989: 336) so cogently asks in reflecting on the problematic concept of authenticity, "What in a culture is *not* staged? What does cultural authenticity consist of?"

Data here are drawn from fieldwork in the Toraja highlands in 1984–1985 and subsequent visits in 1987, 1991, 1992, and 1995. Central to the analysis are two events: the highly publicized funeral ritual referred to at the beginning of this article and a Local Guide Training Workshop in the Toraja highlands that sparked a reverberating emotional debate among Torajans. In different ways, both cases illustrate the issues central to Torajan efforts at ethnic imagery enhancement and address ongoing anthropological discussions about cultural authenticity and the invention of tradition.

The Sa'dan Toraja: Ethnographic Background

The Sa'dan Toraja homeland is in Tana Toraja Regency, a mountainous interior region of South Sulawesi, Indonesia. Traditionally, most Torajans have been wet rice cultivators, although in recent years many farmers have also planted cash crops such as coffee and cloves. Today Torajans can also be found in a variety of occupations, working as teachers, bureaucrats, mining workers, servants, and tour guides in cities throughout Indonesia. In a nation of over 185 million people, the Sa'dan Toraja constitute a small minority, numbering approximately 350,000.

The Toraja people are marginalized by geography, religion, and a diffuse power structure. Their closest neighbors are the Islamicized Buginese and Makassarese peoples, the dominant ethnic groups of South Sulawesi. In contrast to the extensive kingdoms established by these neighboring Buginese and Makassarese, the Toraja never united into a centralized political unit. Traditionally, Torajans lived in scattered mountaintop households, maintaining social ties through an elaborate system of ritual exchanges (Nooy-Palm 1979, 1986). It was not until the arrival of Dutch colonial forces in 1906 that the Toraja were formally brought together under a single political authority.

A few years after the Dutch annexed the highlands, missionaries from the Dutch Reformed Church began proselytizing among the Toraja.[4] Although conversion was initially slow, it gathered momentum in the 1950s and 1960s. Scholars attribute the large number of conversions during this period to two primary factors: inroads made by mission schools, and the newly independent Indonesian government's policy of actively encouraging practitioners of indigenous religions to convert to world religions (Bigalke 1981). Today, over 80 per cent of the Sa'dan Toraja are Christians. (By contrast, over 85 per cent of Indonesia's population describe themselves as Muslims.) Only about 11 per cent of the Toraja people continue to practice the traditional Ways of the Ancestors (*Aluk to Dolo*), which entail the veneration of spirits, gods, and ancestors. Despite the fact that contemporary Torajans are predominantly Christian, they continue to sponsor and partake in elaborate funeral rituals that include pig and water buffalo sacrifices.

Toraja society is hierarchically organized on the bases of descent, wealth, age, and occupation. In precolonial times Torajan society was roughly divided into three social strata: the aristocracy, commoners, and slaves. Status was determined by birth, although economic aptitude or failure permitted some degree of social mobility. Today slavery is outlawed in Indonesia and rank is a delicate topic among Torajans. Not surprisingly, customs pertaining to showcasing rank are a particular focus of many Torajans' reformulation of cultural practices in the context of tourism development, as will be seen in the case immediately following this section.

Tourism to the Toraja highlands is a relatively recent development. Throughout the 1950s and early 1960s, poor roads and Muslim rebellions made it a challenge to travel in South Sulawesi. In the late 1960s, however, President Suharto began to encourage the development of the Indonesian tourism industry. Initially, government officials concentrated on developing and expanding tourism in Bali, Java, and Sumatra. In 1974, however, Indonesia issued its second Five Year Plan, which stressed the promotion of Outer Island destinations, including Tana Toraja (Crystal 1977; Spillane 1987). The touristic marketing of Tana Toraja was a phenomenal success: whereas in 1973 only 422 foreigners voyaged to the Toraja highlands, by 1994 over 53,000 foreign tourists and 205,000 domestic tourists were visiting the region annually.

Both the growing tourist and anthropological literature have helped make Torajans international celebrities, their culture an entity to be studied, dissected, photographed, and packaged for export (Adams 1988, 1990; Volkman 1990). Today's Torajans are increasingly exposed to outsider images of their culture. Local shops offer T-shirts and postcards depicting Torajan burial cliffs, "traditional Toraja villages," and "warrior dancers." Travel agency placards announcing local "funeral parties" and "celebrations of death" line the main street of Rantepao (one of the two major towns in Tana Toraja Regency). Tourism Board posters emblazoned with smiling female dancers beckoning, "Come to Tana Toraja: Land of the Heavenly Kings" decorate local cafes and living rooms. And Torajan villagers devotedly watch Indonesian television variety shows which routinely feature traditionally dressed Torajan singers seated on ornately carved Toraja rice barns. In short, contemporary Torajans are not only ethnically self-conscious, but are also avid consumers, manipulators, and critics of the ethnographic and touristic images of their culture.

Hand in hand with Torajans' emerging ethnic self-consciousness comes an objectification of culture, a tendency that is reinforced by the vocabulary of Indonesian cultural policy. Torajans are extremely fond of commenting to tourists and anthropologists alike that "we Torajans have more culture here." The implicit comparison is with their lowland rivals, the Buginese. Culture, then, becomes a measurable, quantifiable entity, reminiscent of Greenwood's (1977) observations. This objectification of culture has also brought new Torajan concerns about and obsessions with cultural authenticity, as will be discussed below.

Torajan touristic fame not only engenders ethnic self-consciousness, but it also brings a variety of other costs and benefits. On the one hand, it represents a new source of revenue, as well as the opportunity to gain favorable attention and grants from the government. On the other hand, tourism has a tendency to enhance the stereotype of the Toraja as a primitive and backwards people. Many Torajans have voiced the troubling tension they experience between being a celebrated tourist attraction and being portrayed as "primitive" with "joyful funeral festivals." Such tensions have prompted Torajan attempts to reinterpret their customs and reshape outsiders' images of their identity, as the cases discussed below illustrate.

Taming Traditions: Ne' Ke'te's Funeral Ritual

In January of 1987, I returned to Tana Toraja for the funeral of an aristocratic Torajan who had "adopted" me during my initial fieldwork. Ne' Ke'te' had been a prominent local figure, extremely active in civil and religious politics. His funeral promised to be an important event for the entire Torajan community. Traditionally, the Torajan funeral not only provides an opportunity to pay respect and debts to the family of the deceased, but also serves as an important arena for demonstrating one's social status (Crystal 1974, 1976; Nooy-Palm 1979; Koubi 1982; Volkman 1985). The more guests a funeral attracts, and the more water buffalo sacrificed, the more prestige the sponsors attain.[5] Ne' Ke'te's funeral had thus been widely publicized. Thirty-thousand guests including three cabinet ministers, two governors, a foreign ambassador, and van loads of tourists were to attend. My Torajan family was faced with an issue that has confronted Torajans ever since tourism development began in the early 1970s: how to stage a large-scale ritual that would be deemed a success by several very different audiences; by locals, by Java-based government representatives, and by foreign tourists.[6]

Because of the size of the ritual and the amount of attention it was drawing from high-status outsiders, the funeral planning was extensive. The village's architectural transformation for the funeral began months in advance: kinsmen of the deceased built sprawling bamboo complexes around the central ritual arena. These colorfully painted pavilions were to shelter relations and funeral guests over the course of the ten-day ritual.[7] One particularly grand and well-situated pavilion was erected for V.I.P. government visitors (*tamu V.I.P.*). A travel agency paid for the construction of its own pavilion where tourists would be able to rest and reload their cameras away from the bustle of the crowds.

The immense scale of the ritual required complex planning. Emulating government and church organization, a funeral secretary was chosen and some two dozen funeral committees were formed, including an entertainment committee, a clean water committee, a safety committee, and a documentation committee. Evenings in the months and weeks before the funeral ritual began were filled with committee meetings. Individuals who in smaller rituals had labored in a multitude of areas came to view their role in this event in terms of the committees to which they were assigned.

I was also drawn into this frenzy of funeral committee activity. On the evening I arrived in the village, my Torajan family gave me a mimeographed list of funeral task forces and declared that I was assigned to two committees that would put my anthropological training to work: the "Funeral Documentation Committee" and the "V.I.P. Guest Reception Committee." At first I was deeply moved that they had devised a way in which I could participate as a "family member" in the funeral. Only later did I fully comprehend the political dimensions of my assignments. Recognizing the funeral ritual's potential to reinforce outsiders' images of Torajans as primitives, the family had devised a strategy to combat these negative stereotypes. The day before the V.I.P. guests arrived, they instructed me to greet them in traditional Torajan garb at the V.I.P. guest pavilion. They speculated that these guests would initially be amused at the "tourist gone overboard," then become awed (*kagum*) upon learning that I was the deceased's "adoptive daughter and family anthropologist" assigned to explain the funeral ritual to them. The family was explicit about what I was to tell the visiting dignitaries; I was to emphasize that they were not pagans but Christians, and point out the church hymns and ministers officiating at the ritual. As one Torajan kinsman observed, this time no visitors would return home thinking all Torajans were animists.

Moreover, the family was well aware of outsiders' perceptions of their funerary water buffalo sacrifices as wasteful and backwards. Over the years, a number of articles had appeared in the national newspaper, *Kompas,* criticizing Torajans for spending thousands of dollars on funeral ritual slaughters. Disturbed by government officials' and tourists' denigration of their sacrifices, the family stressed that I must not forget to tell the V.I.P. guests that the water buffalo meat would be redistributed, eventually reaching poorer villagers who often do without meat. "They won't believe us if we say it, but they'll believe you," they urged. "You're an anthropologist: you can convince them that our rituals are not wasteful." Finally, they quizzed me on aspects of the ritual itself, wanting to hear how I would explain the various rites to the V.I.P. guests. At one point I was asked what I would say about the palanquin leading the funeral procession. I answered with what I had been told during my fieldwork: that this covered litter held a descendant of a slave. This "slave litter" has traditionally cleared the path for the ensuing funeral party. Hearing this, the family members exchanged glances and quickly concluded that, although essentially correct, this answer would not meet with the approval of the government guests. One commented that a reference to slave descent would prompt disapproval from the government guests, and an elder suggested that perhaps it would be better to call this individual a helper (*pembantu*). After some discussion, this was deemed a suitable explanation.

At the start of the ten-day funeral ritual, family members, distant kin, friends, and other guests began to arrive with gifts of water buffalo, pigs, chickens, sugar, and other offerings. The temporary pavilions were filled with guests and the usually tranquil village was transformed into a bustling bamboo city. The ritual activities of the first three days were punctuated with frequent prayer sessions, water buffalo fights, and, in the evenings, *ma'badong* dances for the deceased. The majority of the visiting dignitaries were scheduled to visit on the fourth and sixth days, which were devoted to the rites termed *ma'pasa' tedong* (parading the water buffalo) and *ma'palao* (moving buffalo and deceased to the ritual field), respectively. Below is an excerpt from my journal recorded on the fourth day of the ritual.

> In front of the tongkonans [ancestral houses] the buffalo herders were busy decorating their buffaloes with red and yellow cloth, gold cutouts, woven bits of grass and slices of squash ... TVRI arrived on the scene equipped with gigantic video cameras and other recording instruments. A few foreign tourists began to show up, along with fleets of Indonesian tourists. Kakak and others sitting in the Secretariat Booth repeatedly made loudspeaker announcements in Indonesian and fractured English that tourists were not to sit on the rice barns, which were reserved for local leaders and their families.... The decorated water buffaloes were then paraded, along with banners of maa' [sacred textiles] and a large gong. Following this procession were the tau-tau [effigy of the deceased], the bereaved family members, etc. I briefly joined the family member section of the procession alongside Sarlota, then circled back to take some pictures, slipping between my roles of participant and observer.... In the early afternoon family members sent me to talk to some of the visiting officials in the V.I.P. grandstand. This group included officials from the Jakarta and Ujung Pandang branches of the ____ Bank. Sure enough, they asked how many pricey buffaloes were to be "wasted" as sacrifices at this "animist" ritual.

The following days brought similar questions from other V.I.P. guests. The family had correctly anticipated the responses their funeral would evoke and the narrative we had rehearsed (that they were Christians, that the buffalo meat would feed many distant villagers, and the euphemistic referral to "helpers" rather than "descendants of slaves") represented an attempt to divest the ritual of all aspects that were expected to prompt the disapproval of outsiders. In short, I was cleverly employed to dispel what they perceived to be negative stereotypes about their culture. Recognizing the power of outsider images over their own claims, they resorted to borrowing the authoritative voice of an outsider to challenge these images. As the Torajans drew on the authority of my discipline, degree, and race to establish the merit of their cultural practices, I became a party to the taming of Torajan traditions.

It is important to underscore that this conscious effort to sanitize Torajan ethnic imagery for an outsider audience did not divest the ritual of its salience. In the eyes of the Torajans, today as in the past, the ritual remained an arena for status enhancement; in this instance, however, it was not only for the deceased's lineage, but for the entire ethnic group. Ironically, the presence of these visiting dignitaries at the funeral both bolstered and weakened the prestige of the family. In deference to the dignitaries, not only were funeral speeches condensed and dances explained, but various rites were juggled, or delayed. For instance, on the seventh day of the ritual (*ma'palao*), the V.I.P.

guests were an hour late. In the traditional past, on that day just after noon the corpse would be transported in an elaborate procession to an ornately carved tower (*lakkian*) situated at the edge of the ritual field. This time several hundred participants waited in the scorching sun until the tardy dignitaries finally arrived in the afternoon and the signal to begin the procession was given. On the sidelines, local guests grumbled that things were not being done in accordance with traditions, that the ritual was not "authentic." Thus, while the very presence of these important officials from far-off places conferred prestige on the family, it also fueled rivals' criticism of their ritual as unauthentic.

As with colonialism, this case shows how tourism development provides a fertile context in which custom is reinterpreted and reframed. Tourism and the attendant attention from the national Indonesian government are prompting new challenges to local forms of meaning, power, prestige, and identity. Examining this carefully staged funeral ritual at close range lends deeper insights into the microprocesses involved in the renegotiation of tradition and the reformulation of ethnic imagery. This case also offers insight into the question raised earlier, namely, how Torajan rituals maintain their salience in the context of touristic promotion and Torajan cultural self-consciousness. Although Torajan rituals are increasingly self-conscious productions, their meaning is clearly not being lost: rather, old themes are being played on a new stage. Touristic celebrity provides the Toraja with new audiences for augmenting their status and a new basis ("authenticity") on which to criticize the rituals of their rivals. In other words, large-scale rituals are now aimed not only at enhancing local status but at increasing Torajan prestige on a national and international level. In this process, aspects of Torajan tradition that outsiders might disdain (e.g., costly water buffalo sacrifices, the heritage of slavery) are either played down or justified in anthropological terms. In this way, controversial traditions are tamed and the image of Torajan ethnic identity is enhanced.

The Local Guide Training Workshop

A second event further illustrates the microprocesses whereby Torajans are actively engaged in renegotiating their history out of concern for their touristic image. In 1985, the South Sulawesi provincial tourism officials determined that the unlicensed "wild guides" (*guide liar*) flourishing in Tana Toraja were a potential liability. These wild guides are for the most part young unemployed or underemployed Torajan men who seek their clients at the restaurants and hotels favored by independent tourists. Although a few of these young men are reputed to be hustlers or rascals prone to overindulging in palm wine, for the most part they are entrepreneurs who have taught themselves one or two European languages and enjoy associating with foreigners. The 1985 decree that only officially licensed guides would be allowed to escort tourists in Tana Toraja was a serious blow to them. As guide-training courses were both costly and distant (eight hours away in the Buginese-Makassarese city of Ujung Pandang), these Torajans recognized that their income from guiding in their own homeland was threatened. In the eyes of many Torajans, this new certification requirement would hasten the encroaching monopoly of Buginese guides in Tana Toraja. As several guides lamented, not only was their livelihood at stake, but now nonlocal guides who knew little about Torajan culture would be controlling what was said about Torajans to tourists. Recognizing these issues, government officials in Tana Toraja Regency organized a Local Guide Training Workshop (*Kursus Pramuwisata Khusus Tator*), designed as a crash course in guiding skills and presentations.

In November of 1985, 88 aspiring Torajan guides and representatives from Toraja's most frequented tourist destinations attended the first such workshop. One of the many goals of the two-week workshop was to develop a uniform Torajan history and mythology to be presented to tourists, thus combating the perceived misrepresentations of Tana Toraja articulated by nonlocal guides. Moreover, for the workshop leaders, the wide regional diversity of Torajan origin myths was troubling; they feared tourists would hear conflicting stories and come to question Torajans' credibility. In essence, the workshop involved an active attempt to achieve consensus on the image of Torajans presented to outsiders. Ironically, what was intended to be a unified move against outside dominance provoked local dissent. The biggest issues debated at the workshop centered on whose version of Torajan history would become "official." Traditionally, each group of Torajan nobles bases its claims to high rank on descent from various heavenly ancestors who descended onto local mountaintops centuries ago. For the nobles present, it was important that their particular celestial forebears be incorporated into the official version of Torajan history told to tourists. Formal recognition of a particular family's mythic history and landmarks meant continued substantiation of their high rank within Torajan society. Moreover, official recognition had the potential to attract to one's village rich, presumably generous, foreign tourists as well as an assortment of concrete touristic amenities, such as paved roads, outhouses, and telephone booths. Given these considerations, the selection of speakers for the workshop became a politically charged issue with not only symbolic but economic ramifications.

Ultimately, several prominent aristocrats in the community who had celebrated reputations as cultural experts, strong political ties, and genealogical links to already established tourist villages were chosen to make presentations at the workshop. Their lecture topics included Torajan history, cosmology, traditional dress, and architecture. The aspiring local guides were then tested on this material and eventually awarded with official certificates. Thus, the aristocratic speakers' particular versions of the Torajan past became the standard text for presentation to outsiders. Not everyone was happy with the situation. Aspiring guides from villages whose myths were not taught grumbled that a false version of Torajan history was being foisted upon them.

One articulate young guide stood up on the final day of the workshop and pointedly asked the moderator, "After two weeks of training meetings, I am left with the question, just what is Toraja? Is it only Ke'te' village or the San-galla region where our speakers come from? Or is it also the other villages over the hill, where many of us here come from? Can we really standardize Torajan history? Won't something be lost?" Not surprisingly, the moderator skirted the question. Although most of the "wild guides" passed the Training Workshop exam and are now certified local guides, the attempt to create a uniform Torajan history at this workshop was not successful. It is notewor-thy, however, that these efforts were motivated by Torajans' concerns with the opinions of outsiders (e.g., their fears that the existence of contradictory versions of Torajan mythic history would prompt tourists to judge Torajans negatively, as "storytelling liars"). Moreover, as evidenced in this case, the attempts of Torajan aristocratic leaders to enhance their culture's image vis-à-vis outsiders prompted some unexpected, disturbing questions about the local distribution of power.

Discussion

The funeral and the Guide Training Workshop reveal some of the political and symbolic issues inherent in the renegotiation of Torajan ritual and his-tory. Suddenly finding themselves in the international spotlight, the Torajans are reexamining their rituals and consciously reshaping their traditions and past. Careful attention to the Toraja case reveals some of the microprocesses involved in the touristic invention of tradition. As we have seen, much of contemporary Torajan sculpting of their customs and history grows out of concerns regarding status, power, and authority. Tourism, like colonialism, creates a fertile context for the reformulation of history and custom, as it ushers in new challenges to local forms of meaning, power, and identity. The Toraja case also emphasized that such self-conscious remodeling of ritual and history hardly comes hand in hand with a divestment in the meaning and emotive power of culture. All too often, discussions in the ethnic tourism literature of staged authenticity leave the reader to mistakenly assume that these processes are invariably tantamount to a collapse in the significance of these ritual performances to local peoples. Though a number of Torajans today are rearranging and condensing aspects of their rituals to accommodate visiting dignitaries, their funerals continue to be vibrant arenas for honoring the dead as well as for establishing a family's local authority. The Toraja case thus lends further support to recent critiques of the concept of staged authen-ticity as an intrinsic aspect of tourism (Crick 1989; Urry 1990; Adams 1996). Whereas other critiques have focused on underscoring the important point that all cultures engage in presumably unauthentic staging, so even staged behaviors entail authenticity, this article makes a companion argument: that self-conscious cultural (re)formulation does not necessarily imply a collapse in meaning or emotive power. In this sense, this article lends support to the growing sentiment that it is time to rethink the discourse of "authenticity" and "staged authenticity."

Moreover, these cases from Tana Toraja offer lessons for ethnic tourism researchers who have typically tended to assume that touristic promotion brings a loss of agency to indigenous peoples (e.g., Greenwood 1977; Erisman 1983; Urbanowicz 1989; van den Berghe 1980, 1994). As this article has illustrated, tourism development does not always entail a complete loss of agency for local people. While Torajans have little control over tourism policymaking and the flow of tourism revenues, they are hardly passive when faced with some of the troubling dimensions of this form of development. Indeed, they are not resigned to accepting representations depicting them as pagan primitives given to inappropriately extravagant funeral rituals, but are actively engaged in ingenious political strategies to adjust and enhance their group's image and vigorously challenge and contest the perceived threats to their identity and power.

Notes

1. This paper is based on research supported by a Fulbright Fellowship and Gowen research funds administered by the University of Washington. Versions of this article were originally presented at the 1987 American Anthropological Association Annual Meeting and at the 1991 Conference on Southeast Asian Studies at the University of California, Berkeley. I thank Carter Bentley, Eric Crystal, Christina Fink, Jill Forshee, Miriam Kahn, Charles F. Keyes, Greg LeRoy, Simon Ottenberg, and Richard Scaglion for their thoughtful comments.

2. Pseudonyms are used throughout this paper.

3. Government tourism officials calculated this figure by comparing the number of tourist ticket sales at the most popular tourist sites with occupancy rates and guest logs at local hotels, inns, and home stays (Rombelayuk, pers. comm.).

4. See Bigalke (1981) for the historical role of the Dutch Reformed Church in fortifying Torajan ethnic consciousness.

5. Given this traditional orientation, the presence of Indonesian government officials, tourists, and other outsiders at Toraja funerals is generally accepted as further evidence of the deceased's drawing power and the success of the ritual. Outsiders, like other funeral guests, are expected to bring gifts (cigarettes, sugar, etc.) to the funeral sponsors. While Torajans acknowledged that tourists who did not bring offerings yet consumed funeral meals could become economically burdensome to their hosts, they tended to be critical of those atypical and few families who charged admission to their funerals. These families, they declared, were going against age-old Torajan values of generosity: to charge admission to funerals was not only an affront to tradition but threatened to give the Toraja a reputation for being greedy. These statements convey their concerns for authenticity and their ethnic image.

6. It is noteworthy that they were least concerned with the opinions of tourists— the opinions of locals and government officials were what really mattered.

7. Save for close relatives of the deceased, most Torajans attend for just a few days, sometimes coming and going between their own homes. Most package tourists generally visit funerals for only a few hours as a part of the day's tour and are bussed back to their hotels in town to eat and sleep.

References

Adams, K. M. 1984. "'Come to Tana Toraja, Land of the Heavenly Kings': Travel Agents as Brokers in Ethnicity." *Annals of Tourism Research* 11(3): 469-85.

———. 1988. *Carving a New Identity: Ethnic and Artistic Change in Tana Toraja, Indonesia.* Ph.D. dissertation, University of Washington. Seattle.

———. 1990. "Cultural Commoditization in Tana Toraja, Indonesia." *Cultural Survival Quarterly* 14(1): 31-34.

———. 1993a. "Club Dead, Not Club Med: Staging Death in Contemporary Tana Toraja (Indonesia)." *Southeast Asian Journal of Social Science* 21(2): 62-72.

———. 1993b. "Theologians, Tourists and Thieves: The Torajan Effigy of the Dead in Modernizing Indonesia." *Kyoto Journal* 22: 38-45.

———. 1995. "Making Up the Toraja? The Appropriation of Tourism, Anthropology, and Museums for Politics in Upland Sulawesi, Indonesia." *Ethnology* 34(2): 143-53.

Adams, V. 1996. *Tigers of the Snow and Other Virtual Sherpas: An Ethnography of Himalayan Encounters.* Princeton: Princeton University Press.

Bigalke, T. 1981. *A Social History of "Tana Toraja," 1870–1965.* Ph.D. Dissertation, University of Wisconsin-Madison.

Clifford, J. 1988. *The Predicament of Culture: Twentieth-Century Ethnography, Literature, and Art.* Cambridge: Cambridge University Press.

Cohen, E. 1988. "Authenticity and Commoditization in Tourism." *Annals of Tourism Research* 15(3): 371-86.

———. 1989. "'Primitive and Remote': Hill Tribe Trekking in Thailand." *Annals of Tourism Research* 16(1): 30-61.

Crick, M. 1989. "Representations of International Tourism in the Social Sciences: Sun, Sex, Sights, Savings, and Servility." *Annual Review of Anthropology* 18: 307-44.

Crystal, E. 1974. "Cooking Pot Politics." *Indonesia* 18: 118-51.

———. 1976. "Ceremonies of the Ancestors." *Pacific Discovery* 29(1): 9-19.

———. 1977. "Tourism in Toraja (Sulawesi, Indonesia)." In *Hosts and Guests: The Anthropology of Tourism,* V. Smith, ed., pp. 139-68. Philadelphia.

———. 1994. "Rape of the Ancestors: Discovery, Display and Destruction of the Ancestral Statuary of Tana Toraja." In *Fragile Traditions: Indonesian Art in Jeopardy,* P. M. Taylor, ed., pp. 29-41. Honolulu.

Erisman, M. 1983. "Tourism and Cultural Dependency in the West Indies." *Annals of Tourism Research* 10: 337-62.

Greenwood, D. 1977. "Culture by the Pound: An Anthropological Perspective on Tourism as Cultural Commoditization." In *Hosts and Guests: The Anthropology of Tourism,* V. Smith, ed., pp. 129-38. Philadelphia.

Handler, R., and J. Linnekin. 1984. "Tradition: Genuine or Spurious." *Journal of American Folklore* 97: 273-90.

Hanson, A. 1989. "The Making of the Maori: Cultural Invention and Its Logic." *American Anthropologist* 91: 890-902.

Hobsbawm, E. J., and T. Ranger, eds. 1983. *The Invention of Tradition.* Cambridge: Cambridge University Press.

Jackson, J. 1989. "Is There a Way to Talk about Making Culture without Making Enemies?" *Dialectical Anthropology* 14: 127–43.

Keesing, R. 1989. "Creating the Past: Custom and Identity in the Pacific." *Contemporary Pacific* 1–2: 19–42.

Keesing, R., and R. Tonkinson, eds. 1982. "Reinventing Traditional Culture: The Politics of Custom in Island Melanesia." *Mankind* 13: 279–399.

Koubi, J. 1982. *Rambu Solo': "La Fumeé descend"—Le Culte des morts chez les Toradja du sud.* Paris.

Linnekin, J. 1983. "Defining Tradition: Variations on the Hawaiian Identity." *American Ethnologist* 10: 241–52.

———. 1992. "On the Theory and Politics of Cultural Construction in the Pacific." *Oceania* 62: 249–63.

MacCannell, D. 1973. "Staged Authenticity: Arrangements of Social Space in Tourist Settings." *American Journal of Sociology* 79(3): 589–603.

———. 1976. *The Tourist: A New Theory of the Leisure Class.* London.

———. 1992. *Empty Meeting Ground: The Tourist Papers.* London.

Nooy-Palm, H. 1979. *The Sa'dan Toraja: A Study of Their Social Life and Religion.* Vol. 1: *Organization, Symbols, and Beliefs.* The Hague.

———. 1986. *The Sa'dan Toraja: A Study of Their Social Life and Religion.* Vol. 2: *Rituals of the East and West.* Dordrecht.

Spillane, J. J. 1987. *Pariwisata Indonesia: Seiarah dan Prospeknya.* Yogyakarta.

Urbanowicz, C. F. 1989. "Tourism in Tonga Revisited: Continued Troubled Times?" In *Hosts and Guests: The Anthropology of Tourism,* V. Smith, ed., pp. 105–18. Philadelphia.

Urry, J. 1990. *The Tourist Gaze: Leisure and Travel in Contemporary Societies.* London.

van den Berghe, P. 1980. "Tourism as Ethnic Relations." *Ethnic and Racial Studies* 3: 375–92.

———. 1994. *The Quest for the Other: Ethnic Tourism in San Cristóbal, Mexico.* Seattle.

Volkman, T. 1985. *Feasts of Honor: Ritual and Change in the Toraja Highlands.* Urbana: University of Illinois Press.

———. 1987. "Mortuary Tourism in Tana Toraja." In *Indonesian Religions in Transition,* R. S. Kipp and S. Rodgers, eds., pp. 161–67. Tucson: University of Arizona Press.

———. 1990. "Visions and Revisions: Toraja Culture and the Tourist Gaze." *American Ethnologist* 17(1): 91–110.

Wagner, R. 1981 [1975]. *The Invention of Culture.* Englewood Cliffs.

White, G. 1991. *Identity through History: Living Stories in a Solomon Islands Society.* Cambridge: Cambridge University Press.

White, G., and L. Lindstrom, eds. 1993. "Custom Today in Oceania." *Anthropological Forum* 6 (Special Issue).

Yamashita, S. 1994. "Manipulating Ethnic Tradition: The Funeral Ceremony, Tourism, and Television among the Toraja of Sulawesi." *Indonesia* 58: 69–82.

20

THE SIMS™ MEET ANTHROPOLOGY

THE USE OF COMPUTER SIMULATION TO HARNESS SOCIAL COMPLEXITY

Lawrence A. Kuznar

Most students of the human condition readily notice that societies, cultures, and even individual people are complicated. Try predicting an election, becoming a millionaire on the stock market, or understanding the object of your affection. Complexity, in a common sense, means having many parts or being hard to understand; individuals and societies certainly meet these criteria. However, "complexity" has a more definite scientific meaning: Complex phenomena are characterized by having many parts that interact in nonlinear ways, producing often unexpected, emergent phenomena. Terms such as "nonlinear" and "emergent" have specific meanings as well that I cover shortly. In this chapter, I demonstrate that the phenomena that interest anthropologists, such as religions, cultures, societies, small groups, and even individuals, satisfy the scientific definition of complexity. Some of the most important scientific developments at the beginning of the twenty-first century involve the use of computer technology to represent complexity in systems, including physical systems, such as galaxies and rockets, as well as ecosystems and social systems (for examples, see Axelrod 1997; Oberkampf, Trucano, and Hirsch 2004). This same computer technology is used to produce complex and entertaining social computer games, like the popular Sims™ and Second Life simulators of virtual lives. This chapter reviews how these computational methods are extended to analyzing the complexity of culture.

In this chapter, I explore how to study social complexity scientifically by recognizing that social complexity has always been on anthropologists' agendas; the founders of the field recognized that explaining social complexity was a central objective of the discipline. I then examine how, until the scientific and technical developments in the late twentieth century, it was all but impossible for anthropologists to represent complexity in our theories and therefore devise rigorous scientific tests of anthropological theory. Next, I describe the basics of computational social science, the methodology for representing social complexity. Even though computational social science provides powerful new capabilities to the scientific anthropologist, a host of new and vastly more difficult problems arise for theory testing, and I describe these challenges. They strike at the core of scientific philosophy and engage some of the most serious and divisive debates to occur in the history of anthropology. To conclude, I present several anthropological examples of computational social science to show the potential future of the discipline.

Social Complexity: Old Wine in a New Bottle

The idea that societies are complex, not just in the common sense but in the scientific sense, is not only nothing new; it also was the core idea at the birth of the social sciences during the early 1800s. Social theorist Herbert Spencer noted in 1860 that societies exhibit four conspicuous peculiarities:

1. Commencing as small aggregations, they insensibly augment in mass....
2. [They have] continually increasing complexity of structure....
3. Their parts gradually acquire a mutual dependence....
4. ... The life and development of a society [are] independent of, and far more prolonged than, the life and development of any of its component units (Spencer 1972: 57).

Spencer (1972: 54) also noted how social institutions, like the division of labor, have unintentionally emerged from the interactions of many small units: "While each citizen has been pursuing his individual welfare, and none taking thought about division of labour, or indeed, conscious of the need for it, division of labour has yet been ever becoming more complete." Spencer's ideas became the foundation for the "organic analogy," the idea that a society functioned like an organism. This metaphor was central to the theorizing of great sociologists such as Emile Durkheim during the late 1800s and anthropologists such as A. R. Radcliffe-Brown in the twentieth century, and it is still widely used by social scientists to address social phenomena as diverse as crime and terrorism (Thomas, Kiser, and Casebeer 2005).

Franz Boas is considered the founder of American anthropology. He presided over the U.S. Bureau of Ethnology during the late 1800s and taught many of the twentieth century's leading anthropologists (Margaret Mead, Ruth Benedict, Ashley Montagu, and many others) at Columbia University. Boas puzzled at the interdependence between individuals and the societies they generate; social institutions emerge out of the complex interactions among individuals, and these institutions in turn condition individuals' lives. The "individual can be understood only as part of the society to which he belongs, and that society can be understood only on the basis of the interrelations of the constituent elements" (Boas 1940: 260).

Bronislaw Malinowski (1944) was another leading anthropological theorist of the early twentieth century. He recognized that more abstract social phenomena, such as value systems and systems of honor and prestige, emerged from the complex interactions of individuals who initially pursued more basic biological and material needs. Because the satisfaction of people's needs nearly always requires that people cooperate with one another, secondary needs (for trust, prestige, honor) often arise in order to guarantee that primary biological and material needs can be met. These secondary needs obtain a life of their own, leading to honor systems in which nonutilitarian items that represent social status become the focus of people's need, driving their behavior.

British anthropologist Radcliffe-Brown was more directly influenced by Spencer's organic analogy and the twentieth-century researchers who used it. Radcliffe-Brown stressed the interrelatedness of social subsystems, such that one could not understand a society's economic system without understanding its kinship system, religious systems of thought, social norms, etc., in addition to how people made a living. Radcliffe-Brown also captured an important element of complexity theory in his discussion of process (what happens in a society) versus structure (what social arrangements result from processes). Structures are ever changing and in themselves are the result of ongoing processes that in turn are influenced by previous social arrangements; "process is dependent on structure and continuity of structure is dependent on process" (Radcliffe-Brown 1965: 12).

In summary, the founders of anthropology recognized that social systems were complex in both the common and scientific senses of the word. This complexity was manifest in the following features:

- Societies have many parts, many of which are small (such as individuals and small communities).
- The small units of a society interact in complicated ways, yielding emergent higher-order phenomena that the participants of a social system may never have anticipated, such as religions, criminal networks, new fads, and many other things that seem to take on a life of their own.
- Emergent phenomena become seemingly stable institutions and belief systems that in turn influence the behaviors of the individuals that created them, often unknowingly.

Therefore, a central challenge for understanding a social system is understanding the dynamic interplay between its constituent units and its larger, more abstract, social structures.

Hitting the Wall: Why Social Scientists Had to Wait to Address Social Complexity

For most, commonsense social complexity is obvious. For those with a little mathematical and scientific training, the scientific complexity of societies and cultures is apparent. It is relatively easy to write about complexity and to admit its existence; it is quite another matter to represent complexity in a theory so that the theory can be used to make predictions about the world and therefore be tested. For instance, it is easy to say that individuals create their social settings and their social settings in turn influence individuals. However, statements such as this are "chicken and egg" arguments that defy testing; the circularity of the statement does not allow a researcher to pin down which phenomena cause others.

As anthropologists amassed information about many societies, past and present, and as they worked hard to unravel the riddles of these many cultures, they often recognized the complexity of society and proposed theories to explain it. However, words are never entirely precise, and anthropological theories have taken on many meanings, making rigorous hypothesis testing extremely difficult. Instead, the norm for anthropological theorizing has been interpretive theory, in which theoretical frameworks were posited (structuralism, postmodernism, interpretivism, and many others), and a researcher's experiences and data were interpreted and given meaning in light of these theoretical frameworks. For example, a structuralist assumes that humans divide social experience into opposites in order to derive meaning. Therefore, when structuralist anthropologist Claude Lévi-Strauss conducted his fieldwork among the Bororo of Brazil, he looked for evidence (e.g., symmetrical village plans) of this basic meaning-producing activity (Lévi-Strauss 1963: 137). Interpretations structure what we think we know about human social life, but they are not tests of a theory—look hard enough, and one is likely to find some kind of evidence that fits a theory, especially when examining a complicated social system.

During the 1960s and 1970s, some anthropologists turned to systems theory in order to provide more rigor to the study of complex social systems (Flannery 1972; Thomas 1973; Thomas, Winterhalder, and McRae 1979). Systems theory is a more holistic approach to studying a large system and has found many applications in fields such as ecology, where tracing out the many interdependencies of the units of an ecosystem is essential for understanding the flow of energy and nutrients throughout the system and why the system has the species it does (Ricklefs 1979). One benefit of systems theory is that it provides an explicit framework for representing a theory: All the units one thinks are important for understanding a system must be labeled, and the connections of these units to other units must be specified. However, in the absence of powerful computing and enough data to characterize each unit, most systems diagrams became tangled webs of connections that cannot be practically tested in a rigorous, quantitative manner. Once again, anthropologists recognized the complex holism of human society but were thwarted in thoroughly and rigorously testing their theories about those systems.[1] Developments in other fields during the late twentieth century began to provide the tools social scientists, including anthropologists, would one day use to represent and test complex theories.

Complexity Theory and Computational Social Science

A system is complex if it is composed of many parts, if these parts interact in nonlinear ways, and if they produce higher-order emergent phenomena. These higher-order phenomena are said to be emergent, meaning that they result from the interactions of the many small units of a system, and once they emerge, they take on properties of their own; their whole is greater than the sum of their parts (Holland 1998: 225). Nonlinear interactions have a disproportionate effect on a system (Epstein and Axtell 1996: 154); for instance, if you add 10 percent of an effect, you may get 50 percent change in the system. Nonlinear interactions often result from feedback loops between a system's variables. In the case of positive feedback, a change in one variable may lead to a change in another variable, which in turn changes the first variable and so on.

Theories that capture genuine complexity are themselves very complex and defy easy representation in language (which is often not precise enough to specify all interconnections and relationships) or mathematical formulas (which cannot easily represent the many contingencies and variables in a complex theory). Researchers have turned to computer simulation because computer code is very precise, yet it allows an extended description of many variables and varied interactions between the variables. Computational social scientists use computer code to represent social theories and run simulations to explore the implications of those theories for social behavior (Axelrod and Cohen 2000; Sallach and Macal 2001). Scientists in many fields have applied computational analysis to represent complexity theories, including mathematics, computer science, physics (at quantum and macro scales), cosmology, biology, ecology, medicine, neuropsychology, art (Axelrod and Cohen 2000: 16–17; Wolfram 2002: 6–12), and, not least, anthropology.

An early example of an anthropological application of complexity theory and computational social science is the Anasazi civilization project spearheaded by the Santa Fe Institute, an institute set up to study complex systems. The project was aimed at understanding how Anasazi civilization in the American Southwest developed and then apparently collapsed in the thirteenth century AD (Axtell et al. 2002; Dean et al. 2000; Gumerman et al. 2003; Kohler, Gumerman, and Reynolds 2005). The researchers created a large simulation model by coding many aspects of Native American life in the Southwest known from historical ethnographic research. They coupled the ethnographic information with data on the environment, past and present, to create a simulated Anasazi civilization that grew on its own. The researchers found that Anasazi social complexity could be generated by the many actions of individual families who unintentionally caused group-level phenomena such as population increases and social collapses (Dean et al. 2000; Kohler et al. 2005). The simulation produced predictions of where Anasazi families would live and how many people would live in the region, and their model results closely matched what archaeologists had discovered in large-scale surveys and excavations (Kohler 2000: 12, 14; Kohler et al. 2005). There is a growing body of computational social science in anthropology. I describe several examples in this chapter, and there are some very good reviews of the work to date (Kohler and Gumerman 2000; Kohler and van der Leeuw 2007; Kuznar 2006).

The Challenges of Complexity Theory

Considering the fact that the founders of modern social science recognized and were concerned with social complexity, and considering the fact that discursive theories and mathematical formulations were unable to capture social complexity adequately, computational social science may represent a genuine scientific breakthrough, and I argue that it does. However, scientific breakthroughs almost always wind up generating more questions and creating more profound problems for scientists to ponder, and this is certainly true of computational social science and complexity theory. These problems involve social data, the mapping of theory to events, the generation of many possible worlds, and fundamental challenges to the notion of scientific theory testing.

The first problem anthropologists have had to confront is their very own data. Many social theories concern aggregate phenomena, such as a population's birthrate, crime rate, shared language and ethnic identity, and kinship system. However, there can be great individual variation in many social variables. Some women produce many children, and others produce none; some people live lives of crime, and others never break a law; and so on. Computer models now can capture this amount of variability. However, social scientists often do not have data at this level of detail. New methods therefore have created new and more stringent requirements for basic data collection. If anyone ever thought that computers meant that we could create human societies *in silico* and not have to do fieldwork, that person was sorely mistaken!

Another problem concerns mapping the implications of a theory to actual social phenomena (see George and Bennett 2005: 10 for a succinct review and excellent examples). One characteristic of complexity theory is equifinality, meaning that many alternative paths can lead to the same event; conversely, multifinality is where many events might have the same underlying cause. Consider your route to your classroom today. Whereas some routes may have gotten you here quicker than others, all were legitimate routes in that they would have gotten you here; this is an example of equifinality. Your desire to "get a good job" may have motivated you to pursue a college education. However, that underlying causal motivation could lead you to choose many different majors and professions; this is an example of multifinality. More traditional social theories tend to posit linear cause-and-effect relationships: Reduce poverty and thereby decrease terrorism, for example. However, complexity theories often lead to many effects and many causes. For instance, a reduction in poverty can actually raise expectations and increase social strife, whereas in other cases it may have its expected effect of suppressing conflict (Collier and Hoeffler 2004; Krueger and Maleckova 2003).

Phenomena such as equifinality and multifinality raise interesting and troubling issues of just how many social worlds exist out there. To be clear, there are not different social realities just because people have different perspectives. There is only one reality, which has the annoying habit of going on despite what we think about it. However, because there are so many unpredictable contingencies in life (whether or not it will rain tomorrow, whether or not you meet someone with whom you have a mutual attraction) that determine life's outcomes (whether or not you drown in a flood, whether or not you marry), and because these events can interact in often unpredictable and nonlinear ways (the paramedic who saves you from drowning becomes your life's love), at any one point in time there are many possible futures that could occur for you. Similarly, there are many possible future worlds that could exist for humanity.

It is great that social scientists now have the ability to model such myriad outcomes. However, this ability to portray social dynamics more realistically presents a daunting challenge to the practice of social science. If scientists test theories by comparing their predictions with outcomes (data), but if the outcomes we can observe are only one of a possibly infinite set of outcomes, then how can we know when a theory has "fit" the data? What if the social affairs we observe are actually a fluke, a highly improbable history that was one of many possibly more probable histories?

This problem is compounded by the fact that complex theories, instantiated in computer code, can be run many times, producing many divergent results. Therefore, computational social scientists do not have one theoretical implication (prediction) to compare with one known reality, but they have many predictions to compare with many potential realities.

Such complex theories can be tested, although social scientists will have to broaden their understanding of what testing a theory means, reduce their expectations for clear and simple answers, and learn to partner with knowledgeable statisticians in order to explore the implications of their theories and gauge the degree to which their theories can predict and explain the social world. One solution is not to worry about making accurate and precise predictions of singular events, but to be able to match the distribution of possibilities between simulations and the worlds we observe. I have employed methods like these by using standard statistical measures for comparing probability distributions to test competing theories of political decisionmaking among tribesmen in highland Irian Jaya (Kuznar 2007). Another solution is to create software that visualizes the realm of possibilities implied by different theories; such techniques have been used to guide policymaking in complex domains, such as what to do about global warming or terrorism (Popper, Lempert, and Bankes 2005).

Advances in computer engineering and complexity theory have given anthropologists new abilities to explore what inspired the founders of the discipline and puzzled generations after. These new capabilities have generated their own technical, scientific, and philosophically challenging problems. The following three examples offer glimpses into the promise that using these methods and overcoming these challenges pose.

Examples

Balinese Water Temples

J. Stephen Lansing's (1993) study of Balinese water temples is a pioneering and now classic study in the use of computer simulation to explore social complexity and unravel a cultural puzzle. The Indonesian island of Bali is known for its exotic puppets, dances, and beautiful landscape, and it is a popular destination for Western tourists. The island's rural economy is based on irrigated rice agriculture. Traditionally, Balinese kings ruled the island, and Western scholars used Bali as an example of how autocratic power could be wielded by a ruler who controlled the flow of water. However, other scholarship cast doubt upon whether or not irrigation was centrally controlled or whether Balinese rice agriculture could even function under central management. Lansing explored these possibilities by simulating the effects of different irrigation control schemes on Balinese rice agriculture in order to identify the scheme that best matched the real outcomes of Balinese agriculture.

Balinese rice farmers are organized in water-using groups called *subaks*. A number of subaks hold collective ceremonies at regional water temples. In addition to worship of ancestral spirits and other religious activity, farmers from the different subaks discuss yearly conditions and make plans for how to coordinate the coming year's planting, irrigation, and harvest schedules. Decisions made at the regional water temples are delegated to the individual subaks and constitute the year's managerial scheme.

Balinese rice agriculture requires some form of management due to two contrasting pressures: irrigation and pests. First, Balinese rice farming requires scheduled irrigation, or the rice plants will die of drought (or at least produce little) and the agrarian economy could collapse. Irrigation must be staggered among the various subaks so that each subak receives adequate water. Second, insect pests can seriously damage crops, and the best method of controlling pests is to have many subaks plant, irrigate, and harvest at a time, which leaves large areas of the land unused, starving out the pests. So there are competing demands for staggered irrigation, which produces a mosaic of rice fields in varied stages of growth that sustains pest populations, versus widespread simultaneous harvest, which suppresses pest populations but would spread water too thinly. The competing demands of Balinese rice agriculture were exacerbated by the introduction of modern, Green Revolution varieties of rice that have potentially great yields but that are particularly susceptible to drought and pest infestations.

Lansing and ecologist James Kremer developed a computational model that simulated the interactions among 172 subaks, 14 water temples, the characteristics of local rivers, the Balinese climate, and pest populations. Their results demonstrated that, on the one hand, centralized control would definitely suppress pest populations, but at the cost of severe deficits in rice production that would threaten the Balinese population. On the other hand, uncoordinated rice agriculture, in which each subak pursued its own irrigation and harvest scheme independently of all other subaks, would yield more rice but would also provide an ideal habitat for pests, which in turn would threaten Balinese rice crops. However, coordination of irrigation, planting, and harvest schedules at the level of regional water temples would minimize pest populations and provided for the maximal rice yield possible.

Lansing and Kremer's simulation demonstrated that kingly control of water was not a tenable system and therefore refuted old, cherished theories of water and power. Their simulations also demonstrated that Balinese agriculture was coordinated, but in an emergent manner—individual subaks came together to produce flexible yearly plans that were manifest as regional agrarian schedules. Furthermore, Lansing and Kremer's work demonstrated that there was much more than ritual to Balinese water temple activities; "the water temples are a social system that manages production, not a ritual clock" (Lansing 1993: 123).

These realizations and results would have been difficult to achieve with the traditional tools of anthropological theorizing and analysis. Balinese rice agriculture and ecology are too dynamic and genuinely complex for a simple set of equations or a verbal theory to capture. Furthermore, Balinese agricultural coordination was too emergent to be represented by a simple model, such as a managerial king, or by the individual independent decisions of rice farmers. However, computer code that could capture the interactions of many small parts of a system provided a realistic and revealing model of Balinese rice agriculture.

The Buzz about Drugs

Michael Agar's (Agar 2005) study of heroin use among the youth of Baltimore is an innovative use of computational modeling to unravel the complexities of how young people decide to experiment with, and possibly get hooked on, illicit drugs. Through Agar's ethnographic work, he came to appreciate the role that talk about drugs played in conveying information to potential drug users and in their perceptions of the risks (or lack thereof) of drug use. However, messages about illicit drug experiences travel dynamically, one is exposed to information about these drugs through face-to-face contacts of friends that can vary tremendously from person to person, not everyone gets the same amount and quality of information, and this information can change dynamically based on one's experiences and those of one's friends and associates. Once again, the social dynamic in question is complex, dynamic, and changing and defies traditional social theory for an explanation, not to mention simple broadcast messages to "Just Say No to Drugs" (Agar 2005: 4.2).

Agar turned to computational modeling to create a program called Drugmart, which models how individuals' attitudes about drugs and risk-taking/ novelty-seeking tendencies impact the spread of information about heroin and its subsequent use. One important point is that, in reality, sometimes drug use spreads and sometimes it does not. This is due in part to the fact that because individuals are not all the same, their risk-taking tendencies and attitudes can be different. Furthermore, their attitudes can change, either in the direction of trying heroin or away from trying heroin based on their exposure to information. In Drugmart, each individual has a risk, a tendency to try something new, and an attitude, which is either favorable or unfavorable toward illicit drugs. Each individual's risk tendency is fixed, although risk tendencies are different for different individuals. Attitude is impacted by interactions, talk, or "buzz" that an individual picks up through interaction with others. Agar incorporates new developments from operational psychology that demonstrate how people weigh negative experience and information more heavily than positive experiences (loss aversion). These elements lend more realism to Agar's simulation of individuals' reactions to the buzz they hear from other individuals. Addiction to heroin occurs after a simulated individual uses five or more times, and as the number of addicts increases in a population, the negative aspects of heroin use become more apparent and more negative buzz is generated.

Perhaps the most important result of Agar's computational experiment is that there is no single, simple result. The spread of heroin use was highly contingent on whether or not a central hub of users randomly formed and on the rate at which addicts were generated in a population. Simulation runs would produce different histories from run to run, based on the same basic set of rules subject to the random contingencies (multifinality), and similar outcomes could be caused by different historical trajectories (equifinality). Often, for various specific causes, a simulation would settle into a low proportion of drug users (around 10 percent) that remained endemic to the population, approximating the situation many cities face (Agar 2005: 6.2). In the end, the value of Drugmart is not that it provides a single cause of illicit drug use that can be attacked and defeated, but rather that it presents an analyst (and, ideally, a policymaker) with the range of possibilities

(Agar refers to this range as the "space of possible outcomes") that we can reasonably expect. Drugmart also provides valuable insight into the power of peer-to-peer information sharing to influence the spread of information about drugs and impact their use.

Genocide: Simulating Hell on Earth

Computational social science can illuminate traditional anthropological puzzles such as the function of Balinese water temples or contemporary social issues such as illicit drug use by young people. Anthropological applications of computational social science can reveal insights into dramatic and often disturbing human phenomena as well, even when the models were not intended to do so.

Genocide is a controversial term, but a widely adopted definition, first codified by the United Nations in 1948, is "any of the following acts committed with intent to destroy, in whole or in part, a national, ethnical, racial or religious group, as such: (a) Killing members of the group; (b) Causing serious bodily or mental harm to members of the group; (c) Deliberately inflicting on the group conditions of life calculated to bring about its physical destruction in whole or in part; (d) Imposing measures intended to prevent births within the group; (e) Forcibly transferring children of the group to another group" (UN OHCHR 1948).

Arguably, each of these acts has occurred in the long and bloody conflict of Darfur in the East African nation of Sudan: Hundreds of thousands of people have been killed, scores of thousands of women have been raped, and 2.5 million civilians have been displaced. The Darfur region has historically been known as a region of conflict, but it was not always this way. In the 1960s, anthropologists working in the region actually reported relative peace and in fact fluid membership among the region's various ethnic groups of "African" Fur, Masalit, Zaghawa, and "Arab" populations of camel and cattle nomads (Haaland 1969). How did things break down so dramatically?

The political turmoil of Sudan is indeed complex, involving numerous political intrigues, ethnic divisions, and international meddling. Julie Flint and Alex de Waal (2008) give an excellent overview of the historical roots as well as the contemporary complexities of the Darfur conflict. However, the conflict is also rooted in tensions in traditional land use practices, exacerbated by global climate tends (UN Environment Programme 2007). Computational modeling provides an excellent tool for teasing out how some of these factors interrelate.

NOMAD is a computational model of the interactions between nomadic people dependent on animal herding and settled villagers who grow crops (Kuznar, Sedlmeyer, and Kreft 2008). For thousands of years, nomads and villagers have lived side by side, locked in relationships that vary from mutual interdependence to mutual fear and distrust. In reality, neither can live without the other: Agriculturalists are often dependent on nomads for trade, and nomads depend on agricultural markets. However, nomads also have the capability to steal what they need from agricultural populations, and agricultural populations, often attached to powerful states, can bring the power of armies against nomads. The result has been centuries of complex, often oscillating conflict between settled agrarian populations and nomads (Barfield 1989).

The NOMAD program models the decisions that agricultural and nomadic families must make as they contend with the vagaries of the environment (drought, snow, disease), the need to find partners for trade, and the opportunities for quick and violent action to gain resources, all in an attempt to procure sufficient calories and protein to sustain their families, to bear children, and to find mates for their children as they grow up. Nomads, in particular, have the choice of trading with agricultural partners or raiding them. Raiding may yield quick riches, but it comes with the danger of death or injury, which can jeopardize a family's survival.

Computational models require data. Even though variables (attitudes, family size, herd size, rice yields) may take on a wide range of values, these values develop through time and need to start somewhere. Therefore, it is very important to choose the initial values for these parameters wisely. The initial NOMAD program utilized environmental, crop yield, family size, fertility, disease, and other data typical of the Middle East, reminiscent of an environment in Syria or northern Iraq. The agriculture was based on wheat and barley, and herding was based on sheep and goat herding typical of the region. The model yielded results consistent with centuries of observations of agriculturalist/nomad interactions. These populations oscillated between periods of low-level raiding and periods of more intense trading, and individual family experiences depended on local circumstances. For instance, a particular nomad family might have joined with others to raid an agricultural family because its herds were afflicted by disease and family members had nothing with which to trade, or they might have raided because a particular agricultural family had a bumper crop, easy for the picking. NOMAD captured the equifinality and multifinality and complex and varied interrelations that astute anthropologists have noted in these kinds of societies.

Once researchers construct and validate a computational model (test and verify that it works), it can be extended to other situations by reparameterizing, or resetting the initial values and parameters to reflect the details of another specific situation or instance. NOMAD was reparameterized into NOMAD-Darfur in order to test the model's implications in another setting. Data on the west Sudanese environment, indigenous crops (sorghum, millet), indigenous herd animals (cattle, camels), and family demography were recalibrated to reflect conditions in Darfur. Initial model results produced the same oscillating pattern of raiding and trading seen in the original NOMAD model parameterized for Middle Eastern conditions, but the oscillations had greater amplitude—periods of raiding were more intense, followed by intense periods of trade. Researchers' examination of individual simulated family decisions indicated that the greater intensity was caused by greater risks and uncertainties in the unpredictable Saharan environment; these increased risks and uncertainties led to more intense problems and behaviors designed to solve those problems.

NOMAD-Darfur produced greater levels of violence than the original NOMAD model had, but it did not produce a genocide. Sudanese researchers have noted that a series of severe droughts in the mid-1980s appear to have led to intense ethnic conflicts between "African" villagers and "Arab" nomads, and that this pattern has been difficult to break ever since (Suliman 1996). To test how such a new pattern of constant conflict could be generated, the intensity of the 1982–1984 Sudan drought was introduced to the NOMAD-Darfur model. The result was shocking. Not only did the drought create intense patterns of violent raiding, but also because of the lasting effects of the drought and of injured agricultural families' inability to recover their economic viability, nomadic herders had no choice but to continue to prey upon an agricultural population that had decreasing capacity to supply its own needs or the needs of the region. Once a family head was killed, a family was taken out of the simulation, effectively creating refugees and regional depopulation. The end result is what complexity theorists call a "phase transition"—the system of oscillating low-level trading and raiding shifted into a system of whole-scale warfare and depopulation from which the system could not return. Tragically, the simulation results appear to trace the recent history of the Darfur region; perhaps more worrisome still, the simulation results did not suggest a way out of the region's current dilemmas (see de Waal and Flint 2007 for a sober assessment).

Conclusion

The founders of social sciences and anthropology recognized the complexity of culture. Many social phenomena that interest scholars—the rise and fall of civilizations, drug use and crime, war and civil strife—seem to come out of nowhere, often emerging from the myriad social interactions of small social groups and individuals. Furthermore, many social phenomena appear to take on a life of their own, behaving according to their own rules, as studies of suicide and ladies' hem length showed a century ago. These sorts of social phenomena have all the hallmarks of mathematical complexity: They occur from nonlinear interactions of many small units, generating emergent phenomena with their own rules of behavior. Furthermore, complex systems are often very sensitive to initial conditions and parameter settings, as Agar's studies of drug use and simulations of genocide demonstrate.

It is extremely difficult to capture the many possible interactions and contingencies of a complex system in a few mathematical formulations. Written theories are often not precise enough to specify the many possible implications that require testing. Computer code provides a flexible alternative for representing complex social theories and testing their many implications. Anthropology's founders, such as Boas, Malinowski, Mead, and Radcliffe-Brown, recognized the complexity of culture, but researchers had to wait until the late twentieth century before computer modeling could capture such theories. The time has arrived, and an increasing number of anthropologists are using computational modeling to address tradition anthropological questions, such as the rise and fall of civilization or the functions of religion and ritual, as well as contemporary policy issues such as illicit drug use, environmental change, and genocide.

Note

1. Many scientific advances came out of systems theory nonetheless. Systems theory reinforced anthropological holism and the attempt to unravel the complicated interdependencies of social phenomena. Also, systems theory encouraged anthropologists to collect data on the many variables they identified in social systems.

References

Agar, Michael. 2005. "Agents in Living Color: Towards Emic Agent-Based Models." *JASSS—Journal of Artificial Societies and Social Simulation* 8, no. 1: 1–19.

Axelrod, Robert. 1997. *The Complexity of Cooperation: Agent-Based Models of Conflict and Cooperation.* Princeton, NJ: Princeton University Press.

Axelrod, Robert, and Michael D. Cohen. 2000. *Harnessing Complexity: Organizational Implications of a Scientific Frontier.* New York: Basic Books.

Axtell, Robert L., et al. 2002. "Population Growth and Collapse in a Multiagent Model of the Kayenta Anasazi in Long House Valley." *Proceedings of the National Academy of Sciences* 99, supplement 3: 7275–7279.

Barfield, Thomas J. 1989. *Perilous Frontier: Nomadic Empires and China.* Cambridge, MA: Blackwell.

Boas, Franz. 1940. "Some Problems of Methodology in the Social Sciences." In *Race, Language, and Culture,* edited by Franz Boas. Chicago: University of Chicago Press, 260–269.

Collier, Paul, and Anke Hoeffler. 2004. "Greed and Grievance in Civil War." *Oxford Economic Papers* 56: 563–595.

de Waal, Alex, and Julie Flint. 2007. "In Darfur, from Genocide to Anarchy." *Washington Post,* August 28, 2007, A13.

Dean, Jeffrey S., et al. 2000. "Understanding Anasazi Culture Change through Agent-Based Modeling." In *Dynamics in Human and Primate Societies: Agent-Based Modeling of Social and Spatial Processes,* edited by Timothy A. Kohler and George J. Gumerman. New York: Oxford University Press, 179–205.

Epstein, Joshua M., and Robert L. Axtell. 1996. *Growing Artificial Societies: Social Science from the Bottom Up.* Cambridge, MA, and Washington, DC: MIT Press/Brookings Institution.

Flannery, Kent. 1972. "The Cultural Evolution of Civilizations." *Annual Review of Ecological Systematics* 3: 399–426.

Flint, Julie, and Alex de Waal. 2008. *Darfur: A New History of a Long War,* 2nd rev. ed. London: Zed.

George, Alexander L., and Andrew Bennett. 2005. *Case Studies and Theory Development in the Social Sciences.* Cambridge, MA: MIT Press.

Gumerman, George J., et al. 2003. "The Evolution of Social Behavior in the Prehistoric American Southwest." *Artificial Life* 9: 435–444.

Haaland, Gunnar. 1969. "Economic Determinants of Ethnic Processes." In *Ethnic Groups and Boundaries,* edited by Fredrik Barth. Boston: Little, Brown, 58–73.

Holland, John H. 1998. *Emergence: From Chaos to Order.* New York: Basic Books.

Kohler, Timothy A. 2000. "Putting Social Sciences Together Again." In *Dynamics in Human and Primate Societies: Agent-Based Modeling of Social and Spatial Processes,* edited by Timothy A. Kohler and George J. Gumerman. New York: Oxford University Press, 1–18.

Kohler, Timothy A., and George J. Gummerman, eds. 2000. *Dynamics in Human and Primate Societies: Agent-Based Modeling of Social and Spatial Processes.* Oxford: Oxford University Press.

Kohler, Timothy A., George J. Gumerman, and Robert G. Reynolds. 2005. "Simulating Ancient Societies." *Scientific American* 293, no. 1: 67–73.

Kohler, Timothy A., and Sander E. van der Leeuw, eds. 2007. *The Model-Based Archaeology of Socionatural Systems.* Santa Fe, NM: School of Advanced Research Press.

Krueger, Alan B., and Jitka Maleckova. 2003. "Education, Poverty, and Terrorism: Is There a Causal Connection?" *Journal of Economic Perspectives* 17, no. 4: 119–144.

Kuznar, Lawrence A. 2006. "High Fidelity Computational Social Science in Anthropology: Prospects for Developing a Comparative Framework." *Social Science Computer Review* 24, no. 1: 1–15.

———. 2007. "Ensemble Computing in Agent-Based Modeling for Transcending Paradigmatic Boundaries in Decision Theory: Understanding Tribal Politics." *Proceedings of the Agent 2007 Conference*: 433–442.

Kuznar, Lawrence A., Robert L. Sedlmeyer, and Allyson Kreft. 2008. "NOMAD: An Agent-Based Model of Nomadic Pastoralist/Sedentary Peasant Interaction." In *The Archaeology of Mobility: Old World and New World Nomadism,* edited by Hans Barnard and Wendy Wendrich. Los Angeles: COTSEN Institute, University of California, 557–583.

Lansing, J. Stephen. 1993. *Priests and Programmers: Technologies of Power in the Engineered Landscape of Bali.* Princeton, NJ: Princeton University Press.

Lévi-Strauss, Claude. 1963. *Structural Anthropology.* Garden City, NY: Doubleday.

Malinowski, Bronislaw. 1944. *A Scientific Theory of Culture and Other Essays.* Chapel Hill: University of North Carolina Press.

Oberkampf, William L., Timothy G. Trucano, and Charles Hirsch. 2004. "Verification, Validation, and Predictive Capability in Computational Engineering and Physics." *Applied Mechanics Reviews* 57, no. 5: 345–384.

Popper, Steven W., Robert J. Lempert, and Steven C. Bankes. 2005. "Shaping the Future." *Scientific American* 292, no. 4 (April): 67–71.

Radcliffe-Brown, A. R. 1965. *Structure and Function in Primitive Society.* New York: Free Press.

Ricklefs, Robert E. 1979. *Ecology,* 2nd ed. New York: Chiron.

Sallach, David L., and Charles M. Macal. 2001. "Introduction: The Simulation of Social Agents." *Social Science Computer Review* 19, no. 3: 245–248.

Spencer, Herbert. 1972. "The Social Organism." In *Herbert Spencer on Social Evolution:*

Selected Writings, edited by J. D. Y. Peel. Chicago: University of Chicago Press, 53–72.

Suliman, Mohamed. 1996. "War in Darfur or the Desert versus the Oasis Syndrome." In *Environmental Degradation as a Cause of War,* edited by Gunthar Bachler and Kurt Spillman. Zurich: Verlag Ruegger, 145–180.

Tegmark, Max, and John Archibald Wheeler. 2001. "100 Years of Quantum Mysteries." *Scientific American* 284, no. 2 (February): 68–75.

Thomas, R. Brooke. 1973. "Human Adaptation to a High Altitude Energy Flow System." Department of Anthropology Occasional Paper No. 7. State College: Pennsylvania State University.

Thomas, R. Brooke, Bruce Winterhalder, and Stephen D. McRae. 1979. "An Anthropological Approach to Human Ecology and Adaptive Dynamics." *Yearbook of Physical Anthropology* 12: 1–46.

Thomas, Troy S., Stephen D. Kiser, and William D. Casebeer. 2005. *Warlords Rising: Confronting Violent Non-state Actors.* Lanham, MD: Lexington.

UN Environment Programme. 2007. *Sudan: Postconflict Environmental Assessment.* New York: United Nations.

UN OHCHR. 1948. "Convention on the Prevention and Punishment of the Crime of Genocide." New York: United Nations.

Wolfram, Steven. 2002. *A New Kind of Science.* Champaign, IL: Wolfram Media.

ABOUT THE EDITORS
AND CONTRIBUTORS

Kathleen M. Adams is professor of anthropology at Loyola University Chicago and adjunct curator at the Field Museum of Natural History. Previously, she held the Mouat Family Junior Endowed Chair in International Studies at Beloit College. She has done fieldwork in Indonesia (Toraja and Alor) and San Juan Capistrano, California.

Howard Campbell is professor of anthropology at the University of Texas–El Paso. He has done fieldwork on the Mexico-U.S. border.

Barbara J. Dilly teaches anthropology at Creighton University. She has done fieldwork in northeastern Iowa and Latin America.

Dimitra Doukas, currently an independent scholar, focuses on the impact of corporate capitalism.

E. Paul Durrenberger has taught anthropology at Antioch College and the University of Iowa (1972-1997), and now he teaches at Penn State. He has done fieldwork in highland and lowland Thailand, Iceland, and the United States.

Suzan Erem is a journalist and writer. She worked as a union organizer and representative in the Midwest and New Jersey and as the opinion page editor of a midwestern newspaper; she now does freelance writing for unions and nonprofit organizations. She has done fieldwork with E. Paul Durrenberger in the Midwest, mid-Atlantic, and southern United States.

Lisa L. Gezon is professor of anthropology at the University of West Georgia. She has done fieldwork in Madagascar, Senegal, and coastal Georgia in the southeastern United States.

Ward H. Goodenough served in the U.S. Army from 1941 to 1945, did fieldwork in Truk and Papua New Guinea, and taught at the University of Pennsylvania from 1949 to 1989.

Andre Gunder Frank (1929-2005), who was born in Berlin, immigrated to the United States in 1940. He studied anthropology at the Center for Economic Development and Culture Change. He taught at Michigan State University until 1961, resigned, traveled, and worked in Africa and Latin America. He then taught in Brazil, Mexico, Montreal, Chile, East Anglia, Amsterdam, Toronto, and Florida.

Marvin Harris (1927–2001) served in the U.S. Army and taught anthropology at Columbia University from 1953 to 1981. In 1968 he sided with the students who occupied the campus. He taught at the University of Florida from 1981 until he retired in 2000. He did fieldwork in Brazil and Mozambique.

Josiah Heyman is professor of anthropology and chair of the Sociology and Anthropology Department at the University of Texas–El Paso. He has done fieldwork on the U.S.-Mexico border.

Emine Onaran İncirlioğlu has taught at various institutions in the United States, England, and Turkey. Her teaching and research interests include the intersection of architecture and anthropology, focusing on the concepts of space, culture, and identity as well as ethnography, basic design education, gender studies, tourism, and "gypsy" (Romani) studies.

Lawrence A. Kuznar teaches anthropology at Indiana University–Purdue University Fort Wayne. He has specialized in the study of traditional herding societies and has done extensive field research in the Peruvian Andes of South America and among Navajo sheepherders and cattle ranchers in the U.S. Southwest.

Bronislaw Malinowski (1884–1942) was born in Poland; did fieldwork in the Trobriand Islands, New Guinea, from 1915 to 1918; and taught at the London School of Economics from 1924 until 1938 and then at Yale University until his death.

Bob Marshall is professor of anthropology at Western Washington University. Since 1990, his research has focused on worker cooperatives in Japan.

Azizur R. Molla received a Ph.D. from Pennsylvania State University in 2005. He has done fieldwork in Bangladesh and the United States.

Gísli Pálsson teaches anthropology at the University of Iceland and has done fieldwork in Iceland, the Canadian Arctic, and the Republic of Cape Verde.

Roy A. Rappaport (1926–1997) served in the U.S. Army and taught anthropology at the University of Michigan. He did fieldwork in New Guinea.

Miles Richardson served in the U.S. military and has done fieldwork in Colombia and the U.S. South. He taught anthropology at Louisiana State University until he retired in 2007.

Alan R. Sandstrom is the director of the anthropology program at Indiana University–Purdue University Fort Wayne. He has done fieldwork among Tibetans in exile in the Himalaya region of northern India and for more than thirty years among the Nahua Indians of northern Veracruz, Mexico.

Eric R. Wolf (1923–1999) was born in Vienna, immigrated to the United States in 1940, and served in the U.S. Army for three years during World War II. He taught at various universities, including the University of Michigan from 1961 to 1971, where he and Marshall Sahlins pioneered antiwar teach-ins and were active in the movement against the Vietnam War. He taught at the

City University of New York from 1971 to 1992. He did fieldwork in Mexico, Puerto Rico, and South Tyrol.

Christian Zlolniski teaches at the University of Texas-Arlington. He has done fieldwork among Mexican immigrants in Northern California's Silicon Valley and in Baja California, Mexico.

CPSIA information can be obtained at www.ICGtesting.com
Printed in the USA
BVOW04s0412211015

423372BV00008B/12/P